THE·STAFF·COLLEGE·LIBRARY

TAM MARTE QUAM MINERVA

Encyclopaedia of the
MODERN
TERRITORIAL
ARMY

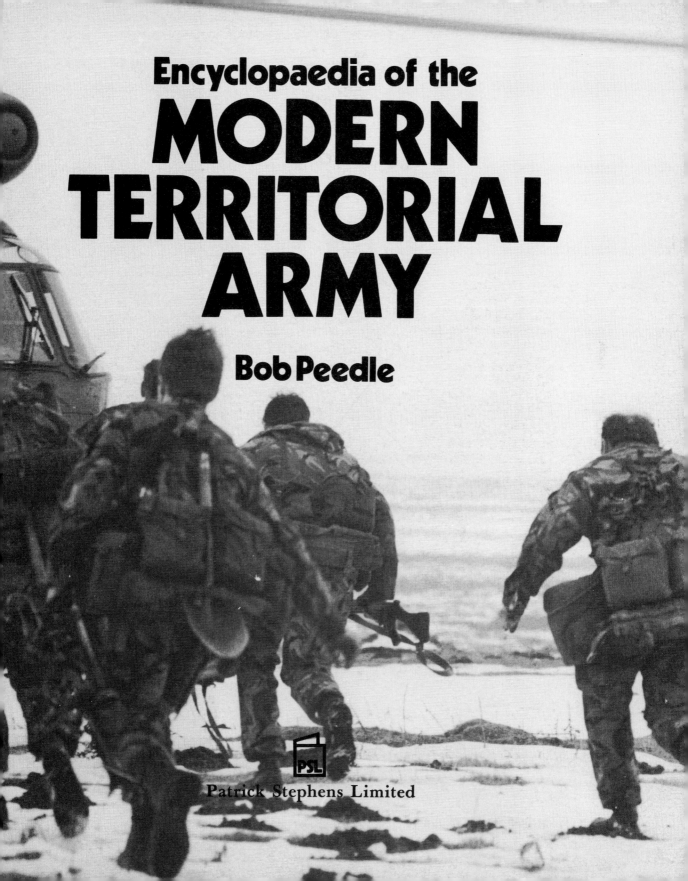

Encyclopaedia of the
MODERN TERRITORIAL ARMY

Bob Peedle

PSL

Patrick Stephens Limited

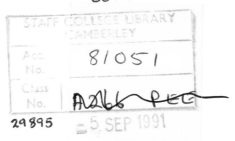
© Military Archive and Research Services 1990

First published in 1990

British Library Cataloguing in Publication Data

Encyclopaedia of the modern Territorial army
    1. Great Britain. Army. Territorial Army
    Peedle, Bob
    355.3'7'0941

    ISBN 0-85059-938-5

Front endpaper: The volunteers from 131
Independent Commando Squadron of the Royal
Engineers prepare to fight their way ashore from
a landing craft.
Rear endpaper: At the end of annual camp, the
members of the recently formed 218 Airfield
Damage Repair Squadron of the Royal Engineers
assemble before returning to their normal civilian
lives — until the next time.

Patrick Stephens Limited is part of the
Thorsons Publishing Group, Wellingborough,
Northamptonshire, NN8 2RQ, England.

Printed in Great Britain by Butler & Tanner
Limited, Frome, Somerset
Typeset by MJL Limited, Hitchin, Hertfordshire

10 9 8 7 6 5 4 3 2 1

Contents

Forewords

By Major The Duke of Westminster, DL
and Major-General M. Matthews CB.

Major The Duke of Westminster DL, Queen's Own Yeomanry.

I was commissioned in the Queen's Own Yeomanry, a medium armoured reconnaissance regiment, in 1972, shortly after the Territorial Army had been re-organized, and am now serving as a Staff Officer, having just completed three years as Squadron Leader.

It was an exacting and exciting task leading a NATO-roled recce squadron. So much has changed during my service that it would be impossible to mention it all here, but something that has not changed as fast as many would have hoped, however, is the level of understanding between Regular and TA as we strive for the one-army concept.

This book, I am convinced, will play an important part toward achieving a better understanding between us. This is a unique work as it takes in some of the past, and also the present; Major Peedle is to be congratulated on this great task. He not only has a great understanding of the TA, but also holds it in great regard, as so many of us do, for the TA is a remarkable organization, surviving against a background of ever-increasing demands of family and work commitments, which limit spare time for training.

To be in the TA is to experience a unique spirit of comradeship and duty, combined with a sense of fun, which has been the hallmark of volunteers over the centuries. I personally have gained much from my involvement in the QOY, much of it indefinable. I have served with soldiers who make great sacrifices to be there, but above all who want to be there for all the right reasons, an essential ingredient for a sub-unit commander who has to lead through sometimes very trying conditions.

The TA can only survive and fulfil its ever-increasingly important role both in the UK and NATO on goodwill, particularly from employers who, for very good reasons in the main, find it difficult in this competitive world to release soldiers for training, whether it be trade training (particularly relevant in my case) or annual camp. To them I merely say that if you, like me, are lucky enough to have people who are prepared to give up their spare time and often holidays to serve their country, surely we have people of rare quality in our midst and they should be encouraged and helped to achieve success in their second career.

In having the privilege of writing this foreword I am acutely aware of the great stalwarts of my old Squadron, those who provided a great backbone and enriched my life: my old troop Sergeant, Mr Cameron, when I was a 'wet behind the ears' troop leader, my Sergeant Major, Mr Parry, my SQMS, Mr Hartley, Corporal Allen who drove me thousands of miles and Sergeant Craig REME, who ensured my vehicle made it. For some sixteen years we served together, years I look back on with great affection. They, like me, have moved on, but we can look back with pride and hope for the future.

This foreword is dedicated to them and the soldiers of the Cheshire Squadron QOY.

I commend this work to you all, I hope that you find it as informative and entertaining as I have.

Westminster, Eaton.

Major-General Mike Matthews CB, Secretary to the Council of TAVRAs.

The volunteer spirit has always been close to the surface of British life. Those who now serve in the Territorial Army keep alive a tradition of voluntary service to the Crown of a kind found nowhere else in the world. From the point of view of military efficiency it is a pity that many of those who serve in the TA, do so for only a short time. The other side of this coin is that every year some 25,000 young men and women don the cap badge of one or other of the Regiments and Corps of the British Army. They all give something and gain something in the course of this service, however short. Major Bob Peedle has done an excellent job in bringing together the profiles of the units of the TA, in a first-class record of this important part of our heritage.

My first real experience of the TA was in 1958 when I became adjutant of 131 Parachute Engineer Regiment (TA), which had its Regimental Headquarters in the Duke of York's HQ, with Squadrons in Scotland, the North of England, Midlands and two in and around London. At that time the Regiment had a strength of 721 all ranks, which I believe made it the largest Regiment in the Army at the time. Its role was to support 44 Independent Parachute

Brigade Group (TA).

For me these were very happy days and I quickly learnt to respect the enthusiasm and efficiency of the volunteer. It seemed to me that the harder you trained them, the more they liked it. One has to remember that TA service is a hobby — some hobby! During my time as adjutant we had little problem with recruiting, as we still had National Service, and on the whole our recruits were trained when they joined us.

I finished my Regular Army career in December 1985, having been Engineer-in-Chief since April 1983. During that period I had many opportunities to see the Territorial Army in action. This involved visits to training centres, weekend training and watching them taking part in major exercises in Germany. They were very well tested, but to my knowledge they never failed to complete a task. Quite a record when you consider the little time that is now available for training and the complexity of modern equipment. Since the end of National Service, recruits now have to be trained from scratch unless they have had previous service in the regular forces.

It was a great pleasure for me to return to the Duke of York's HQ in early 1986 as Secretary to the Council of TAVRAs. The Council co-ordinates the work of all the fourteen TAVRAs who play such an important role in the running of the Reserve Forces.

Also at this time I became Honorary Colonel of 131 Independent Commando Squadron (V) and Southampton University OTC. 131 Commando Squadron is the descendant of 131 Parachute Engineer Regiment and when 44 Parachute Brigade (TA) was sadly disbanded a new role was found for the Squadron, which was to support 3 Commando Brigade, Royal Marines. Honorary Colonels provide a very valuable 'father' figure and continuity in the TA. They can also assist with officer recruiting.

The TA today is expanding to 86,000 by 1990. To reach this figure is a great challenge to all concerned. With increased employment and tighter finance, it is becoming increasingly difficult to find suitable men and women. A National Employer Liaison Committee has been formed whose task is to propose methods of raising the image of the Reserve Forces with the public at large, and in particular with employers. It is essential that this initiative works as·there is a considerable lack of knowledge as to how important the Territorial Army is in the nation's Order of Battle (ORBAT), and therefore our contribution to NATO — forty per cent of the Army mobilized ORBAT, at less than five per cent of the Army's slice of the defence budget — very good value for money!

M. Matthews, Duke of Yorks HQ

Preface by Will Fowler

Returning home on a Sunday evening muddy, tired and with the prospect ahead of a Monday morning at work, many a TA soldier has been asked, 'Why do you do it?' — or a variation on this question, 'If you like it so much, why don't you join the Regular Army?'

The TA soldier may well have asked himself, or herself, the first question as fatigue, cold and rain, by day or night, on a camp, or a weekend, drain almost the last residue of enthusiasm. It can be difficult to explain the motivation of a TA soldier — particularly to someone who has never been involved in any voluntary activity.

The informal explanation which follows is not based on MoD or official TA policy. It does, however, draw on experience gained over nearly twenty years in five TA units in which I served from private soldier to company commander.

Volunteer soldiering and career soldiering have been compared, a little crudely, to the relationship a man enjoys with a girlfriend and with a wife (or a boyfriend and a husband for the WRAC). This may seem a rather simplistic analogy, but it was taken up by a former director of Territorial and Reserves as one way of explaining the difference in outlook between the two forces.

The TA has a career structure like the Regular Army, but has no formal pension scheme or support in domestic matters. As with a girlfriend, the voluntary relationship is one of enjoyment and physical activity — when you are over age, unfit or lose interest, it's time to give it up.

The Regular Army has some of the stability of a marriage: there are the benefits of housing and medical services and a pension on retirement. However, officers and NCOs have the pressure of administration and the full-time responsibility for men and their affairs — in effect, the housekeeping side of the job. Arguably the TA is 'pure soldiering' — training unencumbered by unit administration and the private domestic problems of soldiers and their families.

Former regular soldiers have said that they prefer the TA, since it offers many of the challenges that attracted them to the Army in the first place, without the grind of inspections and administration. Even hard-bitten WO2 or Colour Sergeant PSIs who have been posted, rather reluctantly, to a TA company have grown to like and respect its style of soldiering.

TA soldiers always know that they can 'hang up their boots' and resign, if pressure of work or family life becomes too great. Many men and women in their 20s are involved in career training and exams — TA soldiering is an escape from the pressure of study and preparation. Sometimes, however, this work prevents them from continuing their TA career. For the volunteer, academic or professional exams can be completed in their 20s. However, a Captain or young Major in the Regular Army who chooses to retire and take up a civilian career may have to start professional training up to ten years later than his TA counterpart.

One of the strongest impulses in the volunteer is loyalty — normally to his mates within a small group, or as an NCO or officer to the platoon, troop, squadron or company. The money paid for soldiering is welcome, but a weekend's overtime would probably double what he makes as a soldier — within the hours of 8.00 a.m. to 5.00 p.m. One signals corporal employed full-time by British Telecom listed the extra pay that he would be entitled to if the training weekend were two days' overtime in the rain. There were three extra increments to his basic pay. For some soldiers the bounty is a welcome annual thank-you to the wife and family for putting up with the absences. For some families, however, training weekends can be a welcome break, with the wife free to visit friends and relations without the husband in tow. On Sunday evening the residue of a 24 hour ration pack can be a source of fascination for children who examine the tins, packets and boxes that make it up. For the TA soldier returning from camp or a weekend there is the rediscovery of hot water on tap, privacy and a morning that does not begin with PT or a run.

It can take a real effort of will on a wet Friday evening to leave after five days of a full-time job and become a section corporal or a company commander for the weekend — no less testing, and often more physically demanding, than the full-time job. The officer or NCO may also have taken time off in the evening during the week to plan an exercise or prepare lessons and lectures.

Generally young men and women join the TA looking for adventure. Those who want to be a 'tough guy' will find that there are often a respectable number of men who are stronger and fitter than they are, some of whom have operational experience as former regular soldiers. Very quickly the would-be 'tough guy' discovers that he has a lot to learn and can start the learning process by getting fit. Recruit selection weeds out the medically unfit, physically unsound or those men or women whose educational levels are too low. For some this can be a grave disappointment. I recall a young recruit who had passed the selection, but failed his recruit camp. He sat alone in the stores while his mates paraded to receive their berets as full members of the battalion. We chatted, and as acting second-in-command I urged him not to chuck it in and give up, but to stick with it. It was very cheering some months later to go on exercise and encounter him smeared with camouflage cream, prone in a good fire position, a qualified Rifleman who had not given up but persisted with his training and passed out on the next recruit camp.

Some recruits have been in CCF or ACF cadet forces; some have seen the advertisements and fancy a challenge which will endorse a sense of self respect.

To be frank, if you are in your late teens or early 20s and have a less than exciting job it can be exhilerating to escape at weekends to ride in helicopters or armoured vehicles, to live in the field or navigate across country in the dark. At heart, many grown men still enjoy the sophisticated 'cowboys and indians' of patrolling and fieldcraft. However, after a bit, even these novelties can wear off. What then keeps the soldier in a TA unit are the friends and loyalties he has made. Like the member of a sports team, he knows he will let the side down if he decides not to turn up. Sometimes social and family life can be tested and strained by this commitment. However, the TA soldier is often a happy colleague or employee. He or she may be a bit 'Army Barmy' with their enthusiasm for volunteer soldiering, but often their sense of identity and self respect will be enhanced by the job they do in the TA. The necessary but routine civilian job, which could otherwise be seen as a 'dead end' and produce a discontented employee will be endured if that man or woman can feel that they are a valued part of another separate organization.

The leadership and management value of the TA has been covered elsewhere. Over the years the TA also teaches patience and self control — as when after the long night navigation exercise, the trucks are not at the RV (rendezvous), experienced soldiers have a bit of a growl and then put up a basher and get a brew going. In other words erect a shelter and a make a cup of tea.

The delayed flight, traffic jam or slow train are as nothing compared to the bleak pre-dawn troop movements which begin and end major exercises. 'Hurry up and wait' is not the best way to run an organization, but many a TA and regular soldier has encountered it — the only way to get through is patience and prior planning.

Communication skills in training or in the field are developed in some of the most difficult environments. Try giving a set of orders to a section or platoon as you huddle in the lee of a wood on a rain-swept training area. The outsider may say that no one has to do this in the civilian world — true — but addressing the shop-floor staff, a project team or board meeting in a warm building after you have had plenty of time to collect your thoughts appears, by comparison, almost effortless. The clear sequence in which orders are given, the logical thought processes of a combat appreciation or the way a lecture is structured can be invaluable in the civilian world. The only problem can be toning down instructions so that they do not sound like a set of orders.

The officers and men in the Territorial Army reflect an interesting cross-section of society. There was a criticism of the 'old' TA of the 1950s and early 60s that it perpetuated a 'master and man' attitude, with officers drawn from the professions and men from wage-earning jobs. Much has changed in twenty or more years, and an appetite for adventure and soldiering has always been classless. I recall the bemused reaction of a regular officer when he discovered that the signals corporal of a TA infantry company was a Cambridge MA and had post-graduate qualifications.

TA units which recruit in the big cities contribute in an unintentional way to improved race relations. The comradeship of adversity bonds men, whatever their colour or confession, and when a sub-unit undertakes a task, colour or background are irrelevant when the job has to be done. Anyone who has heard the 'officer's voice' immitated by soldiers, or learned the NCO's nickname, will know that competence, not class or colour, is what counts.

The mix of professional backgrounds can be of benefit to all members of a TA unit. On an exercise in Sennybridge in a break in the action, a young Rifleman received free legal advice about a traffic accident from his company commander, an experienced solicitor. In the civilian world the young soldier would have had neither the cash nor the confidence to contact a solicitor.

Sometimes equipment from the civilian job appears at weekends or camps. One regular Colonel commanding a TA battalion was startled when on exercise in Germany he asked for the platoon commander and the platoon sergeant reached into a bush, and produced, apparently from nowhere, a Telecom telephone hand set: 'Would you like to speak to the platoon commander?' he asked.

Sometimes men and women with professional qualifications do not want to use them as TA soldiers. They join up to get away from the job. Often there can be pressure on, say, a doctor, to become the unit medical officer, or an accountant to became the pay officer.

On exercise in Germany a Chieftain tank broke down near a position held by a company of TA infantry. As the crew peered into the engine and examined the instruments a young TA corporal wandered over 'D'you want a hand?' he asked. The crew shrugged hopelessly and said he could have a go if he wanted. After a few minutes the engine roared into life again. The timing was perfect, for as the infantryman emerged from the driver's hatch, a visiting senior officer was talking to the embarrassed tank crew. None of them knew that in civilian life the corporal was a highly skilled fitter with Mercedes, whom the company would fly to West Germany for updating and training. 'All engines work on the same principles', he explained afterwards.

Platoon funds are strictly not legal in the eyes of the army, so when I was a platoon commander and we levied a modest 50p a man, I was concerned that the book-keeping should be correct. I knew that it would be correctly administered by a junior NCO in the platoon because he was in banking in the City. Little did I expect a bank account with cheque book in the platoon name — in the city branch of the long-established bank favoured by the more traditional army officer. The accounts were a model of rectitude, with details of the exchange rate when we turned some of the funds into Marks before camp in Germany.

This variety of backgrounds is an education for anyone who joins the TA. It can amuse or bemuse the Regular Army, but remains one of the great strengths of the Territorial Army. The reasons why these men and women take up TA soldiering and stick with it are almost as varied as the jobs they do. Ultimately they soldier because they enjoy it.

Will Fowler

Introduction: One Man's Territorial Army

On retiring after twenty five years' service with the Metropolitan Police, it was quite an honour to receive a commission as an officer in the Royal Military Police, TA. At forty four, and too old for most positions in the Army, it was considered that having been a Police Superintendent and a member of the directing staff of the National Police Staff College were sufficient qualifications to raise a new provost unit at Brighton in Sussex. The new life as a freelance broadcaster and travel consultant with the BBC's Motoring and Travel Unit gave me sufficient time to devote to this new and exciting challenge.

The first contact with the TA had been in 1975 whilst serving as the Chief Inspector in charge at Wanstead Police Station in East London. One of the jobs I had was to liaise with other authorities and organizations in the area, especially over security matters. One of these organizations was the Regimental Headquarters of 36 (Eastern) Signal Regiment, a TA unit of the Royal Signals.

We all got on well together, the policemen and the soldiers, and this led to a good social contact. Because of my friendship with the members of their officers' mess, I started to lend a hand on occasions in my off-duty time. It had been necessary in my police service to give some thought and study to the problems of management and leadership, and it was in this field that the Regiment asked me to help. Helping to train their young officers and NCOs meant that I had to put my thoughts into some order and prepare a lecture. This work then formed the basis for another side-line, one that now means that I am often used by the Royal Borough of Kensington and Chelsea to give similar training to those of their staff newly appointed to junior management posts.

Often I visited the Regiment in training at weekends, either to give my presentation, or just to go with the second in command, Major (later Lieutenant-Colonel) Willie Allen to see the management techniques in action. When I started this most enjoyable liaison, the commanding officer was Lieutenant-Colonel John Swindells, who with his training major, Major Mike Alden, both regular officers, delighted in introducing me to the mysteries of the army. Through them I learned the niceties of mess life, as well as many of the courtesies and traditions of the army.

Enduring friendships were forged in those days. The regular Regimental Sergeant Major, Frank Jepson also became a great friend. He left the Regular Army and promptly joined the TA, becoming an officer in the Regiment he retired from, 36 Signals. He is still serving, now as a Major at the Headquarters. His choice of carrying on with the Army in the TA is in itself a tribute to the spirit and enthusiasm of the volunteers, especially when a mature and very experienced Warrant Officer who should have had enough of military life, on leaving the regulars then elects to continue with some form of army service and joins them. One weekend I joined with them as a student on one of their courses. It was a cadre of junior NCOs being trained in various military leadership tasks under Frank's guidance. This was learning how to take charge of soldiers in attack and defence at section and platoon level. It was reasonably physically demanding, and gave us all a chance to learn much about ourselves.

One of the other students was a WRAC non-permanent staff NCO, Val, who not only later married Frank, but also took a volunteer commission in the same Regiment.

By 1981 command of the Regiment had fallen to a TA officer, Willie Allen. When I talked about retirement, it was his idea that I joined the TA. At my age and with a lack of qualifications I felt I had nothing to offer his Corps, but his adjutant Peter McGann, a regular Major, passed on my details to the Assistant Provost Marshal at London District headquarters at Horse Guards in Whitehall. As a result of this there was a telephone call to my office at Enfield Police Station, where after a term on the staff of the Police Staff College at Bramshill, I was serving out my last months in the force. The APM asked me if I would join the Royal Military Police TA.

The author at the Press Launch of the Volunteer Reserve Forces Campaign at the MoD (MARS).

son to move away from London, and a spur to select a place to live. I have always liked Sussex, so all the omens were right.

It wasn't all plain sailing, however. Part of the process all recruits have to go through is the medical. I was declared very fit, but I still failed, having only one kidney. The medical service took pity on me, however, so I was sent off to the Military Hospital at Woolwich where the specialist saw me and subjected me to a number of tests and X-rays. He confirmed the earlier result, that I was fit, and to my relief, fit for military duty, except parachuting and the SAS. He hoped I didn't mind that restriction! I have the greatest respect for those who hurl themselves out of aircraft or subject themselves to the extreme rigours of the SAS, but I am most content to leave that to others.

The medical had not been the only barrier to overcome. As I was still a serving police officer whilst my application was being processed, I needed the written permission of the chief officer, in this case the Commissioner.

The acting Commander of 'Y' District of the Metropolitan Police, Pat Carson, had to do some wheeling and dealing to get the necessary written permission. There is a limit on the numbers of serving civil policemen who are also in TA, and I would have taken that figure over the top. He succeeded on my behalf, however, and the Commissioner, Sir David McNee gave his necessary blessing. It is interesting to note that Sir David has also become involved with the TA, and is the Honorary Colonel of 32 (Scottish) Signal Regiment. Supplied now with the necessary pieces of paper, Lieutenant-Colonel Geoffrey Taylor RMP, the APM, pushed through the rest of the paperwork, and on 3 March 1982, three days after leaving the police, I appeared before a board at Horse Guards, and was accepted for an immediate commission.

My training to convert me from a civilian to a military policeman took place at Chichester, the home of the Corps. This consisted of joining in with the regular recruits, both in the classroom and out in the field on exercise. A day on the ranges and a session in the gas chamber learning about NBC were included. The Company Sergeant Major of the Initial Training Wing also took me under his charge to beast me on the drill square, brushing up on the basics of marching and saluting, as well as giving parade orders.

On 1 April 1982, the new unit was set up at Preston Barracks in Brighton. It consisted of myself as officer commanding, one Permanent Staff Instructor (PSI) who was a regular army Staff Sergeant, and one potential recruit. The next three years saw the unit develop to become effective and take its place along

As a teenager, it had been my wish to join the Army, but instead I followed my father's footsteps into the Police. It seemed that in part my boyhood dreams would at least come true. It was also a very attractive offer to raise and command a brand new provost unit. It didn't need much consideration to accept. Another attraction was that this was to be in Brighton. As a single man for the second time, and after a lifetime in the capital, I was looking for a rea-

with the rest of 253 Provost Company, ready to undertake its wartime role. Within a couple of months there was our first annual camp, and this was to be in Germany. This new officer was taken firmly by the hand by the senior subaltern, Lieutenant George Soper, a TA officer of much experience, having risen through the ranks of the RMP, and having been an RSM before being commissioned. Before he retired from the TA he became a Major and commanded 253 Provost Company. His advice and guidance was invaluable, although the then company OC, Major Burr, kept complaining that I was using Metropolitan Police Radio procedure.

At Brighton the detachment was colocated with a Regular Army unit of the Pay Corps, which has since moved, and a TA Royal Engineers Bomb Disposal Squadron. This was commanded by an old friend, Major Spencer Henry. Both these units kept a friendly eye on our development, especially the Permanent Staff Administration Officer of the Engineers, Captain Brian Batty, who had mastered all the intricacies of TA administration.

Vital to the organization of any unit is the work of the PSI. As a regular, he is at the TA centre most days and provides the vital continuity with both administration and training. The PSI's skill and dedication is soon reflected in the quality of the unit. My second PSI was ideal for the job, and as a former civilian policeman, Staff Sergeant Ken MacLeod brought with his regular army expertise an understanding of ordinary people. Patience with the part-time soldiers, and imaginative training sessions were necessary achievements in such a post. He went on to be the Sergeant Major at the TAHQ of the Corps.

Similarly, at Company level the Permanent Staff Officer is essential to the efficient running of the unit, and in RMP units, this post is filled by a regular career officer.

Theirs is not an enviable job; as with the PSIs, not only do they maintain a presence through the weekdays, so dealing with the great amount of administration, but they also have to be there at training nights and weekends. In short, they are expected to give far more of their time than perhaps in other postings in the army. Two of the PSOs at 253 Provost Company in my time have left on promotion from Captain to Major. These were Roy Bishop, who went on to command the regular Provost Company at Colchester before retiring, and his younger brother Richard, who went on to command the TAHQ at Chichester. It is a coincidence that I later served with their other brother, Lieutenant Colonel Peter Bishop in Public Information.

Another invaluable source of support in the formation of the new unit was the Territorial and Volunteer Reserve Association. As Brighton is in the South East area, the local TAVRA is at Maidstone in Kent. The permanent staff there were headed by Colonel Gerald Mullins, a former regular army officer. He turned out to be an enthusiastic mentor, always at meetings or on the end of the telephone available to help and advise, especially with money matters and problems over buildings or recruiting. The quiet and relentless support the TAVRAs give across the country to the serving volunteers often goes unsung. They are often criticized for being parochial and traditionally conservative, but these are in fact two of their very virtues. By and large they want the best for their own units, and they struggle with politics and red tape to get just that. Being conservative means maintaining standards, and that is just what was being achieved in the South East.

Most significantly at Brighton we were able to see at first hand the benefits that membership of the TA can have for individual young men and women. We recruited some very promising young people, who had no previous military or cadet experience, who then developed in a noticeably beneficial way. They seemed to grow in stature by the time they had finished their two-week recruit course. Confidence to speak and take their own initiative improved, and when they received their first stripe or two as corporals there was an even more pronounced change. For many of them, it is their first chance to give lectures or take charge of other people. They were in fact getting valuable management training, often under quite stressful conditions, especially when on exercise.

Being a small unit, having only one officer and a few senior NCOs, we formed an all-ranks mess. Mess functions were introduced, including ladies nights for all ranks, with mess kit for officers and senior NCOs, best uniform or black tie for the Corporals and recruits. For many of the younger members, these functions were their first experience of a formal dinner, and their first taste of having to act as a host to some important guests. Involved in the growth of a new unit, one does not need the official propaganda to be convinced of the value of the training the TA, and other reserve forces, gives to its members.

Society and employers must surely benefit as well, because people are encouraged to be fitter, smarter, self disciplined and reliable. TA soldiers have to be responsible, taking charge of valuable equipment as well as other people. They have to give as well as take orders, to impose and take discipline, as well as from very early on gain an ability to assess others. These are all virtues of tremendous value, both in business and personally.

Joining with my company on exercise was a novel introduction to a new method of policing. Having to keep traffic moving in convoy on our sections of the major routes was the primary task, as well as to act as police to enforce the law and maintain discipline. This was achieved by groups of NCOs working on their own. The highways and byways of Germany were new to many of us, so we had the opportunity to explore new ground. Although as officers we did not feel superfluous, it became very obvious that the backbone of our operations was the effort by the junior NCOs. There were of course many occasions when, tired and chilled at three in the morning, we wondered what on earth we were doing there, when we could have been back home warmly tucked up in bed. Later on, in the warm glow as dawn breaks, it somehow all seems worthwhile. I discovered the delights of standing in knee high, dew-wet grass alongside a German canal, with a plastic mug of hot sweet tea and an egg banjo. The latter, a fried egg in a roll, was usually accompanied with a sprinkling of burnt grass; still it all went down well, after a chilled night a feast fit for a king. The delights of the compo rations were another new experience, and it is amazing what a tin of curry powder can do to chicken in brown sauce!

After an exercise, the men and women of the new unit had a common experience, something which in the comfort of our mess at Brighton they could regail to the delight, envy, but hopefully not boredom, of friends, relations and newcomers.

After three years on Provost duties with my Corps, someone found out that I was now in broadcasting. The result was a transfer to the TA Public Information Officers' Pool. The villain had been Major Pamela Huggett, a WRAC TA Officer who was then TAPIO for the South East. She had put my name forward to the senior TAPIO, Colonel Alan Protheroe, known to me as the then Assistant Director General of the BBC. He has since moved on to be the Managing Director of SSVC, the Services Sound and Vision Corporation, which among other things is responsible for the British Forces Broadcasting Service.

It was flattering to find out that there was quite a behind-the-scenes tussle, as the Corps did not wish to lose my services. However, I eventually ended up as one of the TAPIOs at London District, including among my TA colleagues, Major Stan Baldwin, an editor on *The Times* and a TA officer for a great many years. My regular army mentor was the Senior Public Information Officer for the District, a retired Guards Officer, Major 'Rags' Courage. Under his guidance I was introduced to the handling of the Press at such major ceremonial events as the Queen's Birthday Parades and the Royal Tournament. The highlight of my time at London District was the two weeks prior to the wedding of the Duke and Duchess of York, when I acted as the public relations officer for the Household Cavalry Regiment. I moved into their mess at their headquarters at Knightsbridge, taking the burden of the Press from the shoulders of the adjutant.

Firstly I had to acquaint myself with the workings of the Regiment, consisting as it does of the ceremonial mounted element of two distinguished Cavalry regiments, the Life Guards and the Blues and Royals. Then it was a case of arranging facilities for the many media reporters and broadcasters who wanted to see the Regiment. During the last few days before the wedding, this meant such as the American CBS fronted by that classic Englishman (in the eyes of the Americans) Roger Moore. The main task on the day itself was to accommodate and help both the BBC and ITV crews, each of whom had a major input from the Knightsbridge barracks. The well-known presenter Sarah Green made quite a few broadcasts on Breakfast television live from the stables, and rooftop predictions were made by the astrologer Russell Grant.

My job with them was to find food and power, arrange for parking and for power lines to be suspended between buildings and over rooftops, and of course to find and prepare troopers, corporals and officers for live interviews.

My army public information experiences were improved by attachments to the office of the Director of Public Relations (Army) at the Ministry of Defence, and to the Public Information branch at HQ United Kingdom Land Forces at Wilton. All this resulted in appointment to a new staff job as SO2, TA Public Information Officer in the MoD with the Director of Army Reserves and Cadets.

I was not quite sure what a job at the MoD would bring: perhaps it would be routine and boring? It certainly has not proved to be so, for although as a TA officer I go to the office only one day a week on average, the job has involved me in many interesting projects, looking at the problems of the TA from a national point of view, as well as getting involved in such as the Home Service Force publicity. My own experience of getting into the Ministry as a TA officer, and being included in the high-level management of the Army, surely indicates that the TA is taken very seriously by the Regular Army, and that TA officers themselves can have a significant influence on policy, not only at a local level, but nationally.

Life in the TA has been full of challenge, and most rewarding. Even the need to pass annual basic fitness tests and regular medical examinations has been a valuable incentive to staying fit and healthy. To be able to write a book such as this has given me an unparalleled opportunity to study the whole of the TA, and to help to some extent to widen the public knowledge, and hopefully respect for this vital part of the defence of the realm. The opening sections of the book are a result of my own research and knowledge, but in those sections dealing with individual units, I have relied heavily on the material that each unit has sent me, my own policy being that I would write very much what each unit would like said about itself.

This means that this work has had many hands, and should truly represent the TA today, including its pedigree. Quite a bit of the history of each unit is included, not merely because in many cases it is of interest, but to illustrate an ancestry, a pedigree, that has a strong bearing on the spirit of the service today. There is tremendous pride in the past achievements of each unit, pride that can generate a healthy rivalry and loyalty.

The inspiration for this book came from John, Diane, and Tony Moore of Military Archive and Research Services from Braceborough in Lincolnshire. The inspiration to actually get down to write it came as much from my wife, Maureen, as from anyone else. I will be forever grateful that the Army gave me this incentive in 1982 to move to Sussex, for whilst living as a bachelor at Lewes I had the very good fortune to meet her. Her part in the production of this book has been significant. The dedication of this work should therefore be to her, and to all the wives, husbands and families of all members of the TA, but it should also be to those millions of men and women over the years who have devoted themselves, and sometimes given their lives, to serving the nation through the Territorial Army.

1 A brief history

It is the love of the people;
it is their attachment to their government,
from the sense of the deep stake they have
in such a glorious institution, which gives
you your army and your navy, and infuses
into both that liberal obedience,
without which your army would be a base rabble,
and your navy nothing but rotten timber.

Edmund Burke

In ancient times, apart from some small groups of paid retainers, there were no standing armies in this country. If the realm needed to be defended, then all free men were obliged to provide manpower. In those days the Militia was the only army, and in Anglo-Saxon England, this was called the Fyrd. It was a force levied locally for the defence of that area, but was later largely replaced by a complex system of feudal duties when the Normans imposed themselves in the eleventh century. For many centuries, members of the Militia joined because they were compelled to, although later some smaller units had members who were volunteers, and later still complete units were formed entirely from volunteers.

When regular armed forces were established, one role of the Militia was to support them in the defence of the country as well as to supplement the army for garrison duties abroad or at home. The Militia were even liable to be called out for service with a field army.

The system was effective to start with, but as the knight in armour arrived on the field of battle, the Militia were less able to cope. Peasants from the fields were no match for trained soldiers, some mounted on chargers.

Following the development of the longbow, it was once again practical to revive the militia system, to enlist peasants quickly trained as competent archers. The introduction of firearms, however, put the military beyond the ordinary man, but when guns became lighter to carry, cheaper to make and easier to master, the Militia again revived. This is how the Militia remained until after Waterloo, when it once more faded away, although it was to exist as a compulsory organization until 1852. It returned as a volunteer force in 1852, until replaced by the Territorial Force in 1908.

The concept of voluntary part-time soldiering goes back for many centuries, and many TA units have records showing direct descent from the eighteenth century, or even earlier. In 1537, Henry VIII granted a charter to the 'Fraternitie or Guylde of St. George; Maisters and Rulars of the Science of Artillerie as aforesaid rehearsed for long bowes, cross bowes and hand gunnes', and today they are called the Honourable Artillery Company, a most distinguished City of London Regiment.

The claim of senior TA Regiment is made by the Royal Monmouthshire Royal Engineers (Militia), which dates from 1577, and has been a unit of the Royal Engineers for well over a hundred years. Although the HAC are older, their service to the Crown was broken by their allegiance to the Parliamentarian cause during the Civil War.

The history of the volunteers is not as old as that of the Militia, but evidence shows that the voluntary military movement developed independently, starting in London, and followed by other cities which raised trained bands of enthusiasts who were ready and willing to defend their immediate localities from hostility.

Loose and often informal voluntary elements grew from the Militia, these associations even electing their own commanding officers. They became regulated nationally in 1794 with the threat of a Napoleonic invasion. Most of these associations were infantry, but volunteer horsemen came forward, to be known as the Yeomanry Volunteer Cavalry. After the victory over Napoleon, the majority of the infantry were disbanded, but the Yeomanry, raised, supported and commanded on a county basis, remained intact.

With a renewed threat of invasion in 1851, the Militia were reintroduced as a volunteer force the

Above *Major Nathaniel Creswick, OC the 4th West Yorks Volunteer Artillery at Sheffield in 1862* (A. F. Flatow).

Below *1874: The Leeds Rifles at Camp at Pontefract. Second from the right is Corporal Braithwaite, who had joined in 1869 and retired as a Major in 1909* (RHQ YORKS).

following year, with an initial establishment of 80,000 men, who each had 21 days' paid training annually. The invasion tension ended with the Crimean War, when France and Britain became allies, but another panic developed in 1859 because of a renewed fear of invasion by yet another Emperor, and it was during this period that volunteer forces really took hold and became established as an auxiliary to the Regular Army. Artillery Volunteers became responsible for the coastal batteries, and Rifle Volunteers had the task of harrassing any invading army.

In an often club-like atmosphere, the new movement thrived, with enthusiasts even paying their own fares to annual camp, drills and the rifle ranges. For sixpence each week they purchased their own, often resplendent, uniforms. Some corps were organized on a county basis, others were urban and very parochial. Many came together because of a profession, such as those of the Inns of Courts, Bankers, Railways, Post Office and the Civil Service. There was even a Freemasons' Corps and a Teetotal Corps. In 1871 the control of the auxiliary forces was taken over by the Crown from the Lord-Lieutenant of each county.

The next development was in 1881 when the Regular Army underwent a dramatic reorganization, known as the Cardwell reforms, after Edward Cardwell, the then Secretary of State for War. He grouped the old infantry regiments into pairs of battalions (those senior to the 26th of the line were already in separate battalions), making them into new regiments. Each new regiment was given a geographical title of a county or city, and the senior of the two battalions in each case became the first and the junior became the second. It was usual for one battalion to

Above *1892: An officer of the 3rd Volunteer Battalion The West Yorkshire Regiment wearing the distinctive Leeds Rifle green uniform* (RHQ YORKS).

Right *1871: a young rifleman with a three-band Enfield Rifle. 7th Yorkshire, West Riding, Rifle Volunteer Corps (The Leeds Rifles).*

serve abroad on a long posting, with the other remaining in Britain. Because they were arranged in geographical association, this brought the volunteers and Militia into closer contact with the Regular Army.

The next two milestones came firstly in 1882, when a group of Post Office Volunteers offered to go on active service in Egypt, and this was accepted, and the second in 1900 with the large surge of volunteers for the Boer War in South Africa. Many thousands volunteered for overseas service in South Africa, and active service companies, each of about 116 men from such as the City Imperial Volunteers and the Imperial Yeomanry, were posted to regular battalions. Of the Yeomanry alone, about 6,000 men served in South Africa during the first two years of this century. Both Egypt and South Africa were special because the Volunteers had been raised to serve only in Britain,

so each man needed to specially volunteer for service abroad.

In May 1904, the Royal Commission on the Militia and Volunteers reported that the Militia 'in its existing condition is unfit to take the field for the defence of this country.' As for the Volunteers, 'neither the musketry nor the tactical training of the rank and file would enable it to face, with prospect of success, the troops of a Continental army.' This Commission did, however, acknowledge in reference to the Boer War that all types of volunteer, as well as the Militia, had 'earned the approval of those under whose command they served.' Their strength at this time was just over a quarter of a million men. Their deficiencies were in transport, equipment and artillery, and were all beyond the control of the members of these forces.

As a result of the efforts of the Royal Commission, the Territorial and Reserve Forces Act of 1907 was

A group of NCOs from The Leeds Rifles pictured in the opening years of the twentieth century. The corporal with the bicycle was a member of the cyclist detachment at Carlton Barracks in Leeds (RHQ YORKS).

passed, and the following year on 1 April, the Territorial Force was born.

Two far-seeing men also set about reforming the Army, which prepared it for the opening of the First World War in 1914. Mr R.B. Haldane, a barrister and philosopher, later Viscount Haldane and Lord Chancellor, together with Field Marshal Lord Roberts VC, set up the General Staff and persuaded the dominions to mesh their defence needs with those of the UK. They also reorganized the auxiliary forces, with the Volunteers and Yeomanry forming the Territorial Force, and the Militia forming the Special Reserve. The first line of defence became the Regular Army, supplemented by a reserve of former regulars who were no longer with the colours, together with the Special Reserve. The second line of defence became the Territorial Force. The 1907 Act brought together the training and administration of the Auxiliary Forces, and with the linking with regular battalions and stronger local associations, an efficient framework existed to create the sort of army that twentieth-century warfare demanded.

A typical infantry regiment then consisted of its first and second battalions of regular soldiers, a third battalion of special reserves (Militia), and the fourth and sometimes a fifth battalion of Territorial Volunteers.

The theory behind this arrangement was that if one of the regular battalions met with heavy casualties, the losses would be swiftly made up by men from the Special Reserve battalion. Once more, the Volunteer

battalions were intended for home defence. The Territorial Force was formed into 14 infantry divisions, each with a Regular Army General in command. Regular officers were also in command of most of the infantry and cavalry brigades.

War with Germany was declared on 4 August 1914, and the next day the Territorials were embodied and told where they had to report for duty. Territorials of the Royal Garrison Artillery went to their heavy guns on the coast, mobile patrols became the responsibility of the Yeomanry, and the Regular Army went to its field positions with the British Expeditionary Force. Once again the offer by Territorial volunteers to serve overseas was accepted and the first complete unit to do so was a battalion of the Middlesex Regiment. Many units went abroad to release regulars for the BEF, taking their places in distant garrisons. The first to get to France was the London Scottish, but the honour of being the first Territorial unit into action fell to the Queen's Own Oxfordshire Hussars, when one of their patrols came across a group of German cyclists in October. On 30 October, the London Scottish were in action and suffered 640 casualties.

Also quickly over the other side of the Channel to join the BEF was the Honourable Artillery Company. By the end of 1914, 23 Territorial Army Battalions were in France. Four months later two complete Territorial Army Divisions were in the field. Back home the volunteers were also busy, the Durham Royal Garrison Artillery engaged units of the German navy

The changing face of transport for the 5th Battalion The Duke of Wellington's Regiment of the Territorial Force: **Above** *Annual camp at Redcar in August 1908, a Maxim machine-gun detachment with horse drawn limber;* **Left** *8 May 1909, the first time that motor vehicles were used in a 'motor mobilization', between Huddersfield and Meltham.* **Below** *8 May 1909: to supplement the motor vehicle, the Battalion also used steam transport.* (RHQ YORKS).

Above *On Strensall ranges near York in August 1912 with a Maxim machine-gun being fired into the stop butt (5th Battalion The Duke of Wellington's Regiment TF)* (RHQ YORKS).

Left *Territorials of the 6th Battalion The West Yorkshire Regiment loading ammunition in August 1914 during the mobilization period at Bradford* (RHQ YORKS).

Above right *Steam transport of the 1st West Riding Brigade arriving at annual camp in 1912 at Hunmanby. The engine was an Aveley and Porter Steam Sapper.*

Right *8th Battalion, The West Yorkshire Regiment TF returning from the assault on Bligny Ridge, for which the Battalion was awarded the French Croix de Guerre.*

in a duel, which created such a din that the battle was heard the other side of the county, in Weardale.

During this war many Territorials gained the VC (see Appendix 2), including two Medical Corps officers who gained bars to their Crosses. Lance Corporal W.H. Coltman of the 6th North Staffordshire Regiment already held the DCM and bar, as well as the MM and bar, when he won his VC in France just a month before the war ended.

After the eleventh hour of the eleventh day of the eleventh month of 1918, when the guns fell silent, it was time to count the dreadful cost. Out of 908,000 British dead, 129,806 were from the Territorial Army.

Throughout the war there had been 56 Yeomanry regiments, but this was too many for the post-war Army. Three were disbanded and of the rest, the senior 14 were allowed to keep their horses. All the others were either mechanized, or changed roles to artillery or signals. They did, however, retain their titles and badges. The horsed regiments were eventually mechanized as well, but this did not happen until 1939, or later in some cases.

The historical background to the TA in Northern Ireland needs special mention. Colonel I.B. Gailey, a TA officer with 74 (Antrim Artillery) Engineer Regiment (V) has explored this aspect of the TA's history*, and his researches go back to before the seventeenth century. Ireland then was very much a tribal society, with very little centralized authority beyond the Pale. Auxiliary military forces therefore developed in a different way to the rest of the country. Irish Lords had produced most of their own soldiers by calling on the 'freemen' within their own domains, who came armed, fought the Lords' battles and returned to their peaceful occupations. For this reason, the wars tended to be of short duration. In 1608 one condition of the Plantation of Ulster was that the 'undertakers', who received grants of land had to 'have ready in their houses at all times a convenient store of arms, wherewith they may furnish a competent number of able men for their defence, which may be viewed and mustered every half year, according to the manner of England'. No Militia in name existed before 1660, and then only in the area of the Pale. Militia saw service in the armies of both James II and William III, but the first Militia Act in Ireland was 1715, and there is some evidence of an array in 1745 and 1756 during the Seven Years' War.

Companies of Volunteers were raised locally by private subscription. They had variously brilliant uniforms and were well armed. Some were in possession of artillery, a move the government of the day was not too happy about.

By the end of 1778, 40,000 volunteers existed. They were a Protestant body, although some of the Companies had admitted a few Roman Catholics. Laws still existed then forbidding 'papists' from possessing arms, so this arrangement came about in a surreptitious way. Colonel Bailey states that 'military organization gave the Irish Protestants a new sense of unity and strength which they now exploited to their advantage. Instead of simply being there to defend the coastline, the Volunteers became a fashionable and extremely effective expression of Protestant political aspirations.'

In the late eighteenth century, the government was anxious to control the Irish Auxiliary Forces, especially as there had been a revival of the volunteering spirit about that time. The Irish volunteers had been tardy in dealing with disturbances, and control over them had proved impossible. The Militia bill of 1793 consolidated the existing laws, setting quotas of men required from each county. An aspect of the new law was that the Corps almost never served, and would rarely be stationed in the county of formation, and another was that Catholics were now officially admitted. The government was to appoint the Colonel for each regiment, and he had to find the other officers, some of whom needed certain property qualifications. There was a ballot in the parishes to select the men, and in some places this led to violence, though it was possible to insure against being selected, and there were always volunteers to take the place of those selected if necessary.

Because of the religious opinions of the majority of soldiers, there were doubts about the loyalties of the Militiamen. An additional force was therefore raised in 1796 as 'District Corps' whose job was local defence, whereas the militia was a counter invasion force. The Infantry and Cavalry were raised almost entirely from Protestants, and the members were exempt from the Militia ballot. This alone was a great inducement to join the new volunteers. As with the rest of the country, the Volunteer Cavalry became known as Yeomen, and the Infantry were called Volunteer Infantry. The volunteers were active during the 1798 rebellion. They were, however, disbanded about 1840. Many Militia men served in England, and it supplied many recruits for the Regiments of the Line, but this was also abolished in 1816.

The Militia was raised again in 1854 on the outbreak of the Crimean War. The new units were artillery as well as infantry. The Militia now, however, was entirely a voluntary body, its volunteers serving for seventy six continuous days' recruit training when they joined, and then a month's embodied service each year. Men from the Irish Volunteers served in the Boer War, as they did again in the First World War, with great distinction.

*In *Royal Engineer Journal*, vol. 97 May 1983.

Right *24 November 1917, at the Battle of Cambrai men of the 62nd Division Machine-Gun Corps filling their gun with water at Graincourt.*

Below *Volunteers of the Duke of Wellington's Regiment serving with the 62nd Division resting in a shell hole after the capture of Marfaux during the Battle of the Marne 1918* (Imperial War Museum).

When the Territorial Army was reconstituted in 1920 following the First World War, it did not apply to Northern Ireland. The circumstances there were special in that the government was bound by a treaty with the new Irish Free State not to raise an army in the Province. It was feared that by raising TA units this would be seen across the border as raising an army. These fears were removed on the condition that the War Office commanded the units and the object of the TA in the Province was for Imperial defence. In the late 1930s, therefore, recruiting restarted, and the exploits of the gallant Ulstermen of the various regiments and corps in the war that soon followed are well known. The TA was popular, and by April 1939 all the units were at full strength.

Meanwhile, the TA in the rest of the country was getting back into its post-First World War stride.

In 1920 the bounty, the annual tax-free award for a year's voluntary service, was a mere £4 for a recruit and £5 for a trained soldier. Through the 1930s, both the regular and territorial armies were short of men, and before the Second World War the TA was poorly equipped. In comparison with the new German Army so were our regular units, with a very weak capability in armour and anti-tank weapons.

The threat of air attack was a major headache for the defence planners. Responsibility for anti-aircraft defence had been given to the TA, and this was expanded into a very large organization, its man-power coming mainly from the TA infantry. Eventually five TA anti-aircraft divisions were formed, their units being either artillery, if equipped with guns, or Royal Engineers if in the searchlight role.

TA recruiting picked up well following Munich in 1938, and in April 1939 the establishment of the TA was doubled. The part-time volunteers of the anti-aircraft units were in uniform and at their gun sites in August that year, and on 1 September the rest of the TA was embodied. It would be many years before they were civilians once again.

For a brief time in 1939 the Militia returned, with young conscripts undertaking six months' training. Before the first intake had been trained, however, war broke out, so they became part of the Army, and the conscripted Militia once again ceased to be.

For the duration of the Second World War, the differences between Regular, TA and Reservist were swept away and all became members of the one army. The county TA Associations, the voluntary bodies who were responsible for recruiting and quartering units locally had handed over an effective army, and they now took over the administration of the Home Guard, known in 1940 as Local Defence Volunteers. By the end of the war this organization had grown even larger than the pre-war TA had been.

The TA were prominent in all three major phases of the Second World War: the BEF's campaign and withdrawal ending with Dunkirk; the defence of the

1938, 66 HAA Regt RA, formerly The
Leeds Rifles, after conversion to the anti-
aircraft role: **Left** a motorized column;
Right learning to use a height predictor.
(RHQ YORKS).

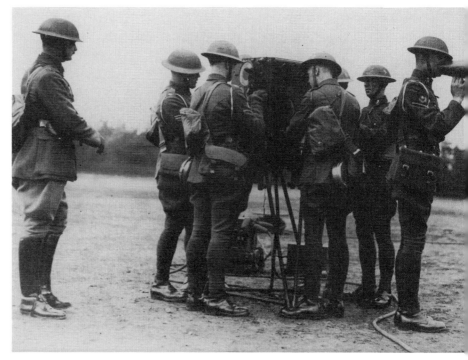

Below 45th Battalion Royal Tank
Corps, TA converted to armour with light
tanks in spring 1938 (RHQ YORKS).

Left *The Leeds Rifles, rebadged to Royal Tank Corps, undergoing machine-gun training in the spring of 1939.*

Below *28 January 1940, somewhere in France, Sergeant Gregson, 4th Battalion The Green Howards, TA, calls the roll on disembarkation* (IWM).

Right *11 April 1943, the 7th Battalion The Green Howards TA; assault of enemy positions at Point 85 in the Gabes Gap area.*

Below *A short rest before the battle for Monte Camino. 6th Battalion The York and Lancaster Regiment TA, 5 December 1943.*

25 June 1944, the Hallams Battalion The York and Lancaster Regiment TA, at Fontenay Le Pesnil after heavy fighting.

August 1943, volunteers from D Company the 6th Battalion The Green Howards TA, advance from Mount Etna towards Messina; seen here entering Letojanni (IWM).

British mainland; and the overseas assaults leading to victory. An early and often boring, mundane task was to guard key points, but three TA divisions landed in France as part of the BEF. One of these, the 51st (Highland) Division was surrounded and captured, despite a courageous stand at St Valery. During the miracle of Dunkirk, many TA were tasked with the defence of the perimeter, and for days the

Queen Victoria's Rifles kept the German thrust from breaking through, but the cost was enormous. The 51st was later reconstituted and engaged the enemy in North Africa, Italy and on the Second Front. In fact on every front, and in every battle the TA did its duty.

After the Second World War, the TA once again revised and reorganized. Until 1967 it consisted of the Territorial Army and the Army Emergency Reserve. This latter reserve was formed of specialist units of various arms, which supported both the Regular and Territorial armies. It was recruited from men and women whose civilian professions or trades meant they had skills the army could not teach them in the limited time a volunteer can give.

A massive upheaval then occurred on 1 April 1967, with the TA and AER combining to form the 'Territorial and Auxiliary Volunteer Reserve'. Many battalions and regiments were obliged to unite into new units, which gave a more compact army. Some severe critics of the time believed that the TA had been carved and hacked about in a merciless fashion. The cumbersome title was changed back to the 'Territorial Army' on 7 August 1979.

The latest changes to the TA consist of an increase in establishment to about 90,000, with new units having been raised and some others enhanced, including the establishment of a 5,000 strong Home Service Force. This improvement is designed to take the army into the twenty-first century.

In the sections of this book dealing with the Regiments and Corps, more detailed histories of the TA will emerge.

In the *Scout*, the magazine of the Scout Movement, of 21 May 1910, an article appeared written by the author's maternal grandfather, Herbert Gardner. He called it 'In Camp with the Terriers', and praised the outdoor life and good food as a health-giving holiday. His description of an ordinary day in camp shows the life of a Terrier as it was before the First World War: reveille at 5 a.m., with the band marching through the lines, followed by 'a good sluice of icy cold water in the fresh morning' to liven one up. Early morning parade before breakfast was followed by an hour cleaning kit. There was then battalion drill, skirmishing, attack practice and training in the field, with an hour's halt for lunch. Later in the day there was sport and outdoor amusements, as well as concerts in the canteen, 'where even the worst singer is allowed to test his voice.' Last Post was the signal to make up the bed, one ground sheet, two warm blankets and the rolled overcoat for a pillow.

The training on a 'Field Day', which consisted of skirmishing and the use of cover, was a far cry from the horrors of the trench warfare to which they were all subjected four years later. Salisbury Plain he referred to as 'one of the finest camping grounds in the world; you can walk for miles and miles without meeting any human being or seeing any human habitation...'; except, of course, when the troops were there, when it was dotted with thickly populated little white cities. Luxuries were provided by the YMCA, from a well-fitted tent, with lounge chairs and everything from halfpenny papers to the best magazines.

Above *At Nijmegen, January 1945, members of A Company, the Hallams Battalion The York and Lancaster Regiment TA unload defence stores at a flooded front-line village* (IWM).

Below *Territorial Force, Gunner Herbert Gardner in 1914.* (B. Gardner).

2 The Territorial Army today

No longer is there a separate Territorial Army, with its own Brigades and Divisions, as once existed. Today there is just one army. This consists of the British Army of the Rhine (BAOR) of which the main fighting force is 1 (BR) Corps, the United Kingdom Land Force (UKLF), and various overseas garrisons. Within UKLF, and to a very small extent BAOR, there are TA units, who dovetail into the Army's organization.

In Germany, there is a small TA contingent created from British civilians who live and work there. The units they form are small components, of platoon or troop size, of major regular army units with permanent bases in BAOR. In time of war these few thousand men can be at their posts very quickly, taking a full role within their major unit, with whom they have been training during peace time.

The bulk of the TA is of course raised and trained within the UK under the command of UKLF, one of whose tasks is to provide reinforcement of BAOR and NATO flanks in time of war.

The Reserves

There are a number of reserves available to supplement both Regular and Territorial Army units in time of war. Regular and Territorial Army officers, when they leave active service are transferred, or volunteer to be transferred, to the Regular Army Reserve of Officers (RARO). For example, those with regular, special regular or certain short service commissions are transferred to this reserve, with an annual training liability for six years, or until they reach 45 years of age. TA and other officers may volunteer for the reserve, but as most of them would have no peacetime training liability, they are encouraged to join in, on a voluntary basis with training or on exercise.

For other ranks, there is the Regular Reserve, which consists of a number of different liabilities, together with the Long-Term Reserve, who have regular training liability. There are also Army Pensioners. These three types of reserve are formed only from former regular soldiers.

The TA not only provides manpower, but also a framework of units into which these reserves can be grafted when necessary.

The Territorial Army

In status each TA unit is equal to its regular counterpart, with a right of a place within the larger organization. Many of the Brigades and Divisions of the Army have their complement of both regular and TA units in varying proportions, for example most of the troops in 15 and 49 Infantry Brigades, part of 2 Infantry Division, are TA, whereas in some other formations the TA complement is much smaller.

Within the TA there are three groups for individuals to join. Group A has the highest call-out liability and training obligations. Group B consists mainly of University Officers Training Corps (UOTC) members, and finally, the newest section is Group C, which consists of members of the Home Service Force (HSF), formed in 1985. The bulk of TA personnel are in Group A.

The role of the TA within the 'one army' concept is to provide units and individuals to reinforce the army committed to NATO, to assist in the defence and security of the UK base, and to provide assistance to the civil authorities at home in time of war, for instance with communications.

Although the TA is considered as one with the regulars, it is still necessary to have some separate control of the policy and administration for them at the Ministry of Defence.

The Ministry of Defence

The Major-General responsible for the management of the reserves, including the TA, is the Director General Territorial Army and Organization (DGTA & Org). The day-to-day executive function is carried out by the Director of Army Reserves and Cadets (DARC), who is responsible for policy matters, management of the TA and the administration of all aspects of the mobilization of reserves. Command of TA units is, however, the same as for regular units, by way of regiments, brigades and districts, and in addition the directors of the various Arms and Services have the same responsibilities for the TA as they do for the regular units. At HQ UKLF the Commander of the UK Field Army, a Lieutenant-General, is also the Inspector General of the TA.

Territorial Auxiliary And Volunteer Reserve Associations

The administration and supply of the buildings, as well as a large amount of the funding for recruiting and some training facilities is the responsibility of the Territorial Auxiliary and Volunteer Reserve Associations (TAVRAs). They are responsible in this respect for all volunteer and cadet forces in their areas.

Their responsibilities in respect of the TA are:
1. the provision and maintenance of accommodation for TA independent units and the furnishing, heating, lighting and cleaning of such accommodation;
2. the administration and maintenance of training areas and ranges vested in them;
3. the provision and administration of married quarters for regular permanent staff in certain cases;
4. recruiting and publicity for units of the TA;
5. liaison with employers, trades unions and local authorities and relations with the public; and
6. welfare.

TAVRAs are able to represent matters directly to Ministers and the higher command of the Army, and by being able to watch over the general wellbeing of the TA, they can raise problems through this route that might not be suitable for consideration through the normal military chain of command. Occasionally the views of the regular soldier and the needs of the territorial volunteer are opposed, so this system ensures that both sides are heard fairly.

Linking the 14 separate TAVRAs is the Council of TAVRAs, which is based at the Duke of York's Headquarters at Chelsea in London. This council acts as the link between the TAVRAs and the Ministry. An example of the value of this council was its efforts resulting in the setting up of the 1978 Shapland Committee, which did a great deal to improve the conditions for the volunteer, including an improved bounty.

Each TAVRA is an autonomous statutory body, established by an Act of Parliament with its own

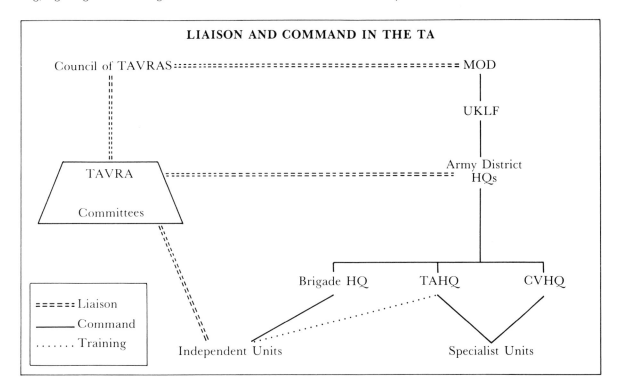

LIAISON AND COMMAND IN THE TA

constitution. The Acts responsible are the Auxiliary Forces Act of 1953 and the Reserve Forces Act of 1980. The TAVRAs are represented by senior members from the Council of TAVRAs on the Advisory Committee of the TA. This is under the chairmanship of an Under Secretary of State from the MoD, and includes in its membership representatives of the CBI, TUC, senior army officers and officials from the MoD.

Heading each TAVRA is a Lord-Lieutenant, and membership is a mixture of the community representing such as the local authorities, employers' organizations and trades unions, as well as serving and retired territorial and regular officers.

The control of the day-to-day function of each TAVRA, and very largely the control of finance, is in the hands of a small permanent staff, some of whom are experienced former regular officers.

These Associations therefore provide an essential link between the Army and the public, and high on their list of concerns is the goodwill of employers and families. Without that goodwill, many valuable and trained TA soldiers would leave the service, or potential recruits be put off from joining in the first place.

Another non-statutory public body that has been recently created to give independent advice on the measures needed to secure the support of such sections of the public as the employers, is the National Employer's Liaison Committee (NELC). This is formed from distinguished people from Industry, Commerce and the Trades Unions, together with representatives from the MoD and the Council of TAVRAs. Each TAVRA is also able to raise its own local Employers' Committee. A major task that both NELC and the local committees have is a Public Relations exercise to persuade the public that not only is it a benefit to the individual to join and serve in the TA, but that the employer benefits as well. The qualities that are highlighted are those of fitness, independence, resourcefulness and smartness. The ability to take and give discipline, and management and leadership training and experience, often under stressful conditions, are also high on the list. New members of the TA also go through a learning experience, because for most of them, they are being introduced to entirely new skills, from drill and care of uniform and equipment to battle skills and weaponry.

Reserve liability

The Reserve Forces Act lays down the types of reserve that can be called out by the Secretary of State:

A — to be called out by the Secretary of State of Defence for service anywhere in the world when war-like operations are in hand or being prepared;

B — to be called out by order of Her Majesty for service anywhere in the world, when danger to the nation is imminent, or a major emergency has arisen;
C — to be called out for Home Defence duties;
D — to be called out by the Secretary of State to aid the Civil Power to preserve the Queen's Peace (this applies only to the Regular Reserve).

All the Reserves, except the Home Service Forces (HSF) come under the call-out in paragraph 'B', and the TA are liable to be called out under any of these headings only if there is an order of Her Majesty, signed under the hand of the Secretary of State, authorizing the call-out. The HSF can be called out as well when this happens, but in all cases their service is confined to the United Kingdom, Channel Islands and the Isle of Man.

In the event of a call to arms, most TA soldiers will report to their local TA Centres. There they will draw weapons and equipment, mount their vehicles and go to their allocated war role. For many, especially those whose task it is to organize and supervise the movement of troops and supplies, such as the Royal Corps of Transport and the Royal Military Police, this transition to the war role must be as fast as possible. Staff Officers and members of specialist units and pools will have received individual instructions as to what to do in these circumstances.

Efficiency of the TA

The situation that applies in the 'one army' is that there is a single chain of command, with both regular and volunteer officers and soldiers appointed to the staff at various formation headquarters. Any comparison between the effectiveness and efficiency of individuals of either type is difficult to make. It is obvious that in many ways the regular must be more effective, after all he is the professional, spending the bulk of his time training and working in the military environment. The volunteer only spends a limited time in the same environment, the amount being restricted by his family, business, job or career commitments.

Many volunteer personnel are as efficient, or even more so than some of their regular counterparts, however, because of their civilian qualifications and experience. Some of these people may be a little lacking in the military niceties, but would be second-to-none technically.

A major problem for the TA is the development of individual and collective expertise, because of the fairly high annual turnover of trained men and women. In any year, about one third of each unit change because of members leaving as a result of personal or business pressures, as well those who leave because of a change of personal attitude towards the

Members of 40th (Ulster) Signal Regiment team taking part in a stretcher-carrying competition (May 1987).

voluntary service. This is the problem that NELC and the TAVRA Employers' Committees are actively tackling.

Some units can only get together to exercise tactically once a year, although many others can arrange this on almost a monthly basis. This means that sometimes battle procedures can be somewhat rusty and the skills and experience of some officers and non-commissioned officers limited by the small amount of time they can personally allocate to military duties. Experience has shown, however, that what the TA may lack in real-time experience, they more than make up for in enthusiasm, improvisation and a quickness to learn and adapt. The survivors in the TA are those who want to be in it. There is no compulsion to remain: if individuals don't like it, they can go.

The economics of the TA

Out of a total defence vote of something in excess of £18,000 million, the Army takes about 30 per cent. Of this amount, about one twentieth is allocated to the TA, and yet the TA provides about a third of the wartime army. Man-for-man, it costs about a ninth of the amount to keep a territorial as it does a regular soldier. This is very good value for money, and without the volunteer reserve forces, in order to meet our current NATO commitment it would be necessary to have a larger regular force. This would be more expensive, and would be a higher call on the nation's purse. There is no difference between regular and TA units in their levels and types of equipment, which ensures the economy of standardization and bulk supply. There was a time in the history of the TA when they were equipped with cast-off equipment from regular units, they were given second best and were way down the list for new kit. Just before the Second World War, units of the Royal Artillery practised with wooden guns. Today it is different. With the need to be instantly ready for war, TA units and Regular units are dealt with according to their role, so many volunteers receive new equipment ahead of some regular units.

Types of Territorial Army unit

The various types of unit need some explanation. That most familiar to the public is the independent unit, which will be found at local Territorial Army Centres (once upon a time these were called 'drill halls'). Each of these may be dedicated to one or more units of varying size, from a Company or Squadron to a detachment of one or more troops or platoons. Members will normally be drawn from those who live or work within a radius of about 30 miles.

These units have the highest training commitment, and soldiers are expected to attend the centre for as many weekly evening training sessions (formerly drill nights) as they can, and this attracts a quarter of a day's pay, an allowance and the reimbursement of any travelling costs. About once each month, sometimes more, there are weekend exercises. These will either start on the Friday evening or early on the Saturday and last until Sunday afternoon or evening. The arrangements for each one depend on the nature of the unit, and can vary from small detachment training to an exercise of a complete regiment or battalion.

It is quaint to hear the press and public use the obsolete term 'manoeuvres' for these weekends. This originated from before the Second World War when major units would be manoeuvred about a major training area, such as Salisbury Plain, like so many pieces on a chess board, far removed from modern warfare. Sometimes these are also erroneously called operations, but that means real war!

Each year a unit will have its 15-day annual camp, and depending on the potential wartime role, this will either be in the UK or abroad. If its role is to support BAOR, there will be a camp in Germany or the Benelux countries every other year or every third year. Others with a role elsewhere could find themselves in parts of Scandinavia. Some have been able to take their camp in more exotic places, such as the USA or Gibraltar. In general terms this camp will consist of a major exercise, together with training centred on a barracks. When there is a major Divisional or Corps exercise, such as BAOR's Exercise Lionheart in 1984, or a major home defence exercise, then most of the annual camp will be taken up with it.

The other major type of unit is the specialist unit. This is not based at a local centre, but has its headquarters at a central location. Most of these are based on a corps which has a specialist role, such as Medical, Transport and Ordnance. Members, who come from all parts of the country, will be on a lower training obligation, but they still have to complete an annual camp.

Specialist units rely heavily on the fact that membership is drawn mainly from those who have a high level of expertise because of their civilian employment. In theory they do not need to be taught their special skills, but merely to practice them in the military environment. There is a wide range of examples of professions, such as all branches of medicine, policemen, engineers, cooks and catering experts, supply specialists, drivers and movements personnel.

Examples of other specialist units are the 'All Arms Watchkeepers' Pool administered by the Royal Artillery, and the Public Information Officers' Pool, administered by HQ UKLF on behalf of the Director of Public Relations (Army).

In the various Corps, responsibility for the TA element is vested either with a Central Volunteer HQ (CVHQ), or a Territorial Army HQ (TAHQ). A CVHQ has responsibility for the specialist units of

the Corps, but a TAHQ also has the task of the special to-arm technical direction of the Independant Units and Pools.

In all types of unit, many volunteers perform far more days' duty than the minimum required. Because a TA unit is expected to operate along the same lines as its regular counterpart, the volunteer officers and NCOs who hold key positions in the command and management structure need to attend more often, to keep the administration ticking over efficiently. Much of the routine work, however, is undertaken by the small cadre of regular officers and NCOs, as well as some civilian staff at each centre.

The level of regular and civilian staff varies with the needs of each unit. Many regiments or battalions are commanded either by a regular or a volunteer Lieutenant-Colonel, perhaps with a volunteer second in command, and regular officers as Training Major, Adjutant and Quartermaster, but most other key command positions are filled by volunteers.

Each unit has its Permanent Staff Instructors (PSIs), who help the officer in command with training and administration, providing a vital link between the regular and volunteer soldier. There are also a number of Non Regular Permanent Staff (NRPS). This strange title denotes those men and women who are in full-time TA posts with military rank, but who are not regular officers or soldiers. Many of them are former regulars, and typical of the NRPS role is the Permanent Staff Administration Officer (PSAO), usually a Captain at a Squadron or Company. Some of the quartermaster and HQ administrative staff are NRPS NCOs.

Training

The training each year is divided between in and out-of-camp training. To qualify for the annual bounty, each volunteer has to undertake a 15-day camp, or its equivalent such as a course, and out-of-camp training appropriate to the unit, which is up to 16 days in independent units. In addition to this, the officer or soldier has to be available for service throughout the year, which is from 1 April to 31 March. Other needs to be fulfilled include a basic fitness test (BFT), firing the personal weapon (APWT), and award of the annual certificate of efficiency by the CO. This certificate is awarded depending on success at certain tests which are designed to ensure fitness for the role. These include personal fitness and weapon handling, first aid, NBC skills and some special to-arm requirements. Some of the out-of-camp training will be designated by the CO as of particular importance, and he can require each officer or soldier to attend a minimum quota of training in order to qualify.

An annual basic fitness test is a must to qualify for the bounty.

Group 'C', which is the HSF, has a lower require-ment for its volunteers. They need only attend a mini-mum of six days' training, be available throughout the year, and gain the certificate of efficiency to qualify for the bounty. This is possible because the HSF is recruited only from trained servicemen who have served at least two years in the regular or volun-teer arms of any of the services, or who were MoD Policemen. This means they already have the neces-sary skills for the job and only need revision and practice.

Recruiting

This is a continuous process for most units in order to make up for wastage and retirement. A potential recruit is attracted either by friends already serving,

or by the various advertisements put out by the units, the TAVRAs or from the MoD. The recruit will go to a TA Centre, usually the nearest to home or work, and ask to join. After the application forms have been completed, most units usually allow potential recruits to come along to the training evenings whilst the paperwork is processed.

This is a useful period for both the unit and the recruit, in which to assess each other. The papers can in some cases take many weeks to process, especially in such as the Intelligence Corps and the Royal Mili-tary Police, where detailed scrutiny is obviously neces-sary. Units have a selection day or weekend, where all potential recruits are put through a series of tests designed to assess whether or not the applicant is fit and suited either to the Army or to that particular unit. A medical examination is needed to prove that health is acceptable, and if all goes well this is fol-lowed by the enlistment. The taking of the oath using the method appropriate to an individual's religious belief is the ceremony that makes a man or woman

Left *All ranks have to be proficient at NBC procedures* (R. Tutt).

Below *'We're the last line of defence, because we're young enough to fight, but a bit too old to run away . . .'. Home Service Force.*

Right *Members of the HSF, 3rd Battalion 51st Highland Volunteers are reminded of the intricacies of the GPMG.*

into a soldier, albeit not yet a trained one. The oath is:

I (name) swear by Almighty God that I will be faithful and bear true allegiance to Her Majesty Queen Elizabeth the Second, Her Heirs and Successors and that I will as in duty bound honestly and faithfully defend Her Majesty, Her Heirs and Successors in Person, Crown and Dignity against all enemies and will observe and obey all orders of Her Majesty, Her Heirs and Successors and of the Generals and Officers set over me.

The next step is the issue of uniform and personal equipment, so that training in earnest can start. Preparation for the two week recruits' course at a depot is next on the agenda.

Members of independent units receive quite a bit of pre-course training with their units, and should at least know how to wear and care for the uniform, undertake simple drill and know the structure of the Army, including the ranks. Success on the course means that the recruit has been trained in all the basics of the common military syllabus, that is basic infantry skills, living in the field, NBC and drill. Each recruit also gets enough of the special to-arm training to qualify as a tradesman at the lowest level of competence. This level of skill is then built up over the years, with tests and courses at various intervals, to ensure a progression not only through the ranks but also to the higher trade ratings.

Recruiting of officers is more complex and takes much longer. One system is the direct entry scheme. Following either a national recruiting campaign or one undertaken by a local TAVRA, applicants are interviewed to screen them, after which they are enlisted as ordinary soldiers. A unit is then found to sponsor each individual. Following success at one of the District Assessment Boards, usually in the course of a weekend at a military establishment, the recruit is granted officer cadet status. Normal recruit training is undertaken with the unit, together with additional training arranged by the District. This is accompanied by any special to-arm training needed.

Following a nine-day tactics and leadership course, the cadet will eventually reach the Royal Military Academy Sandhurst for a two-week commissioning course. All this can take 18 months to two years to complete. Following Sandhurst, the new Second Lieutenant can wear his single shiny star with pride.

Another route to a commission is through service in the ranks. Unless a potential officer has reached Warrant Officer rank, his training and selection is similar to that of direct entrants. Warrant Officers in reaching that high non-commissioned rank will have more than enough experience and background if selected as suitable to be an officer. Ordinary TA and Quartermaster commissions are open to such officers, subject to vacancies. There are of course variations to these procedures for specialists, such as Chaplains, Doctors, Public Information Officers and certain other technical experts, who will find themselves exempt from much of the commissioning procedure and training, and can qualify for an immediate commission, subject to suitable vetting and basic training. This is because they bring from their civilian life all the necessary specialist expertise.

Left Potential officer recruits undergo their arduous selection tests under the watchful eyes of TA officers.

Members of the Territorial Army Commissioning course on their passing out parade at Sandhurst.

There is no hard-and-fast rule concerning age, beyond the need to be over seventeen-and-a-half years old, as well as being fit and healthy. Most recruits are between 18 and 24, the maximum age for most units being 32, or 35 with previous military experience, but for some specialists it is possible to join the TA up to the age of 46.

Volunteers for the HSF are accepted up to the age of 50, and physically fit volunteers can stay until they are 60. Within the rest of the TA the maximum age for remaining in an active post varies with rank and speciality, and after a certain age service is only continued with an annual extension. For some ranks this is 45 years, and others in the 50s.

Pay and Allowances

No one is encouraged to join the TA just because of the financial rewards. Most volunteers can earn between one and two thousand pounds each year at the most. The bounty is a valuable gift each year, as it is tax free, but it is regarded merely as compensation for being available for a whole year for service. Each member of the TA receives a day's pay for each day's training, and this figure is based on the regular army rate for the rank. Expenses and other allowances are paid, so that a volunteer should not be out of pocket. An allowance is paid for each even-

ing training session of two or more hours, as well as a quarter of a day's pay. Travelling expenses are also paid for a volunteer to get himself to the TA Centre or training area from his home or place of work.

TA Career

A recruit who intends to stay as long as he or she can is able to look forward to quite a career, subject of course to their own ability. All the non-commissioned ranks are open to volunteers, and it is possible to become a Warrant Officer Class One or a Regimental Sergeant Major (RSM).

For officers, the highest rank at present available is that of Brigadier. The senior post for volunteers is the Brigadier at HQ UKLF, advisor on TA matters to the Inspector General, and in 1988 Brigadier Ian Sim became the first officer to reach that post without the benefit of regular, wartime or national service experience, having joined the TA as an officer cadet after having been in the Army Cadets. His career as an infantry officer included command of a platoon, a company and a battalion as well as a number of staff appointments.

The Social and Mess Life

As with regular units, all but the smallest TA units

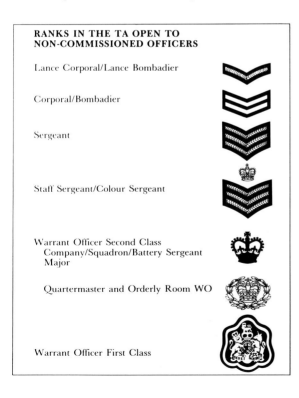

RANKS IN THE TA OPEN TO NON-COMMISSIONED OFFICERS

Lance Corporal/Lance Bombadier

Corporal/Bombadier

Sergeant

Staff Sergeant/Colour Sergeant

Warrant Officer Second Class Company/Squadron/Battery Sergeant Major

Quartermaster and Orderly Room WO

Warrant Officer First Class

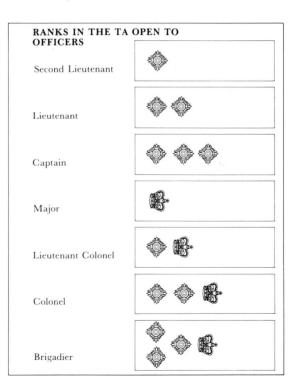

RANKS IN THE TA OPEN TO OFFICERS

Second Lieutenant

Lieutenant

Captain

Major

Lieutenant Colonel

Colonel

Brigadier

have Officers' and Sergeants' messes, with Corporals' and other ranks' clubs. Small units may have just some of these, or operate an all-ranks mess. The major difference between the regular and TA messes is the absence of living-in members. Organization and behaviour within the messes is virtually identical.

Both Officers' and Sergeants' messes will be headed by a President of Mess Committee (PMC). The committee to run each mess is formed from other mess members to take on such roles as secretary, treasurer, wine and house members. In the mess, subject to the Commanding Officer, each PMC rules supreme.

Various mess functions are arranged throughout the year. Some of these, including guest or ladies nights, will require members to wear mess kit, number one dress (blues) or black tie. Officers and senior NCOs in the TA are encouraged to own a mess uniform of their corps or regiment for wear at such events or when attending those of other units. The social side of any unit is an important part of life in the TA, helping to bring members together and enable spouses, parents and friends to share something of the volunteer's pride and enthusiasm in his unit. Dances, barbeques, games nights and outings are typical of the less formal events messes enjoy.

Women in the Territorial Army

The details of the two corps open to women in the TA are dealt with later in this book. In the majority of cases, women join either the WRAC or the QARANC, depending on the role they wish to train for. There are no units in the TA solely for women, and in most units, women take up roles that can be undertaken by either men or women. Major employers of women are the Medical Services and the Royal Signals, although most other arms and services have a WRAC element. There are a few posts where women join other corps, and these are where qualified personnel, doctors and surgeons, are cap badged RAMC or RADC.

Reserve Forces and Leadership Benefits

Mr R. T. S. Macpherson, CBE MC TD DL, Chairman of the National Employers' Liaison Committee has very firm views about the benefits that come from being a member of the reserve forces, not just for the individual but for his or her employer. He has kindly set these views down. In order to fully understand the argument it is necessary to look at

A display of uniforms of volunteers from the Duke of Lancaster's Own Yeomanry.

the state of management and leadership in Britain today. His debate is under four headings:
Criticisms of British management today;
The needs of management training;
Management qualities; and
Where the TA fits in.

Criticisms of British management today: 1987 saw the publication of reports by Hardy and Constable with such devastating criticism of British managers and their performance that the debate on management — partly stilled by the emerging advance of Britain up the ladder of the World economic league — burst out once more in full voice, the loudest voices coming from those professional establishments whose financial interests are touched.

No one doubts that our systems of management training need improvement, even though we suddenly see British managers very much in demand on the world personnel market, and even though there is no doubt the enterprise factors in British management have developed a new cutting edge. This very positive change indicates clearly how much a manager is affected by the social and political climate in which he lives and works. Just a decade ago it was calculated that a third of most managers' time was taken up on labour matters — tensions and disputes — and at least another

Above *recruits from Queen Alexandra's Royal Army Nursing Corps train with male colleagues on their recruits course.*

Below *A WRAC lance corporal checks the weapons of sentries at a communications site.*

third by government-induced uncertainty factors. In addition, the managers worked in a society where risk-taking went unrewarded under penal personal taxation, and where the successful businessman was a prophet quite without honour in his own country.

Now enterprise is publicly and politically admired, and business success is socially applauded. For most managers, good communication in a favourable atmosphere has turned labour relations from a preoccupying burden into a positive and productive element in the job. Government, in turn, is striving not without success to give a physical and political infrastructure supportive to business.

Performance and growth in the economy give a prima-facie judgement that the Hardy and Constable criticisms are to some degree out of date. Nevertheless, it is within the personal experience of all of us that there are many entrenched top managers in industry with permanently defensive strategies, and wholly devoid of the expertise to diagnose their weaknesses and devise improvement. In the City of London, moreover, we have to read into the catalogue of published disasters that many of the new conglomerates are collections of highly able technical operators with no qualified overall management at all.

Further down the line, anecdotal evidence abounds of poorly trained, inadequately motivated, insufficiently informed middle management tiers.

Of course it is one thing to indentify a training shortfall, and quite another to agree how to fill it. **The needs of management training:** The first step must be to get some agreement on the objective — on what a manager needs. The Institute of Manpower Studies recently published a report on what 40 companies felt were basic management skill requirements. These highlighted character qualities like initiative, judgement and motivation, with absorbed qualities like numeracy, planning skills, analysis, organizational skills, language and communication, and so on. The authors of the report drew attention to the remarkable absence in the list of the need for marketing skills, and the need for an understanding of the use of technology and of the implications of technological change. I would suggest these omissions arise from the lack of these qualities in the top managers interviewed — mostly of a generation who didn't know about them.

The obvious training need is for input of the absorbed qualities and techniques. Less obviously, but equally important, are programmes to draw out, develop and improve the character qualities.

In neither case can this be a one-off finite training programme, like an 'A' level or a first degree where, once it is done, that's it for life. Techniques are constantly changing and need updating. Without stimulus, character qualities grow stale, grooved and complacent. My personal rule as a chief executive has been to require my senior people to attend an external course every year, even a short three or four-day seminar, as much to shake their ideas by listening to a new peer group in alien surroundings as to learn from the course subject, beneficial though we hope that to be.

Management qualities: But let's come back to the list of qualities in the Institute of Manpower Studies survey, extended by their reporter's comments. There are surprising and significant omissions — the prime requirements of energy and courage. Energy is the *sine qua non* of successful management; physical and mental demands are constantly at a punishing level. And without courage, there will be no progress; difficult judgements, risk taking, decisions affecting people, possible unpopularity and differences with friends — all these and more call for a high order of moral courage. The final and most crucial omission from the list is leadership. Here is one of the Victorian virtues that is back in fashion in a big way. Suddenly, in a confident, progressive economic atmosphere, people (too often wrongly) take for granted technocratic skills in the boss, and seek real leadership — and respond to it. This is the quality that moulds a team together, that gives direction and purpose, that adds the cutting edge and the touch of flair.

How do we get it? It is far too simplistic to claim that leaders are born not made. Many, many men and women have the seed of leadership inside them, waiting to be nurtured to full flower. Certainly the process will not come from case studies at Harvard or from the best of training at any other management school. Leadership development can only come from exercise of responsibility for people, the direct command of people.

Where the TA fits in: This is where the Armed Forces have a contribution to make, and I refer particularly to the Volunteer Reserve Forces — the Territorial Army, Royal Naval and Marine Reserves, and Royal Auxiliary Air Force. Those who serve as such volunteers are civilians first and foremost, giving priority to their working careers, and serving the Crown partly for patriotic reasons, partly because they enjoy it, partly perhaps because being a spare-time officer is a continuous management and particularly leadership training. The officer takes absolute responsibility for his men. If he fails to make them an efficient and

Typical Programme for Potential Infantry Officer Training

Phase one: This lasts for three to four months and consists of basic training and a recruit course, regimental training and a district assessment board. In detail the training will include weapon training, map reading, first aid, NBC, drill, and this would take place at unit training nights as well as weekends. During this period, the leadership potential is assessed.

Phase two: This will take up the next three to four months, and could include eight weekend training sessions organized on a district basis, as well as continuous training with the unit at evening training sessions. The detail in this phase covers military knowledge, basic tactics, oral orders, service writing, sword drill, service funds, regimental history, platoon commanders' duties and a revision of all the basic training received in Phase One. This should result in a sound basic military knowledge and a development of the leadership capability.

Phase three: This is a nine-day tactics and leadership course held at a regular Infantry Training Depot.

Phase four: This consists of attendance at a two-week commissioning course at the Royal Military Academy at Sandhurst. Between the last two phases, the potential officers continue to attend unit weekend and evening training.

unified team, the failure may be mortal. He has to make positive judgement and clear decisions on matters literally of life and death, and he has to communicate them with unambiguous clarity. He is also likely to be among a company's fittest employees, enjoying less absenteeism, and a physically sound basis for the vital management requirement of energy.

There can be no doubt that the career benefits are great, both individually and perhaps still more for the employer. Where else can he get — and get for free — this sharply-honed leadership training to add to general and specific technical skills, on a continuously tested and extended basis? The cost is minimal — a fortnight's release a year, and most would in any other case be sent on some very expensive external course as part of personnel development anyway.

Of course there is an element of national duty, good old-fashioned patriotism. But in suggesting to employers this course of actively encouraging your planned future top managers to seek Volunteer Reserve commissions, I am pointing you towards the basic Adam Smith principle of enlightened self interest. In no way am I extending the begging bowl, the idea that the services have a problem and please will you come and solve it. The proposition is this: you have a problem, and the Volunteer Forces of the Crown can solve it for you.

These views were set down by Tommy Macpherson and addressed to employers. His background, not only as a most successful businessman, but also as a soldier have made him a good choice as Chairman of the National Employers' Liaison Committee. On 4 June 1939 he was commissioned into the 4th Battalion Queen's Own Cameron Highlanders, a TA unit, and when embodied for the Second World War went to the 5th Battalion. He served throughout the war until 31st October 1945, when he had reached the rank of Major. When the TA reformed in 1947 he was attached to 21 SAS (Artists Rifles) until 1952. After a break, he rejoined as second in command of the 1st Battalion The London Scottish in 1960, taking command of the Battalion as a Lieutenant-Colonel from 1961 to 1964. He was then promoted to Colonel, attached to London District until 1967. From 1968 to 1972 he was a member of the Greater London TAVRA.

Civic Support

In most parts of the country, the TA and other reserve forces enjoy the support of the local civic leaders. In some cases this is shown by their appearance at military functions, but others take a more active part. An example of this activity was shown by Sir Greville Spratt, the Lord Mayor of London during 1987 to 1988. Sir Greville is not only a very respected member of the City, but following regular army service he joined the Honourable Artillery Company as a private soldier, later being commissioned and rising to the rank of Colonel. In his civic role he is by right the President of the City of London TAVRA.

During 1987 and 1988 there was much criticism of the standard of British management in business and government. At their convention in 1987, the Director General of the Institute of Directors said there is a need for leadership training in government and business, people need to be taught to think clearly, boldly and imaginatively. The same message was given by Lord Young, the Employment Secretary, who said '. . .one third of our middle managers have no management training since starting work.' Some learned reports give support to this theme. Professor Charles Handy said 'Management training in Britain is too little, too late, for too few, and despite much progress, a great deal seems to be left to chance in a Darwinian belief that the fittest will survive.'

On 7 March 1988, a report by Wendy Hirsh for the Institute of Manpower Studies highlighted some common characteristics which stand out as being the qualities sought by companies when looking for new managers. These include the ability to communicate, leadership, judgement, initiative, organizational skills, and motivation. Others were planning, innovation, good appearance, interpersonal skills and maturity.

On the same day, Sir Greville Spratt hosted a gathering of some fifty leaders from industry and commerce in the City of London, to ask them to support the TA and the other reserve forces. He asked them to get their companies to make it a policy to allow an extra week's special leave to TA members so that they can attend annual camp. He wanted them to recognize the vital role played by the Reserve Forces in the defence of the country, and to welcome membership of their employees of the TA, RNR, RMR and RAuxAF. His final request was that they made these policies known throughout their organizations.

His message to employers was clear, the TA and other reserve forces are good news. Officers and NCOs develop leadership, get management training, develop good supervising techniques, have the ability to assess subordinates, make decisions often under stress, develop communications skills and instructional ability. As well as this, of course, the volunteer is fit, confident and self-reliant.

This initiative was in line with that of the Prime Minister in launching the National Employer's Liaison Committee (NELC), under the chairmanship of R.T.S. Macpherson, Chairman of Birmid Qualcast. One of the committee's tasks is to provide independent advice on the measures needed to win and maintain the support of employers for the Reserve Forces. Its membership includes leaders of industry, commerce and the trade unions. It had already appreciated that a reliance on national pride was no longer enough to gain employers' support, but that the advantages that employers would gain from their employees' membership of the Reserve Forces in terms of skills learned and personal qualities have to be stressed.

Supporting him that day was Colonel R.R.St.J. Barkshire, a well known figure in the City who had also been a TA officer for many years and who is the Vice Chairman of the City of London TAVRA, who said that it is financially worthwhile supporting the TA. Absence of an effective reserve force could mean extra expenditure on a larger standing army, or an acceptance of not being able to meet our NATO commitment. A larger regular force would mean greater

Young businessmen try their hand at an Executive Stretch.

taxes, and less for other things.

Also in support was Brigadier Dermot Blundell, who then commanded 56 (London) Brigade. He outlined the strengths of the TA, stressing that the regulars are the spearhead of the army, but they would be useless without the power and strength that comes from the shaft. He praised the volunteers: 'Their enthusiasm, initiative and ability to learn fast is quite remarkable. Their diverse civilian skills combine well with a healthy ability to question dogma, let alone military pomposity.'

The TA in the Community

Now and then a TA unit is able to combine its training with something of value to either the community at large or to a small section of it. Very often Royal

Engineer units need to practice demolition skills, and it is far more realistic to have something to blow up, or blow down, especially when its removal can help someone else, such as a charity. Help with building assault courses for youngsters has been another area of value. Aid to the civil authorities, especially in time of severe weather or flood has been freely given when required.

One fairly new way to give something back to the community is in the form of what is known as 'Executive Stretch'. Started in South Wales by 3 RRW, these are weekend courses organized and operated by some TA units. The TA officers and soldiers administer and organize the event, but those taking part will not be TA personnel. They are young executives from local companies, whose employers send them along. Not only does it give them a taste of life in the TA, but it enables them to stretch themselves physically and mentally. Tasks in the field, similar to those for candidates at a Regular Commissioning Board, designed to test teamwork, leadership, preparation and planning, as well as the giving of orders, are accompanied sometimes by the need to fend for oneself as far as food and shelter are concerned.

3 The Yeomanry

In the eighteenth century, various authorized and remunerated fencibles, including cavalry, volunteer light horse and other volunteers existed, but rarely was there any co-ordination, either locally or nationally. When the French declared war on Britain, it proved to be a catalyst that resulted in an Act of Parliament, in 1794. This was to encourage the proper formation of volunteer cavalry. When called out by a High Sheriff or a Lord-Lieutenant, the Gentlemen and Yeomanry Cavalry, as they had become known, were paid as regular troops and subject to military law. Commissions as officers were generally granted to the nobility and gentry, and the other ranks were filled by land-holders and tenant farmers. They had to find their own horses, but saddlery and uniforms were found by the officers, although in some cases they were provided by subscription raised in the county. Some time later, the government provided the arms for these units, consisting of curved swords, horse pistols and some carbines. Not only did membership of the Yeomanry enhance a person's social standing, but it gave exemption from service with the Militia.

Many corps of volunteer cavalry were quickly raised, 28 in the first year, 6 the next and 31 during 1797. The mainstay of the organization was the troop, consisting of between 20 and 50 men and based on a town, village or estate.

Throughout the Napoleonic wars there were false alarms, and rumours were rife, so the Volunteers were often called out. An invasion of sorts did occur in 1797 in Pembrokeshire. A French force, with ships sailing under false British colours and commanded by General Tate, an Irish American employed by the French, appeared off Fishguard on 22 February, and troops were landed. The Castlemartin Yeomanry and other forces gathered between the French and the town. They were joined by many country folk armed with whatever they could get hold of. The French had no stomach for a fight, and apart from a few skirmishes with small groups, they surrendered and laid down their arms at Goodwick Sands under the super-

vision of the Yeomanry. The successor to this Regiment is A Troop of 224 Squadron, 157 (Wales and Midlands) Transport Regiment RCT.

Until well into the nineteenth century, the Yeomanry were often used to police disturbances and quell riots. This was especially so between 1839 and 1847 at the time of the Chartist riots. The need for the civil powers to call for their assistance diminished as more effective police forces were established.

During the nineteenth century most troops of Yeomanry were incorporated into county regiments, and merged into squadrons, in line with the organization of the regular cavalry.

A glorious period for the volunteer Yeomanry came at the turn of the century, when large numbers volunteered for active service in South Africa. Within weeks of the start of 1900, battalions of Imperial Yeomanry were embarked for the Boer War where they proved themselves worthy soldiers and soon adapted to the new style of warfare dictated by the Boers. The Yeomanry and the Boers had farming and country life as a common factor. As a result of the experiences in this war, the 54 regiments of Yeomanry changed their training and equipment. Specialist sections were introduced for such innovations as the machine gun, motor transport and wireless telegraphy (W/T).

The next great test came in 1914, with the start of the First World War. Initially the Yeomanry were concentrated for home defence, in August of that year, but some regiments were soon sent overseas. A few went to France as mounted troops, but there were few opportunities for traditional cavalry action. They were generally held in reserve in case of a major enemy breakthrough, and some even took their turn in the trenches, as infantry. It was on patrolling duties that the Queen's Own Oxfordshire Hussars became the first TA unit to see action in the war.

An example of traditional cavalry action later in the war was the charge by the Northumberland Hussars on the Somme, in 1918. They crossed the valley at Morlancourt at full gallop, and so distracted the enemy that the infantry were able to take some ground. Other Yeomanry regiments served at Gallipoli in 1915, and in Egypt and Palestine.

Between the wars many regiments converted to other arms, such as artillery or signals, or were mechanized in the reconnaissance role. Some regiments disappeared, and only the senior regiments kept their horses.

During the Second World War the only true horsed cavalry action that took place was in the Syrian Campaign against the Vichy French. Spending their time patrolling against the withdrawing French were the regiments of the 5th Cavalry Brigade. This consisted of the Cheshire and North Somerset Yeomanries, and the Yorkshire Dragoons. On 9 June 1941 the Cheshire Yeomanry helped capture a strongly held bridge in the River Litani area, but the last mounted regiment was the Yorkshire Dragoons.

The BEF in 1939 included some of the mechanized Yeomanry, who took their share of the fighting before Dunkirk. Tank and armoured car warfare became the stock in trade of the mechanized Yeomanry in all theatres, such as the Western Desert, Italy, and from Normandy into Germany.

The flexibility and sometimes unorthodox approach of Yeomanry were reflected in the Desert Campaigns. The Long Range Desert Group and Popsky's Private Army both used many such volunteers for their unique approach to desert warfare.

Yeomanry Today

Since 1945 the story of the Yeomanry has been one of constant change and amalgamation. The result is that today five Yeomanry regiments remain in the mechanized cavalry role. Two are in support of our NATO commitment, and the others are for home defence duties.

The Regiments intended for BAOR, the Royal Yeomanry and the Queen's Own Yeomanry, each have four reconnaissance squadrons, all equipped with the Fox Armoured Car as well as the appropriate CVR(T) for SHQs, RHQ, support troops, ambulances and fitters. The three home defence regiments have the civilian model three-quarter ton Land Rover.

The primary role of an armoured reconnaissance regiment is to seek out accurate and useful information about the enemy, his movements and strength. This then has to be passed back to the proper command level as quickly as possible. Any other information, such as the state of the terrain and civilian population, the conditions of the roads, and potential obstacles to our own forces is also necessary.

To fulfil this role, these Regiments need to be masters of fieldcraft and the art of stealth, as well as masters of their equipment. Fire power is a minor consideration, as to use weapons when in this primary role would only betray their presence to a watchful enemy. Some fire power capability is needed, however, in the other roles that the Yeomanry may now undertake. In general terms, their roles are summarized as follows:

a — observing and reporting direction and strengths of enemy forces;

b — covering defensive positions or withdrawing troops;

c — observing obstacles;

d — protection of the flanks of a formation;

e — anti-helicopter or anti-airborne forces operations;

f — advance to contact, seeking out the enemy;

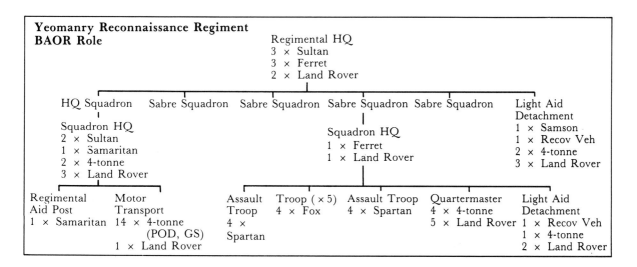

Yeomanry Reconnaissance Regiment BAOR Role

Regimental HQ
3 × Sultan
3 × Ferret
2 × Land Rover

HQ Squadron — Sabre Squadron — Sabre Squadron — Sabre Squadron — Sabre Squadron — Light Aid Detachment
1 × Samson
1 × Recov Veh
2 × 4-tonne
3 × Land Rover

Squadron HQ
2 × Sultan
1 × Samaritan
2 × 4-tonne
3 × Land Rover

Squadron HQ
1 × Ferret
1 × Land Rover

Regimental Aid Post
1 × Samaritan

Motor Transport
14 × 4-tonne
(POD, GS)
1 × Land Rover

Assault Troop
4 × Spartan

Troop (× 5)
4 × Fox

Assault Troop
4 × Spartan

Quartermaster
4 × 4-tonne
5 × Land Rover

Light Aid Detachment
1 × Recov Veh
1 × 4-tonne
2 × Land Rover

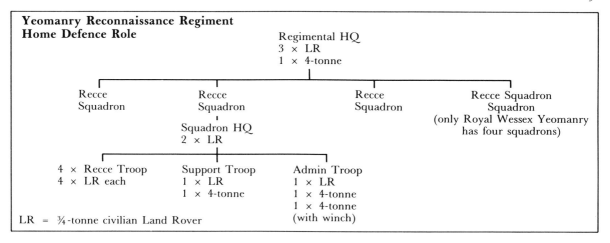

Yeomanry Reconnaissance Regiment
Home Defence Role

Regimental HQ
3 × LR
1 × 4-tonne

Recce Squadron · Recce Squadron · Recce Squadron · Recce Squadron Squadron (only Royal Wessex Yeomanry has four squadrons)

Squadron HQ
2 × LR

4 × Recce Troop
4 × LR each

Support Troop
1 × LR
1 × 4-tonne

Admin Troop
1 × LR
1 × 4-tonne
1 × 4-tonne
(with winch)

LR = ¾-tonne civilian Land Rover

g — disruption in pursuit;
h — escort for convoys and supply echelons;
i — traffic control;
j — NBC reconnaissance.

Another vital role is counter-revolutionary and counter-insurgency operations. The light vehicles of the Yeomanry are particularly valuable in this type of work. On such operations they could find themselves employed on mobile patrol by foot, vehicle or helicopter; setting up observation points; manning road blocks and area cordons; escorting convoys and VIPs; general communications duties; crowd control and dispersal and fire-support for infantry.

Central Volunteer Headquarters Royal Armoured Corps

With its headquarters at Bovingdon in Dorset, CVHQ RAC is responsible for providing certain centralized services and staff, and to this end it administers a pool of TA officers and men, some of whom, as former regulars, retain the cap badge of their regular army cavalry regiment.

The Royal Yeomanry

Regimental badge
Each squadron of the regiment retains the badge of the former regiment whose traditions it carries on.

Royal Honorary Colonel
HM Queen Elizabeth, The Queen Mother.

Deputy Royal Honorary Colonel
HRH Princess Alexandra, the Hon. Mrs Angus Ogilvy.

Regimental march
Quick march is *The Farmer's Boy*.

Stable belt colours
Green, yellow and silver are the regimental colours; however, each squadron also has its own colours.

Squadrons
A (Royal Wiltshire Yeomanry) at Swindon and Trowbridge;
B (Sherwood Rangers Yeomanry) at Nottingham;
C (Kent and Sharpshooters Yeomanry) in Croydon;
D (North Irish Horse) in Belfast;
HQ (Westminster Dragoons) in London;
The Band (Inns of Court and City Yeomanry), also in London.

Affiliated regular army units
A Squadron = The Royal Hussars;
B Squadron = 17th/21st Lancers;
C Squadron = Household Cavalry;
D Squadron = 5th Royal Inniskilling Dragoon Guards;
HQ Squadron = 2nd Royal Tank Regiment;
The Band = Household Cavalry.

General

The Royal Yeomanry is the senior of the five Territorial Army regiments of the Royal Armoured Corps. It is an armoured reconnaissance regiment with a NATO role in BAOR, and is equipped to the same high standards as the Regular Army: In terms of manpower and vehicles it is larger than any other regiment in the RAC. Each squadron represents and keeps alive the traditions of older regiments that came together to form the Royal Yeomanry on 1 April 1967.

A Squadron

Regimental badge

The Prince of Wales feathers mounted within a coronet.

Regimental march

Quick march is *God Bless the Prince of Wales.*

Stable belt

Dark green, red and yellow.

History

On 12 May 1794 a troop consisting of 56 Yeomen had been formed in the village of Bishops Cannings, later to be the Devizes troop. By 1795 there were ten troops, the last being formed at Marlborough. In 1797 these were formed together to form the Regiment of Wiltshire Yeomanry Cavalry. Their first regimental parade was on 13 June 1798 at Beckhampton Down outside Devizes. As the first complete Yeomanry Regiment of Cavalry, they take pride of place as the senior. In common with other Yeomanry regiments, their first action was in support of the civil authority, and in August 1795 the presence of the Devizes troop prevented a bread riot in the town. In 1810 they quelled a mutiny in the ranks of the 2nd Wiltshire Militia in Devizes, and the mutineers were persuaded to surrender without blood being spilt.

In 1830, following decisive action in dispelling rioters at Pyt House in Tisbury, they were awarded the title 'Royal' and this was granted on 24 January 1831. They were the first Yeomanry to be so honoured. The title 'Prince of Wales' Own' came about following the escorting in 1863 of the Prince of Wales, later King Edward VII on a visit to the Marquess of Aylesbury. This had been the first 'Royal' escort provided by Yeomanry. In 1884 Queen Victoria gave first place in the Table of Precedence for Yeomanry regiments to the Royal Wiltshire Yeomanry, and this led to the adoption of the motto *'Primus in Armis'.*

The Regiment's first battle honour was gained in the Boer War, when three companies of the Imperial Yeomanry were found from men of Wiltshire. The battle honour is 'South Africa 1900-1901'. The next action the men of Wiltshire saw was in the First World War; they were mobilized at the outbreak, and ordered abroad in December 1915. They started as horsed cavalry, the three squadrons firstly going to different divisions. Their work was routine, including trench digging, police duties, provision of guards, traffic control, working parties and the building of observation posts. In November 1916 they came together again and in 1917 were involved in the follow up during the German withdrawal to the Hindenburg Line before the Battle of Arras. In September of that year they converted to infantry, with 25 officers and 350 men moving to the 6th Battalion, The Wiltshire Regiment.

After the war, the Royal Wiltshire Yeomanry reformed as mounted cavalry. During the General Strike of 1926, along with the rest of the Territorial Army, they became part of the Regular Army for a ninety-day period, but in the event were not needed to assist in the national effort. HRH The Prince of Wales, later King Edward VIII, then Duke of Windsor, was their Colonel in Chief, a title he retained after his abdication until the Regiment was disbanded in 1967.

The Regiment was again mobilized for the Second World War as part of the 1st Cavalry Division, and spent from 1940 until 1944 abroad, starting as horsed cavalry, then on to searchlights, as motorized infantry, and finally back into a cavalry role as armour. They saw action in Syria and Persia, and made an outstanding contribution at the Battle of El Alamein, where not only did they suffer heavy casualties, but twice lost all their tanks. They continued their war through Italy before their return to England. After the war, the Regiment came to life again in 1947, firstly equipped with heavy tanks, until 1958 when they became an armoured car regiment. Following the disbandment in 1967, one Squadron was reformed as part of the Royal Yeomanry, and in 1971 another Squadron bearing their name was formed for the Royal Wessex Yeomanry as B Squadron at Old Sarum.

B Squadron

Regimental badge

A hunting horn within a circular belt inscribed *NOTTS SHERWOOD RANGERS YEOMANRY*, the whole surmounted by a Crown.

Regimental march

The Sherwood Rangers.

Stable belt

Green and gold.

History

The Sherwood Rangers Yeomanry was formed in the summer months of 1794, the fourth senior regiment of Yeomanry. The Nottinghamshire Yeomanry Cavalry was later formed as part of the various military preparations to meet the threat from France. Apart from various domestic policing escapades, it first saw service when a squadron of the Sherwood Rangers went to South Africa in 1900, followed later by a second squadron. The Regiment went to Egypt in 1914, but in 1915 served dismounted for three months at Gallipoli. Following the First World War, the Nottinghamshire Sherwood Rangers Yeomanry remained as cavalry, and in 1939 went to Palestine. In July 1940 it lost its horses, and as artillery took part in the defence of Tobruk, the battle for Crete and at Benghazi. In August 1941 it became armoured, and as a tank regiment was part of the defensive battle of Alam Halfa. On 24 October 1942 it headed the armoured attacks in the battle of El Alamein, and General Rommel, the German Commander, later implied that this was the only regiment of British troops to breach his defences in the first 24 hours.

The Regiment was the first Yeomanry unit ashore in France on D-Day, 6 June 1944, and its reconnaissance troop was the first British unit to invade German soil. In 1947 the Regiment was revived as an armoured regiment, converting to the reconnaissance role.

C Squadron

Regimental badge

The white horse of Kent mounted on *INVICTA* within a circle inscribed *KENT & COUNTY OF LONDON YEOMANRY*, the crown above and *SHARPSHOOTERS* below.

Regimental march

The Sharpshooters.

Stable belt

The racing colours of the Earl of Dunraven and Mountearl: dark green, yellow and cerise.

History

Until 1920 there were two Yeomanry Regiments in Kent, and in that year the Queen's Own West Kent Yeomanry and the Royal East Kent Mounted Rifles amalgamated to form an artillery regiment. In London, the 3rd County of London Yeomanry had been formed in 1904 after the Boer War, although they had been raised as Imperial Yeomanry in 1899, winning their first battle honour in South Africa. They fought in the First World War in Gallipoli, and as cavalry under General Allenby in 1917. In 1920 they became an armoured car unit, expanding into two armoured regiments in 1938. Both fought in the Desert, Italy and North-West Europe, gaining 42 further battle honours, a figure bettered only by the 11th Hussars.

The two regiments amalgamated to one because of losses at the Battle of Villers Bocage. In 1961 the Sharpshooters amalgamated with the Kent Yeomanry.

D Squadron

Regimental badge

A harp surmounted by a Crown over a scroll inscribed *NORTH IRISH HORSE*.

Stable belt

Green and white.

History

The North Irish Horse was raised in 1902 in the Province of Ulster and attracted many who had served in South Africa with the Imperial Yeomanry. Its original name was 'The North of Ireland Imperial Yeomanry', but in 1905 it became the North Irish Horse. In the First World War they were mobilized, and two weeks after war was declared they landed at Le Havre. In 1916 two regiments of the North Irish Horse were formed, but in September 1917 the second regiment was dismounted and its members served with Irish infantry regiments. The regiments were disembodied, with only one name being shown in the Army List between the wars, becoming known as 'The One-Man Regiment', but in 1939 it was reconstituted as a light armoured regiment. In July 1941 they became an infantry tank unit, and in January 1943, after training and conversion to the new Churchill tank, they sailed for North Africa to join the 1st Army, later joining the 8th Army in Italy. Its first active task was to support Canadian infantry, and as a result the Canadians asked the Regiment to wear the Maple Leaf. In the final advance, the Regiment was the first 8th Army unit to reach the River Po.

Following the war, in 1947 it was reconstituted as an armoured car regiment, but in 1967 reduced to two squadrons, one becoming 69 (North Irish Horse) Squadron of the Royal Signals, and the other joining with the Royal Yeomanry. Its impressive list of decorations for gallantry includes one VC from the First World War.

HQ Squadron

Regimental badge

The Arms of the City of Westminster.

Regimental march

Westminster Dragoons.

Stable belt

Royal clerical purple, gold and maroon.

History

The Westminster Dragoons, 2nd County of London Yeomanry, were raised in 1901 and supplied 800 men during the Boer War to the Imperial Yeomanry. As a result they received the battle honour 'South Africa 1902'. King Edward VII sanctioned the adoption of his royal racing colours as the regimental colours. At the start of the First World War, the Regiment went to Egypt, and their first action against the Turks was in February 1915 at Ismailia. They fought as infantry in Gallipoli, taking part in the capture of Chocolate and Scimitar Hills, and they then remounted in Egypt for a campaign in the Western Desert against the Senussi. After further service in Palestine, they were the first formation of troops to enter Jerusalem on 9 December 1917.

Early in 1918 they trained as a machine-gun battalion, and went to France in June to take part in the bitter fighting at Ypres and Daddizoole, and they were at Menin when the Armistice was declared. They were re-formed after the War, in 1921, as the 22nd London Armoured Car Company of the Tank Corps. For the first two years of the Second World War they operated as an Officer Cadet Training Unit, but by the end of 1940 they re-formed as a fighting unit. As part of 79th Armoured Division they operated minefield clearance tanks, and on 6 June 1944 were the first to land on the beaches of Normandy. With their flail tanks, they were in the forefront of the autumn and winter battles in Holland. After the war the Regiment was re-formed, in 1947, as an armoured regiment, becoming an armoured car unit in 1958. They amalgamated with the Berkshire Yeomanry in 1961, but in 1984 they rebadged as Westminster Dragoons, the other regiment retaining its title within 71 Signal Regiment.

The Royal Wessex Yeomanry

Regimental badge, marches and guidon

The Regiment does not have a collective badge, march or guidon, but each Squadron retains that of its own original Yeomanry Regiment. There is a regimental flag, in the Royal Armoured Corps colours of yellow and red enscribed with the cyphers of the three Yeomanry Regiments from which the Squadrons were descended. When the Squadrons are

paraded together, their guidons are paraded in order of original regimental precedence.

Squadrons

A (Royal Gloucestershire Hussars) at Gloucester;
B (Royal Wiltshire Yeomanry) at Old Sarum;
C (Royal Gloucestershire Hussars) at Stroud;
D (Royal Devon Yeomanry) at Barnstaple;
E (Home Service Force) (Royal Wiltshire Yeomanry) at Old Sarum;
HQ (Royal Gloucestershire Hussars) and the Band at Cirencester.

Affiliated regular regiments

A, B and C Squadrons — The Royal Hussars (Prince of Wales's Own);
D Squadron — 3rd Royal Tank Regiment.

History

The Regiment was formed in 1971 from the cadres of three former Yeomanry Regiments, and on 8th June 1979, Her Majesty The Queen granted the 'Royal' prefix.

General

When it was first formed, the Regiment was used in the infantry role, but in 1981 it was reorganized and is now a home defence reconnaissance regiment, responsible for providing reconnaissance for the United Kingdom Land Forces districts in times of tension or war. Each Squadron is equipped with Land Rovers, extensive communications facilities, and armed with rifles and general purpose machine-guns.

A and C Squadrons

Regimental badge

A portcullis surmounted by a ducal coronet, and underneath a scroll inscribed *ROYAL GLOUCESTER-SHIRE HUSSARS*.

Regimental march

D'ye Ken John Peel.

Stable belt

Beaufort blue and buff.

History

The first troop of Yeomanry formed in Gloucester-shire was at Cheltenham in 1795, and in 1834 the various troops in the county combined to form the Gloucestershire Yeomanry Cavalry under the command of the Marquis of Worcester. He became the Duke of Beaufort the following year, thus starting a tradition of association between that family and the Regiment. The present Duke is the Honorary Colonel of A and C Squadrons and the Band. A lasting tribute to this association is seen in the ceremonial and mess uniforms, which are in the family livery of Beaufort blue and buff, with the badges portraying the family crest.

In 1810 a troop was called upon to quell a riot in Gloucester, and in 1831 two troops assisted regular cavalry to restore order following a serious disturbance in Bristol. On 28 February 1900, a squadron of 125 men left Liverpool for South Africa, gaining the first battle honour for the Regiment. They were mobilized in August 1914 for home defence, but sailed for Egypt in 1915. They saw action as infantry at Gallipoli, and suffered appalling casualties in the legendary attack on Chocolate Hill. In November that year they were reunited with their horses, and became part of the defence of the Suez Canal.

After the Armistice, the Regiment fell foul of the dismantling of the armed services, but in 1922 it came to life again as a TA Company of the Royal Tank Corps, equipped with Peerless Armoured Cars. In the late 1920s they trained for the reconnaissance role and were re-equipped with Rolls Royce armoured cars. In those days communications depended on semaphore and the use of despatch riders. This one company was built up to a full regiment again in 1938.

In September 1939 the Regiment was again mobilized as an armoured unit, and played a vital role in the national defence system until it became a member of the 6th Armoured Division and went to Africa. In October 1941 they arrived in Egypt, in time to take part in General Cunningham's offensive. By then they had become a tank regiment with the Cruiser and Crusader tanks. Throughout this campaign the Regiment suffered heavily, and lost many men. Survivors went on to serve throughout Africa, Italy and North-West Europe until VE Day. After Germany's defeat they were equipped with Churchill tanks and the Crocodile, a flame-throwing version, and stood by to go to Japan, but that war ended before they left. After serving as garrison troops in Austria, they returned to England in September 1946. In 1947 they re-formed as a TA unit, being issued with Daimler armoured cars and scout cars, the latter affectionately known as the Dingo.

In 1967 the role was changed to that of home defence, and in 1969, in line with the massive cuts suffered by the TA, they were reduced to a cadre of three officers and 5 sergeants, whose task was to look after the regimental property and provide a framework on which to build later. The Hussars were always renowned for horsemanship, and this is a tradition that is carried on today.

B Squadron

The badge, march and colours of B (The Royal Wiltshire Yeomanry) Squadron are the same as for A Squadron of the Royal Yeomanry, and up to 1967 their antecedents were the same.

D Squadron

Regimental badge
Within an oval strap inscribed *ROYAL DEVON YEOMANRY*, a hand bearing a rolled parchment, surmounted by the Royal Crown and lion.

Regimental march
There is no official march, however by tradition *Widecombe Fair* has been adopted.

History
On 15 May 1794, the first troop of volunteer cavalry was formed at Pynes near Exeter, and about the same time the East Devon Troop formed at Shute, near Axminster. The Shute troop performed its first service in aid of the civil power, when on 13 April 1795 it assisted to restore order during the Crediton bread riots. By 1798 seventeen troops of Yeomanry had been raised in the county. In 1801 the troops near Exeter were formed into the First Devon Yeomanry, and in 1803 it was granted its 'Royal' title. Soon after, other Devon cavalry units formed, including the North Devon Yeomanry, the South Hams Yeomanry Cavalry, the East Devon Legion Yeomanry Cavalry

Yeomen wearing the Royal Devon Yeomanry cap badge on exercise.

and the Royal East Devon Squadron (the last three were disbanded in 1827).

In 1900 a combined company from the two remaining Devon Regiments volunteered for service in the Boer War, and on 25 March arrived in Table Bay in South Africa. At the outbreak of the First World War in 1914 they were mobilized and moved to the Essex Coast to counter the expected German invasion. In September 1915 they went to the Mediterranean to take part in the ill-fated Gallipoli campaign as infantry. At home, two reserve or second-line regiments were formed. The original Regiment was evacuated to Egypt on 18 December, and on Boxing Day 1915 the two regiments were amalgamated to form a battalion of the Devonshire Regiment, and this new unit took part in the third battle of Gaza against the Turks. In May 1918 they landed in France and played a part in the final defeat of the German army. After the war the two regiments reverted to cavalry, and then to artillery, to be called the Royal Devon Yeomanry Artillery. At the outbreak of the Second World War, a second Yeomanry Artillery Regiment was formed, so once again the Yeoman of Devon were divided between north and south. The new Regiment was 142 Field Regiment, and the original was the 96 Field Regiment. 142 Regiment served in England until July 1943, when it landed in Sicily and undertook a series of operations with their self-propelled guns from there to Padua in Northern Italy, before their eventual disbandment at Resina, Naples. The 96th remained in the United Kingdom until January 1945, when they embarked for Burma.

On arriving in India the Regiment was diverted to Malaya, only to arrive in Kuala Lumpur just in time for the victory parade.

After the Second World War, in addition to the two Yeomanry Artillery Regiments, there were two other RA units in the county. In 1961 they combined to form one Regiment specializing in home defence, but after the disbandment of many TA units in 1967, the Royal Devon Yeomanry was kept alive by a small cadre, until its rebirth in 1971.

The Queen's Own Mercian Yeomanry

Regimental badge
Within a strap inscribed *QUEEN'S OWN MERCIAN YEOMANRY,* a double-headed eagle ensigned with Saxon Crown, the whole surmounted by St. Edward's Crown.

Colonel-in-Chief
The Queen.

Regimental marches
Quick march is *The Light of Foot,* and the slow march is *Scipio.*

Regimental guidon

Crimson silk damask embroidered and fringed with gold. The tassels and cords are of crimson silk and gold, and the guidon is carried on a pike surmounted by the Royal Crest. The badges are borne on both sides, but the battle honours granted for actions in the South African and the Great War are displayed on the obverse and those for action in the Second World War on the reverse. In the centre is the regimental badge, surrounded by the Union Wreath of roses, thistles and shamrocks and surmounted by St. Edward's Crown. Below the wreath is the Honorary Distinction Badge of the Royal Regiment of Artillery, awarded for service in North West Europe 1940 and 1944 to 1945, and in Sicily and Italy 1943 to 1945. The badges in the four corners are those of: The Warwickshire Yeomanry — The Bear and Ragged Staff; The Staffordshire Yeomanry (Queen's Own Royal Regiment) — The Stafford knot and motto *Pro Aris et Focis*; The Shropshire Yeomanry — The Loggerheads, three leopards' faces from the arms of Shropshire; and The Queen's Own Worcestershire Hussars — a sprig of pear blossom.

Stable belt

A gold stripe in the middle, with a royal blue band over and a scarlet band below.

Squadrons

A (Warwickshire and Worcestershire Yeomanry) at Coventry and Stourbridge;
B (Staffordshire Yeomanry) at Tipton and Stafford;
C (Shropshire Yeomanry) at Shrewsbury;
D (Home Service Force) at Telford.

Affiliated regular regiments

A Squadron — The Queen's Own Hussars;
B Squadron — 16th/5th The Queen's Royal Lancers;
C Squadron — 1st The Queen's Dragoon Guards.

History

On 1 April 1971, the cadres of the three Yeomanry Regiments of Warwickshire and Worcestershire, Staffordshire and Shropshire were expanded to form the three Squadrons of the new Regiment of Royal Armoured Corps.

On 25 May 1973, Her Majesty The Queen approved the change of title to 'The Queen's Own Mercian Yeomanry' and in October that year agreed to become its Colonel-in-Chief. On 9 February 1988, the Home Service Force Company rebadged from the RAOC to become D squadron.

General

The Regiment was initially formed in the infantry role for home defence, but in 1982 it was given a new role as a light reconnaissance Regiment, again for home defence duties. Each Squadron consists of four Sabre Troops, each equipped with four long-wheel-base Land Rovers. At the Regimental Headquarters at Telford in Shropshire there are a number of WRAC, who act as drivers, storekeepers and clerks.

A Squadron

Squadron quick march
The Warwickshire Lads.

History

The Queen's Own Warwickshire and Worcestershire Yeomanry was formed by an amalgamation in October 1956 of the two counties' regiments. The origin of the Warwickshire Yeomanry goes back to April 1794, when four troops formed in the county. The Regiment formed from these troops in 1797, and was the second in seniority after the Wiltshire Yeomanry.

The regiment was first called out to help in aid of the civil power in June 1795 at Snow Hill in Birmingham, and it was frequently embodied during the period of industrial unrest between 1827 and 1848. In the Boer War, the Regiment sponsored five companies of Imperial Yeomanry, and a full volunteer squadron went to South Africa in 1900. At the outbreak of the First World War the Regiment was called up and served in Gallipoli and Palestine, taking part in the classic cavalry charge, 'The Charge at Huj', in 1917. The Regiment was again mobilized in 1939, and went with its horses to Palestine. It was motorized in 1941, taking part in the successful Iraqi, Syrian and Persian campaigns against the Vichy French and pro-axis Persia. In 1941 they converted to tanks, and joined the 8th Army. At El Alamein only seven of their sixty tanks survived the battle, where they smashed the enemy gun-line. The Regiment served in Italy, and after the war re-formed as an armoured regiment in 1947, which they remained until amalgamation.

The Worcestershire Yeomanry Cavalry was raised in 1794, and in 1810 helped quell a riot in Worcester. Queen Victoria made the Regiment 'The Queen's Own' in 1837, and then in 1887 the title altered to The Queen's Own Worcestershire Hussars. The Regiment sponsored two companies of Imperial Yeomanry for the Boer War. Mobilized for the First World War, the Regiment saw action at Gallipoli and Egypt.

After one battle, at Quatia on Easter Day, April 23 1916, the Regiment was left with one officer and 54 men, the rest having been killed or captured by the Turks. This Regiment also took part in the charge at Huj, and they entered the City of Damascus three weeks before the Armistice. Following the end of the First World War, in 1922 they ceased to be a cavalry unit and provided two batteries for 100 Field Brigade, Royal Artillery. In the Second World War they went to France with the BEF and suffered heavy losses fighting in the anti-tank role, before being evacuated at Dunkik. Later in the war they became an air-landing light regiment of artillery, and took part in the invasion of France and the airborne crossing of the Rhine. After the war the Regiment was re-created as an anti-tank unit, but in 1950 became part of the Royal Armoured Corps.

B Squadron

Squadron quick march

Lilli Marlene

History

The Staffordshire Volunteer Cavalry was formed on 4 July 1794 in Stafford, with troops in Newcastle under Lyme, Lichfield, Walsall, Stafford and Leek. The Regiment adopted the motto *PRO ARIS ET FOCIS* (For our hearths and our homes). Queen Victoria gave the Regiment the title of The Queen's Own Royal Regiment in the year of her coronation, 1838. In line with other Yeomanry, they sponsored units and sent a contingent to the Boer War.

In October 1915, the Regiment sailed for Egypt as part of the Western Frontier Force. At the end of March 1917, after three months in the Sinai, they advanced into Palestine, playing a part in the two battles of Gaza. The Regiment was again mobilized in 1939, and spent 1940 in Palestine patrolling the Syrian frontier as mounted cavalry. They became armoured in 1941, and moved to Egypt in February 1942. In August that year they were in the Alamein line, where they helped repel Rommel's attack on the Alam El Halfa Ridge, later leading the advance into Mersa Matruh. Later the Regiment was involved in the Normandy landings and the assault over the Rhine. After the war they re-formed as an Armoured Regiment, changing to armoured cars in 1958, which they retained until disbandment in 1969. A small cadre kept the Regiment's name alive, until its rebirth as a Squadron in 1971.

C Squadron

Squadron quick march

The Farmer's Boy

History

The first units of the Shropshire Yeomanry were formed on 11 January 1795 at Market Drayton, and

on 17 April 1795 at Wellington. From the various cavalry troops, some with very individual names such as The Hales Owen Yeomanry, The Brimstree Loyal Legion, and The Oswestry Rangers, three Regiments were formed in 1814.

As with other similar regiments, the first action was in aid of the civil power to quell unrest, such as in the 'Battle of Cinderloo' in the East Shropshire coalfield, which fortunately proved to be bloodless. The South Shropshire and Shrewsbury Regiments later amalgamated as the South Salopian Regiment, whilst that in the north had its name changed to The North Salopian Regiment. These two finally merged in 1872 to form The Shropshire Yeomanry Cavalry. From 1814 these units had been clothed and trained as Dragoons, that is mounted infantry, so called after the 'Dragon', as the musket with which they were originally equipped was called. In 1900 volunteers from the Regiment formed the 13th Company of the 5th Battalion of the Imperial Yeomanry, and gained the first battle honour. In the First World War, whilst serving with the Egyptian Expeditionary Force against the Turks, they dismounted and along with the Cheshire Yeomanry formed the 10th Battalion of the King's Shropshire Light Infantry. On 10 March 1918, Sergeant H. Whitfield of the Regiment won the Victoria Cross at Burj el Lisaneh.

The regiment reverted to horsed cavalry after the war, but again in 1940 they were dismounted to form 75 and 76 Medium Regiments of the Royal Artillery, and as such saw service in the Middle East and Italy. Since 1947 the Regiment survived changes to tanks, armoured cars, scout cars and Land Rovers, and between 1969 and 1971 it was reduced to a small cadre.

The Queen's Own Yeomanry

Regimental badge

A fox in silver, on a scroll inscribed *QUEENS OWN YEOMANRY*.

Regimental march

The quick march is *D'ye Ken John Peel*.

Stable belt

Blue and yellow.

Squadrons

Y (Yorkshire) at York;
A (Ayrshire) at Ayr;
C (Cheshire) at Chester;
D (Northumberland Hussars) at Cramlington;
HQ (Northumberland Hussars) at Newcastle upon Tyne.

Associated Regular Regiments

Y Squadron: 4th/7th Royal Dragoon Guards; 13th/18th Royal Hussars (Queen Mary's Own);
A Squadron: The Royal Scots Dragoon Guards (Carabiniers and Greys);
C Squadron: 5th Royal Inniskilling Dragoon Guards; 16th/5th The Queen's Royal Lancers;

Above left *A fox of the Queen's Own Yeomanry* (MARS).

Above *On exercise Keystone, the codename 'Beaky's Band' was given to this armoured raiding group of volunteers from the Queen's Own Yeomanry and Yorkshire Volunteers.*

D Squadron: 15th/19th The King's Royal Hussars;
HQ Squadron: 9th/12th Royal Lancers (Prince of Wales's); and 4th Royal Tank Regiment.

History

The Regiment formed on 1 April 1971 from the Queen's Own Yorkshire Yeomanry, the Ayrshire Yeomanry, the Cheshire Yeomanry and the Northumberland Hussars.

General

This is one of the two Yeomanry Regiments which support BAOR in the reconnaissance role. For this task it is equipped with Fox armoured cars and Spartan armoured personnel carriers. Its other vehicles include the Sultan, Samson, Bedford 4-tonner, Land Rover, and Scammel recovery vehicles. As well as training, the squadrons take part in many activities, such as skill-at-arms meetings, local shows and recruiting drives. Annual camps are held in Germany and the UK, and at least twice a year the Regiment is able to exercise as a whole. At sport they have entered for the Army's boxing competitions and inter-unit football.

Y Squadron

History

In 1956 the Queen's Own Yorkshire Yeomanry was formed from a number of old regiments. Their antecedents were as follows: The Yorkshire Hussars, who had been raised in 1794 as the Northern Regiment of West Riding Cavalry; the Yorkshire Dragoons, who were also formed in 1794, as the Southern Regiment of West Riding Cavalry; and the East Riding Yeomanry, raised in 1794 as the East Riding Gentleman and Yeomanry Cavalry, which was disbanded in 1801 but re-formed two years later as the Grimston Yeomanry Cavalry, again disbanded in 1814 and re-formed in 1902.

During the Boer War, both the Hussars and Dragoons provided men, and the VC was awarded to Lieutenant A.C. Doxat for his rescue of a dismounted comrade under heavy fire near Zeerust. The Regiments were embodied for the First World War. The Hussars changed to infantry in 1917 and fought at Passchendaele, and the only action by the Dragoons, who remained mounted, was in 1917 helping to push the Germans back to the Hindenburg Line. The East Riding Yeomanry changed to Machine-Gun Corps in 1918. In the Second World War the Yorkshire Hussars sailed to Palestine in 1940 and changed to armour, equipped with Stuart tanks in 1941. The Regiment served in Cyprus and Egypt, returning to England in 1943 to prepare for D-Day. The Dragoons also went to Palestine, and were the last mounted regiment to change to armour, that occurring in 1942. The East Riding Yeomanry sailed to France in 1939 and fought a rearguard action back to Dunkirk. As a result three MCs and five MMs were awarded, and the surviving four officers and 230 men were amalgamated with the 2nd Regiment back in England, returning to France on D-Day.

A Squadron

History

The Ayrshire Yeomanry was raised at Carrick in 1798, and in 1803 the name changed to the Ayrshire Yeomanry Cavalry. They were often used to help restore order in the early nineteenth century, and their first duty abroad was in South Africa, as part of the Imperial Yeomanry.

During the First World War, the Regiment fought as dismounted troops in the Middle East, and during the Palestine campaign the VC was awarded to Sergeant Caldwell. The Second World War brought a change to the artillery role, and they fought in North Africa and North West Europe. In 1947 the Regiment was re-formed in the armoured role.

C Squadron

History

The Cheshire Yeomanry goes back to 1797, and early last century they were used mainly to quell rioting. The most notorious action was at Peterloo on 17 August 1819, when they face a crowd of 60,000 workers, and on that day 11 people died and another 500 were injured. The Regiment sailed for South Africa in 1899 to take part in the Boer War. In the First World War they served as dismounted troops, and then with the Imperial Camel Corps before joining with the Shropshire Yeomanry to form an infantry battalion serving on the Western Front. In the Second World War the Regiment served as mounted cavalry in Palestine, and on 9 June 1941 took part in the last mounted action, against the Vichy French to take a bridge on the River Litani. The following year they lost their horses and became a signals regiment.

D and HQ Squadrons

History

The Northumberland Hussars started life in 1819 as the Newcastle Regiment of Yeomanry Cavalry. The Regiment was used to police civil disturbances, and were mobilized in 1831 for 31 days during a miners' strike. The Hussars saw action during the Boer War, and during the First World War landed in Belgium in 1914. They were present at many battles, including Ypres, Festubert, Loos, Somme, Vimy, Cambrai and the final battles to end the war. They crossed Happy Valley at the full gallop to assist in an infantry advance, and there they suffered heavy casualties.

For the Second World War the Regiment converted to artillery in 1940 as 102nd Anti-Aircraft and Anti-Tank Regiment RA. As such, the Hussars saw action in Greece, Crete, North Africa and Sicily, and in 1944 they landed in Normandy to fight until the end of the war in North-West Europe. After the war they became an armoured regiment, but were reduced to only cadre strength from 1967 until 1971.

The Duke of Lancaster's Own Yeomanry

Regimental badge
A rose within a wreath, laurel on left oak on right; a scroll inscribed *DUKE OF LANCASTER'S OWN* the whole ensigned with a ducal coronet.

Colonel-in-Chief
THE QUEEN

Regimental march
The quick march is *John O'Gaunt*.

Regimental toast
'The Duke of Lancaster'.

Stable belt
A yellow background with one thick stripe of red and another below of blue.

Squadrons
HQ at Chorley;
A at Wigan;
B at Clifton in Manchester;
D at Preston and Blackpool.

Associated regular regiment
14th/20th King's Hussars.

History
The present Regiment was re-formed on 1 April 1971, and has its origins in the various troops of light horse raised in the eighteenth century. The earliest of these was the Bolton Light Horse, formed in 1798, then later there were troops at Furness, Wigan and Worsley. The Regiment assembled in June 1828, and in 1834 King William IV, by special Act, granted the prefix 'Own' and the Sovereign, as the Duke of Lancaster, has traditionally been Colonel-in-Chief. In 1846 another regiment, the Lancashire Hussars, was raised. Both regiments sent a mounted infantry company to the Boer War between 1900 and 1902.

In the First World War, A Squadron of the Duke of Lancaster's Own Yeomanry went to Egypt in 1914, and D and C Squadrons went to France as Divisional Cavalry. Of the Hussars, D Squadron went to France in 1915 and HQ and B Squadrons to Egypt in 1916. C Squadron went to France, and they combined in May 1916 to form VIII Corps Cavalry. In September 1917 the two regiments lost their mounts and became infantry, but after the war one Yeomanry Regiment was re-formed in the county. At the outbreak of the Second World War, the Yeomanry was mobilized as horsed cavalry, but in 1940 was converted to the 77th and 78th Medium Regiments of Royal Artillery. The 78th served in Palestine, Syria and Italy. The 77th languished in Northern Ireland until early 1944, when it prepared for the invasion of Europe. It landed in Normandy on D-Day plus 6, and fought for the Odon Bridgehead and in the battle of the Falaise Gap. It also provided support for the Arnhem drop.

After the war, in 1947, the Duke of Lancaster's Own Yeomanry was re-formed as an armoured regiment. In 1956 its role was changed to that of reconnaissance, equipped with armoured cars, but on 1 April 1967 it combined with the 40th/41st Royal Tank Regiment. In April two years later this new Regiment was reduced to a cadre, until its rebirth in 1971 as an infantry unit. On 1 April 1983 it rejoined the Royal Armoured Corps as a home defence reconnaissance unit equipped with Land Rovers. The Regiment now has a strong WRAC contingent as clerks, drivers and storekeepers.

The Battle Honours of the Royal Wiltshire Yeomanry

South Africa 1900-1901

The Great War

Ypres 1917	Polygon Wood,
Broodseinde	Poelcappelle
Passchendaele	Somme 1918
St Quentin	Bapaume 1918
Lys	Messines 1918
Baillenl	Kemmel
France and Flanders 1918	

Second World War

Iraq 1941	Palmyra
Syria 1941	El Alamein
North Africa 1942	Lisi Valley
Advance to Tiber	Citta Della Peiva
Transimene Line	Advance to Florence

Fighting Vehicle 721 Fox (FV721)

Designed in the early 1960s as a replacement for the earlier Ferret reconnaissance vehicle, the prototype Fox, known as the Combat Vehicle Reconnaissance (Wheeled) emerged with such refinements over the earlier vehicle as aluminium armour and a turret-mounted Rarden 30 mm gun. The prototypes were produced by Daimler at Coventry but the first production version was com- pleted in 1973 by the Royal Ordnance Factory at Leeds. The turret, made by Alvis, is the same as that used by the Scimitar. A Jaguar engine gives it very good road performance, and it has the abil- ity to cross most types of terrain. It is light enough to be carried in threes in the Hercules aircraft, or to be para-dropped in twos together on a special platform. The major role of the vehicle is for high- speed reconnaissance. The two NATO-roled Yeo- manry Regiments are equipped with the FV721, the Royal Yeomanry having 80 of them.

Data: Length: 5.02 metres
Width: 2.13 metres
Height: 1.98 metres
Weight: 6.35 tonnes
Engine: Jaguar 4.2 litre
Maximum road speed: in excess of 100 Km/h.
Armament: 30 mm Rarden can- non and 7.62mm machine-gun.

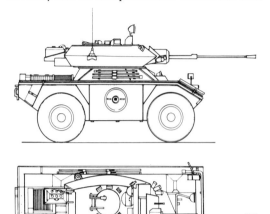

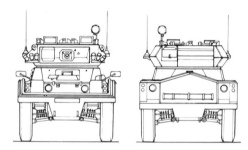

Fighting Vehicle 103 Spartan (FV103)

This vehicle is one of the Scorpion range and is an Armoured Personnel Carrier (APC). Based on the Scorpion hull and suspension it is of an aluminium armoured box design, with space inside for the commander, driver and gunner, as well as four infantrymen. This is a tracked vehi- cle of a family of designs that emerged in the 1970s, the first Spartans having been issued to the Army in 1976. Both NATO-roled Yeomanry Regiments are equipped with these.

Data: Length: 5.13 metres
Width: 2.26 metres
Height: 2.28 metres
Weight: 8.17 tonnes
Engine: Jaguar 4.2 litre
Maximum road speed: in excess of 80 Km/h
Armament: 7.62mm machine-gun

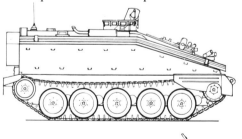

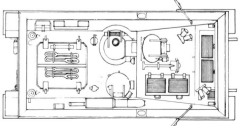

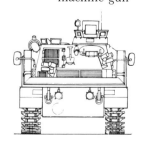

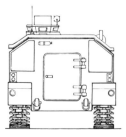

Fighting Vehicle 105 Sultan (FV105)

An armoured command vehicle from the Scorpion family, the Sultan has a box body which can accommodate a crew of a driver, commander and perhaps another four personnel as well as the maps, radios and other equipment needed for command and control. To increase the working area when the vehicle is stopped, there is a collapsible penthouse at the rear. Its interior design and exact internal equipment will vary between units. The two NATO-roled Yeomanry Regiments are equipped with these.

Data: Length: 4.80 metres
Width: 2.25 metres
Height: 2.56 metres
Weight: 8.66 tonnes
Engine: Jaguar 4.2 litre
Maximum road speed: in excess of 72 Km/h
Armament: 7.62mm machine-gun.

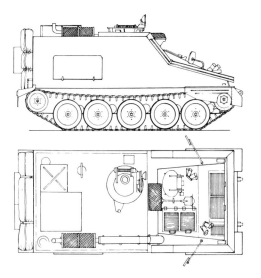

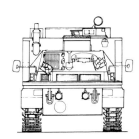
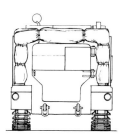

Fighting Vehicle 106 Samson (FV106)

The Sampson was the last of the tracked Scorpion family of vehicles to be produced. This is an armoured recovery vehicle using the basic box structure on a Scorpion type chassis and suspension. Although similar to the FV103 Spartan there are many changes inside to enable it to perform its specialized function. It has an internally-mounted winch driven from the main engine, and this can pull a weight greater than the vehicle itself, up to 12 tonnes. It is fitted with large spades hinging on the rear bulkhead. These dig into the ground, lifting the back of the vehicle up and enabling most effective winching capability. There is a small jib crane, and other special equipment, including a bench vice. The two NATO-roled Yeomanry Regiments are equipped with Samsons.

Data: Length: 4.79 metres
Width: 2.43 metres
Height: 2.25 metres
Weight: 8.74 tonnes
Engine: Jaguar 4.2 litre
Maximum road speed: in excess of 72 Km/h
Armament: 7.62mm machine-gun

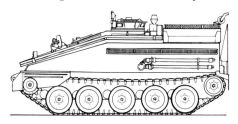

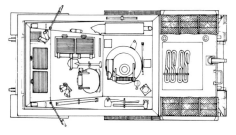

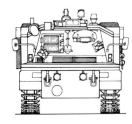
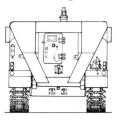

The Last Mounted Cavalry Actions of the British Army

The Charge at River Litani

The arrival of the mounted soldiers of the Cheshire Yeomanry alongside men of the Australian Division in the Middle East during 1941 led to much ribaldry. In a modern war it seemed strange to see men going to war on horseback. In the countryside of the border area between Syria and Lebanon the Yeomen found they did have a role in this war against the Vichy French. On 8 June 1941 the Regiment had ridden more than thirty miles, taking 17 hours, from El Kabri, reaching Tibnine at 5.30 in the afternoon. Although it was not fast progress, both men and horses were tired. On the 9th, the Regiment moved off at 6 o'clock, arriving at Srifa three and a half hours later. Two patrols were sent to investigate the crossings of the River Litani.

The crossing would be no easy task, as the river was in a narrow gorge with a cliff of over 1,000 feet on the north side. Movement through the gorge would have been by narrow tracks, and of course in daylight the horsemen would have presented an easy target for any enemy. One patrol was sent to look at the bridge at Refid, and the other to look at an alternative near Faroun, further to the east.

Lieutenant Rogers with 2 Troop of A Squadron arrived at the bridge at Refid and found that it was covered by the enemy. They came under fire and lost six horses in the engagement. The fact that the bridge was defended was vital information for the Regiment, so Trooper F.E. Mellors was sent back with a message. He plunged into the river and struggled through the torrent to reach the other side and take the track back to Srifa. Having second thoughts about a Trooper on his own without a map making the journey, Lieutenant Rogers sent Corporal Spencer to back him up. He also plunged into the torrent, but the current was too much, and the rider and his mount, 'Little Nell', parted company. The horse lost the saddle, rifle, sword and map case, but her bridle was intact when she emerged on the other side. Corporal Spencer also emerged from the river and then rode bareback to RHQ, where he arrived, still soaked, an hour later.

Lieutenant Shaw with number 3 Troop of A Squadron had in the mean time arrived at Faroun, and found the crossing free of enemy. The Regiment therefore moved off in that direction with C Squadron leading, except the remainder of A Squadron and a section of machine-guns who went to extricate 2 Troop and Lieutenant Rogers at the bridge.

A Squadron found that the enemy had disappeared before their arrival with 2 Troop, so carried on and met the rest of the Regiment at Kakiet Ej Jisr.

C Squadron arrived at the Litani with 4 Troop in the lead. The correct tactic would have been for a section or a troop to have crossed and secured the overlooking hill. There was not time to do this, so perhaps it is fortunate the crossing was undefended. Nevertheless, the Squadron disregarded all possible danger, crossed, and rode straight up the hill to its far side and entered the village of Kakiet Ej Jisr. There was no sign of the enemy.

The 'charge' of the Yeomen was the subject of exaggerated and inaccurate press reporting. The *Daily Express* of June 17 described the action in glowing terms:

> British Scouts crossed the river and ran right into a belt of artillery fire from a strong formation of Spahis who had dismounted and were hidden in the rocks. The British were pinned to the ground. One trooper jumped with his horse straight into the stream, lost his saddle and under machine-gun fire galloped bareback to the rest of his squadron for help. They came on at the full gallop. The Spahis withdrew.

The Regiment had a disappointing day, although matters could have been worse had it not been for the strange withdrawal of the Spahis, the French Algerian Cavalry. Apart from firing on 2 Troop of A Squadron at the bridge, that day, they had avoided contact with the Yeomen and allowed the vital crossing of the Litani virtually unopposed. They had also left the bridge intact.

The following day, the Colonel of the Regiment learned that the French were still in possession of the Litani crossing on the plain and that the expected Commando attack had been postponed because of the rough seas. The next task was to move to the west on the left flank of the French force defending the river and clear the countryside of enemy. Enemy were discovered at the village of Adchite by Lieutenant Shaw and his Troop, who were acting as right flank guard. The Spahis were defending it, and were engaged with Hotchkiss machine-gun and rifle fire by the Yeomen. The defenders were soon seen to gallop away in a cloud of dust. On hearing the sound of gunfire, the Regiment despatched the Machine-Gun Troop to assist them, but the enemy had flown just before they arrived. This had been a fine cavalry action, and was the final incident on their journey.

The final classic cavalry action by the British Army was not to be a breakneck charge with sabres drawn, covering themselves with glory in the face of a determined enemy, but a series of minor engagements. The major value of the Yeomen in this escapade had been psychological. The French had fought desperately, with both the Commandos and Australians trying to cross the Litani, but their aircraft had reported a large and formidable force of British Cavalry threatening their left flank. This proved too much for them, so they retired. This large force of British Cavalry had in fact been the Cheshire Yeomanry, rather thinly spread out over a wide area, but their approach had been the deciding factor in the final victory.

In the title of his book, *The Cheshire (Earl of Chester's) Yeomanry 1898 to 1967*, the author, Lieutenant-Colonel Sir Richard Verdin OBE TD, included the description 'The last regiment to fight on horses.' Their action at the River Litani in the Syrian Campaign up to 10 June 1941 was that last action.

Although this was the last British Army Cavalry action, the last time when British mounted troops charged in the classic cavalry manner against infantry and guns had been in the First World War.

The Affair at Huj

On 8 November 1917, in Gaza, there had been a battle between the British, under the command of Major-General J.S.M. Shea, and the Turks, with German and Austrian support. A well dug-in Turkish rearguard had held up the advance of the British 60th Division at a ridge south of the village of Huj, east of Gaza. It was decided that cavalry was needed, because a move by infantry over 1,000 yards of open ground would have meant many casualties. The cavalry this day consisted of one and a half squadrons from each of the Worcestershire Yeomanry and the Warwickshire Yeomanry. The force was a total of ten troops consisting of 12 officers and 158 troopers. They took part in three separate charges that day, firstly against infantry, whom they dispersed, then against the guns, riding straight at them, and the third charge dispersed some enemy reinforcements.

These three charges went right home, and when the Yeomanry charged the guns, their gunners, who included Germans and Austrians, as well as the Turks, stood to their pieces to the last and were killed by the sword. The Yeomenry captured eleven guns, four machine-guns, and took 70 of the enemy prisoner, as well as killing many of them. All three of the British squadron commanders were killed, in addition to 6 other officers wounded. 26 Yeoman died in the charges with 40 more wounded, and 100 horses out of the 170 that went into battle did not survive.

After these charges, gallantly led by Colonel Cheape, the enemy made no further efforts to defend Huj, and retreated in hopeless disorder, destroying their ammunition and supply dumps as they went.

The first charge against infantry was made by a squadron of the Worcestershire Yeomanry under the command of Major M.C. Albright. The Colonel then ordered a squadron of the Warwickshire Yeomanry

to attack the battery of 75mm guns. Major Albright's squadron, in column of half squadrons, dashed through the Turkish infantry, which streamed away in flight leaving many dead. Because of the desperate situation the other charge was in, Major W.H. Wiggin intervened and stopped the first charge, diverting them to the battle with the field battery. Colonel Cheape had retained two troops of Warwickshire in support, and with these he captured a howitzer battery and an abandoned camel pack battery.

Captain Valintine led his squadron against the guns, with Lieutenant Edwards' two troops on his right. They formed column of half squadrons and galloped towards the guns. Between the start point and the battery, the ground dipped, then rose again, with nearly half a mile under continuous machine-gun fire. Two of the defending Austrian guns were turned round in this short time to face the oncoming Yeomen, but despite their losses the speed of the charge was never checked and they burst, shouting, through the battery, sabreing and riding down the gunners, with only a handful of them getting through to successfully charge the machine guns. At this moment they were joined by the Worcestershires, rallied from their charge against the infantry. The enemy broke and fled northwards in panic. The main feature of this affair was the charge against guns, across open country, without the benefit of artillery support. In his history of military operations in Egypt and Palestine from June 1917 to the end of the war, Captain Cyril Falls says that the charge itself 'must ever remain a monument to extreme resolution and to that spirit of self-sacrifice which is the only beauty redeeming ugly war'. The account of Lieutenant W.B. Mercer, who had been in the leading line of Captain Valintine's squadron, and the only officer not hit, highlights the confusion of such a battle:

> A whole heap of men and horses went down twenty to thirty yards from the muzzles of the guns. The squadron broke into a few scattered horsemen at the guns and then seemed to melt away completely. For a time I, at any rate, had the impression that I was the only man left alive. I was amazed to discover we were the victors.

These two valiant regiments amalgamated later, and are now remembered in A Squadron of The Queen's Own Mercian Yeomanry and 67 Signal Squadron of 37 Signal Regiment.

Where have all the Yeomen Gone?

As this section shows, many of the older Yeomanry Regiments have, by dint of amalgamation, been carried on as squadrons of one of the five modern

Regiments. Many others have their names remembered in other arms of the Territorial Army. This is where some of them are today:

The Royal Wiltshire Yeomanry (Prince of Wales's Own), is A Squadron, The Royal Yeomanry and B Squadron, The Wessex Yeomanry;

The Queen's Own Warwickshire and Worcestershire Yeomanry is A Squadron The Queen's Own Mercian Yeomanry and 67 Signal Squadron, 37 Signal Regiment;

The Queen's Own Yorkshire Yeomanry is Y Squadron, The Queen's Own Yeomanry;

The Sherwood Rangers Yeomanry, is B Squadron, The Royal Yeomanry, and A Company, 3rd Battalion The Worcestershire and Sherwood Foresters Regiment;

The Staffordshire Yeomanry (Queen's Own Royal Regiment) is B Squadron, The Queen's Own Mercian Yeomanry;

The Shropshire Yeomanry is C Squadron The Queen's Own Mercian Yeomanry and 95 Signal Squadron, 35 Signal Regiment;

The Ayrshire Yeomanry (Earl of Carrick's Own) is A Squadron The Queen's Own Yeomanry;

The Cheshire Yeomanry (Earl of Chester's) is C Squadron The Queen's Own Yeomanry and 80 Signal Squadron 33 Signal Regiment;

The Leicestershire and Derbyshire (Prince Albert's Own) Yeomanry is C Company 7th Battalion The Royal Anglian Regiment;

The North Somerset and Bristol Yeomanry is part of the 6th Battalion The Light Infantry (Volunteers);

The Queen's Own Lowland Yeomanry is 225 Squadron, 154 Regiment, Royal Corps of Transport;

The Northumberland Hussars are D Squadron, The Queen's Own Yeomanry;

The Pembrokeshire Yeomanry were amalgamated into 4th Battalion The Royal Regiment of Wales, but the traditions of the Castlemartin Yeomanry are carried on by A Troop, 224 Squadron, 157 Regiment, Royal Corps of Transport;

Kent and County of London Yeomanry is C Squadron, The Royal Yeomanry;

The Royal Gloucestershire Hussars is A and C Squadrons, The Wessex Yeomanry;

The Berkshire Yeomanry is 94 Squadron, 71 Signal Regiment;

The Westminster Dragoons is HQ Squadron, The Royal Yeomanry;

The Fife and Forfar and Scottish Horse Yeomanry were amalgamated into The Highland Yeomanry;

Royal Devon Yeomanry is D Squadron, The Wessex Yeomanry;

The Highland Yeomanry is 239 Squadron, 153 Regiment, Royal Corps of Transport;

Inns of Court and City Yeomanry is 68 Signal Squadron, 71 Signal Regiment and the Band of The Royal Yeomanry;

The West Somerset Yeomanry is part of 6th Battalion The Light Infantry (Volunteers); and

The North Irish Horse is D Squadron The Royal Yeomanry and 69 Signal Squadron, 32 Signal Regiment.

The Yeomanry Regiments that had been converted to Artillery are now:

The Essex Yeomanry (Royal Horse Artillery) is 70 Signal Squadron, 71 Signal Regiment;

The South Nottinghamshire Hussars Yeomanry (Royal Horse Artillery) is 307 Observation Post Battery, Royal Artillery;

The Surrey Yeomanry (Queen Mary's Regiment) is D Company 6th/7th Battalion The Queen's Regiment;

The Flintshire and Denbighshire Yeomanry is B Company 3rd Battalion The Royal Welch Fusiliers.

One Yeomanry Regiment that converted to Royal Signals was The Middlesex Yeomanry and is now 47 Signal Squadron, 31 Signal Regiment.

4 The Artillery

In the modern battle, the role of the Artillery is vital to success. It provides a range of weapons from the long-range missile to short-range, close support weapons. It is obvious that weapons such as the nuclear warhead are in the hands of the regular army units, but nevertheless, the TA has a wide range of skills, and the most sophisticated of equipment vital to the war-time expansion of this arm.

Briefly the function of the Artillery is:
1 indirect fire, to bring about disruption and delay, and to destroy the enemy before coming into contact with friendly forces; especially to destroy the effectiveness of the enemy artillery;

2 to provide close artillery support for ground forces, by neutralizing the enemy in the close contact battle; and
3 air defence.

The TA Artillery commitment in time of war is to provide BAOR with extra field regiments. These units are currently equipped with the 105mm light gun. Two of the eight field regiments in the UK are from the TA, as well as four Blowpipe and Javelin air defence regiments.

The two TA light gun field regiments, each having three six-gun batteries, are 100 (Yeomanry) Field Regiment and 101 (Northumbrian) Field Regiment.

TA gunners man their light gun.

The air defence regiments of the TA are 102 at Newtonards, 103 in Lancashire, 104 at Newport and 105 in Edinburgh. There are three Observation Post Batteries, 266 at Bristol, 269 in Leeds, and 307 at Nottingham, and a TA Battery which will become part of 29 Commando Regiment RA in time of war, 289 Commando Battery, is at East Ham in London. The Honourable Artillery Company also supplies personnel for observation posts and various headquarters functions. Other TA artillery specialists are provided for a variety of tasks from the Central Volunteer Headquarters RA at Woolwich.

Honourable Artillery Company

Regimental badge

Beret badge: on a wreath, a dexter arm embowed in armour, the gauntlet grasping a pike in bend sinister between two dragon's wings each charged with a cross. This is the Company's crest, which is worn over a black patch on a khaki beret by all except the Corps of Drums, who wear the forage cap badge with no patch. Forage cap badge: a grenade with monogram *HAC* on the ball.

Captain General

THE QUEEN

Regimental marches

The quick march is *British Grenadiers*; the slow march is *Duke of York*; the canter is *Bonnie Dundee*; the trot is *The Keel Row*; and the walk is *Duchess of Kent* (named after its composer, who was Queen Victoria's mother).

Regimental Colours

The Colours of the HAC are unique in that they depict the battle honours of both the Artillery and Infantry divisions of the Regiment. The design of the Queen's Colour is based on the Union Flag. The Regimental Colour, which was crimson until 1783, is now blue, and depicts the HAC's coat of arms. The poles for the Colours are both charged with a crown.

Stable belts

RHQ, HQ Squadron, Training Wing and Band: — scarlet and navy blue, edged with narrow gold stripes;
1 Squadron — red;
2 Squadron — green;
3 Squadron — royal blue;
Gun Troop — blue with a narrow gold stripe in the centre, as for E battery, 1 RHA; and
Corps of Drums — three equal stripes of navy blue, crimson and navy blue, as for the Household Division.

History

The HAC claims to be the oldest regiment in the British Army, and although the actual date of origin is not known, in 1537 Letters Patent were granted by Henry VIII and it was embodied as the Fraternity or Guild of St. George. There are indications, however, that this merely laid down rules and regulations for an existing organization. Whether or not it is the senior unit of the TA is hotly disputed by the Royal Monmouthshire Royal Engineers (Militia), who precede the HAC in the Army List, and whose service was not broken by the Civil War, the City of London having been staunchly behind the Parliamentarian cause. From the Guild of St. George, the name of the Regiment went through a series of changes, including London's Hopeful Artillery, and its present name came into common use by 1668. The headquarters has been at Armoury House, adjacent to the City of London, since 1641, the main portion of the building constructed thanks to the generosity of King George I.

The word 'Artillery' in the title is used in its obsolete sense, which meant any missile weapon or weapon of volley, such as crossbows or muskets, and until 1973 the HAC maintained an Infantry element, which is carried on today by its two companies of Home Service Force volunteers.

A unique tradition carried on today is that, since 1611, all members of the HAC have had their names recorded in the 'Vellum Book'. Another tradition is that of 'Regimental Fire', used when toasting or cheering another member of the Company. It consists of a ninefold shout of the word 'Zay' accompanied by movements of the right hand, thought to stem from either the movements required to ignite a grenade, or an eighteenth century toast-drinking ceremony. Guests are toasted with Silent Fire, where the first eight 'zays' are silent. As well as the TA side to life in the HAC, there are other sections of the Company, including the Old Comrades, Veterans, the HAC Detachment of the Metropolitan Special Constabulary, the Company of Pikemen and Musketeers and the Light Cavalry. There is also a TA Band of the HAC. The civil affairs of the Company are governed by a Court of Assistants, which was first set up in 1633. Associated with the Company is a Masonic Lodge for members of the HAC only.

Two other distinctions of the Company are that, following the Letters Patent of Henry VIII, members are not empanelled for Jury service within this Realm, and King Edward VII bestowed the distinction of a special Medal Ribbon to the Volunteer Decoration (now the Territorial Decoration) and the Volunteer Long Service Medal (now the Territorial Efficiency Medal). The colour of this ribbon is as that for the RHQ stable belt. In 1781 the Corporation of the City of London allowed £150 for the purchase of two three-pounder battalion guns for the company. These were the type of guns used by the Infantry, and were to show the City's gratitude for the Company's firm stand in the earlier Gordon Riots. As a result, the Artillery Division of the Company was formed. In the South African War the HAC provided all the officers and two-thirds of the men for the Battery of City Imperial Volunteers, as well as detachments for the Infantry and Mounted Infantry. As a result the Company received its first battle honour.

During the First World War, units of the Company served in France, Egypt, Aden and Palestine, and on 23 April 1917 Victoria Crosses were awarded to Lieutenants Haine and Pollard at Arras. In that war, 12,847 HAC members served, with 4,950 being wounded and 940 killed in action or dying on active service. The Company earned 42 battle honours and its members gained 255 gallantry awards.

One honour to the Company between the Wars was that in 1938 the Infantry Division formed the guard at Buckingham Palace, the first TA unit to do so. In the Second World War the HAC was involved in defence duties in London, and units saw action in North Africa and Italy, from Knightsbridge and El Alamein to Cassino and Senio. They also took part in the invasion of Normandy and through North-West Europe to the Rhine. The Company earned 17 more battle honours, and its members were awarded 453 honours and decorations, although at a loss of 723 lives.

In both wars members of the HAC were often gazetted to other regiments on commissioning, and two former members were awarded the VC. They were Captain T.T. Pryce, serving with the 4th Battalion of the Grenadier Guards at Vieux Berquin on 23 May 1918, and Major R.H. Cain with the South Staffordshire Regiment (Airborne) at Arnhem on 2 November 1944.

Following the Second World War, the HAC formed two Royal Horse Artillery Regiments and one Infantry Battalion, but one of the Artillery units was disbanded in 1955. The Company formed in its present structure and role in 1973, that is three squadrons

with a BAOR role, a training squadron, the band and a gun troop. The two HSF Companies formed in 1985.

The Company carries out a number of ceremonial duties in the City of London. Guards of Honour are provided for State Visits when the Lord Mayor holds a banquet in the visitor's honour. Commands for Royal Salutes on these occasions are still addressed to 'Gentlemen of the Honourable Artillery Company'. The other duties are the Royal Salutes fired by each Squadron and the Gun Troop in turn, with four 25-pounder salute guns from the Tower of London. Sixty-two guns are fired on Royal anniversaries, and 41 on Royal or State occasions.

Royal Regiment of Artillery

Regimental badge
A gun between two scrolls, that above inscribed *UBIQUE*, that beneath inscribed *QUO FAS ET GLORIA DUCUNT*, the whole ensigned with the Crown all gold.

Captain General
THE QUEEN

Regimental marches
The quick march is *The RA Quick March,* and the slow march is called *The Royal Artillery Slow March.*

Regimental Colours
The Royal Artillery does not have standards or guidons as other regiments; the guns are their colours, and are given the same respect and compliments.

Stable belt
Stripes of red, blue and yellow.

History
Artillery pieces of various types have been used by armies far back into the middle ages, but it was not until the beginning of the last century that, under threat of a possible Napoleonic invasion, various volunteer artillery units were formed. Until 1924 the

Above *The TA's light guns are air portable for maximum tactical flexibility in time of war* (Eastern Daily Press).

Above right *Preparing to load, TA gunners on exercise.*

Regiment was divided into three basic distinctions. These were the Royal Garrison Artillery (Heavy, Coast and Pack), the Royal Field Artillery and the Royal Horse Artillery. Between 1924 and 1938 they were all considered part of the one Regiment, but then it was reconstituted into two branches, one being field artillery and the other covering coastal defence, anti-aircraft and anti-tank artillery.

Today the Regiment consists of The Royal Artillery and the Royal Horse Artillery. There is no TA element of the RHA now, although they had links with the former HAC artillery division. This is recognized in that the saluting detachment of the HAC, when firing salutes at the Tower of London, are still addressed as 'Honourable Artillery Company, Royal Horse Artillery'.

Central Volunteer Headquarters Royal Artillery (CVHQ RA)

The CVHQ RA commands and administers two specialist Pools, members of which are on the lower annual training commitment. It was formerly called headquarters Army Emergency Reserve Royal Artillery TA, and was responsible for RA and Army Air Corps individual reinforcements. In 1967, on reorganization, it obtained its present title and it no longer has responsibility for the AAC.

Royal Artillery Specialist Pool (V)

This pool consists of officers and soldiers who are specialists in a number of fields:
Naval gunfire liaison officers;
Field Branch Artillery (officers);

Rapier Air Defence Systems (officers and soldiers);
Artillery Meteorological Systems (soldiers);
Artillery Intelligence Analysts (officers and soldiers).

These personnel either train at the Royal School of Artillery at Larkhill, or with the Royal Navy, and they take part in all major exercises held in the UK and BAOR each year. Individuals are permanently affiliated to major formations or regiments, and return to them annually for their 'in camp' training.

The All Arms Watchkeepers and Liaison Officers Pool (V)

This Pool consists of TA officers who have substantive ranks from Captain to Lieutenant-Colonel. They are permanently affiliated to a major formation, either in the UK or abroad, for duty as liaison officers and watchkeepers in all the staff disciplines. These include ground liaison officers with both fixed wing and support helicopter RAF Squadrons.

Members of the Pool retain their own corps or regimental cap badge and dress, and some may return to their original unit after a three to five-year tour as a watchkeeper. CVHQ RA is responsible for their weekend training, which usually takes place at Woolwich, consisting of radio, log-keeping and map-marking exercises, as well as all other aspects of staff duties as presented by the Junior Division Staff College, Arms Schools and Staff Officers from the formations to which these watchkeepers are attached. The Pool has also received recent authorization to employ WRAC TA officers in this work.

100 (Yeomanry) Field Regiment, Royal Artillery (V)

Royal Honorary Colonel
His Majesty Olav V, King of Norway.

Batteries
200 (The Sussex Yeomanry) at Brighton and Reigate;
201 (The Hertfordshire and Bedfordshire Yeomanry) at Luton and St Albans;
202 (The Suffolk and Norfolk Yeomanry) at Bury St Edmunds, Ipswich, Norwich and Swaffham;
HQ (Home Counties) at Grove Park, South East London.

General
The Regiment was formed in 1967 by the amalgamation of a number of former Yeomanry Regiments who had converted to artillery. It is equipped with the 105mm light gun and has a key role to reinforce BAOR in time of war.

Members of the Royal Artillery specialist pool receiving instruction on the towed Rapier missile from the Royal Artillery Specialist Pool.

200 (The Sussex Yeomanry) Field Battery

History
This Battery is based in Brighton, with a Troop in Reigate, and it can trace its history back to 1794 when four troops combined under the title the 'Sussex Troops of Gentlemen and Yeomanry'. They took part in the Napoleonic Wars, and then went into suspended animation until 1901, when the Sussex Imperial Yeomanry saw action in the Boer War. The Sussex Yeomanry Brigade fought in both World Wars but was later reduced to a Regiment in the mid-1950s until 1967 when the present battery was formed.

In 1985 200 Battery received the freedom of the county town of Lewes.

Members of 200 Battery with a director, which is used for sighting guns.

201 (The Hertfordshire and Bedfordshire Yeomanry) Field Battery

History

In 1794 five troops of Hertfordshire Yeomanry were raised, the Bedfordshire Yeomanry following three years later. Both county Regiments served in the First World War, the Hertfordshire Yeomanry being dismounted, but the Bedfordshires retained their horses to start with and later fought in the trenches dismounted. They both saw service in many theatres during the Second World War. At Arnhem they were among the few batteries of artillery available to support the Airborne troops. The Pegasus badge is still proudly worn by members of the Battery to commemorate this. By 1961 the two county Regiments were amalgamated into one, and in 1967 it was reduced to its present size.

202 (The Suffolk and Norfolk Yeomanry) Field Battery

History

The predecessors of this battery are the Loyal Suffolk Hussars and the Norfolk Yeomanry, one time the Royal Norfolk Yeomanry Cavalry. The Suffolk regiment started life in 1793 as the Loyal Suffolk Hussars, being renamed in 1893 as the Duke of York's Own Loyal Suffolk Hussars after George Duke of York, later King George V. The Norfolk Yeomanry was formed in 1902 as the King's Own Royal Regiment Norfolk Yeomanry.

The background to the Norfolk Yeomanry starts in 1782 when troops of The Norfolk Rangers were raised, and by 1828 there were three regiments, 1st West, 2nd Mid and 3rd East. It was reconstituted as one Regiment in 1831, consisting largely of men from the former 2nd Mid Regiment, but was disbanded in 1849. A new regiment was raised in 1901 and in the First World War they saw service in Gallipoli and Egypt, and as infantry took part in the Palestine campaign of 1917. The Regiment converted to artillery in 1920, and in 1942 became the 65th Anti-Tank Regiment RA, serving in the Middle East and at El Alamein. After the Second World War they were reformed as the 389th Light Anti-Aircraft Regiment, but in 1961 amalgamated with the Suffolk Yeomanry as the 308th Field Regiment.

The Loyal Suffolk Hussars provided two companies of Imperial Yeomanry in the Boer War, and in the First World War it served in 1915 in Gallipolli. On withdrawing to Egypt it was dismounted and used to defend the Suez Canal, being redesignated the 15th

Gunners of 202 (Suffolk and Norfolk Yeomanry) Field Battery RA.

Battalion, The Suffolk Regiment in 1917. Following service in Palestine, the Regiment moved to France in May 1918. After the War it was converted to artillery in 1920, providing two batteries to 103 Brigade RFA. Nineteen thirty-eight saw a conversion to the anti-tank role, and in 1942 four batteries were regimented as 55th Anti-Tank Regiment, landing in Normandy on D-Day plus 6. They fought in North-West Europe until the end of the War. In 1947 they became the 308th Anti-Tank Regiment, amalgamating with the Norfolk Yeomanry in 1961.

Headquarters (Home Counties) Battery

History

The Battery derives its origin from a small detachment which formed in 1915 as Headquarters Royal Artillery, 44 (Home Counties) Division. This TA Division fought in both World Wars and survived until 1967, when it ceased to exist.

101 (Northumberland) Field Regiment, Royal Artillery (V)

Batteries

203 (Elswick) at Blyth;

204 (Tyneside Scottish) at Newcastle upon Tyne;
205 (3rd Durham Volunteer Artillery) at South
Shields;
HQ at Gosforth.

History

The Regiment in its present form was raised in 1967
from a number of artillery TA units in the North East
of England. It was originally a Medium Regiment,
but in 1978 was redesignated a Field Regiment and
re-equipped in 1980. The Regiment is able to trace
its history back to 1803 when the threat of invasion
from France meant that volunteer artillery units were
needed. The first was under the command of the
Duke of Northumberland, and was the Northumberland Volunteer Artillery. After 1815 their activities
were suspended. In 1859 another volunteer corps was
raised, and on 2 August the 1st Northumberland
Volunteer Artillery was born. On 23 December the
same year, in South Shields, the 3rd Durham Volunteer Artillery was formed.

In the early days, volunteers had to buy their own

uniforms, and Officers and NCOs were elected by
the members of the unit, although the Commission
of an Officer was granted by the War Office on
recommendation of the Lord-Lieutenant. Over the
next few years more batteries were raised, on both
sides of the Tyne.

In 1900 it was decided that Volunteer Artillery
should not be sent to South Africa. Messrs Armstrong
Whitworth, however, made six twelve-pounder field
guns which were presented to Field Marshal Lord
Roberts. He directed that the guns should equip the
'Elswick Battery', named after the ordnance works,
and that they should be manned by the men who built
them. It became the most effective artillery unit in
the Boer War; this is commemorated in the name of
203 Battery of today's Regiment. One of the Elswick
guns is in the Museum at RHQ. When 203 Battery
was formed in 1967, it did so with personnel from
Q Battery 324 Heavy AA Regiment and P(the
Elswick) Battery, 272 (Northumbrian) Field Regiment RA(TA) both based in Blyth, and initially they
were equipped with 5.5 inch guns.

203 (Elswick) Field Battery driving past The Queen in May 1983.

A gun commander stands by.

In 1914 both the Northumberland and Durham TA were mobilized. Among the men from the North East in the opening of the Battle of the Somme at La Boiselle on 1 July 1916 were four service Battalions of Tyneside Scottish; they were decimated by the German machine-guns. On 1 April 1939, although these gallant men had not been TA, the name in their memory was continued in a newly-formed TA Regiment, the 12th (Tyneside Scottish) Battalion, The Durham Light Infantry, which on 1 January 1947 became the 670th Light Anti-Aircraft Regiment RA (Tyneside Scottish, The Black Watch) TA. After two more changes of name this became 204 Battery, and to this day they march behind a pipe band and wear the Tam O'Shanter. In the Second World War gunners from both sides of the Tyne served in every theatre of battle.

The Durham gunners fought in both Wars as part of 50 Northumbrian Division. In 1967 274 Field Regiment and 463 LAA Regiment were disbanded, and members from the two formed 205 Battery, which commemorates the name of the original Volunteer Artillery of the County. The latest honour to 101 Regiment was the granting of the Freedom of the City of Newcastle upon Tyne in October 1980.

General

The Regiment has a major role in support of BAOR in time of war. Its three Batteries each have eight Light Guns, and there are three Cymbeline Mortar Locating Radars.

102 (Ulster) Air Defence Regiment Royal Artillery (V)

Batteries

206 at Coleraine;
215 at Newtonards;
HQ at Newtonards.

History

The office of 'Ordinance and Traine of Artillery in Ireland' was first recorded in 1684, being stationed at Charlemont, Londonderry and Carrickfergus. The first regular Artillery Company was formed in 1756. Some 20 Companies were formed and divided into two, the 1st and 2nd Battalions. The 1st became part of the Regular Army and the 2nd, stationed in Ulster, formed the Antrim Militia Artillery in 1854. After several changes in title the Province provided the 3rd (Ulster) Anti-Aircraft Brigade (Supplementary Reserve) in 1939 and it served in Africa, India and Italy, as well as providing AA defence for the Battle of Britain and the withdrawal from Dunkirk.

Following the overall demobilization after the Second World War, two Artillery units eventually remained in Ulster; these were 245 Light Air Defence Regiment and 661 (Ulster) Field Regiment. In 1967 these were incorporated into 102 (Ulster and Scottish) Light Air Defence Regiment, but in 1986 the Ulster portion of the Regiment was increased and took its present title.

General

The Regiment is trained to provide low-level air defence of the Army in Germany in the event of war. This highly-mobile Land Rover-borne unit is equipped with the Javelin missile system.

103 Air Defence Regiment Royal Artillery (V)

Batteries

208 at Liverpool;
209 in Manchester;
213 at St Helens and Widnes;
216 in Bolton;
HQ (Kings) at Liverpool;
Lancashire Artillery Volunteer Band at Bolton;
A (HSF) Battery at Liverpool, St Helens and Widnes.

History

The Lancashire Artillery Volunteers were first raised in 1859 as 23 companies of Artillery. In Manchester

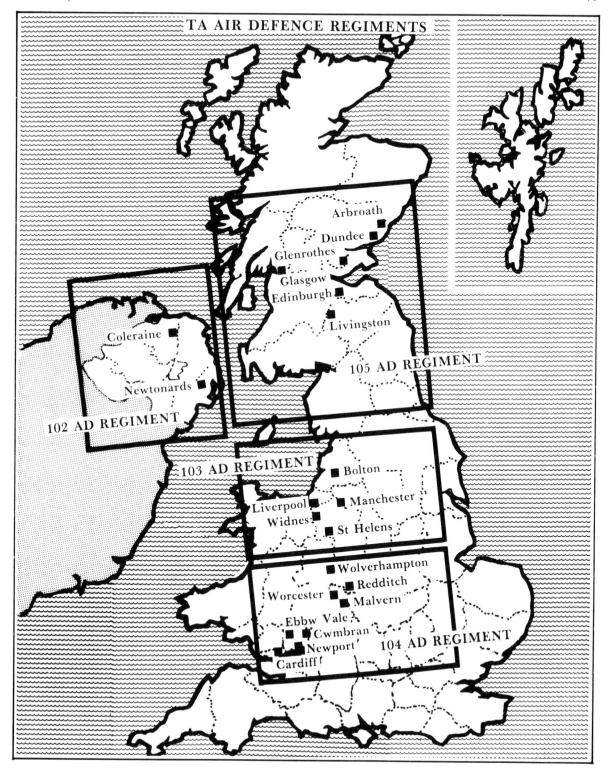

TA AIR DEFENCE REGIMENTS

Arbroath

Dundee

Glenrothes

Glasgow

Edinburgh

Livingston

105 AD REGIMENT

Coleraine

Newtonards

102 AD REGIMENT

103 AD REGIMENT

Bolton

Liverpool

Widnes

Manchester

St Helens

Wolverhampton

Redditch

Worcester

Malvern

Ebbw Vale

Cwmbran

Newport

Cardiff

104 AD REGIMENT

some elements had existed earlier, as in 1804 the Duke of Gloucester inspected the Heaton Artillery Volunteers. At the same time the Lancashire Hussars, the Irish Rifle volunteers and the Liverpool Rifle Volunteers were being raised. Later on, these, and some battalions of the Kings Regiment, a battalion of the Prince of Wales volunteers and the Liverpool Scottish, were all rebadged as Lancashire Gunners. In the First World War there were 15 Artillery Brigades or Infantry battalions, and during the Second World War 17 Artillery Regiments from the county. Until 1967 seven of these remained, but they were amalgamated to form 103 (Lancashire Artillery Volunteers) Light Air Defence Regiment. These Regiments had particularly distinguished records, and two Victoria Crosses were awarded, one to Sergeant Gourley of the 2nd West Lancashire Brigade, Royal Field Artillery at Cambrai in 1917 and the other to Lieutenant Baxter of the Liverpool Irish, leading a bombing party known as the 'Forty Thieves' in 1916. The Bolton Artillery at Serapeum in February 1915 were the first volunteers in the First World War to fire a shell in anger. The Regiment took its present title in 1977, being equipped with Blowpipe, converting to Javelin in 1987.

General

The Regiment is trained in the low-level air defence role and is equipped with Javelin. For mobility they rely on Land Rovers, and in time of war have a role supporting the Army in BOAR.

104 Air Defence Regiment Royal Artillery (V)

Batteries

210 (Staffordshire) at Wolverhampton;
211 (South Wales) at Cardiff, Ebbw Vale and Newport;
214 (Worcestershire) at Worcester, Malvern and Redditch;
217 (County of Gwent) at Cwmbran;
HQ at Newport.

History

The origins of the Regiment in the Midlands stems from the Staffordshire Rifle Volunteers, formed in 1860, and the Worcester Volunteer Artillery Corps, formed in 1864. The Welsh batteries descend from the First Monmouthshire Artillery Volunteer Corps raised in 1860, the Glamorgan Artillery Militia in 1854 and the Glamorgan Artillery Artisans in 1859.

General

The Regiment is employed in the low-level air defence

role and was originally equipped with Blowpipe, the shoulder launched missile system, but this has been replaced in 1988 with the updated Javelin system. This Land Rover-borne unit is earmarked for service with BAOR in time of war.

105 (Scottish) Air Defence Regiment Royal Artillery (V)

Batteries

207 (City of Glasgow) at Glasgow;
212 (Highland) at Arbroath and Glenrothes;
218 (Lothian) at Livingston and Edinburgh;
219 (City of Dundee) in Dundee HQ (City of Edinburgh) in Edinburgh.

History

The Regiment was formed in 1986 from two Batteries, 207 and 212, of 102 (Ulster and Scottish) Air Defence Regiment, the Ulster Batteries forming 102 Regiment, and the Scottish Batteries being joined by two new batteries. It is regarded as the successor of 445 (Lowland) Light Air Defence Regiment, which had been disbanded in 1967 but had its roots in the expansion of the TA in 1938. It also can claim the antecedents of The Lowland and Highland Regiments Royal Artillery. Through the Lowland Regiment the history can be traced back to the Artillery volunteers of the nineteenth century in Lanarkshire, Ayrshire, Dumbartonshire, Edinburgh City, Renfrewshire, and Bute, Ross and Cromarty.

Through the Highland Artillery Regiment, the Regiment can claim descent from those early volunteers such as the 1st Aberdeenshire, The Highland, Fifeshire, Forfarshire and 1st Edinburgh. All the constituent antecedent Regiments of both the Highland and Lowland Regiments changed their titles and roles many times, and served with distinction in the two World Wars.

General

The Regiment formed for low-level air defence role in Germany on 1 April 1986, with 219 Battery being formed one year later. It is equipped with Land Rovers and the Javelin missile system.

266 (Gloucestershire Volunteer Artillery) Observation Post Battery, Royal Artillery (V)

History

The origins of the Battery go back to 1859 with the

Gunners from 105 Air Defence Regiment with Javelin on exercise in BAOR.

formation of the 1st Gloucestershire Volunteer Artillery. It fought as part of 240 Medium Field Brigade during the First World War and as 76th (Gloucestershire) AA Brigade in the Second World War. The Artillery Ground at Whiteladies Road in Bristol is a famous city landmark, and owes its name to the battery founded there in 1859.

General

This battery has its headquarters in Bristol, and in time of war supports Royal Artillery units in BAOR by providing observation post parties. As well as OP parties, the Battery has a troop of its own guns to enable it to practise fire control.

269 (West Riding) Observation Post Battery, Royal Artillery

History

The Battery was formed in 1975 and is descended from three Yorkshire TA Field Artillery Regiments. 269 and 270 Regiments were amalgamated to form 249 Regiment, and this was then disbanded, leaving no Artillery units in Yorkshire from 1967 until this battery was formed. To help foster the 'family' atmosphere, strong links are maintained with former members of the old regiments. The Battery had the honour of firing a Queen's Birthday Salute in York. In 1986 a team raised a large sum for charity by entering the Horsforth Half Marathon. They have held the King George V Cup awarded annually by the National Artillery Association.

General

The Battery, which has its headquarters in Leeds, would provide observation post parties for units in BAOR in time of war. It has a troop of guns for practice use. The full range of military training is undertaken, including infantry skills and co-ordination of Divisional Artillery. Members have taken part in various survival training and major exercises in BAOR.

The Battery maintains close links with 45 Field Regiment RA, whose recruiting area is West Yorkshire. As well as gunners, the Battery has the usual complement of supporting corps members from REME, ACC and RAPC, as well as WRAC, whose tasks include cooking, clerical work, safety for live firing and driving.

307 (South Notts Hussars Yeomanry, Royal Horse Artillery) Observation Post Battery, Royal Artillery (V)

History

The unit traces its history back to 9 August 1794, when the first of the Yeomanry Troops was formed in the county. As with other Yeomanry regiments it was used extensively in policing civil disturbances in the early nineteenth century. Its first recorded action was in the Market Square in Nottingham in 1811, when it quelled a Luddite riot. In 1826 there was Royal approval for the new title, The South

Nottinghamshire Yeomanry Cavalry, uniting the five troops into a single regiment. In 1900 the Regiment mobilized as a Hussar Regiment, forming part of the Imperial Yeomanry, and sailed to South Africa. It was once again mobilized for the First World War and served in Egypt, Gallipoli, Macedonia and Palestine, but in 1918 the Regiment surrendered its horses to become a Machine-Gun Battalion in France. After the war, in 1922, it was converted from the cavalry role once more to become 107 Field Brigade, Royal Artillery, and it was again mobilized in 1939 for the Second World War.

In 1940 the Regiment once more sailed to Egypt, and during two years' fighting in the desert it forged strong links with 1 RHA, an association that is commemorated in the unit's current title. In June 1942 at the Battle of Knightsbridge the casualties were so heavy that it was not possible to reform 107 Field Regiment until 1944. A second South Notts Regiment, the 150th, had been formed. All South Notts Hussar units were disbanded after the war and were reformed as one Gunner Regiment.

General

The headquarters of the Battery is at Bulwell in Nottinghamshire, and in time of war it provides observation posts for the Royal Artillery in support of 3 and 4 Armoured Divisions in BAOR.

289 Commando Battery, Royal Artillery (V)

History

The history of the Battery is traced back to the various Middlesex and Essex Artillery Volunteers and Kent (Royal Arsenal) Volunteers of 1860. The Commando role was adopted in 1977 after 20 years as 289 Parachute Regiment and Battery RHA(V). It is worth going deeper into the history of this Battery, as it is representative of the other Artillery Volunteers and in this case is drawn from three major counties. When artillery volunteers were first raised to counter the threat of Napoleonic invasion, they received pay for completing two days' drill out of seven, but they were in most respects civilians. Their main benefactors were wealthy businessmen, rather than the Government.

These volunteers became almost private armies, with their benefactors designing and paying for their uniforms. During 1859 authority was given to Lord-Lieutenants to raise Artillery Volunteer Corps for home defence duties with a main function to man coastal defences — 'To aid, in the most efficient manner in the manning of batteries erected for the protection of our coastal towns so that the Royal Artillery and Militia may be, to as great an extent as possible,

disposable for other services.' The term 'battery' in those days meant a single gun, and a volunteer corps was of rather indeterminate size, varying from 30 to over a thousand strong. Ten corps were formed by the end of 1859, and 35 had been authorized. The smallest unit in an average corps was a 'sub-division', with about 30 men under the command of a Lieutenant, and on an increase to 50 men it became a company, with a Captain. If four companies were formed, it became a Brigade. On 1 March 1860, Colonel Tullock, a superintendent at the Royal Arsenal, raised four companies of volunteers, and later that year the 10th Kent Artillery Volunteers became known as the 10th Kent (Royal Arsenal) Artillery. Just before this, in November 1859 at Harwich, the 1st Essex Artillery Volunteer Corps was formed and in February 1860 they amalgamated with the 2nd Essex. The 3rd Essex was established at Barking and, later renumbered the 2nd Essex, it moved to Grays at about the same time as the new 3rd was formed in June 1861 at Plaistow.

In Middlesex, the 1st, 2nd and 3rd Middlesex Artillery Volunteer Corps were formed, the 3rd having been raised by Lord Truro in November 1860 at 111 Regent Street in London's West End, but in October 1861 it moved to 3 Hanover Square. Much is known about the 3rd Middlesex, and in its early days it was equipped with the 64-pounder rifled muzzle-loaded gun on a garrison standing carriage, and the 40-pounder Armstrong rifled breach-loaded gun on a travelling siege-carriage. Later on, number 1 Division was at Clerkenwell, number 2 at Kennington and number 3 at Marylebone and later Paddington, with Brigade HQ at Cockspur Street at Charing Cross and subsequently at Great Scotland Yard off Whitehall. The uniform of the 3rd Middlesex was distinctive, consisting of a Racoon Skin busby with a scarlet cloth busby bag hanging over the right side and a white plume on the left. The undress cap was the old 'pill box' type, with a scarlet cloth band edged top and bottom with silver wire braid and a silver wire button on the crown. In front of the cap was a white grenade. The tunic was blue, with white cord facings top and bottom of the scarlet cloth collar and white metal grenades on either side of the collar opening. The cuffs had white cord Gordian Knots. The distinctive head dress gave rise to the nickname 'Truro's Tigers'.

Volunteer forces as a general rule wore silver cords, rather than gold which at that time was only worn by regular army units. The 3rd varied from tradition on the jacket facings, which were usually red not white. The Corps had a good gunnery tradition, and in 1869 won several prizes at the 'Tir Nationale' at Liège, and they were presented with commemorative medals by HM King Leopold of the Belgians. Their practice camp took place at Whitsuntide at Sheerness at Garrison Point Fort, so that they could drill on the 9, 10, 11 and 12-inch rifled muzzle-loaded guns of the coastal artillery, and for practice with field guns at Barton's Point at Sheerness. They also attended annual camp at Shoeburyness for competition against other units, winning the Queen's Prize for the first time in 1870.

These then are the three roots of today's battery at East Ham, but many changes were yet to come. The various corps and batteries were amalgamated, or disappeared. Many famous or notable men served in these units, in addition to Lord Truro with the 3rd Middlesex. At one stage the 3rd Kent (Royal Arsenal) Artillery Volunteers were commanded by Lieutenant-Colonel H.M. Hozier, a notable soldier and future father-in-law of the late Sir Winston Churchill. A memorial to him stands in the Territorial Army Centre at Rochester Row in London.

In 1891 the volunteers were redesignated as 'Artillery Volunteers' and all the various titles changed accordingly. At this time equipment changes were made, and in 1892 the 3rd Middlesex trained with the then new field and position armaments, which consisted of the 9-pounder rifle muzzle-loaded gun, and the 13-pounder and 40-pounder guns. In 1891 His Royal Highness the Duke of York, later King George V, became Honorary Colonel of the 3rd Middlesex. For the Boer War, out of 1,000 volunteers required, the 3rd Middlesex alone provided 400 officers and men. The first volunteer officer to lose his life in South Africa was Lieutenant-Colonel Hoskier, who was commanding the 3rd Middlesex. He had gone there in an independent capacity as a War Correspondent attached to Montmorency's Scouts, and was killed on 23 February 1900 whilst on reconnaissance. There is a plaque to his memory at the TA Centre at East Ham.

In 1902 all Volunteer units were restyled Royal Garrison Artillery (Volunteers), and on 1 April 1908, with the coming of the Territorial Force, the volunteers were disbanded, although the older units continued to serve, but under new titles and with a new organization. The Territorial Force was organized into 14 Divisions, each having four Artillery Brigades. Each of these was about the size of a Regiment of today, and this was the set up when the TF was mobilized in 1914.

Following 1921 there were many changes of title and reorganization within the TA, mainly because of the gradual mechanization of the Armed Forces. For the first few years there was much improvization, and at practice camp in 1922 at Larkhill, one Battery was almost entirely horsed with long-tailed undertakers' funeral blacks, which they nearly succeeded in killing one day on the ranges. In 1924 the

Brigades of Royal Field Artillery were renamed as Field Brigades Royal Artillery (Territorial Army). With the pre-Second World War re-organization of the TA, the Brigade became a Field Regiment of three troop Batteries, each troop having four guns, and in April 1939 along with the rest of the TA their numbers were doubled. Four regiments from the South East were available at the start of the war. 92nd were the first to taste action with the BEF in France, and fought in the retreat to Dunkirk, which was reached at five o'clock on 31 May 1940, with only 12 guns remaining. It was evacuated and returned to England, leaving 12 of their fellows killed in France.

One unit formed from two batteries of the 92nd was less fortunate and 140 men were captured, the remainder of 140 (5th London) Army Field Regiment making their way to England by way of Dunkirk. In 1942 they re-formed and became part of the new 1st Army, seeing service in Algeria, Tunisia, Italy and the Balkans.

The 85th (2 East Anglian) Army Field Regiment with men from Stratford in East London and Romford in Essex spent the early part of the war on dull routine duties, but in September 1942 they sailed from Liverpool on HMS *Highland Monarch* to Port Tewfik in Egypt, by way of Freetown and Durban, and eventually at midnight on 26 November they arrived at Camp 19 El Tahag. Six weeks later they went to Iraq as part of the Persia and Iraq Forces (PAI Force). In 1943 the Regiment moved to Tripoli as a Mountain Regiment, their 25-pounder guns going to other units, and the 3.7-inch howitzers, pack mules, and Basuto soldiers joined them. In February and March 1944 the Regiment went to Italy to come under the command of 4th Indian Division. Through the Italian campaign the Regiment was mainly with the 4th and 10th Indian Divisions, and was very successful, members being awarded six MCs, six MMs, and 36 mentions in dispatches. 134 (E. Anglian) Field Regiment, after two years at home, went to India and saw service in Burma.

After the war, in 1947 all artillery regiments, regardless of function, were renumbered and re-organized, the prefix 2 denoting TA Regiments. The regiments of the South East were then part of 16th Airborne Division (TA), and three regiments were formed, 285 (Essex) Airborne Light Regiment, 292 (5 London) Airborne Anti Tank Regiment, and 291 (5 London) Airborne Anti-tank Regiment. The Airborne Division was disbanded in August 1956 and replaced by 44 Independent Parachute Brigade Group, so 285 and 292 amalgamated to become 289 Parachute Regiment.

291 Regiment converted to ground troops. Thus the number 289 made its first appearance, and it is said that it came from the average between 85 and

92, rounded up, as 288½ would never do! It was fortunate in having the late Admiral of the Fleet Lord Louis Mountbatten, Earl Mountbatten of Burma, as its Honorary Colonel. In 1960 he received on behalf of the Regiment the status of 'Royal Horse Artillery'.

In 1967 as part of the general TA re-organization, 289 was reduced in size to a Battery, equipped for a short time with 25-pounder guns and later a new 105mm Pack Howitzer. At this time it relocated at East Ham in East London. 1 April 1977 saw yet another change, when the Battery became part of 29 Commando Regiment RA and the following year was equipped with the new 105mm Light Gun. The close links with the City of London were established again when the Battery formed an association with the Worshipful Company of Basketmakers.

General

With its headquarters at East Ham in East London, the Battery is one of four belonging to 29 Commando Regiment, Royal Artillery. The Regiment is a regular army unit and 289 is its Territorial Army component. In addition to its HQ, there is a TA Naval Gunfire Support (NGS) troop at Poole in Dorset, trained to direct naval gunfire in support of the Com-

mandos. The Battery is currently equipped with the 105mm Light Gun, which can be deployed either by road or helicopter. The Commando role means that the battery trains for possible deployment on NATO's northern flank. Each January the Battery joins with the rest of the Regiment for Arctic training, and the annual camp is held in Norway or Germany every few years. The arctic training includes skiing, and there is a parachuting requirement for the NGS troop and OP parties.

The prime achievement of all new recruits to the Battery is to gain their Green Beret. This is awarded by the Royal Marines after success at the two-week Commando course held at the Commando Training Centre in Devon. The build-up to the course for the volunteers takes many months, and only those who are fit and totally committed are able to complete the programme. As a result, new recruits have to gain a good knowledge of basic Commando and Infantry skills, they have to be able to live and operate in difficult and mountainous country. This means learning skills such as working with helicopters, landing craft, parachuting and skiing, as well as the art of survival in areas of extreme climate, such as Northern Norway or the tropical areas of Central America.

Gun, 105mm

This is usually called the Light Gun L118, and is now the standard gun for the UK-based field regiments. It replaced the earlier 105mm Pack Howitzers in 1978. It is light enough to be air-portable in the Hercules transport or under a helicopter. The normal ground-towing vehicle is the 1 ton Land Rover, with another acting as a limber, carrying additional ammunition. The gun is capable of firing the full range of ammunition, and in the Falklands proved its worth by firing over 400

rounds each gun each day during the final battle for Port Stanley. It is 105mm calibre, weighing 4,100lbs (1,860 kg) and has a maximum range of 17,200 metres. It has a crew of six men, and from its folded towing position takes two minutes to get into action, half that if it is already unfolded. The ammunition available includes HE 35lb (16kg), HESH, smoke, illuminating and marker. It has a muzzle velocity of 709 m/s and it can fire at six rounds a minute.

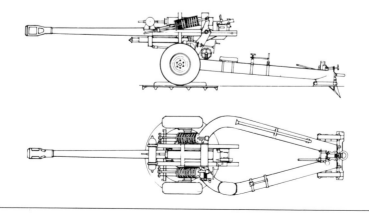
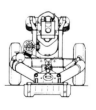

Javelin

This system is accepted as an improved Blowpipe, however it has a different type of guidance system. SACLOS is semi-automatic command to line of sight, and all the operator has to do is maintain the aiming mark on the target, and a micro-computer does the rest. It is slightly longer than its predecessor. It was first fired at the end of 1984 and is now being issued to TA anti-aircraft Regiments. This is a short-range, shoulder-launched guided weapon for close air defence and its primary job is to protect combat units and static locations against low-level attack. It is carried on a Land Rover and trailer, but it is man-portable over short distances. The maximum impact is over four kilometres, at up to 1,000 metres altitude. The missile is powered by solid fuel and reaches a speed of Mach 2.

Honourable Artillery Company: Captains General

Sir Christopher Morres, 1st Master and Ruler, 1537-44,

Sergeant Major General Phillip Skippon, Captain 1639-47, Captain General 1657-60,

James, Duke of York (afterwards James II) Colonel-in-Chief 1660-64, Captain General 1664-90,

William III, Captain General 1690-1702,

Henry Howard, Duke of Norfolk, Captain General 1690 during William III's absence in Ireland,

George, Prince of Denmark (Consort of Queen Anne), Captain General 1702-08,

George, Prince of Wales (later George II), Captain General 1715-60,

George, Prince of Wales (later George IV), Captain General 1766-1830,

William IV, Captain General, 1830-37,

Augustus Frederick, Duke of Sussex, Captain General and Colonel 1837-43,

Albert, Prince Consort, Captain General and Colonel 1843-61

Albert Edward, Prince of Wales (afterwards Edward VII) Captain General and Colonel 1863-1910,

George V, Captain General and Colonel 1910-36,

Edward VIII, Captain General 1936,

George VI, Captain General 1936-52,

Elizabeth II, Captain General 1952-

289 Parachute Regiment, Royal Horse Artillery TA (now 289 Commando Battery, RA (V)): A Peacetime George Cross.

On 16 January 1965, Lance Bombardier Brian Spillett, a volunteer soldier of 'P' Battery died in hospital from burns he received trying to rescue a neighbour from a fire in Lodge Crescent, Waltham Cross, Hertfordshire. The citation reads:

'A fire broke out at a house, the home of a man and his wife and their child and the grandfather. The fire had reached an advanced stage when the family were aroused, and it was only with great difficulty that the wife and child and the grandfather escaped. The father was still in the house when Mr Spillett, attracted by shouting, came from his house a few doors away. He arrived only partly dressed. When he reached the door of the house, both downstairs and upstairs were a mass of flames. Mr Spillett enquired whether everyone was out of the house and on learning the father was still in it on the first floor, he ran straight into the flames. Attempts to hold him back were brushed aside. Mr Spillett reached the first floor, but was unable to rescue the father. By now the inside of the house was a blazing inferno and he only managed to escape himself by jumping through a first-floor window.

'He was found some time later in the garden of an adjoining house, very extensively burnt and with other serious injuries. He died in hospital a week later. Mr Spillett sacrificed his life in an effort to save that of a neighbour.'

He was awarded the George Cross, posthumously.

The Brave TA Gunners

Extracts from citations for 85th (2 East Anglian) Army Field Regiment, Royal Artillery TA

'On 9 September 1944, Lieutenant (Temporary Captain) Wintringham was Forward Observation Officer for 337 Battery with 1 Royal Sussex in the operations round Pain De Castello. Early in the morning he went forward with a platoon to capture the ridge north-west of the village. The platoon was held up by spandau fire in the dark, and Captain Wintringham worked his way along round the flank to a position whence he could observe the enemy. Having noted their positions he tried to rejoin the infantry but found they had withdrawn. He thereupon went forward again, and from first light onwards passed back information about the enemy and brought down observed fire on their positions, close to himself. Later he returned safely. For this action he was awarded the Military Cross.'

'On 11 October 1944 near Montecodruzzo, Gunner Belcher was a member of an Observation Post party which walked into a minefield during the hours of darkness and set off a mine. Despite heavy artillery fire, from which he sustained injury, he cleared the area of casualties at great risk to himself. For this total disregard for danger and for his coolness and unselfish devotion to his comrades he was awarded the Military Medal.'

Cymbeline Radar

Radar FA number 15, marks 1 and 2 are mortar-locating radar systems. During the Second World War, enemy mortars exacted too high a toll of casualties on our forces, so a major priority was to find a suitable method of detecting them quickly to enable the artillery to neutralize the menace. Radar was chosen and Green Archer, Radar FA number 8, was developed. This is now replaced by the smaller and lighter system. Both marks of radar operate on the same principle, that is when a bomb is fired it rises at a steep angle, so it can be detected by radar. The radar then automatically switches to a higher angle and using the two readings rapidly calculates the location of the firing point. Counter fire can be directed on it in very short time. It has an operating range of about 20 kilometres and is mounted in a Land Rover-towed trailer. The normal crew is four men, with two spotting in a forward area to give warnings of mortars firing. It can also be used for other jobs, such as detection and control of helicopters or light aircraft, detection of rocket firing locations and limited artillery control and survey.

One TA Gunner's Story
(As told to the author by former TA Gunner, Bert Gardner.)

In 1937, my father said to my brother and I, 'Now listen, I want you to join the Territorial Army, it'll make men of you.' We weren't particularly keen on this idea, but he was so insistent we made our way one evening down to the TA Drill Hall in Colindale. We didn't go in, but walked past the door and back home to lie to our dad that they wouldn't take us, we were too short. He had been in the TA before the First World War and served throughout the war in the Royal Artillery; later when the Second World War came along, he got back into uniform with the Royal Air Force. He was very keen that we should join, and threatened to drag us back there the next day. Reluctantly we went back and both joined 317 Company, 36 Middlesex Regiment, Royal Engineers, a searchlight unit. We both entered into the spirit of it, but after only about four months, my brother Ted left and joined the regulars, serving right through to the post-war years, when he retired as a Warrant Officer in the Royal Artillery.

Although we were badged Royal Engineers, it was later when the war started that we changed to Artillery, when searchlights became part of Anti-Aircraft Command. After Ted left, I carried on as a TA sapper, attending camp and training. In 1938 at the time of the Munich crisis, we were all called up, and had a camp lasting a month, but when it died down we went back home and to our civvy jobs.

In about August 1938, we moved Drill Hall from Colindale to a brand-new purpose-built building in Edgware Road at Edgware. One morning we were all summoned to appear in our best spit-and-polish uniforms, and we lined up in the street outside as Lord Hore-Belisha, the Secretary of State for War, opened our new premises. At the time I had made progress, and was now a bugler in the unit band.

Our uniform was the heavy, First World War style, with puttees and heavy greatcoats. We did, however, have a walking-out uniform of 'blues', and each Sunday I would put mine on, and parade the streets of Edgware and Burnt Oak, showing off to the girls! Most enjoyable.

In 1939, we were all called up again to set up our searchlights in various parts of the country. I went to a farmer's field in Cambridgeshire. We were under canvas, and it was pouring with rain. On the third or fourth Sunday the farmer ran out and called us in to listen to the radio. It was the Prime Minister announcing that we were at war — the date 3 September 1939. Our reaction was strange, something of a panic I suppose, all running round looking for our tin hats. Nothing happened for quite some time. It was a good job it didn't, all we had were sticks and dummy guns. It was a red letter day, however, when we were issued with a Lewis machine gun. We were thrilled to bits with it. It was erected on a pole, surrounded by sandbags, and we all did two-hour stints standing behind it, using our binoculars to scan the sky looking for enemy.

We did try to fire it a few times, but each time it jammed. It was a full-time job reassembling it again and again, as it didn't work properly.

When called up this time, I loaded everything I could possibly carry into my kit bag. When I said goodbye to Mum, I had the kit bag, a suit case, and my old piano accordian over my shoulder. I couldn't play all that well, but enjoyed a tune. I went to the drill hall and fell in line with all the others. We got sorted out and on to the lorries to take us away to our country posts. One officer,

Lieutenant Lebus, made a bit of a fuss about coming to war with an accordian slung over my back. He must have relented, because it ended up with me in Cambridgeshire, and was very useful, especially during the phoney war, with nothing doing and it pouring with rain all the time.

One early problem we had in TA units called up for the war, was the absence of cooks. All the guys on the site used to have to take turns to do the cooking. I remember making uneatable porridge that the spoon stood up in, it was dreadful stuff. Also no one knew how to make a good cup of tea in a pail, but somehow we all survived, and in fact it was quite good fun.

It was Mr Lebus who got me into driving. One day he asked for volunteers to drive him to Brigade HQ. Being a bit bored, I suppose, I volunteered. The catch was that, apart from motor bikes, I had never before then driven anything.

I got in and Mr Lebus said 'Away you go.' I started the engine up, put it into gear and drove off. It was a terrible drive, and quite a hairy experience, but from then on I was driving almost permanently, everything from motor cycles as a despatch rider, to a variation of a Sherman Tank with a 25-pounder field gun mounted on it. In the early days, I had to learn to drive an enormous lorry, a Thomas Tilling. It had a searchlight mounted on it, and when you stopped, by pushing various switches the engine would run as a generator suppling power for the light. Some of these were very old, a few with solid tyres, but it also had an early form of automatic gearbox, which was most strange.

One day a lorry pulled up on the site, and unloaded what looked like a load of cardboard tubes, stuck together on a frame. In fact they were metal tubes, the latest rocket-firing weapon, well the latest thing for 1941. We had to load it with its rockets, then run away, lie down and push a button on the end of a long cable. The whole thing sort of blew up in your face. It was very exciting at the time, but perhaps that is because life was still very boring on a searchlight site in those early days.

I had a good war, learnt how to drive, saw plenty of this country as well as the Middle East. It had been boring to start with, but livened up later in the War. For the first couple of years we had stuck together as the original TA unit, the same mates and officers. Heaven knows where I would have ended up if I hadn't joined the TA and relied on the lottery that call-up became.

5 Corps of Royal Engineers

Regimental badge

The Royal Arms and Supporters, *Ubique* and *Quo Fas et Gloria Ducunt*.

Colonel-in-Chief

THE QUEEN.

Regimental march

The quick march is *Wings*.

Stable belt

Deep red with two blue parallel bands.

General

The Corps is unique because of the number and variety of tasks it has undertaken, and many of the specialist skills it has evolved have developed into other organizations. The RE 'babies', as they are sometimes called, include the Royal Corps of Signals, the Royal Electrical and Mechanical Engineers, and to a large extent the Royal Air Force. The Boer War saw a great increase in field engineering, with bridging and demolitions playing an increasingly major part in their work, and Field Companies became even more valuable components of infantry and cavalry divisions. The RE part in the operation of railways became vital to the flow of supplies over long lines of communication. Sappers were also needed to build a network of blockhouses and camps for Kitchener's army.

During the First World War, on the Western Front the Royal Engineers faced a long period of trench warfare. They settled into this type of war, dealing with such needs as grenades, pumps, camouflage screening, trench mortars and the construction of roads and railways. Tunnelling companies developed mining operations beneath the enemy lines. The production of maps was an RE task, the survey battalions producing a new situation map every day. Ports, coastal craft, railways and inland water transport were an RE responsibility, until they handed operational control over the Royal Corps of Transport in 1965. In the Middle East, sappers built a pipe for carrying water from the Nile, and a railway to run alongside it. In the UK, RE units manned the searchlights.

The Second World War brought the sappers into even greater prominence on the battlefield, dealing with everything from bridges and construction, to demolitions and unexploded bombs. On every battlefield the men of the Royal Engineers, including those from the TA, played vital and indispensable roles in assault, defence and survival.

The Corps has the main task of providing military engineering support to the three services. This means they help our forces to fight, live and move, and at the same time deny the same functions to an enemy. The modern combat engineer is a capable and skilled tradesman and technician, who is versatile in a very wide range of roles. He is firstly a trained soldier able to cope with the skills of an infantryman. He is also trained as a combat engineer, with a basic grounding in bridging, demolitions and the construction of defences.

In the Royal Engineers, therefore, the same skills are found as are present in any major civil engineering concern; they include those required for tasks such as bridging, road building and mending, battlefield constructions, and life support constructions such as water supply and shelters. There is also mine warfare and anti-tank obstacles, as well as surveying, postal services, diving and bomb disposal.

At the Central Volunteer Headquarters at Blackwater in Camberley, Surrey, there are a number of specialists, including a major pool of highly-qualified engineers, many of whom in time of war will work as part of the Military Works Force (MWF). This pool is the Engineer and Transport Staff Corps, with its headquarters at Maidenhead in Berkshire. The latest development for the Royal Engineers is that CVHQ has raised a new squadron on behalf of the States of Jersey of specialist combat engineers. The new squadron is the Jersey Field Squadron, Royal Engineers, (The Royal Militia of the Island of Jersey) (V), and a new independent unit has been formed at Stafford known as HQ 30 Engineer Brigade Artisan Troop.

History of the Engineer Volunteers

The formation of a Volunteer Force of Engineers was approved on 12 May 1859, and this was conveyed from the Government to Lord-Lieutenants of counties. The formation was under the provisions of the Act of Parliament of 5 June 1804 which had raised volunteers for the wars against Napoleon. Regulations were laid down in January 1861 outlining the formation of the companies. These should be of between sixty and a hundred enrolled volunteers, including engineers, masons, joiners, quarrymen and railway employees. The seniority of these Engineer corps was to be decided by the number allocated to each corps by the Secretary of State for War. County precedence was settled according to the date on which the first company in the county was formed. Middlesex was the first, and therefore the senior, with Lanarkshire as second. The remaining twenty-two were in this order: Edinburgh City; Lancashire; Newcastle on Tyne; Yorkshire (West Riding); Gloucestershire; Cheshire; Denbighshire; Tower Hamlets; Cumberland; Surrey; Hampshire; Glamorgan; Essex; Devonshire; London; Flintshire; Northamptonshire; Durham; Somersetshire; Aberdeenshire; Sussex and finally Bedfordshire. After 1860, the companies were merged into 'administrative battalions'. The total force was known as 'Engineer Volunteer Corps' until 1888, when they became 'Engineer Volunteers, Fortress and Railway Forces, Royal Engineers'.

Before the formation of the Territorial Force in 1908, the Engineers suffered two further changes of name, to 'Volunteer Engineers, Fortress and Railway Forces, Royal Engineers' in 1891 and finally to 'Royal Engineers (Volunteers)' in 1896.

The Royal Monmouthshire Royal Engineers (Militia)

Regimental badge

The Prince of Wales plume, cornet and motto *Ich Dien* surmounted by a crown, on either side of the plume the letters *R* and *E*, below a scroll inscribed *ROYAL MONMOUTHSHIRE*.

Honorary Colonel

HRH The Duke of Gloucester.

Regimental Colours

The Regiment is the only engineer unit to have its own Colours, and has trooped them. In 1914 the Colours of the East Monmouthshire Militia, direct antecedents of the Regiment, were presented to the Regiment for 'safe keeping' by the Lord Lieutenant of Monmouthshire by order of The King.

Stable belt

Members of the Regiment wear the RE stable belt, but with a green 'Militia Flash'.

Squadrons

100 at Newport in Gwent;
108 (Welsh) at Swansea;
225 (City of Birmingham) at Oldbury;
HQ at Monmouth in Gwent.

History

The Regiment is listed first in the Army list as the senior Regiment of the TA. The HAC claims earlier antecedents, but because of their continued loyalty to the Crown in the Civil War, the Royal Monmouthshire Royal Engineers (Militia) take precedence. The Regiment is a survivor of the Militia regiments, and traces its origins back to the trained bands and general levies of medieval and Tudor times. It claims ancestry back to a Posse Comitatus of 1539, which became a Trained Band on 21 March 1577. This was when the general levy was extended to Monmouthshire by Henry VIII, on the abolition of the Marcher Lordship. During the eighteenth and nineteenth centuries it was embodied on several occasions, notably the Seven Years' War (1760), the American War of Indepence (1778), the Napoleonic War (1803 to 1815) and the Crimean War (1854 to 1856). It did not in fact go to Crimea as a Regiment, but 300 officers and men served there with the Royal Welch Fusiliers. The

Monmouth and Brecon Militia received its 'Royal' honour in 1793, changing its title to the Royal Monmouthshire Militia in 1820. In 1852 it changed again to the Royal Monmouthshire (Light Infantry) Militia, but in 1877 under the Cardwell reforms it became a part of the Corps of Royal Engineers, acquiring its present title in 1896. This title gives it the unique privilege of two 'Royals' in its designation.

In 1899 it was once more embodied, for the South African War, and two companies served there with a bridging battalion. The First World War saw it again mobilized with several Siege and Railway Companies, and during the war its members were awarded five DSOs, eight MCs, twelve DCMs and sixteen MMs.

In September 1939 it mobilized 100 and 101 Field Companies, which went to France with the BEF, both companies having to fight as infantry during the withdrawal to Dunkirk. The two companies were in the van of the fighting until VE day, in North-West Europe, and were among the first Sappers to cross the river obstacles of the Seine, the Rhine and the Weser. After the war, in 1948, the Regiment reformed with three Field Squadrons, but in 1967 two of these were disbanded, leaving only 100 Squadron. At the same time the Regiment took over 108 (Welsh) Field Squadron, the remnant of 53 (Welsh) Division Engineers and 225 (City of Birmingham) Field Squadron, the remnant of 48 Division Engineers. Now that Monmouthshire has been absorbed into the county of Gwent, the Regiment provides the sole reminder of the centuries-old county name.

General

In time of war the role of the Regiment is to support BAOR. To undertake this role, their equipment includes that for bridge-building and road-laying. The latest addition to the establishment includes some posts for WRAC, who are used in certain administrative trades. For many years the Regiment has been affiliated with 6 Field Squadron of the Royal Canadian Engineers, based in Vancouver, and where possible, personnel are exchanged for training. Included amongst its honours the Regiment has the freedoms of Monmouth and of Swansea, and 225 (City of Birmingham) Squadron has the freedom of Smethwick.

The Regiment regularly enters a team for the Cambrian Patrol Competition, and in 1986 they were runners up and winners of their section. The cooks have also brought honour in their efforts in Exercise 'Combat Caterer' over many years, finishing second in the UK finals in 1986. There is a very successful shooting team which competes in the annual RE Rifle Association meeting, the Wales Skill-at-Arms meeting, Bisley and the Hechler & Koch Small Bore competition.

71 (Scottish) Engineer Regiment

Squadrons

102 (Clyde) at Paisley and Irvine;
104 (City of Edinburgh) at Edinburgh and Livingstone;
124 (Lowland) Field Squadron at Coatbridge and Cumbernauld;
HQ at Glasgow.

History

The Regiment formed on 1 April 1967 from a number of older units. The RHQ and HQ Squadron in Glasgow were formed from 80 (Scottish) Port Regiment. 102 Squadron formed from 102 Field Engineer Regiment, which had been raised in 1947 from a number of squadrons with histories dating back to 1884. They had been involved in submarine mining, and 49th (Coast Battalion) Company was a Fortress Unit in the defence of the Forth and Clyde during the First World War. 238 Company were the first troops to enter Tripoli in January 1943 and captured the Governor's standard, which is now housed in the Royal Engineers Museum.

104 Squadron started life as the 1st Edinburgh City Engineers Volunteers in 1860. They became involved in submarine mining, with their headquarters in a floating hulk called *Dido*; the Squadron retains its links with the present day HMS *Dido* of the Royal Navy. The Squadron saw service in the Middle East in 1916 and took part in the battles on the Somme, Ypres and Cambrai. When the TA reformed in 1947, 585 (Edinburgh) (Independent) Field Squadron became part of 155 Brigade Group, but in 1950 joined 124 Field Engineer Regiment. In 1961 a light Anti-Aircraft Artillery Regiment in Edinburgh rebadged as 432 Corps Engineer Regiment, and 585 Squadron transferred to it. This Regiment became today's 104 Squadron.

124 Squadron has its roots with the 2nd Lanarkshire Royal Engineers (Volunteers) formed in 1903. During the First World War, its 1st Lowland Field Company became one of the most decorated of any Territorial Army Engineer unit, gaining amongst its honours one Victoria Cross, thirteen Military Crosses and thirty Military Medals. During the 1950s, 124 Field Engineer Regiment (TA) formed, becoming 52 (Lowland) Division Engineers in 1961.

General

The Regiment's wartime role is in support of 29 Engineer Bridge and 2 Infantry Division, and to undertake this work it is equipped to the same standard as a regular unit.

72 (Tyne Electrical Engineers) Engineer Regiment

Squadrons

103 (1st Newcastle) Field Squadron at Gateshead and Newcastle upon Tyne;
106 (West Riding) at Sheffield and Dewsbury;
118 (Tees) at Hartlepool, Middlesbrough and Sunderland;
HQ at Gateshead.

History

The Regiment traces its history back to 1884 when it was formed to defend the Tyne using sea mines, later using searchlights in the trenches to bring down Zeppelins during the First World War. In the Second World War it was employed on Air Defence duties and served in the Middle East. The title of 'Tyne Electrical Engineers' was granted in 1907.

General

As part of 29 Engineer Brigade, whose headquarters is at York, the Regiment provides support to 1 (BR) Corps in Germany. It has affiliations to 28 Amphibious Engineer Regiment in BAOR and 72 Pioneer Regiment of the German Reserve Army (VBK).

73 Engineer Regiment

Squadrons

129 (East Riding) at Hull and Goole;
217 (London) at Holloway and Wandsworth;
575 (Sherwood Foresters) at Chesterfield, Derby, Buxton and Mansfield;
873 Movement Light Squadron at Acton in West London;
HQ at Bilborough, Nottingham.

History

The Regiment, which took its present form on 1 January 1969, can trace its roots back to the revival of the volunteer forces in Nottingham in 1859, when the Nottinghamshire (Robin Hood) Volunteer Battalion was formed as infantry. It has had many changes of name, and fought in the First World War as two battalions of infantry. During the 1930s they changed to the searchlight role and became Royal Engineers. In 1940 they changed cap badge again to become 42 (Robin Hood Sherwood Foresters) Searchlight Regiment, Royal Artillery. They merged with another Regiment to become a heavy artillery unit, and in 1961 reverted to sappers as 350 (Robin Hood) Field Squadron RE. In 1967 they made their seventh change in 19 years and became infantry again, until reduced to a cadre of only 8 men in 1969. Some personnel, however, became the nucleus of RHQ 73 Engineer Regiment on its formation.

The unit at Hull was first formed in 1884 as the Humberside Submarine Miners RE. It served in France during the First World War, and for the first three years of the Second World War was employed on construction work in the UK. Later in the war it served in Tunis, Sousse, Naples and Rome, before finally moving to Palestine. The Squadron based at Holloway in North London started life as the First Tower Hamlets Engineer Volunteer Corps in January 1860, and during the First World War served in South Africa. At the start of the Second World War the East Enders were some of the first to France with the BEF on 13 September 1939, and in May the following year in the face of the enemy they demolished the bridges over the River Lys in Belgium. After Dunkirk, the unit became part of the Guards Armoured Division, landing back in France in the third week after D-Day, and among the first troops to enter Brussels. The youngest Squadron is 873 Movement Light Squadron, formed in 1947. It is the only remaining searchlight unit in the British Army, and many tattoos and major events have used its lights and expertise.

General

The Regiment is earmarked to reinforce BAOR in time of war and usually takes one camp in three abroad.

74 (Antrim Artillery) Engineer Regiment

Squadrons

112 (Antrim Fortress) at Bangor, Carrickfergus and Belfast;
114 (Antrim Artillery) at Antrim, Belfast and Ballymena;
272 (West Riding) Field Support Squadron at Bradford;
HQ at Belfast.

History

The Regiment can trace its history back to the Royal Antrim Artillery Militia, which formed in 1854 to man the coastal defences of Belfast Lough. During the Crimean War of 1854 to 1856, and the Boer War, 1899 to 1901, there were periods of embodied service. In 1902 the name was changed to The Antrim Royal Garrison Artillery (Militia), and in 1908 on the formation of the TF it was one of the two Royal Garrison Artillery units transferred to the Special Reserve. The Regiment manned the defences of

Belfast Lough in the First World War until the end of the War, and in 1919 it was placed in suspended animation. In 1937, 188 Antrim Heavy Battery RA(TA) and the Antrim Fortress Company RE(TA) were the first Territorial Army units to be formed in Northern Ireland. In 1940, 188 Battery expanded to become 525 Coast Regiment RA, and had the task of manning coastal defence batteries. The Fortress Company became 591 (Antrim) Parachute Squadron RE and served as part of 6th Airborne Division for the Normandy landings, and in the battles in the Ardennes and the Rhine.

Post war, the successors of these two units were 146 (Antrim Artillery) Corps Engineer Regiment (TA) and 591 (Antrim) Independent Field Squadron RE (TA), which combined in 1967 to form 74 (Antrim Artillery) Engineer Regiment (V). 272 (West Riding) Field Support Squadron joined the Regiment in 1977. 188 (Antrim) Heavy Battery claims to have been one of the first to fire its guns in the Second World War, have fired across the bows of an incoming ship three hours before war was declared on 3 September 1939. This ship had not carried out the approved recognition procedure when trying to enter harbour. The Pipes and Drums of the Regiment were granted the right to wear the family tartan of MacDonald of the Isles.

The history claimed by 272 Squadron originates with the formation of the Volunteers in the West Riding of Yorkshire in 1859, which became the 2nd (Bradford) Corps Yorkshire (West Riding) Artillery Volunteers the following year. During the First World War as part of 49th (West Riding) Division, the unit served on the Western Front from April 1915 until the Armistice, and among the principal actions were Aubers Ridge 1915, Somme, Thiepval 1916, Ypres, Poelcapelle 1917, Lys and Bailleul 1918. In the Second World War another unit, 6th West Yorkshire Regiment (The Prince of Wales' Own) converted to the searchlight role and became RE and then RA, and the Artillery unit remained a Field Regiment serving in France, North Africa and Italy. These two Regiments were re-established after the war and amalgamated to form 370 Field Regiment RA (TA) in 1955. In 1969 it reduced to a Cadre later absorbed into 272 Squadron.

General

To equip the Regiment for its role, its members train in Germany and Denmark, as well as the UK, although individuals have been as far afield as Canada, Kenya and Falkland Islands. Amongst the specialists are those skilled at mine warfare, demolition, provision of water supply, bridging dry and wet gaps, and as some of their equipment floats, watermanship and the handling of high-speed assault craft are also some of the skills.

75 Engineer Regiment

Squadrons

107 at Birkenhead, Huyton and St Helens;
202 Field Squadron at Clifton in Manchester, Preston and Burnley;
HQ at Failsworth in Manchester.

History

The Regiment in its present structure formed in 1969; however, 107 Field Squadron can trace its history back to 1864. In that year the 1st and 2nd Lancashire Engineers (Volunteer) were raised. The number 107 was first used only in 1947 on the formation of 107 (West Lancashire) Engineer Regiment. In 1949 it amalgamated with 130 Army Construction Regiment and 128 Corps Engineer Regiment. During the 1967 re-organization, this Regiment merged with 113 Cheshire Field Squadron and was reduced in size to its present form.

202 Field Squadron was formed in the First World War as part of 30 Division County Palatine Engineers, but was disbanded in 1919. The following year it was re-formed as part of 42 East Lancashire Divisional Engineers. During the Second World War it was detached to 52 Highland Division until a second disbandment in 1946. The following year it was once again re-formed, as part of 123 Field Engineer Regiment. This Regiment lasted 20 years, being disbanded in 1969 with the title of 42 Divisional Engineers. 202 was brought back to life in its present role in 1969.

The Regimental Workshop REME at Oldham also has a remarkable record. It started life in about 1859 as the 31st Lancashire Rifle Volunteers, but later changed to being part of the Manchester Regiment. In 1938 it was rebadged, becoming 41st Battalion, Royal Tank Corps, converting to the 1st Scorpion Regiment RAC in 1942. As such it saw action in North Africa, Tunis, Sicily, Italy and the Adriatic. In 1947 the unit was retitled the 41st (Oldham) Royal Tank Regiment, later being reduced in size to become A Squadron of the Duke of Lancaster's Own Yeomanry (Royal Tank Regiment). Its final rebadging came in 1969 when it became a workshop, its members now wearing the REME badge.

In 1974 as an example of the Military Aid to the Civil Community (MACC) scheme, six engineering projects were taken on during the second week of annual camp that year.

Although these were minor projects, they were regarded as suitable training, and were:
at Hunters Crescent in Perth, two playground shelters erected by 107 Field Squadron;

at Bonnybridge in Falkirk, an improvised steel
footbridge erected by 107 Field Squadron;

at Brodic Castle, Isle of Arran, the erection of an
improvised wooden footbridge by 202 Field
Squadron;

at Rogart, Sutherland, a river diversion scheme for
local farmers by 202 Field Squadron;

at Letterfinlay, Inverness, improvised water supply
for the local community by 125 Field Support
Squadron;

at Braemar, bridge approach roads for Highland
Rescue Organization by 125 Field Support
Squadron.

General

The Regiment has a role in BAOR in wartime, so
much of its training is in Germany. It is equipped
to carry out all minor and many of the major military engineering tasks, and has its own plant unit and
wheeled tractors and dump trucks. 107 Field Squadron has the honour of the Freedom of both St Helens
and Birkenhead. Teams from the Regiment can be
found entering for two major annual events, the Cambrian Marches and the Nijmegen Marches.

101 (London) Engineer Regiment (Explosive Ordnance Disposal) (V)

Squadrons

579 at Stone in Dartford;

Lieutenant Julie Owen, the TA's first WRAC Bomb Disposal Officer, describing her role to the Secretary of State and Mr Tommy Macpherson at a Press Conference in London.

Using liquid nitrogen to freeze the mechanism of a practice bomb.

583 at Brighton;
590 at Rochester;
591 at HMS Collinwood at Chatham;
HQ at Stone in Dartford.

History

The Regiment is one of the newest in the British Army, being formed on 1 June 1988, although its component Squadrons have been going some time. Until then, the four Squadrons were all part of 33 Engineer Regiment (EOD), which is a Regular Army unit. During the Second World War, RE Bomb Disposal (BD) Units were formed in many parts of the UK, but after the War they were run down, and by the later 1950s consisted of HQ BD Unit (UK), the Army BD School and HQ BD (Army Emergency Reserve), the first two being Regular Army units. Following the reorganization of the TA all BD AER units were disbanded, together with two Independent TA Squadrons, 579 and 583 at Chatham and Dover. Following this, 590 Specialist Team RE (BD)(V) was formed at Rochester and quartered in Fort Clarence.

In 1969, to comply with standard NATO titles, both regular and territorial army bomb disposal units were redesignated as Explosive Ordnance Disposal (EOD). In September 1975 590 STRE (EOD) (V) amalgamated with another EOD unit which had been recently formed, 591 STRE, and formed 590 EOD Squadron. 591 STRE had been formed as a sponsored unit in 1973. During 1978 the Army Board accepted the advice of the 'Plummer' report which called for 33 Engineer Regiment (EOD) to expand in three phases between 1973 and 1981. This was com-

pleted by the target date with the re-formation of 579 and 583 Squadrons as EOD units, and 591 being formed from part of 590 Squadron. As most of the EOD expertise was with 590 a great deal of cross-posting was necessary to ensure that the other three squadrons each had a cadre of trained and experienced personnel on which to establish themselves.

The heavy peacetime commitment of 33 Regiment led to the idea that the TA units should form a regiment of their own. In manpower terms they were more than large enough for this, so in April 1988 approval for the formation of 101 Regiment was granted. The new Regiment claims the ancestry of 101 Regiment back to the Middlesex Engineers, who were the senior corps of Engineer Volunteers during the last century.

The first company had been raised on 6 January 1860 by the staff of the South Kensington Museum. Volunteers from the Middlesex Engineers served in the Egyptian war of 1882, and two sections served in South Africa in the Boer War. After the formation of the Territorial Force, a Headquarters and two companies, 3rd and 4th London Field Companies, moved into the Duke of York's Headquarters near Sloane Square. A third Field Company was raised at the outbreak of the First World War number 2/3rd. Later second and third-line units were also formed. After the war when the TA was re-formed, only two London Divisions were formed, the 47th and 56th. Divisional engineers were needed for both. In 1935 the two divisions were broken up and a new London Infantry Division took their places, the Engineers remaining as divisional engineers of the new division. A second division was formed following the Munich crisis. Early in the war the numbers 47 and 56 were reintroduced for the two London divisions. In 1947, after a distinguished war record, the Engineer Regiment reformed under the new name of 101st Field Engineer Regiment as part of 56th (London) Armoured Division. The title of London was added in 1954, but on the reorganization of the TA in 1967 it was disbanded, the title remaining dormant until taken up again on 1 June 1988 by the new EOD Regiment.

591 Squadron can trace its own history back to before the Second World War when it started life as 591 (Antrim) Field Company, a TA searchlight unit in Northern Ireland, and between 1942 and 1945 all members wore the 'red hand' badge on their uniforms. In 1942 the unit became airborne as a Parachute Squadron as part of 6th Airborne Division, taking part in the assault on Normandy. The Squadron was disbanded in 1945, and the number did not appear again until 1973, when it designated the newly formed Specialist Team, and subsequently a squadron.

583 Squadron claims its history back to Number 3 Company, Kent Light Engineers TA, which was redesignated 583 Field Company on 12 August 1940. In June 1943 it joined three other companies to form 15th Kent GHQ Troops RE. Number 1 Platoon of the Company was involved in the assault crossing of the Seine during the nights of 25 and 26 August 1944. The first two boats, ferrying soldiers of the 5th Battalion the Wiltshire Regiment grounded on shoals about thirty yards from the enemy, and came under heavy machine-gun fire. One boat and crew were lost. The operation continued the next day until all the infantry, including their jeeps, were safely across. From 28 August 1944 until April the next year, the 15th Kent GHQ Troops RE were responsible for the building of seven major bridges in France, Holland and Germany, with a total length of over one and a half miles. The unit was placed in suspended animation on 10 June 1946, and re-formed as 583 Construction Squadron of the TA at Northfleet in Kent on 1 January 1947. It changed role to BD on 1 July 1950, and was granted the Freedom of Gillingham in Kent in 1952. It was disbanded on 1 April 1967.

General

The nature of bomb disposal work means that the units work in small teams, each headed by an officer and senior NCO. This means that the officer and senior NCO level within EOD Squadrons is higher than many other units. Training for the role is involved, starting with normal recruit training before the basic trade skills are taught. In addition the combat engineer trades, as required throughout the Royal Engineers, are need for promotion, as well as signalling, driving and other military skills. A well-motivated sapper would take at least a year to become a trained BD Engineer. For officers, however, this process is longer, and it would take some two to three years to fully qualify as a Bomb Disposal Officer (BDO). The Regiment had its first WRAC officer qualify as a BDO in 1988. Mainly, however, the tasks of WRAC in EOD units are confined to those of clerks, drivers and signallers, but they receive introductory BD Engineer training similar to their male colleagues.

Each Squadron of the Regiment has similar kit, including hydraulic jacks and lightweight shafting equipment. Each section has an ultra lightweight excavator, and the Squadrons are all equipped with the latest bomb trepanning equipment. All equipment is anti-magnetic.

As with other units, they take part in the major exercises both in the UK and abroad. Members also enter for such as the Courage Trophy, a London District Military skills competition, and the Cambrian Marches.

583 Squadron is a good example of where a TA unit is able to combine training in its specialist field with doing some good for the community. As with many other TA units, it became involved in the extensive clearing-up operation following the devastation of the October 1987 hurricane. The massive trees that were its victims in Sussex became excellent engineer projects, in terms of the movement, transport and disposal of large, awkwardly-shaped obstacles. They have been able to use both explosives and construction skills in their various projects over the years. In February 1982 they removed dangerous roofs from Second World War gun emplacements at Newhaven, and a year later went back there to reinstate an old six-inch coastal defence gun at Fort Newhaven. In September 1983 they constructed an assault course at Cuckfield, raising over £1,000 for the NSPCC. Brighton charities benefited from the £1,500 raised from another assault course built by them at Newhaven in May 1984. Back to Cuckfield the following September, they increased the money for the NSPCC by another £2,000. A good bit of war-role training was the clearance of some unexploded ordnance found in a dewpond at Ditchling in May 1986, and on visits to Scotland in June 1986 they built a footbridge at Cawdor Castle at Inverness. At the same time they blew up some 'eyesore' buildings at Dalbeattie, a task they were able to repeat twice the following year.

The job of the Regiment is to dispose of all enemy air-dropped weapons, booby traps and other devices, including everything from terrorist devices to chemical weapons.

105 (Tyne Electrical Engineers) Plant Squadron RE(V)

History

The history of this Squadron has much in common with that of 72 Engineer Regiment, in that they both stem from the Tyne Electrical Engineers. Volunteer Engineer units in the North-East of England can trace their descent from 1860 when, because of the threat of war with France, defence of naval and commercial ports by submarine mines was engaging the attention of the War Office. In 1884, following successful trials by the Jarrow-based 1st Newcastle upon Tyne and Durham Engineer Volunteers, the Tyne Division Submarine Miners (V) was formed in Cliffords Fort, Tynemouth. Subsequently a further eight similar units were established around the British coast. The skills of the engineers, both in mechanical and electrical matters were ideal for the development of this kind of coastal defence, and in 1890 the use of searchlights was added to complement the submarine mining. In 1904 the Royal Navy took over responsibility for all mine defences, so by 1907 as submarine mining came to an end, the unit was renamed Tyne Division Royal Engineers (Volunteer) Electrical Engineers. A period of uncertainty then followed with changes of duties and titles; however, by 1911 there was some stability with the formation of the Tyne Electrical Engineers.

In the First World War, searchlight detachments served from Cromarty in Scotland to the banks of the Piave in Italy. On mobilization in 1914 three of the four companies moved to Haslar Barracks in Portsmouth, to man the coastal lights in that area. By the end of the war 60 subordinate units had formed and included such as anti-aircraft searchlights. In France, many Tynesiders saw exacting and dangerous service using man-portable lights to detect raiders crossing no-man's land, and they were nicknamed the 'suicide brigade'.

From 1915 the amount of machinery on the battlefield had increased so much that a special RE company was formed. Selected men from the Tyne and the London Electrical Engineers formed the basis of No 1 (London and Tyne) Electrical and Mechanical Company RE, and it deployed in France later that year. Its job was to instal, operate and maintain all electrical lighting and mechanical installations, this included a large printing press and the development of the first trench locomotive. Water supply and trench drainage became increasingly important aspects of their work. From the experience of the first Somme offensive, a further four E & M Companies were formed in early 1917, giving one for each of the 5 Armies. Officers and men from the Tyne Electrical Engineers served in each of them.

After the war, the unit at Cliffords Fort was reconstituted as the Tyne Electrical (Fortress) RE with a Works Company and an Electric Lights Company. Coastal illumination was a major role, but in 1924 the Works Company changed to Anti-Aircraft illumination duties. In 1932 many regular Fortress Companies RE were reduced, with the TA taking on some of their responsibilities. As a result the EL Company was enlarged to include a works section and its title became No 1 (Electric Light and Works) Company Tyne Electrical Engineers RE(TA).

When the Second World War was declared, the Company was deployed on the fixed defences in the Tyne area, but in October 1940 their title was changed to 128 Electrical and Mechanical Company RE (Tyne Electrical Engineers) TA. After three months' training in Scarborough they spent nine months building two secret harbours at Gareloch in Scotland. On 1 December 1941 they boarded the troopship RMS *Andes* in Liverpool, bound for Basrah in Iraq. They reached their destination the following February, after calling at Durban and Bombay, and spent the next two

years in Iraq and Persia. This was followed by service in Palestine, Egypt and Libya on such tasks as petroleum storage and distribution, power-station construction, maintenance and operation, and water supply. By the end of 1945, the unit's war tasks having been completed, most of the unit had become civilians again. The unit reformed as 128 E & M Company RE after the war. In 1953, the Coronation year, the Borough of Tynemouth adopted the Company at a ceremony on Sunday 31 May. In 1955 the unit was reorganized and became 128 Corps Field Park Squadron RE (TA) Tyne Electrical Engineers and was affiliated to 105 Corps Engineer Regiment, and their role switched to Field Engineering. On 1 April 1967 the unit was disbanded and promptly reformed as 105(Durham) Plant Squadron RE(V) at Frenchmans Fort in South Shields, and initially came under the command of 72 Engineer Regiment based in Gateshead. On 2 November 1973 the title 'Durham' was changed to Tyne Electrical Engineers. Since 1975 it has been an independent Squadron.

General

The Squadron is located at Frenchmans Fort in South Shields, Tyne and Wear, and in time of war its job is to provide Engineer Plant support to 29 Engineer Brigade in BAOR. To do this there is equipment issued to the unit valued in excess of £2.7 million, which would double in time of war. The equipment held in the UK is used extensively on training exercises involving military aid to the civil community in North-East England and Scotland. Work of this nature has been undertaken for the Highland Development Board, the Year of the Disabled, National Trust in Scotland, Forestry Commission in England and Scotland, various local councils and authorities, the Scouts, Museums such as the Beamish/Tanfield railways, and any local clubs or deserving charities. In the case of a charity this work is not charged for, provided it is of some training value to the Squadron. Work is not undertaken that ought to be done by local contractors on a commercial basis. The Squadron is sports-minded, with entries in the Army Cross-Country Championships and the International CIOR Triathlon Competition.

117 (Highland) Field Support Squadron RE (V)

History

The Squadron traces its origins back to the Tay Submarine Mining Company in Dundee and the 1st Aberdeen Royal Engineer (Volunteers) in Aberdeen. They became the 51 Highland Divisional Engineers on the formation of the TF in 1908. During the First World War the two units served in France and

Belgium, and immediately after the War in North Russia. At the start of the Second World War, the Dundee and Aberdeen Companies, (239 Field Park and 237 Field Coys) were part of the BEF at the Maginot Line. They were in action in the withdrawal from France, and involved in a series of key demolitions on the Bresle River before the Battle of Abbeville. They also took their turn as infantry.

239 Field Park Company remained with the reformed 51st Highland Division and fought with it through the Western Desert and Northern Europe, ending the war in Bremerhaven. 237 Field Company was attached to 11 Infantry Brigade and fought in Algiers and the North African Campaign. Among their achievements was the building of a 100-foot Bailey Bridge over the River Medjerda near Tunis, the first to be built under fire.

In the 20 years following the end of the War they underwent a series of name and role changes, ending in the present formation in 1968. From 1979 until 1983 they raised an Airfield Damage Repair detachment at RAF Leuchars, to trial the concept of TA Sappers supporting the RAF in the Airfield Damage Repair (ADR) role in the UK. This trial was a success, and 227 Squadron was formed at the airfield as a result.

General

The Squadron is at three locations, with headquarters and Workshops Troop at Dundee, the Resources Troop at Glenrothes, and the Plant Troop at Bridge of Don, Aberdeen. Its role as an Independent Field Support Squadron as part of 29 Engineer Brigade is to provide support to 2nd Infantry Division in BAOR, to set up and operate a forward Engineer Store Park. The tasks would include the unloading and issue of engineer's stores from railheads and stores dumps. In addition, it has a responsibility to assist in the maintenance of supply routes and to manufacture and repair engineer equipment.

125 Field Support Squadron RE(V)

General

The Squadron headquarters is at Stoke-on-Trent, with a detachment at Cannock. Their role is basically similar to that of 117 (Highland) Support Company.

131 Independent Commando Squadron, RE (V)

History

The Squadron was formed in 1947 as 131 Airborne Engineer Regiment TA, with a role in 16 Airborne Division. In 1956 when 16 Airborne Division was reduced in Brigade size to become 44 Independent Parachute Brigade, the Regiment remained unchanged. It became probably the largest TA unit in

Preparing to fight their way ashore.

the early 1960s, with over 1,000 active volunteers. In 1964 the Regiment had their annual camp in Aden; sadly, two members were killed on the Yemen Frontier. In that incident the Medical Officer received the MBE for his gallantry. In 1967 in the second major post-war reorganization of the TA, 131 was reduced to Squadron size. Their saddest day was on 28 September 1975, when 11 members were drowned at Cromwell Weir on the River Trent. In December 1975 the Squadron lost its parachute role, and it suffered a few years of uncertainty. This ended when the Royal Marines took the Regiment into the order of battle of 3 Commando Brigade.

General

The Squadron has its headquarters at Kingsbury in north west London, and has troops located at Plymouth, Birmingham and Hull. Its task is to provide engineer support to 3 Commando Brigade, Royal Marines. The frontline combat support is provided by a regular unit, and 131 are responsible for assisting the logistic units. As the Brigade's role is on NATO's northern flank, men are sent each year to Norway to train with the regulars in Arctic conditions. All members are taught basic ski and survival techniques. A number of the Squadron have to be parachute and diver-trained. To qualify to join 131 and to wear the coveted green beret, all ranks must undergo Commando training, passing a tough two-week course at the Commando Training Centre run by the Royal Marines. The Commando tests include a six-mile speed march in 60 minutes; a tarzan/assault course in 13 minutes; the endurance course in 71 minutes; climbing a 30-foot rope, and completing a 200-metres fireman's carry in 90 seconds. All these tests are carried out in full fighting order, including a rifle.

Each troop has a specialist role that it has to become particularly proficient at, in addition to general combat engineer tasks. For example one troop specialize at bridging and building dug-in command posts.

The troop in Plymouth has built live ship-to-shore commodity fuel farms, and another troop is proficient at the construction of water points, prisoner-of-war cages, mine warfare and demolitions. There are also sections specializing in plant, resources, MT and signals. During 1988, volunteer members of the Squadron visited Norway, Kenya, France, Holland, Luxembourg and Guernsey.

135 Topographical Squadron RE (V)

History

The Squadron's history goes back to 1949, when 135

Field Survey Regiment RE (V) was formed, but this was disbanded on 31 March 1967 and the new Squadron was formed the following day. The Squadron took its current title, to conform to NATO standards, on 13 February 1985. Mapping and surveying have been Royal Engineer skills for many years, and in the First World War, as well as providing a new situation map each day, the RE Survey companies produced some 34 million maps of all kinds. Large-scale plans were prepared for the artillery, fixing the positions of guns and targets. Once again in the Second World War, artillery survey was transferred to the RE, except for the main triangulation work.

General

The Squadron headquarters is at Ewell in Surrey, and it provides geographic support for all three services. Surveying, printing and distribution of maps are vital functions in support of the Army, and the specialist technicians include survey, photographic, cartographic and print personnel. Training for this role includes weekend exercises, NATO exercises, and various military and technical training, including specialist courses. Noteworthy in the unit's recent achievements are the production and printing of a new Guernsey map and its subsequent revision, and the production of a new map for Gibraltar.

Airfield Damage Repair Squadrons

A recent addition to the Royal Engineer role is that of Airfield Damage Repair (ADR). The job is to repair aircraft-operating surfaces, to keep an airfield operational despite damage from either enemy action or accident. To train for this role, the Squadrons exercise their skills with over £4 million worth of plant and equipment. Volunteers have to develop a variety of abilities, from combat engineering and plant operation to driving heavy goods vehicles and bricklaying. Along with members of the RAF Regiment, other army units or the HSF, they take their part in the defence of the airfield as well. Among the skills and trades in which a volunteer can receive training are: plant operator, HGV driver, welder, fitter, clerk, electrician, signaller, carpenter and joiner, bricklayer, and vehicle mechanic. WRAC are also recruited for some of these trades.

The following are the ADR Squadrons of TA: 212 at RAF Wattisham; 216 at RAF Marham; 218 at RAF Honington; 219 at RAF Coningsby; 234 at RAF Leeming; 236 at RAF Kinloss; 267 at RAF Waddington; and 277 at RAF Leuchars.

History

In 1966 the responsibility for Airfield Damage Repair

218 Field Squadron at the end of annual camp 1988.

passed from the RAF to the Royal Engineers.

Some of the squadrons claim interesting histories. 218 at Honington can trace its origins back to the 1st Tower Hamlets Engineer Volunteer Corps, which was raised at Bethnal Green in 1861 from the 1st Middlesex Volunteer Engineers, who ran the unit until 1867. The Volunteer Corps was raised from and largely funded by the Truman, Hambury and Buxtons brewery, and saw service in the Boer War, by which time it was known as the East London Engineer Volunteer Corps, and contained a Railway Reserve Company raised in 1890 from men employed by the Great Northern Railway Company. Thirty-three of these men saw service in South Africa from 1899 to 1902. On the formation of the Territorial Force in 1908, the unit became the 1st London Divisional Engineers, and in the First World War served in France and Flanders. There was, however, a unit 218 Field Company RE which had no connection with East London and was not a TF unit. Between the wars 218 Field Company was part of the 1st London Division at Victoria Park in Bethnal Green, and at the outbreak of the Second World War became part of 56th Division and went to France with the BEF. Only half the Company's strength managed to escape

through Dunkirk, the rest being killed, wounded or taken prisoner. The Company re-formed in Leeds in 1941 and saw service in Gibraltar, where, amongst other things, they worked on the airfield. Shortly before the end of the war with Japan, the Company went to the Far East. After the war 218 was re-formed at Bethnal Green, but disbanded in 1956 until the designation was resurrected on 1 April 1984 for ADR with 12 Engineer Brigade.

When 218 was formed as ADR it did so at Waterbeach, the old home of the RAF Airfield Construction Branch which moved to Honington during 1986. 219 Squadron formed there the same day as 218, and claim the same background as 218, except its number existed from the formation of the Territorial Force and in the First World War it served with 32 Division, but was disbanded after the war. In 1939 it was re-formed as a Corps Troops Field Park Company and remained at home until 1942, when it went to India to join 15 Corps in Bengal, staying there until December 1945. It moved to Singapore and then to Johore Bahru in Malaya in 1946. 219 Squadron re-formed as part of 114 (1st London) Engineer Regiment (TA) in 1947, only to be disbanded again in 1967. Revived in the ADR role, they moved from

Royal Engineers — Airfield Damage Repair

A typical list of special equipment required by an ADR Squadron is:
3 ADR Compactors;
1 Excavator WM Heavy;
1 Tractor, Wh EM Lt;
3 Tractors, Wh EM Lt;
2 Mat Carriers;
6 Lighting Towers;
2 De-watering pumps;
2 Sweepers, rotary vac SP;
2 Saracens for reconnaissance;
6 Dump Trucks, heavy;
2 Grader Mot Universal;
4 Tractors Wh EM Med;
2 Trailer Generator sets;
2 Screed Beams;
10 Mixing Machines;
2 Roller SP Vib;
The vehicle list includes four Land Rovers and four 4-tonne trucks.

Waterbeach to RAF Coningsby during the winter of 1985.

234 Squadron formed on 1 April 1986, but can trace its history to before the Second World War when it was part of 105 Engineer Regiment (Tyne Electrical Engineers). 236 Squadron at Kinloss started life as 236 Army Troop Company, raised on 2 October 1915, by the Mayor of Stockton on Tees and on 9 March 1916 it went to France. The number was next used in December 1922, when 236 was raised as 236(H) (City of Aberdeen) Field Company as part of 51 Highland Division. In the Second World War it became part of 55 Highland Division, and served in France. After Dunkirk, the Squadron re-formed at Aldershot, and in 1942 went to Madagascar, East Africa and South Africa, before moving to India on 26 January 1943. Four months later it was in Burma, returning to India in 1945. After the war it was re-formed as 236 (Aberdeen) Field Squadron in 117

(Highland) Field Engineer Regiment, but absorbed into 117 Squadron on 1 April 1967.

267 Squadron was twice formed as a second-line Company to 225 Company RE. In the First World War it formed as 478 fighting with 61 Division in France, and as 267 Field Squadron started the Second World War at home, moving to the south of England in 1940 with 61 Division in case of invasion. In 1941 it served in Northern Ireland, but by the end of the war 61 Division had been broken up to reinforce front-line units. In 1947, 267 Construction Squadron was a unit of 112 Construction Regiment at Erdington, but was never actually raised, because of lack of numbers. The number was reintroduced on 1 April 1985 for the ADR Squadron at Waddington.

277 were the original ADR Squadron, formed from a detachment from 117 (Highland) Field Support Squadron set up with 1 officer and 12 other ranks in 1979 as a pilot scheme. On 1 April 1983 the Squadron was declared a properly constituted and independent TA Squadron under the command of 12 Engineer Brigade. The last Squadron to use the number 277 had been based in Fife for many years, and this Squadron is back in Fife, at RAF Leuchars.

Royal Engineers Postal and Courier Services

The military post has been in existence in some form or other since the early thirteenth century. Since those times, and as more servicemen and women began to use the post, the system has developed into the tri-service organization that exists today. The Royal Engineers now provide four regular Postal and Courier Regiments, to give a worldwide postal and classified courier service for the Navy, Army and RAF.

In war there are four TA PC Regiments allocated to the Home Defence role, each having three Squadrons, and another seven PC Squadrons are allocated to support BAOR and overseas roles. These units are located throughout the UK and recruit mainly, but not exclusively, from within the Post Office Corporation. They carry out the normal TA specialist unit training of a minimum of two weekends and one two-week training camp each year.

The Territorial Army

Variety: the spice of life

Above *Members of the HAC in tunic order at a Press Launch at the MoD* (MARS).

Below *On Salisbury plain, Tyneside Scottish gunners on exercise.*

Above left *A Javelin detachment from 105 (Scottish) Air Defence Regiment Royal Artillery (Volunteers) on exercise in Germany.*

Above right *All commando troops need to be good skiers* (131 COMMANDO SQUADRON RE).

Below *The Colonel-in-Chief visits 31 Signal Regiment in Belgium.*

Above *A section from 6 RRF deploy to protect a helicopter landing area.*

Below left *Number 4 Guard drawn from D Company 3/51 HIGHLAND is inspected by Her Majesty The Queen.*

Below right *Practice in the Training Centre on a GPMG in the anti-aircraft role* (5 QUEENS).

Left *A youthful fusilier at FIBUA training* (6 RRF).

Below left *The Regimental Colours are borne on parade with pride* (4 QLR).

Below *Live mortar firing at night* (2 YORKS).

Above *Exercise Brave Defender saw men of 4 PARA in a defensive role* (MARS).

Right *Volunteers in a Chinook before a jump* (10 PARA).

Right *Para-badged HSF protect Northolt Airfield on exercise* (MARS).

Above *Supply of POL is vital to front line troops, a major task of the RAOC* (COI).

Left *Volunteer craftsmen becoming familiar with an armoured fighting vehicle* (COI).

Below *The TA RMP units have both men and women, who have to be capable of dealing with military offenders as well as policing major military routes* (COI).

Right *Catering in the field. Hungry soldiers demand the very best from their cooks* (38 SIGNAL REGIMENT).

Right *WRAC live in the same conditions as the men* (38 SIGNAL REGIMENT).

Below *Milan training* (2 YORKS).

Above *6 Bn, Royal Anglian Regiment prepare for a helicopter pick-up near Bodney during Exercise Brave Defender* (MARS).

Left *A member of the HAC HSF Company at a key point on the same exercise* (MARS).

Below left *Members of 10 PARA taking part in their eight-mile cross-country stretcher race in fighting order.*

Below right *Helicopter abseiling* (10 PARA).

6 The Royal Corps of Signals

Regimental badge

The figure of Mercury holding a Cadeceus in the left hand aloft, poised with the left foot on a globe all silver, above the globe a Scroll inscribed *Certa Cito* and below on each side six laurel leaves all gold, the whole ensigned with the Crown in gold.

Colonel in Chief

HRH The Princess Royal, GCVO

Regimental marches

The quick march is *The Royal Signals March*, based on the traditional airs, *Begone Dull Care* and *Newcastle*; the slow march is called *HRH The Princess Royal.*

Stable belt

Horizontal bands of light blue at the top, dark blue in the centre and dark green at the bottom. These represent sky, sea and land.

Corps motto

Certa Cito (swift and sure).

History

The role of the Royal Corps of Signals in today's army has changed little since it was formed in 1920. Before that, signals were a task undertaken by the Royal Engineers.

In the European wars in the late eighteenth century, there was an increase in the size of armies in the field. Wider fronts of battle, more sophisticated weapons, more complicated administration, longer lines of support, gave rise to the need for efficient communications. Among the first in this field was Wellington, who introduced a despatch system using dragoons detached for this duty from their regiments. Although there were some visual telegraph machines, runners and horsemen were the main method of communicating. The various early visual signalling systems included the Venerable Lord George Murray's 'Lettering' system, which employed the use of a shutter. There was also Gamble's Machine, which was primarily for alphabetical signalling. The invention in 1837 of the Morse Code, which virtually coincided with the perfection of the electric telegraph, brought a new era to the field of communications. In 1854, the electric telegraph was used for the first time in war, and by the end of the Crimean campaign 21 miles of cable had been laid and there were eight signals offices in the circuit. In 1870, a Royal Engineers Telegraph Troop was formed at Chatham, and in 1884, the Telegraph Battalion RE came into being.

The early part of this century brought about more changes to communications. By 1907 wireless had been accepted, and that year the first two wireless companies had been formed.

In 1908, as a result of the earlier Evelyn Wood Committee, it was decided that rather than form a new corps, the service would be provided by an organization called the Royal Engineer Signal Service. In the Reserve Army there had been telegraph representation for many years, for example in the Militia there had been Post Offices volunteers who had seen service with the Telegraph Battalion in Egypt, the Sudan and South Africa. Volunteer telegraph sections had been formed at various times from 1880. In 1908, the Regular Army Signal Service was supplemented by five Territorial Force Companies for Line of Communications and Army Troops, and 14 for the Infantry Divisions.

TA signallers played a full part in both World Wars. Since the formation of the Corps in 1920, first the Middlesex Yeomanry, then Princess Louise's Kensington Regiment formed part of the Corps. As a result of further changes since 1969 more TA Regiments have converted to the signals role, including The Queen's Own Warwickshire and Worcestershire Yeomanry; The Royal Gloucestershire Hussars (part); The Berkshire Yeomanry; The Essex Yeomanry; The North Irish Horse (part); The Inns of Court and City Yeomanry (part) and the East Lancashire Regiment.

General

The Corps has to provide and maintain a rapid, accurate and above all reliable system of communications for the Army. This job is as necessary in peace as in war. Although the task has changed little over the years, the means to do it have kept pace with scientific developments, and the modern army makes full use of computers, satellites and the very latest in electronic technology.

The importance of signals can be seen in the fact that over eight per cent of the army strength is devoted to this vital task. A more modern additional role is that of Electronic Warfare (EW). EW is a complex branch of warfare, and includes such as monitoring enemy signals systems, locating their source, jamming their radio transmissions, deception of the enemy using electronic interference, and generally denigrating the efficiency of an enemy's communications systems. EW is intended not only to provide effective intelligence, but also to disrupt an enemy's command and control systems. Defending oneself from an enemy's EW is a skill that has developed as well.

TA Signals Regiments provide support in both BAOR and at home. 11 Signals Brigade, with its headquarters at Liverpool is responsible for TA units under NATO command, and 12 Signals Brigade with its headquarters at Chelsea supports BAOR. Wartime communications within the UK are the duty of other signals TA units.

31st Signal Regiment (V)

Squadrons

41 (Princess Louise's Kensington Regiment) at Coulsdon;
47 (Middlesex Yeomanry) at Harrow;
83 at Southfields and Cobham;
HQ at Hammersmith.

History

In 1967 the 31st (Greater London) Signal Regiment (V) was formed, but the title 'Greater London' was discontinued on 1 April 1987. The history of the constituent squadrons goes back to Napoleonic times. 41 Squadron continue the name of the Princess Louise's Kensington Regiment, which was a distinguished rifle and then machine-gun Regiment, which converted

to the signals role in 1947. It goes back to 1859 although it was preceded by a volunteer Corps dating back to 1798. Its very first colours were presented in 1799 by the then Duchess of Gloucester, and these hang in St Mary Abbots Church in Kensington. A section of the Regiment went to South Africa with the City Imperial Volunteers in 1900 thus gaining the first battle honour. In 1905 it was adopted by the Royal Borough of Kensington with permission to use the arms and motto *Quid Nobis Ardue* (Nothing is too hard for us), and so it became The Kensington Rifles. In 1908, HRH The Princess Louise, Duchess of Argyll, who resided at Kensington Palace, gave her consent to the use of her name in the Regiment's title. In August 1914 it went to war.

Three battalions of the Regiment were raised, the 1st went into the line and by the end of February 1915 had suffered 96 casualties. Many hundreds of West Londoners serving in the Battalion became casualties in the many battles, and it was decimated with 436 casualties at Aubers Ridge on 9 May 1915. By November 1918 only 83 men were able to march to Mons and Victory. The 2nd Battalion served at home and in Ireland before going to the Middle East, and was at the capture of Jerusalem in December 1917. After the First World War the Regiment continued, but in 1937 became part of the Middlesex Regiment and the following year became a machine-gun unit. Two battalions fought in the Second World War, and many were captured before Dunkirk. The 1st Battalion saw service in Sicily and Italy, moving to Greece after the war, and the 2nd Battalion provided a machine-gun Company for the First Guards Brigade and served in Iceland, England and then Normandy in June 1944. On reaching Nijmegen, the Kensingtons received a very warm welcome, and a street in the town has been named after them.

After the War, in 1947 the Regiment became part of the Royal Signals and its new title was Army Phantom Signal Regiment (Princess Louise's Kensington Regiment), and they retained the right to wear the Kensington badges and buttons and to carry its colours. As a 'Phantom' unit it was unique, being the ears and eyes of an army Commander in time of war. 1961 saw another reorganization, absorbing other units to become 41 (Princess Louise's Kensington) Signal Regiment TA, but losing its 'Phantom' role. In 1967, the colours and drums were placed in the Officers' Mess at Hammersmith and the present Regiment has custody of them.

The Middlesex Yeomanry, whose name is carried on by 47 Squadron, was at one time one of the premier volunteer cavalry units, including in its title 'Duke of Cambridge's Hussars', and serving with great gallantry in the Middle East during the First World War. The Regiment converted to the signals

Captain Paul Fredericks, a troop commander with the Middlesex Yeomanry Squadron, briefs some of his key personnel before an exercise. Captain Fredericks is a manager with British Telecom.

role in 1920 on the formation of the Royal Corps of Signals, and distinguished itself in the next war, especially in North Africa, providing communications for a part of the 8th Army.

Following its historical links with 47th (London) Division, 83 Squadron has the right to wear a unique badge in the form of a Dutch Tile.

General

The present role of the Regiment is as part of 11 Signal Brigade, and provides supplementary telephone and teleprinter communications for SACEUR. Every other year the Annual Camp is in North-West Europe. In common with other TA Royal Signals units, many recruits, especially technicians, come from British Telecom, with a few more from the various manufacturers of communications equipment. About one-quarter of the strength is found from the WRAC, and they participate in most trades, including HGV drivers, and among the officers are WRAC Troop Commanders and others second in command of Squadrons.

The Regiment is affiliated with the Worshipful Company of Innholders. This is most appropriate, as it was the Innholders of the City of London who originated regular postal services, by way of the stage coaches operating in and out of the capital.

32 (Scottish) Signal Regiment (V)

Squadrons

51 (Highland) at Aberdeen;
52 (Lowland) at Glasgow;
61 (City of Edinburgh) in Edinburgh;
69 (North Irish Horse) in Londonderry;
HQ at Glasgow.

History

The Regiment was formed in 1967. 51 (Highland) Divisional Signal Regiment was reduced to squadron size, and its history goes back to the formation of the 1st Aberdeen Engineer Corps in 1898. 52 (Lowland) Divisional Signal Regiment was also reduced to

Squadron size, and its history stems from 1895 when the 1st Lanarkshire Volunteer Military Engineers were formed. Their TA Centre was built in 1894 and is still in use today by the Squadrons based in Glasgow. Before and during the First World War, the Honorary Colonel of the Regiment was Field Marshal Earl Kitchener of Khartoum.

A younger unit taken over in 1967 was 61 (City of Edinburgh) Signal Regiment (V), which had started life in 1939 as the 2nd Anti-Aircraft Divisional Signals. The North Irish Horse did not join the Regiment until 1969, when 'B' Squadron North Irish Horse rebadged to Royal Signals, having been originally raised as a Yeomanry Regiment in 1902. The Regiment is also commemorated in the name of D Squadron of the Royal Yeomanry in Northern Ireland. During the Second World War the Regiment fought with great distinction alongside the Canadians in Italy in 1944, and for their gallantry, the Canadians gave its members the right to wear a silver maple leaf on their service dress, a custom continued today.

General

The role of 32 (Scottish) Signal Regiment is to provide the communications needed by the Army and certain civilian establishments in Scotland and Northern Ireland in time of war. WRAC provide up to 40 per cent of the strength, and undertake most trades. On its formation in 1967, Lord Strathspey gave his permission for the Regiment to adopt the Red Grant tartan, and this is worn today by the Pipe Band, by WRAC members for their skirts, and as a patch behind the cap badge on the beret and glengarry. The Queen's Gurkha Signals are affiliated to the Regiment.

33 Signal Regiment (V)

Squadrons

42 in Manchester;
59 in Liverpool;
80 (Cheshire Yeomanry) at Gilwern in Chester;
HQ at Huyton in Liverpool.

History

The Regiment formed on 1 April 1967, incorporating 42 and 59 Signal Regiments, and 80 Squadron, taking on the designation of a former Army Emergency Reserve Signal Regiment. This Squadron incorporated the Cheshire Yeomanry title in 1973, the Regiment also being continued in the title of C Squadron of the Queen's Own Yeomanry. 33 Signal Regiment's history therefore goes back to 1880 with the raising of the 1st Lancashire Volunteer Battalion RE in Liverpool. This converted into Signal Companies

in 1912 and provided contingents for overseas tasks in the early part of the First World War. In 1920 the unit re-formed as 2nd Western Corps Signal Company, and the following year as 55th (West Lancashire) Divisional Signals. At the outbreak of the Second World War, a second regiment was raised as 59th Motor Divisional Signals. 55 Regiment served throughout the war in the UK, but 59 went to the 8th Army and served at El Alamein, Tunis, Sicily and Italy, finishing the war in Austria. 42 Divisional Signals went to France in 1940 and was evacuated from Dunkirk. In 1941 it converted to armour, only to be disbanded in 1943. In 1947 the original unit was reborn as 42 (Lancashire) Infantry Divisional Signal Regiment.

59 Signal Regiment started life as the 4th Anti-Aircraft Divisional Signals in 1939 and it was engaged continuously during 1940 and 1941. In 1955 Anti-Aircraft Command was abolished, so the Regiment became an ordinary signals unit. In 1960 the WRAC element was transferred to 42 Signal Regiment, and this allowed 59 to take on the role of a Trunk Formation Signal Regiment in support of BAOR.

The Cheshire Yeomanry was formed in 1797, and the history of 80 Squadron is therefore the same as that for C Squadron of the Queen's Own Yeomanry, except that 80 Squadron was based on the original Regiment's Signal Section. Both units wear the Cheshire Yeomanry badge on the collars of service dress uniforms. This badge consists of the Prince of Wales's feathers with the motto *Ich Dien* over a scroll bearing the words *Cheshire (Earl Chester's) Yeomanry.*

General

The role of the Regiment is the provision of mobile support communications facilities within SHAPE. For this role its equipment includes radio relay, HF radio, switchboards and teleprinters. This is a mixed Regiment, with WRAC playing a full part, and one of the Squadrons has had a WRAC Major in command. On 18 April 1980 the Regiment was granted the Honorary Freedom of the Borough of Knowsley, with the privilege of Freedom of Entry.

34 (Northern) Signal Regiment (V)

Squadrons

49 (West Riding) at Hull and Leeds;
50 (Northumbrian) at Gateshead and Darlington;
90 (North Riding) at Middlesbrough;
HQ at Middlesbrough.

History

The Regiment formed on 1 April 1967 by the amalgamation of 49 (West Riding) and 50 (Northumbrian) Divisional Signals Regiments and 90 Signal Regiment AER. 49 Squadron can therefore trace its history back to 1861 and the formation of the 2nd West Riding of Yorkshire Royal Engineers (Volunteers) in Leeds. After seeing service in the Boer War the unit converted in 1908 to Northern Command Telegraph Companies (Army Troops) RE (TF) of one wireless, one cable and one air-line Company. When the First World War started, these were formed into a Signals Depot at Biggleswade which then raised a number of Signals units for France and the Middle East. In 1920 the unit was raised again as 49th (West Riding) Infantry Divisional Signals TA, and in 1939 it raised the duplicate 46th (North Midland) Divisional Signals TA. Early in 1940 49 Signals took part in the Norway operations, and then became Iceland (C) Force Signals, returning in 1942 to the UK, taking part in operations in North-West Europe from 1944 until the end of the war. Another part of 49 when it was no longer needed in Iceland became part of 7th Air Formation Signals, serving in North Africa, Sicily and Italy.

46 Signals went to France with the BEF and became heavily embroiled in Dunkirk, being evacuated with the rearguard. Early in 1943 they took part in the North African operations and served out the war in Italy and Greece. Both 49 and 46 Signals were disbanded in 1946, re-forming at Leeds the following year as 49th (West Riding and Midland) Armoured Divisional Signal Regiment TA and 51st (North Midland) Air Formation Signal Regiment. Later the 49th converted into an Infantry Divisional Signal Regiment and in 1961 was changed again to 49th Division/District Signal Regiment. At this time WRAC joined it for the first time.

50 Signal Squadron goes back to the reorganization after the Boer War, when in 1908 the TF was formed and previously existing volunteer units were brought together to create the Northumbrian Divisional Telegraph (later Signal) Company RE (TF). During the First World War it served on the Western Front from 1915 until the war ended. The unit re-formed in 1921 as 50th (Northumbrian) Divisional Signals TA and in 1939 raised 23rd Divisional Signals TA as a duplicate. Early in 1940 50 Signals joined the BEF in France, and was evacuated through Dunkirk. It then went to the Middle East, seeing service in Syria and the Western Desert. After taking part in the invasion of Sicily in 1943 it returned home and was allocated to 21 Army Group for the invasion of Europe. It was in the spearhead of the assault and was engaged in the whole of the North-West Europe campaign. 23 Signals did not see action, but converted into a training unit for NCOs at Harrogate. In 1947 elements of both units were united into the

50th (Northumbrian) Infantry Divisional Signal Regiment TA, with a further reorganization in 1960, when elements of the disbanded 60th Signal Regiment were incorporated.

General

The role of the Regiment today is as part of 12 Signal Brigade, to provide an area communications system in BAOR. WRAC are employed in the Regiment, taking such roles as data telegraphist, switchboard operator and clerk. The Regiment has received the honours of freedom of Leeds, Darlington and Middlesbrough.

35 (South Midlands) Signal Regiment (V)

Squadrons

48 (City of Birmingham) in Birmingham;
58 (Staffordshire) at Newcastle under Lyme;
89 (Warwickshire) at Rugby;
95 (Shropshire Yeomanry) at Shrewsbury;
HQ at Sutton Coldfield.

History

The Regiment was formed on 1 April 1967. HQ and 89 (Warwickshire) Squadrons are able to trace their antecedents back only to after the Second World War, with the formation of 9 Independent Armoured Brigade Signal Squadron (TA), which was disbanded in 1956 but re-formed the following year as 2 Port Task Force Signal Squadron. With another change of name in 1961 as a Guards Brigade Squadron, it formed the basis for the two new units in 1967. 48 (City of Birmingham) Squadron can trace its past back to 1862 and the formation of the 2nd Gloucestershire Regiment (V) which became an RE unit in 1880, converting to a Telegraph Company in 1908. For the First World War it became the South Midlands Divisional Signals Company. In 1915 the number 48 was first used. After the war it was reconstituted as 48 (SM) Divisional Signals (TF). Following the Second World War it became 1/20 (SM) Army Signals Regiment, changing to 48 Signal Regiment again in 1959. The South Midlands title was changed in 1986 to the current title.

58 (Staffordshire) Squadron has history only since the Second World War, but 95 (Shropshire Yeomanry) Squadron goes back to the formation of Yeomanry Cavalry in the County early last century, and in 1872 both the North and South Salopian Yeomanry Cavalry formed the Shropshire Yeomanry Cavalry. In 1940 they converted to Artillery and become a Signal Squadron in 1969.

General

In wartime the Regiment provides communications facilities for SACEUR's reserve, so exercises in Germany every other year. WRAC undertake a variety of jobs, including most of the Signals trades. On 12 September 1970 the Regiment was granted the Freedom of the City of Birmingham, and exercises its right to march through the streets 'with drums beating, bands playing and bayonets fixed' every second year.

36 Signal Regiment (V)

Squadrons

44 (Cinque Ports) at Gillingham;
45 (Essex) at Colchester and Warley;
54 (East Anglian) at Cambridge, Bedford and Norwich;
56 at Eastbourne and Folkestone;
HQ at Wanstead in East London.

History

The present Regiment was formed in 1967 from three Regiments, each of which has its name continued in a Squadron title. They were 44th (Home Counties) Signal Regiment (Cinque Ports); 45th (Essex) Signal Regiment and 54th (East Anglian) Signal Regiment. Through their antecedents the history can be traced back to the trained bands raised within the Cinque Ports in 1692. 44 Squadron has undergone twenty one changes of title since those very early days. They became artillery in 1859, and until they became a signal regiment in 1957, they changed roles from Coast, to Garrison, then Field, Anti-Aircraft and finally heavy Anti-Aircraft Artillery. As gunners they saw action in both World Wars. The number 44 was given only in 1961, but the Cinque Ports title goes back to the earliest days.

54 Signal Squadron has its origins in the RE Telegraph Company formed in Bedford at the turn of the century. This unit, which it is said was raised by a German Officer, went to France in the First World War. The number 54 appeared in the title in 1915, and between the wars it was an East London Signal Regiment, based at Stratford. It had the horse-drawn cable waggons for some time after the Regular Army had mechanized, and they were a frequent sight for the East Enders, exercising on Wanstead flats. In 1938 the TA was doubled in strength, and 54 Regiment formed a second Regiment, 4 Divisional Signals. It was supposed to move into a new Drill Hall at Wanstead after Summer Camp in 1939, but while they were away the TA was mobilized for the Second World War the old sweats claimed they had a six-year camp instead of two weeks. Part of 54 went to Singapore to form yet another Regiment, but arrived there

just in time to be captured. 4 Divisional Signals went to France and were evacuated through Dunkirk. Following the war, a Signal Squadron was raised in Cambridge to cover the East Anglian area, and this claimed the 54 number, because Bedford housed one of its troops. The East London Signals at Wanstead had been established as 2/20 Army Signal Regiment. This changed to 1st (Essex) then 45 (Essex) in 1959. This Regiment was granted the Freedom of the Borough of Wanstead and Woodford in 1963, a right that is maintained by the present Regiment with the London Borough of Redbridge. In 1969 when 45 Squadron moved into the TA Centre at Ilford, it incorporated the former members 4/5 Essex Regiment into its ranks.

General

36 Signal Regiment deploys to Germany in time of war as part of 12 Signal Brigade to provide an area communication system between the channel ports and the Rear Corps boundary. To train for this, the Regiment deploys to Germany for annual camp every other year. The Regiment was re-equipped in 1988 with a sophisticated and modern communication system, which was deployed directly from the manufacturers, and has been introduced to service with the TA in advance of any regular unit. 56 Signal Squadron is administered by 36 Signal Regiment, but in time of war it goes off on its own for an HF task in BAOR.

Apart from 56 Squadron, WRAC are recruited to most trades and WRAC officers have commanded troops and squadrons. Despite a heavy training commitment, HQ Squadron has found time to enter the London District Orienteering competitions, which it won two years running, even beating teams from the SAS.

37 (Wessex and Welsh) Signal Regiment (V)

Squadrons

43 (Wessex) at Bridgwater and Exeter;
53 (Welsh) at Cardiff and Brecon;
57 (City and County of Bristol) at Bristol and Cheltenham;
67 (Queen's Own Warwickshire and Worcestershire Yeomanry) at Stratford and Stourbridge;
HQ at Bristol.

History

The Regiment was formed on the reorganization of the TA in 1967 from 43, 53 and 57 Signal Regiments. A fourth Squadron was formed from The Queen's Own Warwickshire and Worcestershire Yeomanry eight years later. 43 Squadron can trace its history back to The Devon and Somerset Volunteer Engineers, formed in 1860, the same year as the formation of The Severn Defence RE (V), from which 53 Squadron originates.

57 Squadron has a more recent history, coming as it does from 2 Coy 5 Anti-Aircraft Division Signals of 1939. The Transmitter and Brigade Headquarters Troop of 57 Squadron has a much older pedigree, however, going back to 1795 and the formation of the Cheltenham Troop of The Loyal Gloucestershire Corps of Gentlemen. The oldest ancestry is held by the newest component of the Regiment, that is 67 Squadron. It claims descent from the Warwickshire Yeomanry and the Queen's Own Worcestershire Hussars, both formed in 1794 and which were amalgamated to form one Regiment in the 1950s. The Warwickshire Yeomanry was the second most senior Yeomanry Regiment. Elements of both Regiments served in the Boer War with the Imperial Yeomanry, but their finest hour was during the First World War, in the advance towards Jerusalem in 1917, when they were involved in what was probably the last classic cavalry charge, at the village of Huj in Gaza. (See chapter three for a full description of that action.)

In the Second World War at El Alamein in 1942, the Warwickshire Yeomanry spearheaded Operation Supercharge, launched after the battle had become bogged down in front of the German gun lines. The Regiment went into battle with 70 tanks and emerged with only seven undamaged, but the German line had broken.

When the two Regiments merged they became a Reconnaissance Regiment equipped with armoured cars, and as a special honour Her Majesty The Queen is their Colonel. To this day, in the Squadron the Loyal Toast is 'Gentlemen, the Honorary Colonel'. The traditions of this Regiment are also carried on by A Squadron of the Queen's Own Mercian Yeomanry, who hold the old guidon and claim the battle honours. 67 Squadron maintains some of the dress traditions of the old Regiment, which include the Bear and Ragged Staff collar badges, the old Warwickshire county badge, and 'WWY' shoulder titles. Corporals and above wear the Worcestershire Yeomanry badge, a pear blossom, on the sleeves of numbers 1 and 2 dress. On Regimental parades all ranks wear the dark blue Royal Signals dress hat, but on Squadron parades officers and men wear the Warwickshire Yeomanry white-topped hats, copied from the 13/18 Royal Hussars. The Royal Signals cap badge, however, is, worn on all head dress. Officers and Senior NCOs of the Squadron may also wear the distinctive Yeomanry mess kit.

General

The role of the Regiment in time of war is to provide essential communications in the United Kingdom. To do this it specializes in HF, VHF, and UHF radio, teleprinters and telephone systems. WRAC are recruited, and they undertake most roles. The Regiment is proud of its abilities on the ranges, and the shooting team has achieved substantial success in both District and National (Bisley) levels, winning major trophies, including the TA Royal Signals trophy, the Mercury Cup.

38 Signal Regiment (V)

Squadrons

46 (Derbyshire) at Derby and Leicester;
64 at Sheffield;
87 (Nottingham) at Nottingham;
93 (East Lancs) at Blackburn and Manchester;
HQ at Sheffield.

History

The Regiment formed in 1967 with the amalgamation of the old 64 and 46 Signal Regiments TA. 46 (Derbyshire) Squadron can trace its history back to 1908 when the North Midland Telegraph Company RE formed at Stoke-on-Trent. At the outbreak of the First World War it was embodied at Derby and went to France as the 46th (North Midland) Divisional Signal Company RE, serving on the Western Front

The Colonel in Chief visited 38 Signal Regiment in 1980, accompanied by the TA Commanding Officer. He is wearing the Territorial Decoration.

Left *A WRAC date telegraphist of 38 Signal Regiment at work.*

Above *40 Signal Regiment camouflage their vehicles.*

In 1947 elements of both these units re-formed into the 21st (North Midland) Corps Signals Regiment, with units at Derby, Chesterfield and Nottingham. In 1959 it was renamed 46th (North Midland) Signal Regiment. 87 Squadron at Nottingham has origins with both original Regiments, having been formed from 337 Brigade Signal Squadron, which was part of 46, and from the Nottingham Squadron of 64 Signal Regiment. 93 Squadron is the most recent, having been formed in 1969 from a cadre of the 4th Battalion, The East Lancashire Regiment, and it takes its number from that unit.

General

As part of 2 Signal Brigade, the Regiment has a home defence role, providing communications in the UK. The men and women of the Regiment are trained in all aspects of Royal Signals work. Members find time to enter the Cambrian Patrol Competition, the Nijmegen marches and local half-marathons, and they are encouraged in various forms of adventure training, such as skiing, sailing, survival and abseiling. As the unit usually has its annual camp in this country, as a variation at times soldiers are attached to regular army units overseas for exercises.

throughout the war. In 1920 it was reconstituted as a Royal Signals unit, equipped with horse-drawn wagons with linemen and despatch riders mounted on horses. In 1936 it became the North Midland Corps Signals, and on the outbreak of the Second World War formed two units for 3 and 4 Corps. 3 Corps went to France in 1940, and after Dunkirk became 10 Corps Signals serving in Syria and the Western Desert. It served in Greece, at El Alamein and the invasion of Italy. The 4th Corps unit remained at home until late in 1941, when part of it formed the 11th Armoured Divisional Signals and the rest joined a new 4 Corps in Iraq and served in Assam and Burma.

39 (City of London) Signal Regiment (V)

Squadrons

2 (Dundee) in Dundee;
3 at Tunbridge Wells;
5 (Queen's Own Oxfordshire Hussars) at Banbury;
HQ in the City of London.

General

The Regiment's role is to provide special long-range communications facilities for the armed services as needed in time of war. It recruits both men and women, and WRAC are trained in most Royal Signals trades.

40th (Ulster) Signal Regiment (V)

Squadrons

66 and HQ at Clonaver Park, Belfast;
85 at Clonaver Park, Belfast and Lurgan.

History

The Regiment formed in 1967 by combining 66 (Ulster) Signal Regiment with 81 Signal Regiment (AER) and 302 Infantry Brigade Signal Squadron. A number of other volunteers with suitable qualifications were absorbed at the same time from other disbanded units in Ulster. The Regiment's history goes back to 1939 when the first Volunteer Signal unit was raised in Northern Ireland, along with the formation of the 3rd Anti-Aircraft Brigade. About 75 per cent of the volunteers were from the Post Office Engineering Department. The unit was at annual camp when the Second World War broke out and it was mobilized, taking over communications tasks with the gunners. It embarked for France in December 1939 as part of BEF Headquarters. In the retreat to Dunkirk the unit had some casualties, and most members of one of the sections were captured.

The rest of the unit evacuated through Dunkirk, Cherbourg and St Nazaire. Back in the UK, the HQ and two sections re-formed as 2nd Anti-Aircraft Brigade Signals, going to the Middle East in November 1940 and serving with the 8th Army in North Africa, Sicily and Italy. The remaining section in 1940 stayed in the UK until August 1941, when it embarked with 83 HAA Regiment for the Middle East. It served with PAI Force in Persia and Iraq. The unit later moved to Tripoli, where it remained until the end of the War.

In 1947 with the post-war reconstitution of the TA,

35 (Ulster) Anti-Aircraft Independent (Mixed) Signal Squadron was formed. The number in the title was changed from 35 to 51 in 1952 and it continued until Anti-Aircraft Command was disbanded in 1955. The Squadron then re-formed as 11 (Ulster) Signal Liaison Squadron changing its role from line to radio communications. The WRAC element was separated from the Squadron to form 57 Signal Squadron WRAC, renumbered 324 in 1959. 11 Squadron became 323 (Ulster) Independent Signal Squadron in 1959. In 1961 a new Regiment was formed with the amalgamation of 323, 324 and elements of 328 (Ulster) Battalion WRAC into 66 (Ulster) Signal Regiment. Its duties were to assist the civil authorities in time of war.

The Regimental records note an amazing feat of communications in 1964. An 'at home' was held at the headquarters in Belfast on 28 June, and one attraction was for visitors by buy hydrogen-filled balloons, write their names on them, and release them. At Catterick in Yorkshire, the Royal Signals Training Brigade were holding an Annual Reunion for old comrades the same day. A balloon released by Warrant Officer Earnshaw in Belfast arrived 5½ hours later at Catterick, where it was captured by Corporal Meek.

In 1947, the 107 Independent Infantry Brigade Signal Squadron was formed in Belfast, changing its name to 302 Signal Squadron in 1959. Its job was to provide communications for a TA Infantry Brigade.

General

As part of 12 Signal Brigade, the Regiment has a wartime role in support of BAOR. To train for this, some annual camps are taken in Belgium. WRAC form about a quarter of the strength of each Squadron.

71 (Yeomanry) Signal Regiment (V)

Squadrons

70 (Essex Yeomanry) at Chelmsford, Harlow and Southend;
94 (Berkshire Yeomanry) at Chertsey, Windsor and Southampton;
68 (Inns of Court and City Yeomanry) at Lincolns Inn, Whipps Cross and Bexleyheath;
HQ at Bexleyheath.

History

In 1969 the Essex Yeomanry, formerly an Artillery Regiment, was re-formed as a Squadron of 71 Signals. Its history goes back to 1797 when the volunteer cavalry was first raised in the County. During the First World War it fought as mounted cavalry, but in a dismounted action Lance-Corporal Harold Mugford won the VC at Monchy, for keeping his machine-gun in action despite having both legs broken, as well as other wounds. In 1921 the Regiment converted to artillery and during the Second World War fought in most theatres of battle as 104 Royal Horse Artillery. A second Regiment of Essex Yeomanry was formed in the Artillery role in 1939, numbered 149 RHA, and fought with great distinction through France, Belgium, Holland and Germany, where it was disbanded in 1945. After the War the Regiment re-formed as 304 (Essex Yeomanry) Regiment Royal Artillery.

94 Squadron keep alive the traditions of the Berkshire Yeomanry. This Regiment had been amalgamated with the Westminster Dragoons from 1961 to 1984, but now the Dragoons form part of the Royal Yeomanry as HQ Squadron. Another link is that both 68 Squadron and the band of the Royal Yeomanry carry on the traditions of the Inns of Court and City Yeomanry.

General

The role of the Regiment is to provide the vital communications in the UK in time of war. About one-third of soldiers are WRAC. Through the Essex Yeomanry, the Regiment has the Freedom of both Chelmsford and Colchester. Another link with the past is that members of 70 Squadron have the privilege of retaining the Essex Yeomanry green berets with a red background to the Royal Signals cap badge.

63 (SAS) Signal Squadron (V)

This is an independent Squadron with detachments at Poole, Southampton, Gosport, Chichester and Portsmouth. Its role is to provide the specialist communications required in support of the Special Air Service Regiments. The intensive training not only includes the technical and communications skills, but also parachuting and fitness. It is fair to say that they recruit only men of above average calibre. Training and exercises often take members to countries such as Denmark, France, Germany, Belgium, Italy, USA, Peru, Kenya and Norway. A typical year's training will include helicopter ditching, parachuting, abseiling, skiing, assault boat drills, shooting, orienteering and hill walking, as well as a full range of military skills. After a probationary period, a recruit to the Squadron is presented with his distinctive beige beret.

The Origins and Titles of 44 (Cinque Ports) Squadron 36 Signal Regiment (V)

1692 Western Regiment of Trained Band of Soldiers;
1779 to 1783 Cinque Ports Provincial Militia;
1794 to 1800 Cinque Ports Volunteer Company;
1803 The Regiment of Cinque Port Volunteers;
1810 to 1816 Cinque Ports Militia;
1859 1st (Cinque Ports) Artillery Company;
1861 1st Admin Brigade (Cinque Ports) Artillery Volunteers;
1880 3rd Volunteer Artillery Bde (CP) Division;
1887 1st (CP) Artillery Volunteers;
1902 1st (CP) Royal Coast Artillery;
1903 1st (CP) Royal Garrison Artillery (Vol);
1908 1st (Home Counties) (CP) Bde Field Arty (TF);
1921 1st (HC) (CP) Field Bde RA;
1938 to 1945 75 (HC) (CP) A.A. Regt RA TA;
1947 to 1956 259 (Mobile) H.A.A. Regt (HC) (CP) TA;
1957 Home Counties District (Mixed) Signal Regt;
1959 62 (Mixed) Signal Regt;
1960 62 (Mixed) Signal Regt (CP);
1961 44 (Home Counties) Signal Regiment;
1962 to 1967 44 (HC) Signal Regiment (CP).

Today, to commemorate the Cinque Ports connections, officers and senior NCOs wear a Cinque Port Flash on their mess uniforms.

Wavell

Wavell is a battlefield Automatic Data Processing (ADP) facility which helps formation headquarters personnel to carry out command and control. Operators can input, retrieve, update and delete information held in the database. Updated information is automatically distributed to other holders with the same records. Bruin or Ptarmigan communication systems each have two channels reserved to enable automatic communication between Wavell terminals. Its great value is the saving of time and manpower resources in circulating, switching and receiving routine data and reports, and as it stores information it is available for retrieval of data as required.

Ptarmigan

Ptarmigan is a very flexible communications system for the battlefield which is mobile, secure and digital. It is the latest in technological area communications networks that will meet the tactical requirements of the armed services. As it is a digital system, switching and message routing can be carried out quickly and reliably using solid state techniques. It is not unlike a modern telephone system in that each unit has its own special number. To contact a unit the number is transmitted by radio and this code is picked up by several nodes, or switching stations and it is directed along a path to its receiver. The path chosen will be the best at that time, perhaps changing during a transmission because of changing conditions. This system can deal with voice as well as Wavell, facsimile, video, and teleprinter traffic.

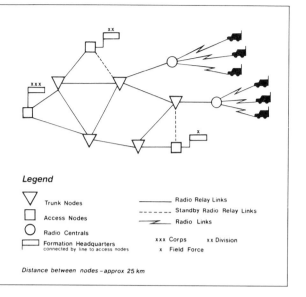

Legend

▽ Trunk Nodes

☐ Access Nodes

○ Radio Centrals

⌐ Formation Headquarters
connected by line to access nodes

——— Radio Relay Links

– – – – Standby Radio Relay Links

⌁ Radio Links

xxx Corps   xx Division

x Field Force

Distance between nodes – approx 25 km

A signals corporal from the Territorial Force late in the First World War (B. Gardner).

Today's signaller mans a radio equipped Land Rover.

7 The Infantry

The Infantry remain as ever the major manpower strength of any army. They are the men who possess the ground for which a battle is fought. Gone, however, is the old view that the Infantry are mere cannon-fodder whose lives may be thrown away in the pursuit of a government's or a General's folly. Today each infantry man is a technician, not only schooled in basic tactics and military skills, but capable of dealing with the complex machinery and electronics that make up his weaponry, communications and life-support systems. He does not blindly obey orders, but today is expected to use his own initiative, and to be able to react to the rapidly-changing circumstances that a modern, mobile war will bring.

The Regimental system of the British Army is unique amongst the world's armies, and is one of its great strengths. Each regiment has its own distinctive titles and traditions, badges and styles of uniform. The loyalty and pride these differences encourage are almost a secret weapon in our Army's arsenal.

From the formation of the Regular Army in 1660 until about 1743, most infantry regiments were known by the name of their Colonel; later, numbers were officially allotted to regiments of the line in their order of seniority. Today, a hundred years after the abolition of the numbering system, some of the present titles have had them restored.

The Infantry Battalions of the TA have their origins either as additional battalions of Regular regiments, or from purely volunteer sources, or from the militia. As with the Regular units, the volunteers are divided into 'Divisions'. The term 'division' in this sense is not to be confused with a fighting formation, of which they may be part, but is an administrative and organizational system.

The TA battalions allocated to the various divisions are as follows:

The Scottish Division

1st and 2nd Battalions 52nd Lowland Volunteers; 1st, 2nd and 3rd Battalions 51st Highland Volunteers.

The Queen's Division

5th and 6th/7th Battalions The Queen's Regiment; 5th and 6th Battalions The Royal Regiment of Fusiliers; 8th Battalion The Queen's Fusiliers; the 5th, 6th and 7th Battalions The Royal Anglian Regiment.

The King's Division

4th Battalion King's Own Royal Border Regiment; 5th/8th Battalion The King's Regiment; 4th Battalion the Queen's Lancashire Regiment; 1st, 2nd, 3rd and 4th Battalions Yorkshire Volunteers; 4th and 5th Battalions The Royal Irish Rangers.

The Prince of Wales's Division

4th Battalion the Devonshire and Dorset Regiment; 1st and 2nd Battalions The Wessex Regiment; 3rd Battalion The Staffordshire Regiment; 3rd Battalion The Cheshire Regiment; 3rd Battalion The Royal Welch Fusiliers; 3rd and 4th Battalions The Royal Regiment of Wales; 3rd and 4th Battalions The Worcestershire and Sherwood Foresters Regiment.

The Light Division

5th, 6th, 7th and 8th Battalions The Light Infantry; 4th and 5th Battalions The Royal Green Jackets.

These are not the full titles of each Regiment; in each of them the word 'Volunteer' appears, as do many historic numbers or additional titles. The Parachute Regiment, which is also infantry, is separate from these groupings.

Helicopters play a vital part in battlefield transport. Infantry deploy into an RAF Puma.

Regimental Colours

The origin of the custom of carrying Colours goes back to when tribal chiefs fixed the family badge or coloured flag to a pole. This was held up to show the rallying point for the clan or family, and to identify themselves to their allies. Knights of mediaeval times used armorial bearings on shields and banners for the same purpose. These origins led to the idea of a flag or colour for each regiment. In 1751, the Infantry Regiments were permitted to have two colours, the King's and the Regimental, and this has continued ever since. Colours are smaller today than before, as their use has now become more ceremonial rather than as an actual rallying point in the dust and confusion of battle. Until the Boer War, Colours were taken into battle, and these were defended at all costs, since a regiment that lost its Colours would probably be routed. There were sound reasons, therefore for instilling into soldiers of the day the belief that the Colours embodied the spirit of the regiment. In each regiment today they are treated with the greatest of respect, and when uncased are given full honours.

The design of Colours is similar for each Regiment, in that the Queen's Colour is based on the Union Flag, but each of the Colours is decorated with the Regiment's own battle honours and the Regimental Colours have battle honours and distinctions and mottoes. The ceremony of Trooping the Colour at regular intervals is practiced in many battalions. This stemmed from the need to show all the soldiers what their rallying point looked like before going into battle.

The Scottish Division
52nd Lowland Volunteers

Regimental badge

Upon a Saltire, thistle within a circulet inscribed *NEMO ME IMPUNE LACESSIT.*

Regimental march

The quick march is *Scotland the Brave.*

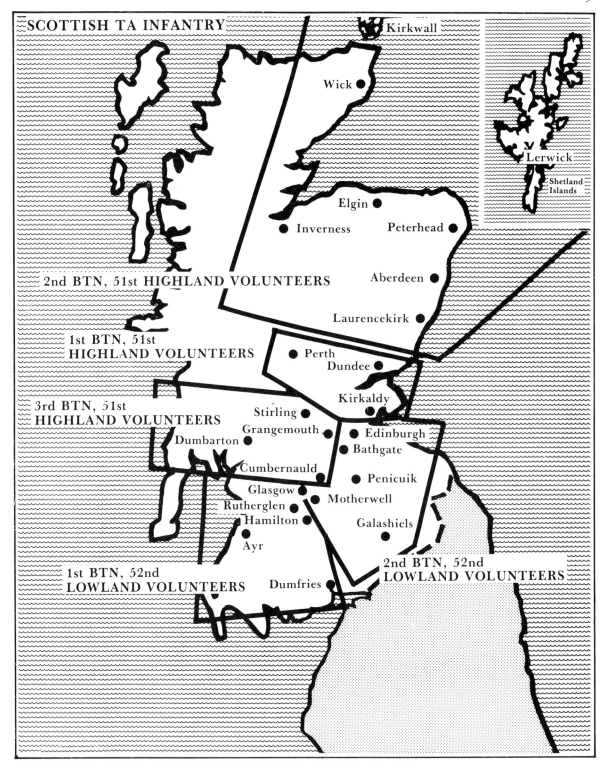

SCOTTISH TA INFANTRY

Kirkwall

Wick

Lerwick

Shetland Islands

Elgin

Inverness

Peterhead

2nd BTN, 51st HIGHLAND VOLUNTEERS

Aberdeen

Laurencekirk

1st BTN, 51st HIGHLAND VOLUNTEERS

Perth

Dundee

3rd BTN, 51st HIGHLAND VOLUNTEERS

Kirkaldy

Stirling

Grangemouth

Edinburgh

Dumbarton

Bathgate

Cumbernauld

Penicuik

Glasgow

Rutherglen

Motherwell

Hamilton

Galashiels

Ayr

1st BTN, 52nd LOWLAND VOLUNTEERS

2nd BTN, 52nd LOWLAND VOLUNTEERS

Dumfries

1st Battalion

Companies

A (Royal Highland Fusiliers) at Rutherglen;
B (Royal Scots Fusiliers) at Ayr;
C (King's Own Scottish Borderers) at Dumfries;
D (Cameronians) at Hamilton;
E (Highland Light Infantry) in Glasgow;
HQ (Glasgow Highlanders) in Glasgow;
2 Companies of HSF: F at Ayr and G in Dumfries.

Regimental dress

All companies wear the dress of the 'parent' regiment, with the exception of the cap badge, and for A, B, E and HQ Companies, these are The Royal Highland Fusiliers and the Mackenzie Tartan; for C Company, The Kings Own Scottish Borderers and the Leslie Tartan; and for D Company, The Cameronians, and the Douglas Tartan. Stable belts are not worn.

History

The 1st Battalion was formed in 1967, its recruits coming from Glasgow and the West Lowlands as far south as the border. The name, 52nd Lowland, commemorates the 52 Lowland Division, a TA Division which fought with great distinction in both World Wars. In the First World War, the Division saw action at Gallipoli, Palestine and the attack on the Hindenburg Line. In the Second World War, after a brief stay in France in 1940, it eventually saw action on Walcheren Island in the Scheldt estuary, and was thereafter continually involved in the campaign in North-West Europe until the assault on Bremen in 1945.

General

In time of war the Battalion has a role in support of NATO.

2nd Battalion

Companies

1 (Royal Scots) at Penicuik;
2 (Royal Scots) in Edinburgh and Bathgate;
3 (King's Own Scottish Borderers) at Galashiels;
4 (Cameronians) at Motherwell;
HQ in Edinburgh;
5 (HSF) in Edinburgh.

Regimental dress

As with the 1st Battalion, each company wears the accoutrements applicable to their 'parent' regiment, except for the cap badge. Stable belts are worn in the appropriate tartan. The tartans are: 1, 2 and HQ Companies, Royal Scots, with the Hunting Stuart tartan; 3 Company, King's Own Scottish Borderers with

the Leslie tartan; and 4 Company, Cameronians with the Douglas tartan.

History

The 2nd Battalion of the Regiment was raised in 1971, and in the titles of its Companies commemorates the TA involvement of The Royal Scots, The King's Own Scottish Borderers and the Cameronians (Scottish Rifles). The first two of these still have Regular Army units, but on 31 March 1987 the Cameronians were placed in the disbanded units section of the Army List. Strong ties are maintained with the parent regiments, and in 1983 this Battalion provided a Guard for the march through Edinburgh of The Royal Scots in their 350th anniversary year. HRH The Princess Royal, Colonel-in-Chief of The Royal Scots, presented the 2nd Battalion's first colours in 1985.

General

The Battalion has a home defence role in time of war. At its HQ Company, 30 members of the WRAC are included on strength and serve in the MT, Signals and Intelligence sections, and as cooks.

51st Highland Volunteers

Regimental badge

Upon a saltire, a stag's head above a scroll inscribed *CUIDICH'N RIGH* (Help the King).

Regimental marches

The quick march is made up of *Highland Laddie* and *51st Highland Division of Wadi Akarit*, and the slow march is *Callin Mo Ruinsa*.

1st Battalion

Companies

A (Black Watch) at Dundee;
G (London Scottish) at Westminster in London;
K (Black Watch) in Kirkcaldy;
V (Liverpool Scottish) in Liverpool;
HQ (Black Watch) in Perth:
Z (HSF) at Perth, Kirkcaldy and Dundee.

Regimental dress

A, K and HQ Companies wear the Black Watch tartan, G Company wears Hodden Grey tartan and V company the Forbes tartan.

History

The Battalion took its present form in 1971 when the original Highland Volunteers were divided into two to form the 1st and 2nd Battalions. It has a distinguished history, and as a result of action in the First World War, members of K and HQ Companies wear the ribbon of the Croix de Guerre on their shoulders and the officers and senior NCOs wear a distinctive lanyard. These commemorate the award of the medal to the 6th Battalion, the Black Watch, from whom they are descended. V Company at Liverpool is associated with a double VC, that of Captain Noel Godfrey Chavasse RAMC, who was a Regimental Medical Officer with the Liverpool Scottish Regiment during the First World War. The London Scottish were the first TA Infantry unit to see action during the First World War, at Mersines on Hallowe'en, 1914. The title 51st, of course, commemorates the famous 51st Highland Division that saw action with the BEF in France in the Second World War, where it was captured at St Valery after Dunkirk. When re-formed it more than avenged that insult, in battles in North Africa and again in North-West Europe.

General

For their wartime role in support of BAOR, training takes place both in the UK and in Germany. A team from the Battalion takes part in the annual Army Ski Championships, and it has been known for its boxing team to beat Regular Army challengers. This Battalion also administers the 51st Highland Volunteers band, which includes three WRAC members.

2nd Battalion

Companies

A (Queen's Own Highlanders and Lovat Scouts) at Wick;
B (The Gordon Highlanders) at Peterhead;
C (Queen's Own Highlanders) at Inverness;
D (The Gordon Highlanders and Lovat Scouts) at Aberdeen;
HQ (Queen's Own Highlanders and Gordon Highlanders) at Elgin;
Y (HSF) at Elgin, Inverness, Stornoway, Wick and Kirkwall;
X (HSF) at Aberdeen, Lerwick, Peterhead and Laurencekirk.

Regimental dress

Stable belts are not worn by this battalion, and the

Men of the 32nd Battalion 51st Highland Volunteers on exercise.

tartans are: B, D, and elements of HQ Companies, the Gordon tartan; A, C and elements of HQ Companies, the Mackenzie of Seaforth tartan; and the platoons on Orkney and in the Shetlands wear the Fraser tartan.

History

The Battalion was formed from the companies of the Highland Volunteers in the North Highlands and Islands in 1971. It carries on the TA traditions of the Seaforth Highlanders, the Cameron Highlanders, the Gordon Highlanders and the Lovat Scouts, and can trace its history back to the Militia, Volunteer and

Territorial units formed in the middle of the last century. Its final reorganization came in 1982, when it took its present structure.

General

The mobilization role is in support of BAOR, and in order to train for this, annual camps are taken at intervals in Germany. Because of the spread of units over the Highlands at 17 different locations, from Lerwick in the north to Stornaway in the west and Fort William and Laurencekirk in the south, there are often many problems in getting together for training. Much of this is undertaken on private land in the Highlands, although units are able to get together at least four times each year, as well as at the annual camp. The parent Regular Army regiments from whom permanent staff are drawn are the Queen's Own Highlanders and the Gordon Highlanders. The Battalion boasts many fine shots who take part in the Army in Scotland Skill at Arms meetings and at Bisley, and in 1985, HQ Company team were the Scottish champions. A welcome change from routine training came in 1985 when 'A' Company went to Gibraltar to relieve a Regular unit guarding the Rock.

3rd Battalion

(Full title 3rd Battalion 51st Highland Volunteers (The Argyll and Sutherland Highlanders)).

Companies

A at Stirling;
B at Cumbernauld;
C at Grangemouth;
D at Dumbarton;
HQ at Stirling;
W (HSF) at Stirling, Dumbarton and Grangemouth.

The 7th and 8th Battalions of the Argyll and Sutherland Highlanders on parade for the last time.

Regimental dress

The tartans and dress customs are the same as The Argyll and Sutherland Highlanders, except for the badge. The tartan is the Argyll and Sutherland Highlander tartan, otherwise known as 'Government Tartan Number 1a'. Stable belts are of the regimental tartan.

History

The Battalion was formed in 1975, and suffered its final reorganization in 1981. It is the direct successor to the 7th and 8th Battalions of the Argyll and Sutherland Highlanders. The 7th Battalion started life in 1859 in the counties of Stirling, Clackmannan and Kinross, and was eventually established as two Volunteer Battalions, the 1st Stirling Rifle Volunteer Corps and the Clackmannan and Kinross Rifle Volunteer Corps. In 1887 they were retitled the 4th and 7th Volunteer Battalions of The Argyll and Sutherland Highlanders. Volunteer Companies made up from men of both Battalions served in the Boer War. On the formation of the TF in 1908 the two battalions ceased to exist and their place was taken by the 7th Battalion of the Regiment. In 1914, the Battalion went to France and fought with the 51st Highland Division, a total of 54 Officers and 898 other ranks losing their lives. The 7th re-formed in 1920 as a TA unit and was mobilized again for the Second World War. Early in 1940 it went to France with the 51st Division, where it was overwhelmed in a disastrous battle on the Somme, when 23 Officers and 500 men were either killed or captured. The Battalion was reformed back home and it then fought with the reconstituted 51st Division in the Western Desert at the Battle of El Alamein, and at Wadi Akarit in Tunis where on 6 April 1943 the Commanding Officer, Lieutenant-Colonel Lorne Maclaine Campbell, won the VC. It then fought at Gerbini in Sicily, before moving to the battles in North-West Europe where it was involved in the assault crossing of the Rhine. During the war 32 Officers and 472 other ranks lost their lives. The 7th was re-formed as a TA unit in 1947, but disbanded in 1967.

In 1860 various separate Corps of Rifle Volunteers had formed in Argyll. These were absorbed into the 1st Administrative Batallion, Argyll Rifle Volunteers by 1867. By 1883 the 'Rifle' title had been discontinued and it became the 5th Volunteer Battalion, The Argyll and Sutherland Highlanders. Sixty men from Argyll served with the 1st Battalion in the Boer War. In 1908 the 5th became the 8th (Argyllshire) Battalion of the Regiment. It served in France from 1915 to 1918 as part of 51st Division, fighting in the labyrinth at Vimy, at Beaumont Hamel, Arras, Ypres and Cambrai, during which the total casualty list was 230 officers and 4,000 men. Between the wars the 8th

Her Majesty the Queen presents new colours to the 3rd Battalion; here the Regimental Colours are taken by Second Lieutenant D.R. McNeil.

remained a TA unit and in February 1940 went to France where it was involved in the battles on the Somme and at St Valery. It re-formed back home and went to North Africa as part of the 78th Division, gaining a reputation for itself in the battles at Green

Hill and Longstop Hill. These were followed by service in Sicily and Italy, finishing in 1946 at Klagenfurt in Austria. It re-formed in 1947 but was disbanded in 1967.

On 21 March 1918, at Marteville in France, Second-Lieutenant John Crawford Buchan was killed in an action for which he was later awarded the VC. Another posthumous VC was awarded to John Thomas McKellar Anderson at Wadi Akarit in Tunisia on 6 April 1943, the same day as Lieutenant-Colonel Campbell of the 7th Battalion won a VC.

The Colours for the new battalion were presented by Her Majesty The Queen, Colonel-in-Chief of the Argyll and Sutherland Highlanders, on the esplanade outside Stirling Castle on 16 July 1986.

General

The Battalion has home defence duties in time of war, and to supplement training, members take part in the Cambrian March Competitions, and reached fourth place in 1986. A section under the command of a subaltern has been to the Falkland Islands to experience life with the Regular soldiers of the 1st Battalion, Argyll and Sutherland Highlanders, where they carried out the same duties. The Battalion has an affiliation with HMS *Rothesay* and HMS *Repulse*.

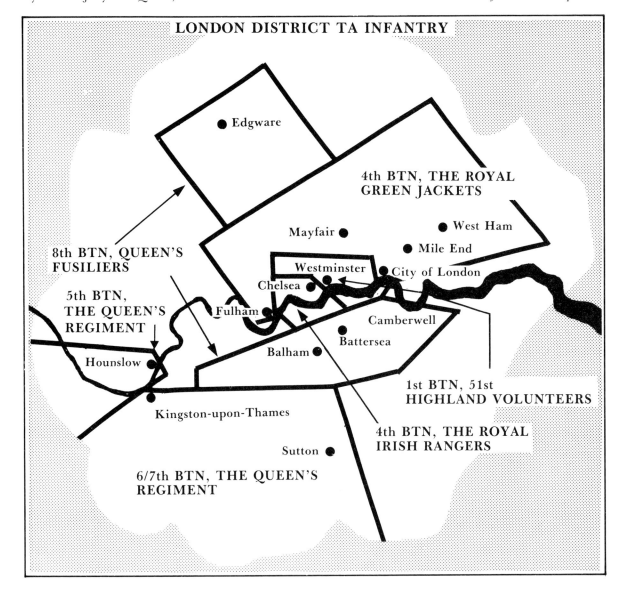

LONDON DISTRICT TA INFANTRY

- Edgware

4th BTN, THE ROYAL GREEN JACKETS

8th BTN, QUEEN'S FUSILIERS

Mayfair ●   ● West Ham

   ● Mile End

5th BTN, THE QUEEN'S REGIMENT

Westminster   ● City of London

Chelsea ●

Fulham

Camberwell

Battersea ●

Balham ●

Hounslow

1st BTN, 51st HIGHLAND VOLUNTEERS

Kingston-upon-Thames

4th BTN, THE ROYAL IRISH RANGERS

Sutton ●

6/7th BTN, THE QUEEN'S REGIMENT

The Queen's Division
The Queen's Regiment

Regimental badge
A Dragon upon a mount within the Garter. Above the Dragon and superimposed on the Garter the Plume of the Prince of Wales.

Motto
Unconquered I Serve.

Regimental marches
The quick march is *The Soldiers of the Queen* and the slow march is *The Caledonian*.

Allied Colonels-in-Chief
Her Royal Highness Princess Juliana of the Netherlands, and Her Majesty Queen Margrethe II of Denmark.

Regimental dress
Collar badges on uniforms are the White Horse

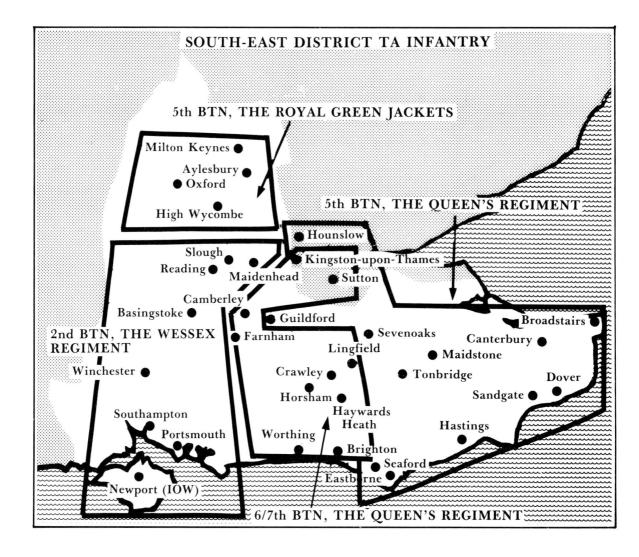

rampant, from the badge of The Queen's Own Royal West Kent Regiment and later The Queen's Own Buffs. This is mounted in a scroll on a star, and above this a single plume, which commemorates The Royal Sussex Regiment. Uniform buttons bear the Paschal Lamb, the oldest of all regimental badges, known to have been worn by members of The Queen's Regiment before 1685. This is superimposed on the star from the Order of the Garter, as a reminder of The East Surrey Regiment. The stable belt is a plain blue colour.

5th Battalion

Companies

A at Guildford and Hounslow;
B at Broadstairs, Dover and Sandgate;
C at Hastings, Eastbourne and Seaford;
E at Tonbridge, Sevenoaks and Maidstone;
HQ at Canterbury.

History

The Battalion formed on 1 April 1967 and carries on the TA traditions of the 4th and 5th Buffs (Royal East Kent) Regiment, the 3rd Battalion The Royal Surrey Regiment, 4th/5th The Royal Sussex Regiment and the 5th Battalion The Middlesex Regiment.

General

In time of war the Battalion has a role in support of BAOR.

6th/7th Battalion

Companies

A (Salerno) at Farnham and Camberley;
B (Somme) at Brighton and Worthing;
C (Quebec) at Crawley, Haywards Heath and Lingfield;
D (Tangier) at Sutton and Kingston upon Thames;
HQ (Alamein) at Horsham

History

The Battalion was formed on 1 April 1975 by the amalgamation of the 6th and 7th Battalions of the Regiment. Both these Battalions had been formed on 1 April 1971, the 6th from cadres of the Queen's Surreys, Middlesex, Royal Artillery and The Surrey Yeomanry (Queen Mary's Regiment), and the 7th from cadres of the Royal Sussex, The Buffs, The Queen's Surreys and the Queen's (West Kent), the latest addition being B Company, formed at Brighton in 1986. The TA Battalions of the Queens have been responsible for four of the many VCs won by the Regiment. One of the greatest achievements of the Second World War was in Burma, the defence of

Top *A section about to take part in a platoon attack* (5 QUEENS).

Above *NBC practice is an essential part of training* (5 QUEENS).

Kohima by the 4th Battalion The Queen's Own Royal West Kent Regiment. It held out for 15 days against a complete Japanese division, buying enough time for two British divisions to arrive and prevent the intended Japanese invasion of India. From then on the Battalion was often at the head of the column that drove the enemy back to Rangoon and beyond. At Kohima Lance-Corporal Harman won the VC by first killing an enemy machine-gun crew and capturing the gun single-handed, then rushing another post alone and killing all five of the enemy. He was then killed by a burst of enemy fire.

General

The role of the Battalion is that of home defence in war, with special responsibility for safeguarding the facilities necessary to the effective conduct of a European war and the maintenance of democratic government in the UK.

At this point it is as well to look at the sort of training that 6th/7th QUEENS undertakes in the home defence role, as an example of all other similarly-roled battalions. The training is wide and varied, and the specialist skills developed are:
1. Patrolling — the aims of which are to obtain accurate and up-to-date information, to dominate an area to prevent enemy infiltration, and to destroy or disrupt the enemy forces;
2. Observation — this is necessary to gain the maximum information about the enemy, its strengths, movements, positions and likely intentions;
3. Escort duties — this involves providing a secure route for anything which is sensitive or vulnerable, such as troops, supplies, ammunition and VIPs. It may also involve the reconnaissance and clearing of routes necessary for such movement;
4. Vehicle check points, which are set up to control access to military establishments and also to control

the movement of arms, ammunition, explosives and personnel;
5. Cordon and search, which is the securing and isolation of a suspected enemy position to prevent movement in and out, to allow the area to be searched and the enemy 'flushed out'.

The Royal Regiment of Fusiliers

Regimental badge
St. George and the dragon within the Garter.

Regimental marches
The regimental quick march is *The British Grenadiers*,

Training for a home defence role means the volunteers need to adapt infantry tactics to fighting in a built up area. Old army married quarters provide an excellent training ground (6/7 QUEENS).

An indication of the life of a regular officer serving with a TA unit between the two World Wars is the experience of the late Lieutenant-General Sir Brian Horrocks. This was outlined in Philip Warner's book Horrocks *(Sphere, 1985)* about this modest and likeable wartime leader. Things have improved vastly, of course, since then.

The part-time soldiers were a territorial battalion of the Middlesex, the 9th. As his own battalion had now gone overseas, with all his friends, he faced what he thought was a bleak future. He soon found he was mistaken. His appointment as Adjutant to the 9th Middlesex began in January 1927; the regimental headquarters was in Willesden.

Maintaining enthusiasm among these men, who came to be dubbed 'Saturday night soldiers', was by no means easy. Volunteers had to be encouraged, and those already in retained (unless found to be more of a liability than an asset). If the equipment of the Regular Army was inadequate and dated, that of the TA was worse. The task of the adjutant and his senior Warrant Officer was to be imperturbable, cheerful, and full of enthusiasm. When Horrocks arrived he knew next to nothing about the Territorial Army, and even less about the civilian world and its preoccupations. Soon he found himself totally immersed in fresh interests, not merely in his own job, but also in the jobs and attitudes of those in the unit. He confessed himself amazed at the enthusiasm shown by many. Later, in the Second World War, he found this experience with the TA a valuable asset. He understood the prejudice which existed on both sides.

Horrocks spent three years with the 9th Battalion. The unorthodoxy of his career was instilling in him an understanding of the people who would later be proud to be called 'Horrocks' men'. In his German POW camps, and during the hard times in Russia, he had had ample opportunity to see how different types reacted under stress; he also learnt his own strengths and weaknesses. With the 9th Battalion he learnt that in certain circumstances you can do more by cheerfulness and resourcefulness than you can by authoritarianism; if he had tried the latter the Battalion would probably have melted away. When a man missed an essential parade it was useless trying to discipline him; all you could do was to make him feel sorry and decide he would not miss the next one. And above all, the work of the 9th Battalion must seem interesting and important.

a second being *The New Fusilier.* Other authorized marches played when in the appropriate regimental area are: Northumberland, *Blaydon Races,* Warwickshire, *Warwickshire Lads,* London *Fighting with the 7th Royal Fusiliers* and in Lancashire, *The Minden March.* The slow march is *Rule Brittania!* in slow tempo. The second slow march is *De Normandi* and others that are played on appropriate occasions are *St George, Macbean's Slow March,* and *The Lancashire Fusiliers' Slow March.*

Colonel-in-Chief
Major-General HRH The Duke of Kent KG.

Mascot
The Antelope Mascot has been adopted by the Royal Regiment of Fusiliers from the Royal Warwickshire Fusiliers. The mascot may be allotted, together with its handlers, by the Colonel of the Regiment to any Battalion. The Antelope wears livery bearing the insignia of the Regiment.

Regimental flag
The flag is the red cross of St George on a white background, and at the centre of the Cross is the regimental emblem.

Regimental day
St George's Day, 23 April each year is regarded as the anniversary of the birth of the Regiment and is specially marked. On this day red and white roses are worn by all ranks in uniform or civilian clothes. The Colours remain uncased all day, the drums and Drum Major's staff are all garlanded with red and white roses. Other days traditionally observed include Gallipoli Day (25 April), Albuhera Day (16 May), Normandy Day (6 June), and Minden Day (1 August).

Hackle
All RRF members wear the red and white hackle.

Stable belt
Rose and primrose.

5th Battalion

Companies
A and B at Birmingham;
C in Ashton-under-Lyne
D at Bury and Rochdale;
HQ at Coventry.

History
The Battalion formed in 1968 and carried on the traditions of the TA units of the Royal Fusiliers, Royal Warwickshire Fusiliers and the Lancashire Fusiliers.

Above *A Fusilier machine-gunner.*

Below *A weapons check is a vital part of the duty officer's work.*

Below right *Company signallers check equipment before an exercise* (6 RRF).

General

In time of war the Battalion is part of 49 Brigade of 2 Infantry Division, with a role to support BAOR.

6th Battalion

Companies

W at Berwick-upon-Tweed and Alnwick;
X at Newcastle upon Tyne and Hexham;
Y at Longbenton, Newcastle upon Tyne;
Z at Ashington and Tynemouth;
HQ, Support and the Band at Newcastle upon Tyne;
St Lucia Company (HSF) at Newcastle upon Tyne (note Battalion HQ is at Alnwick).

History

In 1975 the Battalion was formed from two companies of the 5th Battalion Royal Regiment of Fusiliers and two companies of the Northumbrian Volunteers. The traditions of the 5 RRF are carried on by X and Z Companies, and of the Northumbrian Volunteers by Y and HQ Companies. Following a reorganization in April 1978, W Company was raised. The Volunteer Battalions of the Northumberland Fusiliers provided Volunteer Service Companies and saw action in South Africa during the Boer War. In the First World War, many TA soldiers in 14 NF TA Battalions from the area saw action, and Lieutenant James Johnson was awarded the VC whilst serving with the 36th Battalion in 1918.

In the Second World War, 7 RNF was a machine-gun unit with the 51st Highland Division, and fought the rearguard action at St Valery. An unusual award of the Distinguished Conduct Medal was made to Fusilier Joe Purvis from Ashington, for his escape as a prisoner of war. He escaped from Poland, and by way of Switzerland into France where he fought with the Maquis until the Americans took over the area after D-Day. In 1966, TA members of the 6th and 7th Battalions volunteered for and served with the Regular Army in Aden during the unrest. The strong ties of this Battalion with the North-East of England are shown in that their Honorary Colonel was the late Colonel The Duke of Northumberland KG, who was also a holder of the Territorial Decoration.

General

In time of war the Battalion becomes part of 15 Brigade of 2 Infantry Division with a task in support of BAOR. Annual camps work in a three-year cycle, two being in the UK and the third with BAOR. The only WRAC members of the Battalion are found serving with the band. Teams have entered the Cambrian and Nijmegen Marches and a team from Ashington won Exercise Martial Merlin in 1986 and 1987. This is 15 Brigade's march, shoot and military skills competition. Honours have also come to the Battalion's drivers in winning Exercise Hard Drive in 1986 and 1987, and to the cooks, who won Exercise Grebe Grey in 1988. On four occasions the North England Public Relations Trophy, the Fairclough Trophy, has been won by the Battalion.

The Royal Regiment of Fusiliers has many honours, including the Freedoms of London, Birmingham, Coventry, Salford, Newcastle upon Tyne, Warwick, Leamington Spa, Bury, Rochdale, Stratford upon Avon, Rugby, Morpeth, Berwick-upon-Tweed, and Sutton Coldfield. The 6th Battalion was presented with an illuminated address by Alnwick District Council in 1978.

8th Queen's Fusiliers (City of London)

Companies

A (Highwood) at Camberwell, South East London;
B (Albuhera) at Edgware, Middlesex;
C (City of London) at Balham, South-West London; and
HQ at Battersea, South-West London.

History

The Battalion formed on Albuhera Day, 16 May, 1988, and is part of both the Queen's Regiment and The Royal Regiment of Fusiliers, taking precedence after 6/7 QUEENS. It took under command the two London Volunteer Companies of the two Regiments,

and formed a third Rifle Company and HQ Company. HQ Company members are badged either *Queens* or *RRF*, depending on individual preference. A Company is badged *Queens* to show its pedigree from the 21st (County of London) Battalion The London Regiment (1st Surrey Rifles), and D Company 6/7 QUEENS.

B Company is also badged *Queens,* and was B Company 6/7 QUEENS, although it can trace its history back to the Middlesex Rifle Volunteers of 1859. C Company is badged *RRF* and was most recently C Company 5 RRF, and its TA Centre was originally that of 9th (2nd City of London) Battalion The Royal Fusiliers (City of London Regiment).

General

Many of the 20 Battalions from whom the Battalion descends served in 56 (1st London) Division from its formation at Hallencourt on 8 February 1916, so it is fitting that today 8QF serve as part of 56 London Brigade, which perpetuates that Divisional title. In time of war, however, the Battalion would have a role in support of BAOR.

The Royal Anglian Regiment

Regimental badge
The Castle and Key of Gibraltar upon an eight-pointed star.

Colonel-in-Chief
HM Queen Elizabeth the Queen Mother.

Deputy Colonels-in-Chief
HRH Princess Margaret, Countess of Snowdon; and HRH Princess Alice, Duchess of Gloucester.

Regimental marches
The quick march is *Rule Brittania!* and *Speed the Plough,* the slow march is *The Slow March of the Northamptonshire Regiment.*

Stable belt
Blue with a red middle portion and a yellow line in the centre.

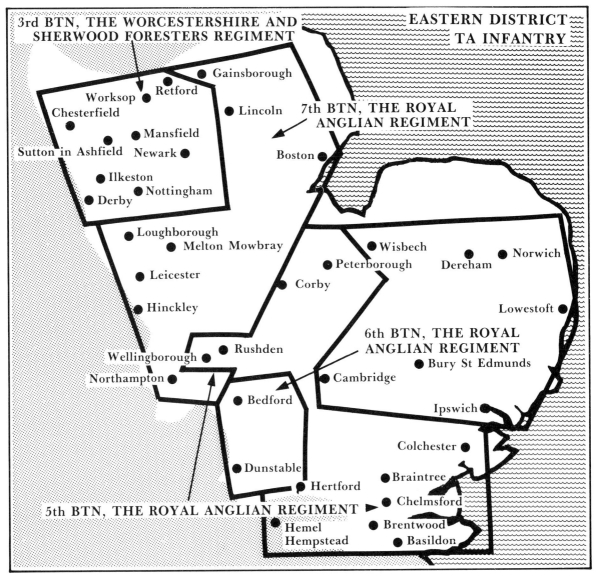

5th Battalion

Companies

1 (Essex) at Basildon and Braintree;
2 (Northamptonshire) at Wellingborough, Rushden and Corby;
3 (Essex) at Brentwood, Chelmsford and Colchester;
4 (Hertfordshire) at Hertford and Hemel Hempstead;
HQ and Heavy Weapons at Peterborough.

History

The Battalion formed on 1 April 1967 on the re-organization of the TA into the TAVR. It was an amalgamation of the County Regiments and other Corps in East Anglia. Battalion HQ and HQ Company were made up from the 4th/5th Battalion The Northamptonshire Regiment, with elements of the Suffolk and Cambridgeshire Regiments. 1 Company was made up of The Royal Norfolk Regiment and elements of The Suffolk and Cambridgeshire Regiments; 2 Company were from the 4th/6th The Royal Lincolnshire Regiment; 3 Company came from the 4th/5th The Essex Regiment; 4 Company were formed from 4th/5th The Leicestershire Regiment; and a 5th Company was added in 1969 from The Bedfordshire and Hertfordshire Regiment.

That is how the Battalion remained until a major shake-up in 1978 when the 2nd and 4th Companies left and were replaced by C Company of the Northamptonshire Regiment, becoming 2 Company. In 1985, 1 Company left and was replaced by a Company from The Essex Regiment. After having been a Home Defence unit, the Battalion was given a specific role as part of 7 Field Force with a commitment in BAOR, its first exercise in North-West Europe being Crusader in 1980. In 1984 this role changed to becoming part of 49 Brigade, 2 Infantry Division and in this role its first exercise was Lionheart.

General

The Battalion retains its role with 49 Brigade and takes annual camp in the UK, Germany and Gibraltar. Training has also been undertaken in the USA and Kenya. Dress of the Battalion varies, in that 1 and 3 Companies wear the purple lanyard and beret after 3 R ANGLIAN, and 2, 4, HQ and Heavy Weapons Companies wear a black lanyard and side hat, after 2 R ANGLIAN.

6th Battalion

Companies

A (Norfolk) at Norwich and East Dereham;

Right *A 6 R ANGLIAN mortar team in action.*

Below *On a major home defence exercise, the TA of the 6 R ANGLIAN working alongside regulars of the USAF security troops.*

B (Bedford) at Bedford and Dunstable;
C (Suffolk) at Ipswich and Lowestoft;
D (Cambridgeshire) at Cambridge and Wisbech;
HQ (Suffolk) at Bury St Edmunds.

History

The Battalion formed in 1971 and has the same kind of pedigree as the 5th Battalion. Because of their associations with the former Suffolk and Cambridgeshire Regiment, they have a part to play in the Minden Day celebrations. This commemorates the battle on 1 August 1759 when the 12th Foot marched through rose gardens before the battle, and on this day red and yellow roses are worn by all ranks of the 1st Battalion of the Regiment.

General

In time of war the Battalion has a home defence role. There are about 40 WRAC members, usually working in Company HQs as signallers or part of the intelligence cell or MT.

7th Battalion

Companies

A at Scunthorpe and Grimsby;

B (Lincolnshire) at Lincoln, Gainsborough and Boston;
C (Leicester and Derbyshire Yeomanry) at Loughborough, Melton Mowbray and Hinckley;
D (Northamptonshire) at Northampton;
HQ at Leicester.

History

The Battalion formed in 1971 from small cadres keeping alive the traditions of The Leicester and Derbyshire Yeomanry (Prince Albert's Own), The Royal Lincolnshire Regiment, The Royal Leicestershire Regiment and the Northamptonshire Regiment.

General

In time of war, the Battalion is part of 49 Brigade, as part of 2 Infantry Division. To train for this, annual camp is taken either in Germany or the UK. Training has also taken place in the USA, Cyprus, Norway and Iceland. There are many sporting interests, and teams have taken part in soccer, rugby, badminton, orienteering and shooting, including Bisley. Among the adventure training activities are climbing and fell walking.

A section advances under cover of smoke.

Above *In defence on Exercise Keystone (7 R ANGLIAN).*

Right *A torchlight briefing on exercise in Germany (7 R ANGLIAN).*

The King's Division

4th (V) Battalion King's Own Royal Border Regiment

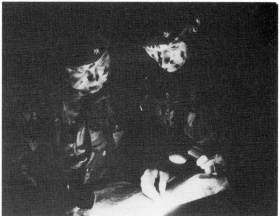

Peel, The Lass of Gowrie and the *Corn Riggs are Bonnie*; the slow march is *And shall Trelawney Die?*

Stable belt

Bands of blue, yellow and blue.

Regimental dress

The buttons showing a dragon and the word *China* commemorate the 55th Regiment's service in China, where they captured the Imperial Dragon Standard. Officers, however, wear the Bath Star of the Border Regiment on the buttons of their number one Dress Caps, Side Hats and Mess Dress waistcoats. Officers

Regimental badge

Within a laurel wreath, a lion and crown.

Regimental marches

The quick march is an arrangement of *D'ye Ken John*

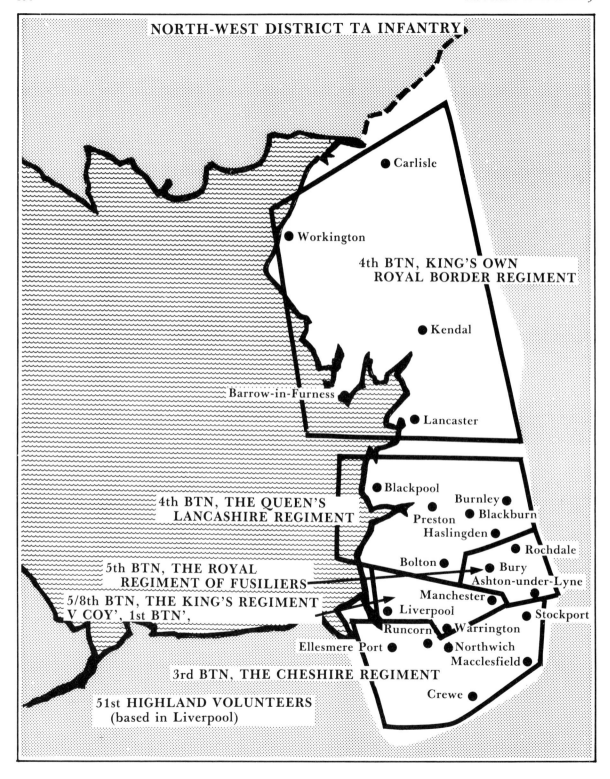

NORTH-WEST DISTRICT TA INFANTRY

● Carlisle

● Workington

**4th BTN, KING'S OWN
ROYAL BORDER REGIMENT**

● Kendal

Barrow-in-Furness

● Lancaster

● Blackpool

Burnley ●

**4th BTN, THE QUEEN'S
LANCASHIRE REGIMENT**

● Preston

Blackburn

Haslingden ●

● Rochdale

**5th BTN, THE ROYAL
REGIMENT OF FUSILIERS**

Bolton ●   ● Bury

Ashton-under-Lyne

**5/8th BTN, THE KING'S REGIMENT
V COY', 1st BTN',**

Manchester ●

Liverpool

● Stockport

Runcorn ●   ● Warrington

Ellesmere Port ●   ● Northwich

Macclesfield ●

3rd BTN, THE CHESHIRE REGIMENT

Crewe ●

**51st HIGHLAND VOLUNTEERS
(based in Liverpool)**

also wear a third *China* button in a triangular form on the cuff of number one Dress, this being a long standing tradition from the Border Regiment.

Companies

A Carlisle
B Kendal and Lancaster;
C at Burrow-in-Furness;
D at Workington;
HQ at Lancaster;
E (HSF) in Lancaster, Kendal and Carlisle.

History

The 4th Battalion was formed in 1975. The Regular Army regiment, of which this is the TA component, was formed on 1 October 1959 by an amalgamation of The King's Own Royal Regiment (Lancaster), and The Border Regiment.

General

In time of war the Battalion mobilizes for home defence duties. Annually one Company undertakes overseas training, and venues have included Cyprus and Gibraltar. Individual soldiers also regularly join the 1st Battalion for training abroad. The Battalion has a number of WRAC on its strength in non-combatant roles, with duties such as signals. Amongst its training activities, the Battalion takes part in the North-West TAVRA Derby Trophy Competition, the Cambrian Marches and the German Patrol Competition.

Leadership training is a virtue gained in the TA. Here 22 year old Lance Corporal Stephen Cottam shows the way (4 KINGS OWN BORDER).

A patrol is briefed (4 KINGS OWN BORDER).

5th/8th (V) Battalion The King's Regiment

Regimental badge
The White Horse of Hanover superimposed upon Fleur de Lys, below this a scroll with *KINGS*.

Colonel-in-Chief
HM Queen Elizabeth the Queen Mother

Regimental marches
The quick march is *Kingsman*, although *Zakmi Dil* may be played prior to the march past, and the slow marches are *The English Rose* and *Farewell Manchester*.

Regimental flags
Three flags are available for use, but only one is flown at any one time. The Colonel's Flag is only flown when the Colonel of the Regiment is in the barracks or on parade, and this is deep green with the Regimental Badge at its centre. The Lieutenant-Colonel's Flag is the Regimental Flag and is deep green with a deep red St George's Cross edged with white and the Regimental Badge at the centre of the cross. The Major's Flag is flown when command of the Battalion or rear party is on someone other than the Commanding Officer. It is also flown by a Company detached from the Battalion. The design is the same as the Lieutenant-Colonel's flag but has a white flame running from the upper dexter canton towards the centre.

Regimental dress
On the beret, the regimental badge is worn on a red cloth backing. The regimental side-hat is worn straight on the head, with the front one-inch above the brow. It is maroon with a deep green piping to the front and rear folds. The regimental badge is backed in green, and the cap has no buttons. Officers and Warrant Officers Class 1 wear a blue/grey shirt when in shirt-sleeve order. These officers also wear a pullover in green wool with a V-neck and green detachable epaulettes with brass badges of rank and *KINGS* titles.

Regimental customs
The rank of private in the Regiment is designated 'Kingsman' (abbreviated to Kgn); the word 'Private' is not used in this context. Nine Regimental Days are celebrated: 28 February is Ladysmith (1900); 16 March is Italy (1944); 2 April is Francilly Salency (1917); 15 May is Burma (1943/45); 10 June is Guadeloupe (1795); 1 July is Somme (1916); 13 August is Blenheim (1704); 14 September is Delhi (1857); and 5 November is Inkerman (1854).

Companies
A and B at Liverpool;
C in Manchester;
D in Warrington;
HQ at Warrington;
E (HSF) at Warrington and Manchester;
The North West Infantry (TA) (King's) Band is at Warrington.

History
In 1957 the Regular Army regiments were re-organized, and about this time the amalgamation took place of The King's Regiment (Liverpool) and The Manchester Regiment under the title the King's Regiment (Manchester and Liverpool). In 1969 the two city names were dropped from the title. Despite this, the TA side of the Regiment continued with one Battalion of The King's Regiment in Liverpool, two in Manchester and one in Ashton-under-Lyne.

Following the disbandment of the TA in 1967, the TA Battalions of the King's Regiment and The Manchester Regiment became companies of the new battalion formed in Lancashire, The Lancastrian Volunteers. In 1972, the reserve forces were expanded with a second Battalion being raised in Lancashire at Preston and at Ashton-under-Lyne. Further expansion in 1975 aligned the TAVR Battalions with their Regular Army sponsors, so the companies of the Lancastrian Volunteers, whose origins were The King's and Manchester Regiments, formed the current Battalion. It is recognized as being the successor to the 5th Battalion The King's Regiment (Liverpool) and 8th (Ardwick) Battalion The Manchester Regiment. When the volunteer movement started in 1859, the 1st Lancashire Rifle Volunteer Corps was founded and it was renamed the First Volunteer Battalion The King's (Liverpool) Regiment in 1888, taking the number '5' in 1908. Detachments were sent to South Africa for the Boer War, and in the First World War, in February 1915, it was with the 2nd Division on the Western Front. Private Arthur Herbert Proctor gained the VC for his action on 4 June 1916 at Ficheux. During the Second World War the Battalion served in the UK until the Normandy landings in 1944.

Guarding key points on land and water on a home defence exercise (5/8 KINGS).

The 8th had a similar history, having been formed in 1860 as the 33 Lancashire Corps, becoming the 20th in 1880, and the 8th (Ardwick) Battalion of The Manchester Regiment in 1888. It also served in the Boer War, and in the First World War served at Gallipoli and Egypt, before moving to the Western Front in 1917. In 1940 it saw service with the BEF and then in Malta, Syria, Egypt, Italy and Palestine.

General

For its wartime role in support of BAOR, the Battalion is organized into four Rifle Companies, with mortar, Milan anti-tank, and reconnaissance platoons. To train for this, annual camp is held in alternate years in Germany, but individual volunteers have exercised with Regular units in Cyprus, Orkney, the West Indies, Kenya and Gibraltar. There are no WRAC serving with the Battalion.

4th (V) Battalion The Queen's Lancashire Regiment

Regimental badge

The Red Rose of Lancaster.

Motto
Loyally I serve.

Colonel-in-Chief
THE QUEEN.

Regimental marches
The quick march is *L'Attaque/The Red Rose,* and the slow march is *Long Live Elizabeth,* from selection No 2 *Merrie England.*

Stable belt
Maroon.

Regimental dress
A yellow and primrose backing to the soldier's beret badge.

Companies
A at Burnley;
B at Blackpool;
C at Bolton;
D at Blackburn and Haslingden;
HQ at Preston (plus mortar and recce platoons).

History
The Battalion was formed in 1974, and carries on the TA traditions of the 4th Lancashire Regiment and 5th The Loyal Regiment (North Lancashire).

General
In time of war its task is to support NATO. The Regiment enjoys the honour of the freedoms of Burnley, Warrington, Mascingden, Blackburn and Preston.

Yorkshire Volunteers

Regimental badge
The White Rose of Yorkshire, ensigned with St Edward's Crown, below a scroll inscribed *Yorkshire.*

Honorary Colonel
Honorary Major General, HRH The Duchess of Kent.

Regimental march
The quick march is *Ilkley Moor.*

Stable belt
Red with a double white stripe.

Regimental dress
The only peculiarity of dress of the Regiment is that on officers' Mess Dress, at the rear of the cuff, one, two, three or four small anodized buttons denote the Battalion of the wearer.

1st Battalion (Cleveland)

Companies
B (The Green Howards) at Middlesbrough;
D at Harrowgate, Northallerton;
G (the Green Howards) at Guisborough and Loftus;
K (The Green Howards) at Coulby Newham;
HQ at York.

History
The Battalion was formed on 1 April 1967 and can trace its history back to the Corps of Yorkshire Rifle Volunteers, raised in 1859 in the North Riding of Yorkshire. In 1860 all the Yorkshire Volunteers were organized into twelve battalion-sized units, which remained virtually unchanged for a century. Although they were consolidated, many retained local identities with their names. Between 1883 and 1887 the Volunteer Battalions were aligned to Regular units, and it was during this time that two of the Battalions became The Green Howards. Detachments fought in the Boer War gaining the 'South Africa' battle honour. In the First World War the Volunteers were mobilized as part of the 50th York and Durham Brigade. From 1915 they saw service in France and Flanders. All the Yorkshire Regiments fought with great distinction, but with many casualties. Again for the Second World War, the Volunteers were mobilized and fought on all fronts. After the War, the Yorkshire Drill Halls came to life again, and by 1961 there were five Yorkshire Battalions. These were reduced to only a small cadre in 1967, except for one Company from each Regiment, which formed the Yorkshire Volunteers.

Fortunes revived in 1971, and this Battalion became the basis for an expansion. The cadres of the other regiments were reinforced with those from the former Yorkshire Artillery Volunteers, to raise the 2nd and 3rd Battalions.

General
In time of war this Battalion is mobilized in support of BAOR, and annual camp is spent both in the UK and Germany.

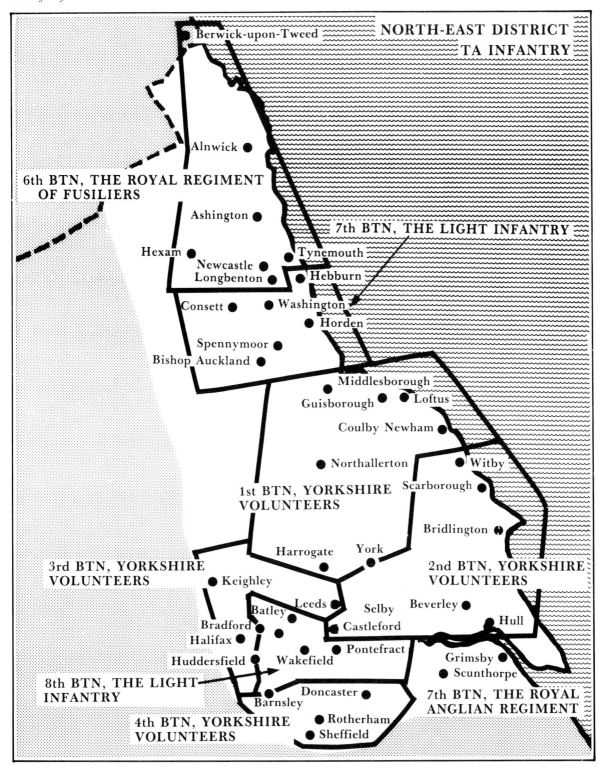

NORTH-EAST DISTRICT
TA INFANTRY

Berwick-upon-Tweed

Alnwick

6th BTN, THE ROYAL REGIMENT
OF FUSILIERS

Ashington

7th BTN, THE LIGHT INFANTRY

Hexam
Tynemouth
Newcastle
Longbenton
Hebburn
Consett
Washington
Horden
Spennymoor
Bishop Auckland

Middlesborough
Guisborough
Loftus
Coulby Newham
Northallerton
Witby
Scarborough

1st BTN, YORKSHIRE
VOLUNTEERS

Bridlington

Harrogate
York

3rd BTN, YORKSHIRE
VOLUNTEERS

2nd BTN, YORKSHIRE
VOLUNTEERS

Keighley

Selby
Beverley
Leeds
Hull
Batley
Bradford
Castleford
Halifax
Pontefract
Huddersfield
Wakefield
Grimsby
Scunthorpe

8th BTN, THE LIGHT
INFANTRY
Doncaster
7th BTN, THE ROYAL
ANGLIAN REGIMENT
Barnsley

4th BTN, YORKSHIRE
VOLUNTEERS
Rotherham
Sheffield

2nd Battalion (Yorkshire and Humberside)

Companies

A at York and Selby;
B at Hull;
C at Castleford;
D at Scarborough, Whitby, Bridlington and Beverley;
HQ at York.

History

This was one of the two Battalions formed in 1971 from the cadres of the old Yorkshire Regiments, including the Yorkshire Artillery Volunteers.

General

The wartime role calls for support of BAOR.

3rd Battalion (West Yorkshire)

Companies

A at Keighley and Bradford;
B at Leeds;
C at Huddersfield;
D at Halifax;
HQ at Huddersfield.

History

The Battalion was formed in 1971 alongside the 2nd Battalion, and carries on the TA traditions of the Duke of Wellington's Regiment, The Leeds Rifles, and the West Riding Artillery Regiments. Through them, the Battalion history goes back to the middle of the last century.

General

The wartime role of the 3rd Battalion is for home defence, so most training is taken in the UK. There are 60 WRAC included in the strength, undertaking such roles as clerks, drivers, signallers, cooks and medics. The Battalion's running team has had success, having won the TA Championships in 1986 and 1987. The Rifle team has competed successfully in District, TA and National Rifle Association events at Bisley. The Battalion enjoys the honour of the freedoms of Mirfield, Huddersfield, Leeds, Halifax, Keighley and Morley.

4th Battalion (South Yorkshire)

Companies

A (Hallamshire) at Barnsley;
B (Sheffield Artillery Volunteers) at Rotherham;
C (York and Lancaster) at Doncaster;
D (Hallamshire) at Endcliffe Hall, Sheffield;
HQ (Sheffield Artillery Volunteers) Endcliffe Hall;

The volunteers had captured the town on Exercise Keystone, so a sweep of the streets of Ottenstein was needed to secure the area (2 YORKS).

H (York and Lancaster) (HSF) at Endcliffe Hall, Doncaster, Rotherham and Barnsley.

History

The 4th Battalion was started on 1 January 1987 with D Company from the 1st Battalion. So that it could be constituted on 1 January 1988, the other Companies were added: A was formerly D Company 3 YORKS; B was formerly B Company 3 YORKS, and C was formerly E Company 1 YORKS. The Battalion is considered the direct successor to the Hallamshire Battalion of the York and Lancaster Regiment and Sheffield Artillery Volunteers. Among the distinguished history of its antecedents, the Hallamshire Battalion was engaged in the ill-managed campaign in Norway in 1940, when they provided the final rearguard for the evacuation by Lord Louis Mountbatten's Fifth Flotilla. They garrisoned Iceland from then until D-Day.

General

The Battalion is a Home Defence unit, and WRAC are included in non-combatant roles.

Above *3rd Volunteer Battalion of The West Yorkshire Regiment parade for Queen Victoria's Jubilee* (RHQ YORKS).

Below *1912: the machine-gun detachment of the Leeds Rifles at annual camp at Hunmanby* (RHQ YORKS).

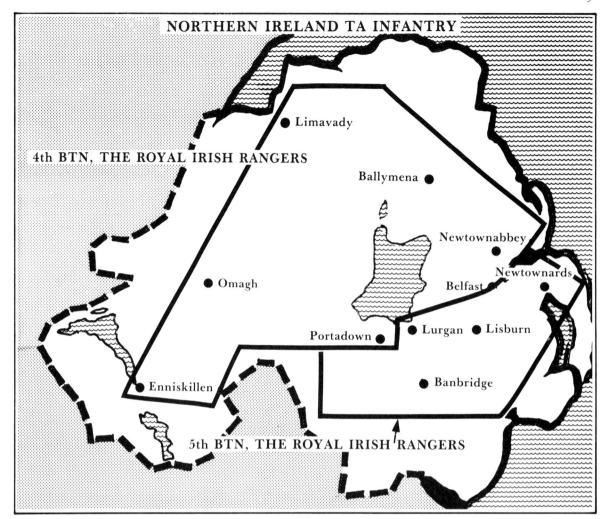

4th (V) Battalion, The Royal Irish Rangers (North Irish Militia)

Regimental badge
Tara Harp in silver.

Regimental marches
The quick march is *The Regimental March of the Royal Irish Rangers* and *Killaloe*, and the slow march is *Eileen Allanagh*.

Motto
Faugh a Ballagh (Clear the way).

Companies
A (Royal Inniskilling Fusiliers) at Omagh, Co. Tyrone, and Enniskillen, Co. Fermanagh;
B (Royal Ulster Rifles) at Newtownabbey, Belfast;
C (Royal Irish Fusiliers) at Ballymena, Co. Antrim, and Limavady, Co. Londonderry;
D (London Irish Rifles) at Chelsea in London, and Hillingdon, Middlesex;
HQ at Portadown, Co. Armagh.

History

In 1967 the four Irish TA infantry battalions were reduced to company strength. These were the 5th Royal Inniskilling Fusiliers, 6th The Royal Ulster Rifles, 5th The Royal Irish Fusiliers and The London Irish Rifles. These then came together to form The North Irish Militia. On 18 April 1978 the title changed to that in use today. Each company maintains the traditions of its former Regiment by including it in its title and wearing its collar badge.

The regimental history of the London Irish, now D Company, records that the football team of the 1st Battalion, 18th (County of London) Battalion, the London Regiment (London Irish Rifles), kicked a football across no man's land in an assault on the German line at the Battle of Loos on 25 September 1915. The ball, which led the assault and found its way into the German front line, was later recovered, and is now preserved in the Regimental Museum.

On 9 June 1988, to celebrate the 21st anniversary of the Regiment, the Regimental Colour was trooped at the Redford Cavalry Barracks in Edinburgh. The Bugles, Pipes and Drums of the Battalion, supported by the Northern Ireland (TA) Staff Band provided the music for the event. This unusual grouping of Bugles, Pipes and Drums is unique to The Royal Irish Rangers, and is part of regimental tradition.

Above *4(V) R IRISH on parade in Service Dress.*

Below *Teamwork means helping your mates along to reach the end* (4 R IRISH).

General

To train for its war role in support of BAOR, annual camp is taken either in the UK or in Germany. The riflemen have to master all the infantry skills, with members of the Anti-Tank, Mortar and Reconnaisance platoons having to be capable of operating their specialist weapons systems.

5th (V) Battalion, The Royal Irish Rangers (27th (Inniskilling) 83rd and 87th)

Regimental badge

An Irish Harp and crown above *Royal Irish Rangers.*

Regimental marches

The same as for the 4th Battalion.

Stable belt

Green, with black leather.

Regimental dress

The uniform of the Royal Irish Rangers reflects those of its predecessor regiments, two of which were Fusiliers and one Light Infantry. The black buttons and leather crossbelt (for officers) of the Rifles are worn, but the crossbelt is brown rather than black.

Companies

A at Lisburn;
B at Newtownards;
C at Lurgan;
D at Belfast;
HQ and Support Weapons Platoons at Banbridge.

History

On 1 April 1972, the Battalion was formed incorporating the cadres of the 6th The Royal Ulster Rifles and the 7th The Royal Irish Fusiliers. Initially Battalion HQ and a Command and Admin Platoon were established at Armagh, with B Company at Killyleagh and C Company at Lurgan. There was some opposition to the formation of the unit in the first place, with an attitude of 'it will never live'. Fortunately the doubters were overruled and the Battalion has flourished. It gained its BAOR role in 1978, and has participated in two major exercises since then, Crusader in 1980 and Lionheart in 1984. On 26 August 1981, the Battalion was presented with its own Colours by HRH Princess Alice, Duchess of Gloucester at a ceremony at Ballymena. Since its formation there have been a number of changes. In 1978 a detachment of B Company formed in Bangor. In 1981, C Company from 4 R IRISH transferred to this Battalion as A Company. 1982, B Company moved to Newtownards and HQ Company with the Support Weapons Group moved to Banbridge, but Battalion HQ remained in Armagh. In 1986 D Company formed in Lisburn, but two years later it moved to South Belfast. Also in 1986, the Recce Platoon formed in Armagh.

On 5 March, the Battalion celebrates Barrosa Day. This commemorates the Battle of Barrosa which was fought in 1811 by the 2nd Battalion of the 87th Regiment, who were later to become the Royal Irish Fusiliers, and whose number is commemorated in todays Battalion's title. At Barrosa the 87th were commanded by a Major Gough, promoted to Lieutenant-Colonel after the Battle, and later becoming Field Marshall and the first Viscount Gough. The Battle was a major engagement in the Peninsular War against Napoleon's French Army in Spain. Despite the fact that the French numbered twice the British Forces, it was a victory against them. The Eagle Standard of the French 8th Regiment of Infantry was captured by Sergeant Masterson of the 87th with the immortal cry, 'Be jabers, boys, oi have the cuckoo'. Ever since, the Battle has been commemorated at a formal dinner in the Officer's Messes of the Regiment, and the Royal Irish Rangers have continued the tradition since the amalgamation of the Irish infantry regiments. There are two particular ceremonies peculiar to Barrosa night. Tradition has it that after the battle, the officers retired to their mess waggon for refreshment, only to discover that an accident had smashed all the bottles, leaving their various contents mixed together in the bottom of the vehicle. Undaunted, they availed themselves of the mixture, drinking it all. This is commemorated by the Barrosa Cup, a potent mixture of wines and liqueurs, the recipe of which is a closely-guarded secret, passed down by the Mess Sergeants. It is passed round the table with each officer making the toast to 'Barrosa' until the cup is empty. During this ceremony the officers sing a mournful poem recounting the details of the Battle.

The other highlight of the evening is the Barrosa speech, which is delivered by the latest-joined subaltern. He relates the story of the Battle, but has to include the names of currently-serving officers in the order of battle. The speaker is credited with complete innocence, so there is much pre-speech priming, and many senior officers manage to get a few rude comments included. The honour of holding the dinner is rotated yearly between the two TA Ranger Battalions and the Regimental Depot in Ballymena.

General

The Battalion's war role is with BAOR, and this means frequent annual camps in Germany. High levels of skill are demanded for this role, in addition to specialist skills needed to operate the 81mm mortar, and the Milan anti-tank weapon, both of which are used by the Battalion.

The Prince of Wales's Division

4th (V) Battalion The Devonshire and Dorset Regiment (1st Rifle Volunteers)

Regimental badge

The Sphinx superimposed upon the Castle of Exeter.

Colonel-in-Chief

Major-General HRH The Duke of Kent, KG.

Regimental marches

The quick march is an arrangement of *Widecombe Fair, We've Lived and Loved Together* and *The Maid of Glenconnel.*

Stable belt

Brunswick Green with a tawney stripe, and fastened on the left side.

Regimental Dress

Senior NCOs and Officers wear a green lanyard on the left side, and all ranks wear the Croix de Guerre at the top of each sleeve.

Companies

A at Plymouth;
B at Paignton;
E in Exeter;
HQ in Exeter;
G (HSF) in Plymouth (from 1989).

History

The Battalion formed on 12 October 1988, but as a part of the Devonshire and Dorset Regiment it carries on the same traditions. Its regimental badge is a mixture of features from both the old Devonshire and Dorset Regiments. The Castle of Exeter and the motto, *Semper Fidelis* (Ever Faithful) both come from the Devonshire badge, and the Sphinx and Battle Honour 'Marabout' from the Dorset Regiment. The Dorset's motto, *Primus in Indus* is also on the badge. Both regiments have Regular Army history back to the seventeenth and eighteenth centuries, and Territorial Battalions of each regiment served with distinction in both World Wars.

The Regiment has maintained close connections with the Duchy of Kent since 1802 when the 54th (Dorset Regiment) was stationed in Gibraltar, where the first Duke of Kent, HRH Prince Edward, was the Governor. On Boxing Day 1802, elements of the Army on Gibraltar mutinied, but the 54th stayed loyal. To protect Prince Edward they had to open fire. This incident was particularly significant, because on 24 May seventeen years later, the Duke and Duchess of Kent gave birth to a daughter who, at the age of 18, became Queen Victoria. Prince Edward presented a magnificent silver Rose Bowl, and this is still used in the Mess. Her Royal Highness Princess Marina, Duchess of Kent, was Colonel-in-Chief of the Dorset Regiment from 1953, and when the Regiments amalgamated on 17 May 1958 she graciously agreed to continue as Colonel-in-Chief of the new Regiment, which she did until her death in 1968.

General

The Battalion has been raised for home defence duties, and WRAC are recruited for administrative and supporting roles. The Regiment has freedom of a number of cities, boroughs and towns, through which it is allowed to march with drums beating, bayonets fixed and Colours flying. These are Lyme Regis, Barnstaple, Poole, Dorchester, Blandford, Exeter, Bridport, Torbay, Weymouth, Christchurch and Plymouth.

The Wessex Regiment (Rifle Volunteers)

Regimental badge

The Wessex Wyvern on a plinth inscribed *Wessex*.

Regimental march

The quick march is *The Farmer's Boy*.

1st Battalion

Battalion motto

'Their Land to Defend'.

Stable belt

Cambridge Blue, with the Wyvern Badge on the buckle.

Companies

A at Gloucester, Bristol and Cinderford;
B at Swindon;
C at Dorchester and Weymouth;
D at Poole and Bournemouth;
HQ at Devizes, Gloucester, Andover and Cheltenham.

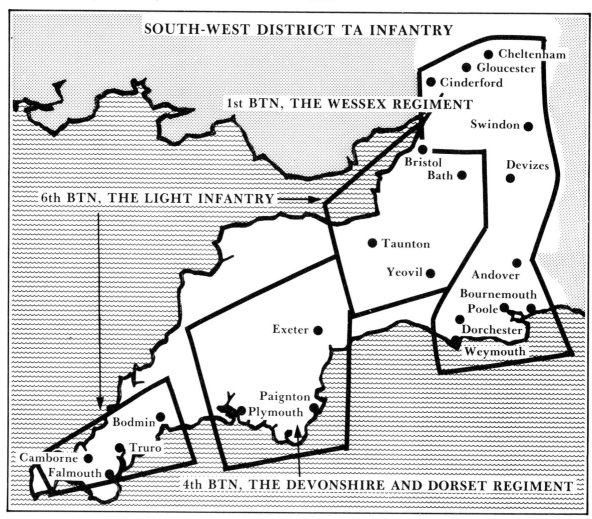

Trying out the new SA80 personal weapon (1 WESSEX).

History

In 1967 the Battalion was formed from the former TA battalions of the county regiments of Devon, Dorset, Gloucestershire, Hampshire, Berkshire and Wiltshire. The Regimental Badge, the Wessex Wyvern, was made famous during the Second World War as the badge of the 43rd (Wessex) Division. The mythical figure has been used by fighting men from the West Country since the sixth century; King Harold used it at the Battle of Hastings, and it is featured on the Bayeux Tapestry.

In 1971 the Battalion was redesignated the 1st Battalion The Wessex Volunteers, and granted its full title the following year.

Through C Company it can trace its origins back to 1573, when the Shire Levies were raised in Dorset and Dorchester. The Dorset Militia became the first regiment to enroll in 1757 and to receive arms under Pitt's Militia Act; as a result, for many years the figure '1' was used on their badges and appointments. In 1814 the Militia and Volunteers were disbanded, but in 1830 the Regiment of Dorset Yeomanry Cavalry was raised again. In 1859 No. 3 Corps (Dorchester) Rifle Volunteers formed in Dorchester. In 1881 the Dorsetshire Regiment, 1st Volunteer Battalion, was in existence, with C (3rd) Company Dorset Rifle Volunteers joining them. In 1899 volunteers saw service in South Africa, and the following year a company of Imperial Yeomanry Cavalry was raised in the county.

General

In time of war the Battalion has a role to support NATO, and it is one of the few 'teeth arm' TA units that is part of a Regular Army Infantry Brigade as part of the UK Mobile Force. This gives it a unique role, and training for this takes place in the UK and in Germany. To train for their role, they rely a great deal on the RAF, with whom they have developed a good relationship, as mobility in time of war is provided by helicopters. The Battalion is active in various inter-service events and D company send a team to take part in the annual Ypres Marches. Shooting teams from the Battalion are also regular winners at Bisley. A group of volunteers went to Canada in 1983 to train with the 1st Battalion The Gloucestershire Regiment, and other soldiers have served with the 1st The Duke of Edinburgh's Royal Regiment on a UN tour in Cyprus.

2nd Battalion

Companies

A at Portsmouth;
B at Winchester, Southampton and Newport I.O.W.;
C at Maidenhead, Slough and Basingstoke;
D at Reading;
HQ at Reading;
E (HSF) at Reading, Maidenhead, Winchester and Portsmouth.

History

The Battalion carries on the TA traditions of the Royal Berkshire and the Royal Hampshire Regiments.

General

In time of war it has a home defence role and for training uses many of the UK training areas, usually taking annual camp in this country. In 1986, one company trained at Fort Indiantown Gap in

Pennsylvania as part of an exchange with the US Army National Guard. The training covers all infantry work, including combat survival, patrolling and operating with helicopters. Each man has to be efficient at his personal weapon, and field firing at platoon level usually includes support from the Battalion's own 81 mm mortars. Each of the TA centres is equipped with its own miniature rifle range. Members of the WRAC serve in such tasks as signallers, cooks, drivers and medical assistants. Teams have entered the annual Ypres Marches as well as the Cambrian Marches and the Devizes to Westminster Canoe Race. In 1987 the WRAC team won the district's WRAC cross-country competition.

The Cheshire Regiment 3rd (Volunteer) Battalion (The 22nd (Cheshire) Regiment)

Regimental badge
An Acorn leaved and slipped.

Colonel-in-Chief
HRH The Prince of Wales and Earl of Chester, KG.

Regimental marches
The quick march is *Wha wadna fecht for Charlie?* and the slow march is *The 22nd Regiment Slow March 1772.*

Stable belt
Three bands, of cerise, buff and cerise.

Companies
A at Stockport;
B at Macclesfield;
C at Ellesmere Port;
D at Crewe and Northwich;
HQ at Runcorn.

History
The Cheshire Regiment was raised in the Wirral and in the area of Chester in 1689, and has never been amalgamated with any other Regular Army regi-

ment, remaining active until this day. It is the County of Cheshire's infantry regiment and has borne the county title since 1782.

The volunteers in the county started in 1859 with the 1st Cheshire Rifle Volunteers at Birkenhead and Wirral, 2nd in Chester, 3rd in Northwich, 4th in Stockport and the 5th in Congleton and Macclesfield. These became Volunteer Battalions in 1882 and by the First World War had become the 4th at Birkenhead, 5th at Chester and Mid-Cheshire, 6th at Stockport and 7th at Macclesfield. These same Battalions fought in the Second World War. In 1947 the 5th and 6th Battalions were disbanded, and the 4th and 7th continued as TA units in West and East Cheshire respectively until they amalgamated into one as the 4th/7th Battalion in 1967. This lasted only two years, and was disbanded in 1969. The only remaining TA infantry unit in the county was A company of the Mercian Volunteers in Stockport, until 2 MERCIAN raised a company in Ellesmere Port. These two companies formed the basis for the new Battalion when it was raised on 5 April 1988, and its formation was completed by early 1989, the 300th anniversary of the Regiment, when both the Regular and TA Battalions received new Colours.

General
In time of war the role of the Battalion will be in home defence. The Regiment has the freedom of Chester, Macclesfield, Birkenhead, Stockport, Crewe, Nantwich, Ellesmere Port and Neston.

3rd (V) Battalion the Royal Welch Fusiliers

Regimental badge
A Grenade Flamed, proper, within, the crest of The Prince of Wales.

Colonel-in-Chief
THE QUEEN.

Regimental marches
The quick march is *The British Grenadiers,* and the slow marches are *The War Song of The Men of Glamorgan* and *Forth to the Battle.*

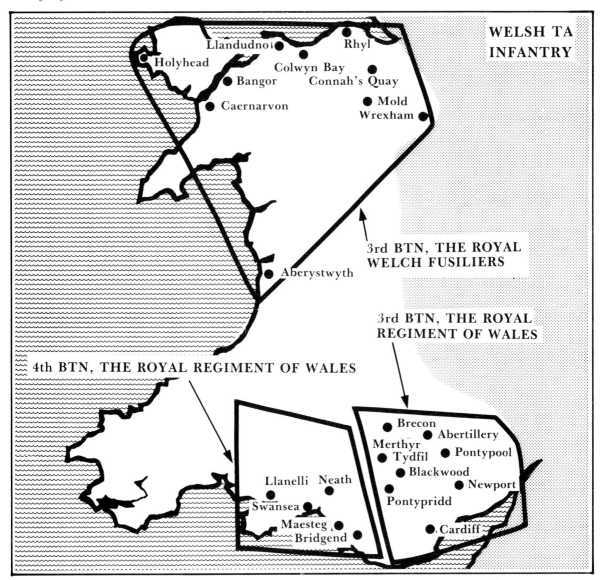

WELSH TA INFANTRY

Holyhead
Llandudno
Rhyl
Colwyn Bay
Bangor
Connah's Quay
Caernarvon
Mold
Wrexham

3rd BTN, THE ROYAL WELCH FUSILIERS

3rd BTN, THE ROYAL REGIMENT OF WALES

4th BTN, THE ROYAL REGIMENT OF WALES

Aberystwyth

Brecon
Abertillery
Merthyr
Tydfil
Pontypool
Blackwood
Llanelli Neath
Newport
Swansea
Pontypridd
Maesteg
Bridgend
Cardiff

Companies

A at Aberystwyth;
B at Colwyn Bay, Llandudno and Rhyl;
C at Connah's Quay and Mold;
D at Caernarfon, Bangor and Holyhead;
HQ at Wrexham.

Stable belt

Maroon and blue.

Customs and traditions

The five black ribbons that a Royal Welch Fusilier wears on the back of his collar in service dress make him unmistakeable. They are a vestige of the days when soldiers wore pigtails, which were powdered and greased. To protect the tunics or coatees, the pigtail was worn in a bag, known as the 'queue bag'. The 'queue' for British soldiers was abolished in 1808, but at that time the Regiment was serving in Nova Scotia, and because of the poor communications of the day, they were probably the last to wear it. The ribbons which secured the queue were retained, and became know as the 'flash', this being the old slang word for a wig. It is recorded that in 1834 when the Regiment arrived at Gosport from Gibraltar, a General ordered the flash to be removed, but the

Colonel of the Regiment rushed to London and returned within twenty-four hours with a letter announcing that His Majesty King William IV had been pleased to grant the flash as a 'peculiarity whereby to mark the dress of that distinguished Regiment.'

The custom of wearing a White Hackle originated in 1702 when the 23rd Foot was formed into a regiment of Fusiliers, and therefore adopted the same pattern of head dress as the Grenadier companies of line Regiments. About 1709 the officers of the Regiment began to wear feathers in their hats, this being officially approved in 1789 when it was laid down that the hackle would be white.

A tradition of the Regiment is the Regimental Goat, a custom which was already long standing as far back as 1777. The first Royal Goat was donated by Queen Victoria in 1844. It is never referred to as a mascot.

In messes, the Loyal Toast is never proposed except on St David's Day, nor do the officers and their guests stand when the National Anthem is played at the conclusion of the band's programme in the mess. This custom has no written origin, but His Majesty King George IV is said to have expressed the wish that the Loyal Toast should be dispensed with. This was following the address of loyalty from the Royal Welch Fusiliers after they had refused to join the Mutiny at the Nore in 1797.

St David's Day is celebrated religiously by the Regiment. Leeks are worn, and those who have never eaten one are required to do so, and when the toasts are proposed on that day, they are all concluded with the words 'and St David'. It is still traditional to include on the toast list 'Toby Purcell, His Spurs and St David', Toby Purcell having been the Regiment's first Second-in-Command, who distinguished himself at the Battle of the Boyne in 1690, his spurs having been worn by successive seconds-in-command, until they were lost in 1842. It is tradition that after the dinner, the Goat is led around the table followed by a drummer, fifers and the drum major carrying a silver salver on which are leeks. The mess sergeant also follows with a loving cup filled with champagne. This procession halts at the chair of the most recently joined Subaltern, who stands on his chair, places his right foot on the table, and eats a leek. While he is eating, the drummer plays a continuous roll. He then drinks from the loving cup for a toast to St David. All present, including guests, who have not eaten leek are expected to do so before they leave the mess.

The same ceremonial is carried out in the Sergeants' Mess and the other ranks' dining hall.

The spelling of Welch with a 'c' is left over from the old English spelling, but the Regiment clung to this form when other Regiments changed to the new form of 'Welsh'. Army Order 56 of 1920 confirmed the 'c' spelling.

History

There have been a number of Territorial battalions of the Regiment, and in the Second World War, after landing on the Normandy beaches, they fought with the Army across Northern Europe. Because of their fighting at s'Hertogenbosch and in the Reichwald, the people of that town still honour the Regiment. After the war, some of the TA units were converted to anti-aircraft or anti-tank gunners and parachutists, but the Regiment was reduced to a cadre, before being re-formed as the 3rd (V) Battalion.

The Royal Regiment of Wales (24/41st Foot)

Regimental badge

The Prince of Wales's Feather, and the collar badges are a wreath of immortelles with the Welsh Dragon superimposed.

Colonel-in-Chief

HRH The Prince of Wales KG.

Regimental marches

The quick march is *Men of Harlech* and the slow march is *Scipio*.

Stable belt

Bands of green, red, white, red and green.

3rd (V) Battalion

Companies

A at Abertillery and Blackwood;
B at Newport and Pontypool;
C at Pontypridd and Merthyr Tydfil;
D at Cardiff;
HQ at Maindy Barracks in Cardiff;
E (HSF) in Cardiff and Brecon.
Anti-tank Platoon is at Pentre, mortar platoon at Cwmcarn and the band in Cardiff.

History

The Battalion was formed on 1 April 1971 and can

trace its ancestry back to the earliest volunteer forces in Wales. In 1859 the various Welsh companies were formed into battalions on a county basis, including the 1st, 2nd and 3rd Monmouthshire Rifle Volunteer Corps. In 1881, following the Cardwell reforms, the 1st Glamorgans became the 2nd Volunteer Battalion The Welch Regiment, the 2nd Glamorgans became the 3rd Volunteer Battalion The Welch Regiment, and the 3rd Glamorgans retained their old title, The Swansea Rifles. At the same time the Monmouthshire battalions became the 2nd, 3rd and 4th Battalions The South Wales Borderers. The further reorganization in 1908 established the 1st, 2nd and 3rd Battalions The Monmouthshire Regiment, the Glamorganshire RHA and the 5th and 6th Battalions of The Welch Regiment. In 1914 all these units went to war, serving in France and the Middle East. On the re-forming of the TA from 1920 onwards, four battalions of infantry and one searchlight regiment RE were formed. During the Second World War the battalions saw action again, and two VCs were gained. These were to Lieutenant Tasker Watkins of the 1/5th Welch for his actions on 16 August 1944 at Martigny in France, and Corporal Edward Thomas Chapman at the Dortmund Ems Canal on 2 April 1945.

In 1947 TA units once again formed in South Wales, and in 1967 a new regiment was raised as The Welsh Volunteers, but this ceased in 1971, and on further reorganization this battalion came into being, the latest change being in 1984 when D company was added.

The Battalion usually celebrates St Davids Day on 1 March each year, and Gheluvet Day on 31 October. This commemorates a battle which took place on 31 October 1914 around Gheluvelt which involved the 2nd Battalion The Monmouthshire Regiment as well as two other Welsh Regiments, the South Wales Borderers and The Welch Regiment. The Germans made a supreme effort to break through to Ypres and on to the Channel ports, but the Welshmen held the village, despite repeated infantry attacks and appalling casualties, especially for The Welch Regiment. Although Rorke's Drift Day, 22 January, is not celebrated by the Battalion as a whole, it is commemorated by B Company, who claim a link with B Company 24th Foot who fought in the action.

General

The role of the Battalion in time of war is to support NATO, so annual camps are often taken abroad. To supplement training, detachments have trained with the regular Battalion, and in 1987 joined them in Canada. Two junior officers were able to take part in Operation Raleigh. On the sporting side, numbers of the Battalion have won the Welsh 1000's cross-

country competition for five years running, and are the TA champions at the sport. Teams also enter for the Cambrian Patrol competition and the Wales Skill at Arms Championships.

4th (V) Battalion

Companies

A at Llanelli;
B at Neath;
C at Bridgend and Maesteg;
D (City of Swansea) in Swansea;
HQ in Swansea.

History

The Battalion in its present form goes back to 1971, and it enjoys, with the Regiment, the Freedom of the Boroughs of Llanelli, Swansea and Dynevor. The origins, however, go back to 1859, and since then its names have changed often:
1859 Milford Haven Volunteer Company;
1860 1st Pembrokeshire Rifle Volunteers;
1881 1st Volunteer Battalion The Welch Regiment;
1908 4th Battalion The Welch Regiment;
1960 Cadre 4th (Territorial) Battalion The Welch Regiment;
1967 4th (Carmarthenshire) Battalion The Welch Regiment (TA);
1971 4th (V) Battalion The Royal Regiment of Wales.

64 officers and men went to the Boer War under the command of Captain Picton Evans from Carmarthen, who was mentioned in despatches for his special and meritorious services. Called up for the First World War, there was action at Gallipoli, and from there to the Western Desert until the end of the war. Mobilized in 1939 at Gowerton for the Second World War, the Battalion trained in Northern Ireland, then back to Southern England for the invasion of France.

After landing in Normandy on 17 June 1944, the first action of the Battalion in the last war was at Grainville sur Odon on 30th June 1944 and before first light it had repelled three strong counter attacks. The anti tank platoon 'killed' a Tiger tank with the first rounds of ammunition fired in action. The Battalion broke through the Seigfried Line in the Reichwald between 9 and 13 February 1945, and remained in action until the end of the war, when it was on the outskirts of Hamburg.

General

In time of war, the role of the Battalion is in Home Defence. Members often undertake exchange training with the United States National Guard. Companies have visited Virginia and Massachusetts, and the National Guard have been hosted at Sennybridge. On

Guarding key points in South Wales (4 RRW).

a regular basis a company goes to Gibraltar to take over guard duties from the resident Regular Battalion. Every two years the West German Army Reserve send some officers to join in with the summer exercises. WRAC are part of the Battalion, taking on such roles as cooks, pay clerks, drivers, signallers and as part of the Intelligence Section. Teams from the Battalion have taken part in the Nijmegan and Cambrian Marches, and the Welsh 1000's cross-country competition.

The Worcestershire and Sherwood Foresters Regiment

Regimental badge
A Maltese cross Pommettee charged with the Garter in gold encircling a stag in silver lodged on water proper thereunder a plinth inscribed *FIRM* in gold, the whole upon an elongated star of eights in silver.

Colonel-in-Chief
HRH The Princess Royal GCVO.

Regimental marches
The quick march is an arrangement of *Young May Moon* and *Royal Windsor*, and the slow march is *Duchess of Kent*.

Stable belt
Three equal bands of Lincoln Green, Maroon and Lincoln Green.

Regimental dress
The only peculiarity is that officers wear the sword frog with the Sam Browne belt when in service dress.

Honours
The Regiment has the freedom of a number of cities and towns: Chesterfield, Nottingham, Derby, Ilkeston, Mansfield, Newark, Worksop, East Retford and Buxton.

3rd (V) Battalion

Companies
A (Sherwood Rangers Yeomanry) at Mansfield and Retford;
B (Leicestershire and Derbyshire Yeomanry) at Sutton in Ashfield and Ilkeston;
C (Derby Foresters) at Derby and Chesterfield;
D (Robin Hood Foresters) at Beeston in Nottingham;
E (Notts Foresters) at Worksop;
HQ at Newark;
F (Nottinghamshire HSF) at Worksop, Mansfield and Beeston;

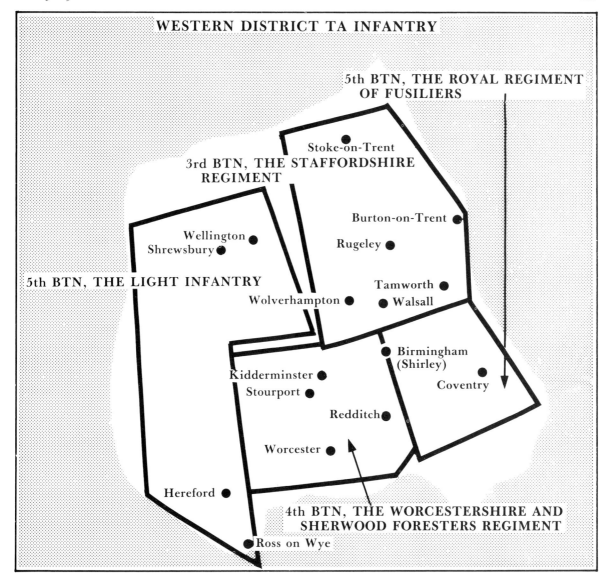

WESTERN DISTRICT TA INFANTRY

5th BTN, THE ROYAL REGIMENT
OF FUSILIERS

Stoke-on-Trent

3rd BTN, THE STAFFORDSHIRE
REGIMENT

Burton-on-Trent

Wellington
Shrewsbury

Rugeley

5th BTN, THE LIGHT INFANTRY

Tamworth

Wolverhampton

Walsall

Birmingham
(Shirley)

Kidderminster

Coventry

Stourport

Redditch

Worcester

Hereford

4th BTN, THE WORCESTERSHIRE AND
SHERWOOD FORESTERS REGIMENT

Ross on Wye

G (Derbyshire HSF) at Derby and Chesterfield.

History

The Regiment formed on 28 February 1970 by the amalgamation of The Worcestershire Regiment and The Sherwood Foresters Regiment. The 3rd Battalion was raised in 1971 by including the cadres of Yeomanry Regiments and Infantry Battalions that had survived the 1967 reorganization, and it is based solely in Nottinghamshire and Derbyshire. It carried on, therefore, the TA traditions of The Sherwood Rangers Yeomanry, The South Notts Hussars Yeomanry, the 5th (Derbyshire) Battalion The Sher-

wood Foresters, the 7th (Robin Hood) Battalion The Sherwood Foresters, and the 8th (Nottinghamshire) Battalion The Sherwood Foresters. Originally in deference to their previous roles, the Sherwood Rangers Yeomanry became A Squadron, and the South Notts Hussars Yeomanry became B Battery. A further change took place four years later and B Battery went and A Squadron became A Company. A fifth Rifle Company was raised in 1978 and this was designated B (Leicestershire and Derbyshire Yeomanry) Company.

On 1 January 1980 a full HQ Company was authorized and this formed up on 1 March 1980. Each year, the Battalion takes part in three parades, Remembrance Sunday, St George's Day and Crich. In 1987, instead of the usual St George's Day parade, the Battalion trooped its Colour in the presence of their Colonel-in-Chief.

Because of their work as air defence artillery in the low countries in the Second World War, 7th Foresters, now D (Robin Hood Foresters) Company, were awarded the Belgian Croix de Guerre.

General

In time of war the Battalion, as part of 54 Brigade, has home defence duties. The 1st Battalion of the Regiment provides the Permanent Staff Instructors, as well as necessary Regular officers and RSM. To train for its role, it mainly uses UK training areas, but it has taken its annual camp in the Isle of Man, and has sent composite companies on three occasions to Gibraltar and once to Cyprus in 1987. Individuals have also undertaken exchange visits to the USA and Germany. Small parties have attended short periods of training with the Regulars of the 1st Battalion and also in Canada. Whilst Lieutenant (now Captain) Peter Platt was on an exchange visit to the USA, he was awarded their Army Achievement Medal for giving first aid at the scene of an accident involving a US Army vehicle and personnel of the 1st Battalion, 104th Infantry. Members of the WRAC are serving with the Battalion as clerks, in the QM's department, as mess staff and with the signals platoon.

4th (V) Battalion

Companies

A at Worcester and Stourport;
B at Kidderminster;
C at Shirley;
D in Nottingham;
HQ at Redditch in Worcestershire.

History

The origins of this Battalion go back to 1967 when the TA Battalions of the Cheshire, Worcestershire, Staffordshire, Nottinghamshire and Derbyshire Regiments were disbanded into cadre form. Many of these contributed considerably to the creation of the new Regiment of the Midlands, 'The Mercian Volunteers'. A number of new Home Defence Battalions were formed in 1971, and one of these was the Light Infantry and Mercian Volunteers. This new Regiment disbanded in 1975 and the 2nd Battalion The Mercian Volunteers was raised in its place. On 5 April 1988 the title 'Mercian Volunteers' was replaced and it rebadged to its new Regiment. The original battalion in 1971 had a number of different cap badges, and even different rates of marching between Com-

panies, light and heavy infantry paces. These matters were standardized with the 1975 reorganization.

General

In time of war the Battalion supports BAOR and annual camp therefore takes place either in the UK or Germany. Its shooting team had success at Bisley in 1983, carrying off the China Cup. They also take part in the Cambrian and Nijmegen Marches.

3rd (V) Battalion The Staffordshire Regiment (The Prince of Wales's)

Regimental badge

The Prince of Wales's Plume within the Stafford Knot.

Regimental marches

The Quick March is *The Staffordshire Regiment,* an arrangement of *Come Lassies and Lads* and *The Days we went a gipsying,* and the slow march is *God Bless the Prince of Wales.*

Stable belt

Plain black.

Companies

A at Tamworth;
B at Stoke-on-Trent;
C at Burton on Trent and Rugeley;
D at Walsall;
HQ at Wolverhampton.

History

On 5 April 1988 the Battalion took its present title, having been the 1st Battalion The Mercian Volunteers until that date. They had originally been raised on 1 April 1967, and became the direct successors to the early TA battalions of the County Regiments of Cheshire, Staffordshire, Worcestershire and Nottinghamshire. The name and cap badge were derived from the Kingdom and crest of Leofric, Earl of Mercia, better known through his wife, Lady Godiva.

General

The wartime role is to support BAOR, and as such it is equipped to the same level as a Regular Army non-mechanized infantry Battalion, and training takes places in the UK and Germany.

The Light Division
The Light Infantry

Regimental badge

A bugle horn, stringed, in silver.

Colonel-in-Chief

HM Queen Elizabeth the Queen Mother.

Deputy Colonel-in-Chief

HRH Princess Alexandra the Hon. Mrs Angus Ogilvy GCVO.

Regimental marches

The quick march is *Light Infantry* and the regimental double-past is *The Keel Row.*

History

During the North American wars in the 1750s, light armed troops were formed by General Wolfe. Men were hand-picked for their efficiency, toughness, high standard of intelligence and ability to move quickly, quietly and use individual initiative without necessarily waiting for orders. They were lightly equipped and dressed in brown and russet green, colours that blend naturally with the countryside. In 1803 Sir John Moore had the task of training 'light' formations. To this day the Light Infantry retain many old customs, for example marching with the rifle at the trail at 140 paces to the minute. They have bugles instead of drums, and use special drill calls of their own, and on ceremonial occasions they perform the double past.

Light Infantry traditions

In regimental messes in The Light Infantry, the loyal

The Light Infantry wear the distinctive badge showing a bugle horn.

toast is not drunk. This was a privilege earned by the Duke of Cornwall's Light Infantry (32nd Regiment) because of their defence at Lucknow. It was also conferred on the 85th, later the 2nd Battalion The King's Shropshire Light Infantry, by King George IV after officers of that Regiment had dealt with rioters who had insulted him in a theatre in Brighton. The privilege also applied to the Durham Light Infantry who, during their campaign in the West Indies, were awarded the designation of 'Faithful', since when it was not necessary to drink a toast to demonstrate their loyalty to the Sovereign.

Bayonnets are not used on parade, and drill movements are started and finished from the at ease position. When leaving a parade the Light Infantry double away. On uniforms, instead of a lanyard as other regiments, a whistle cord is worn. Red sashes when worn are over the left shoulder, and an 'Inkerman' chain is worn on the red sash. One unique custom is in the regimental spelling of the NCO rank of Serjeant. Another tradition is the wearing of a white rose to celebrate Minden Day.

The regimental day of The Light Infantry is 22 July, the date of the Battle of Salamanca in 1812, known as Salamanca Day. It was a significant event in The Light Infantry history.

Stable belt
Green.

Regimental Colours
The Colours of the Light Infantry consist of a Queen's Colour and a Regimental Colour for each Battalion. The Queen's Colour is the Great Union Flag with the St. George's Cross in the centre, with a crimson circle and the words *The Light Infantry* in gold. The battalion's number is shown in the centre of the circle in roman numerals. The Battle Honours of the First and Second World Wars are on the horizontal and lower vertical arms of the St George's Cross. The 5th Battalion have the word 'Volunteers' instead of a Roman numeral, this was because at one stage they were the only TA battalion of The Light Infantry. Future colours of this Battalion will bear the roman number V, instead.

The Regimental Colour has a field of blue because it is a Royal Regiment. The fringe is gold and blue and the tassels crimson and gold. The pike is surmounted by a Royal Crown in gilt. The title, Light Infantry, is in gold on a Crimson circle within a union wreath of roses, thistles and shamrocks, with the regimental badge in silver on a crimson ground. The whole is ensigned with the St Edward's Crown. The battalion number is in Roman numerals in the top corner nearest the pike. The honorary distinctions are: bottom left corner the Sphinx superscribed *Egypt*;

and bottom right corner a Mural Crown superscribed *Jellalabad*. The Battle Honours worn on the Colour are embroidered on the branches of the wreath. Underneath are the mottoes:
Aucto Splendore Resurgo; Cede Nullis; and *Faithful.*

The Sphinx and the Mural Crown are inherited from the Somerset and Cornwall Light Infantry, and the three mottoes from The King's Shropshire Light Infantry, The King's Own Yorkshire Light Infantry and The Durham Light Infantry.

5th (Shropshire and Herefordshire) Battalion

Companies
A at Shrewsbury;
B at Wellington;
C at Hereford.
D at Ross on Wye;
HQ at Shrewsbury.

History
This is the natural successor to the 4th Battalion The King's Shropshire Light Infantry, and can trace its history back to The Regiment of Shropshire Volunteer and Association Infantry of 1795. The 4th Battalion The King's (Shropshire Light Infantry) formed in 1908 when the TF was started, and it served with distinction during the First World War, forming four separate battalions. For the action at the Battle of Bligny Ridge on 6 June 1918, the Battalion was awarded the Croix de Guerre avec Palme, and today the flash of the medal is worn on the uniform. Bligny day is celebrated each 6 June. On that day the 1/4th KSLI was ordered to counter-attack an enemy position. They dashed forward and after heavy fighting won the day and took prisoners. The position had been the key to the whole line of defence, and its recapture had been considered extremely critical.

In 1920 the title became the 4th Battalion, The King's Shropshire Light Infantry, and as such fought in the Second World War. It re-formed after the War, until 1967 when as part of the major reconstruction of the TA, it was reduced to merely the Battalion HQ and HQ Company of a new Regiment, The Light Infantry Volunteers. In 1972, this new Regiment became 5LI, with Companies at Shrewsbury (HQ), Truro (A), Wakefield (B), Hereford (C) and Durham (D), with a new Company at Wellington (E) in 1975. The Companies at Truro and Durham transferred to 6 LI and 7LI respectively, and the Companies in Ross on Wye and Wakefield transferred from those two Battalions to 5 LI on 31 March 1981. B Company moved to Pontefract in April the following year. In 1986 8LI was raised in Yorkshire. A and B Companies transferred to it, and a new Company, originally called X, now A Company, was raised at the old Light Infantry Depot at Copthorne Barracks in Shrewsbury, and E Company was renamed B.

The units in Herefordshire can claim ancestry from the old Herefordshire Light Infantry. This dates back to 1797 and the formation of the Herefordshire Volunteers, who were disbanded after the Peace of Amiens in 1802. The volunteers re-formed in 1806 as the Archenfield (Hereford) Local Militia and two battalions of The Herefordshire Regiment. They were only short-lived and were disbanded in 1816 after Napoleon's defeat at Waterloo.

The Regiment was raised again in 1860, when the Herefordshire Volunteers were revived. In 1880, together with the Radnorshire Corps, they became The 1st Herefordshire Rifle Corps, affiliated to The King's Shropshire Light Infantry, with whom two companies served in the Boer War. In 1908 they became the 1st Battalion The Herefordshire Regiment and adopted the motto *Manu Forti* (with a firm hand), the family motto of the then Commanding Officer, Colonel Scobie. The Battalion was mobilized in August 1914, and for its actions at the Suvla Bay landing was mentioned in despatches by General Sir Ian Hamilton. The Battalion re-formed in 1921 and for the Second World War became part of 159 Infantry Brigade of the 53rd (Welsh) Division, until the summer of 1942 when it joined the 11th Armoured Division as lorried infantry. Its principal battles in North-West Europe were the River Odon bridgehead on 26 and 27 June 1944; Caumont 30 and 31 July 1944 (Black Sunday), and finally the arrest of the Doenitz Government in Flensburg on 23 May 1945. The principal trophy in this last action was the capture of the Grand Admiral's pennant and standard.

After the War the 1st Battalion re-formed on 29 April 1947 as The Light Infantry Corps, taking the title of 1st Battalion The Herefordshire Light Infantry (TA). It ceased to exist in 1967 but is carried on today in the Light Infantry at Hereford and Ross on Wye.

General

Members of the Battalion have the distinction of wearing a cockade on the left side of their number one dress hat. In time of war it is in support of BAOR, so annual training takes place both in Germany and the UK.

6th (Somerset and Cornwall) Battalion

Companies

A at Bath and Midsomer Norton;
B at Yeovil and Taunton;
C at Falmouth and Camborne;
D at Truro and Bodmin;
HQ at Bath;
E (HSF) at Bath;
F (HSF) at Truro.

History

The Battalion was formed on 1 April 1971 when the cadres of The Somerset Yeomanry and Light Infantry and The Duke of Cornwall's Light Infantry each became two companies. In 1975 the Cornish companies amalgamated and a company of The Light Infantry and Mercian Volunteers from Ross on Wye was transferred to the Battalion. On 1 February 1981, the new company from Herefordshire became part of 5 LI and their company at Truro and Bodmin was taken over by this Battalion.

The North Somerset and Bristol Yeomanry had been formed by the amalgamation of The North Somerset Yeomanry and The 44th Royal Tank Regiment in November 1956. The 44th had formerly been 6th Battalion The Gloucestershire Regiment.

The history of The North Somerset Yeomanry goes back to 1794, and apart from being used to suppress riots during the first century of its existence, its first taste of action came as part of the 7th Battalion Imperial Yeomanry in the Boer War. In 1901 it was chosen to provide the personal escort of cavalry to Lord Roberts, the Commander in Chief. The Regiment served as cavalry during the First World War as part of the 6th Cavalry Brigade from August 1914 until April 1918, when it ceased to exist because of the devastating number of casualties it had received. It was re-formed in 1922 and for the Second World War became part of the 1st Cavalry Division, and after seeing action in Syria, it was re-formed in 1941 as Air Formation Signals. In this new role it saw service in the Western Desert, Sicily, Italy and North-West Europe. In 1947 the Regiment changed roles once again, becoming an armoured unit of 16th Airborne Division, which it remained until amalgamation in November 1956.

The 44th Royal Tank Regiment had been formed from the 6th Battalion The Gloucestershire Regiment, when it converted to armour in 1938. It first saw action on 15 November 1941 in support of the New Zealand Division at the relief of Tobruk. It continued to see action in the Western Desert in the battles of Sidi Omar, Bardia, Sidi Mufta and the first and second battles of Alamein. It carried on into both the Sicilian and Italian campaigns until the end of 1943, when it was withdrawn back to England. In 1944 it was again in action, this time in France with the 4th Armoured Brigade taking part in many battles in North-West Europe, including the Falaise Pocket, the Rhine Crossing, Bremen, Hamburg and many other other battles. At the end of the war, the Regiment remained operational in Schleswig Holstein, before being disbanded in 1946, to be re-formed in 1947 as a TA armoured unit until it joined with the Yeomanry. After amalgamation, the new Regiment remained armoured until 1967, when it became part of the Somerset Yeomanry and Light Infantry.

On 25 July 1794 The Royal Corps of Voluntary Cavalry was formed in West Somerset, later becoming The Western Regiment of Somerset Gentlemen and Yeomanry, The West Somerset Regiment of Yeomanry Cavalry and finally The West Somerset Yeomanry. In March 1900 a squadron strength of the Regiment sailed to South Africa as part of the Imperial Yeomanry, and it was later awarded the distinction of 'South Africa 1901' on its Regimental Crest. In 1914 it started the First World War as Yeomanry Cavalry, but later became an artillery unit, serving with the Anzacs as RHA, returning to the Western Front in 1918 after serving in Egypt, Gallipoli and Palestine. In 1920 it was re-formed into an Artillery Brigade. A reorganization in 1927 saw two batteries of the Yeomanry brigaded with two of The Queen's Own Dorset Yoemanry as 94th Brigade RFA. Following its mobilization for the Second World War, it was stationed in England until landing in North-West Europe as part of The Guards Armoured Division, taking part in the battles for Carpiquet Aerodrome, Caen and Villers Bocage, staying with the Division until the German capitulation at Cuxhaven.

In 1947 when the TA re-formed, it became 255th Field Regiment RA and remained so until February 1967, when it was absorbed into The Somerset Yeomanry and Light Infantry.

The Somerset Light Infantry (Prince Albert's) formed two battalions from the earlier three volunteer battalions in 1908. These were the 4th and 5th, and in 1914 on the outbreak of the First World War, each Battalion formed second battalions. Initially they replaced Regular units in India, but later saw service in Mesopotamia, Palestine, Egypt and France. After the First World War they were again reduced to two battalions, but with the doubling of the TA in 1938, the 6th and 7th Battalions were added. During the War only the 4th and 7th Battalions saw any action. As part of the 43rd Wessex Division, they took part in all the battles from Normandy to the River Elbe. More battalions were formed during the war, and the 10th fought in France and Germany as the 7th (Light Infantry) Battalion of the Parachute Regiment. All these battalions were disbanded at the end of the war, except the 4th, which was re-formed in April 1947. In 1954 it took the title 4/5th to retain the identity of both its pre-war parent Battalions. It was amalgamated with the Duke of Cornwall's Light Infantry in 1959 to form the Somerset and Cornwall

Light Infantry, but the 4/5th retained its county name and title.

The Royal Cornwall Militia was raised in 1760 and appeared in the Army List of 1799 when embodied for service against the French. The Cornwall Rifle Volunteers, the direct ancestors of today's Cornish TA, were not raised until 1859. The first Rifle Company was raised at Penzance that year, and the last to be formed was number 22 at Saltash in 1865. These twenty two companies were formed into two Battalions, the first being the western half of the county, and the second in the east. In 1881, because of changes in the Regular Army, the 1st and 2nd Battalions of The Duke of Cornwall's Light Infantry were formed, so the two volunteer battalions were renamed as the 1st and 2nd Volunteer Battalions, the militia becoming the 3rd (Special Reserve) Battalion DCLI. On the formation of the TF in 1908, the two volunteer battalions became the 4th and 5th respectively. At the outbreak of the First World War, the 4th went to India, later serving in South Arabia, Egypt and Palestine. A second battalion formed from the 4th also went to India, where it remained throughout the War. The 5th Battalion, with 984 Cornishmen out of a total strength of 999, joined the 61st Division in France, where they served until the end of the War. The 4th and 5th Battalions were established again for the Second World War, and the 5th as part of 43 (Wessex) Division landed in Normandy shortly after D-Day and was conspicuous in the fighting near Caen at Hill 112 (Cornwall Hill), and later in the attempt to relieve Arnhem and at the battle in the Reichswald. After the War, one battalion, the 4/5th, was formed at Bodmin, until reduced in 1967.

The 6LI, through its predecessors, has very strong links with the City of Bath, where it has its present day headquarters. The first volunteers formed in the City in 1745 and the Somerset Fencible Cavalry formed there in 1794. The 1st and 2nd Somerset Rifle Volunteer Corps were raised in Bath in 1859, and on their reorganization in 1882 the HQ and two companies of the 1st Battalion remained in the City. This continued after the formation of the TF in 1908, when the 1st was redesignated as the 4th. The North Somerset Yeomanry Cavalry had formed in 1818 with two Bath companies. The ladies of Bath presented Colours to the Bath Volunteer Regiment in 1803, and the Mayor presented the same Colours to the 1st Volunteer Battalion Somerset Light Infantry in 1887, who carried them until the formation of the TF, and the presentation of new Colours the following year, 1909. These new Colours were carried by 6LI until Her Majesty Queen Elizabeth, The Queen Mother presented new ones to replace the 70-year-old set in 1979. The old Colours are laid up in the 6 LI TA Centre.

General

The Battalion has the honour of the freedom of Taunton, Bath and Wells. In time of war its role is home defence. Two members of the Battalion were selected to represent the Reserve Forces in the United Services Rifle Match, and Lieutenant Bateman was awarded the Cambridgeshire Trophy and NRA Gold medal for his outstanding shooting, when he gained the highest aggregate score of all Commonwealth Reservists.

7th (Durham) Battalion

Companies

A at Horden;
B at Hebburn and Consett;
C at Washington;
D at Bishop Auckland;
HQ at Bishop Auckland;
E(HSF) at Bishop Auckland, Horden and Washington. The Light Infantry Burma Band is at Chester-le-Street. The Mortar Platoon also is at Chester-le-Street, and the Anti-Tank Platoon is at Spennymoor.

History

The Battalion formed on 1 April 1975 from the HQ and 3 companies from the Northumbrian Volunteers, and from the 2nd Battalion the Yorkshire Volunteers. It was joined by an Air-portable Company from 5LI. The Northumbrian volunteers had only been formed four years earlier in 1971, from cadres left over from the disbandment of the TA in 1967 from 4 KOYLI, 6/8 DLI and the Durham Artillery Regiment, formerly 463 (7DLI) Light AA Regiment RA (TA), all expanded to form Companies. Through these, the Battalion can trace its history back to the Territorial Administrative Battalions of the mid-nineteenth century and the Volunteer Battalions of the DLI formed after 1885. In the First World War the DLI raised 32 battalions, which were often used to tunnel under the German lines to explode mines.

General

The wartime role is in support of BAOR as part of 15 Infantry Brigade, 2 Infantry Division.

8th (Yorkshire) Battalion

Companies

A at Wakefield;
B at Pontefract;
C at Batley;
D at Barnsley;
HQ at Wakefield;
Anti-tank (Milan) Platoon is at Wakefield and the

A mortar bomb on way to its target (8 LI).

Mortar Platoon at Minden House in Pontefract. The Officers and Sergeants' Messes are also at Minden House.

History

The Battalion formed on 1 January 1987 and inherited two companies from the 5th Battalion. There are strong links in Yorkshire, especially in the Wakefield and Doncaster areas. The Battalion is directly descended from the 4th and 5th Battalions, The King's Own Yorkshire Light Infantry, both of whom played major parts in both World Wars. The volunteer movement in the West Riding started in 1859 when, because of a threat of war resulting from the ambitions of Napoleon III, Volunteer Rifle Corps were raised.

It started life as the 9th West Riding Yorkshire Rifle Volunteers, and in 1880 changed to the 5th West Riding Yorkshire Rifle Volunteers. Later it joined with the 1st Volunteer Battalion of the South Yorkshire Regiment to form the 1st Volunteer Battalion of The King's Own (Yorkshire Light Infantry). In 1908, this became the 4th KOYLI, and at the same time the 5th KOYLI was formed at Doncaster. At the outbreak of the First World War, both Battalions were in camp at Whitby. They then both saw action during the War, and in 1920 both re-formed, at Wakefield and Doncaster respectively.

During the First World War, the 4th Battalion saw plenty of action and was in the thick of the fighting at Hooge, in 1916 took part in the Battle of the Somme, in April 1917 at Neuve Chappel and in October fought in the grim battle of Passchendaele. The story of the 5th Battalion was very similar. In March 1918, Lieutenant-Colonel Watson, commanding the 2/5th was awarded a posthumous VC for his gallantry at Rossignol, and in the last phase of the war Serjeant Calvert earned a VC at Havrincourt.

At the beginning of the Second World War, the 4th Battalion split into two. 1/4th served in Norway in 1940 and after evacuation spent a month in England before going to Iceland. In 1942 it returned home and trained for the invasion of France where it went four days after D-Day. It was involved in the heavy fighting around Caen and remained in action until the German surrender, ending the war in Utrecht.

The 2/4th Battalion saw action in France in 1940 and fought a rearguard action on the Seine before evacuation from Cherbourg. In January 1943 it sailed for North Africa and fought through to Tunisia. It then took part in the invasion of Italy, and was one of the early units ashore at Salerno.

The 5th Battalion became 53 Light AA Regiment in 1939 and served in France, giving invaluable support right up to its evacuation from Dunkirk. In 1947, the 4th Battalion re-formed at Wakefield, but the 5th was kept alive only in the names of two artillery regiments.

General

The wartime role of the Battalion is to support NATO as part of 15 Infantry Brigade. Annual camp is taken either in the UK or abroad. The Battalion enjoys the privileges of the freedoms of Doncaster, Leeds, Wakefield, Batley and Pontefract.

The Royal Green Jackets

Regimental badge

A Maltese cross inscribed with selected battle honours thereon a bugle horn stringed and encircled with the title of the Regiment all within a wreath of laurel ensigned with the Crown resting upon a plinth inscribed *Peninsula*; across the tie a Naval Crown superscribed *Copenhagen 2 April 1801* all in silver.

Colonel-in-Chief

THE QUEEN.

Regimental marches

The quick march is an arrangement of *Huntsman's Chorus* and *Italian Song,* and the regimental double-past is *The Road to the Isles.*

Stable belt

Rifle green.

4th (V) Battalion

Companies

B at Fulham;
C in The City of London;
F at Mile End Road, East London;
G at West Ham;
HQ in Mayfair.

History

The Battalion was formed on 1 April 1967 by the amalgamation of the TA Regiments of the former King's Royal Rifle Corps, Rifle Brigade and Oxfordshire and Buckinghamshire Light Infantry. Through the Queen Victoria's Rifles, the Battalion traces its history back to 1792. The Queen Vic's moved to the Mayfair headquarters in 1888, the site having been donated by the then Duke of Westminster. The drill hall was destroyed by German bombs in 1941 and rebuilt in 1952. The Queen Vic's fought in Calais in May 1940 and later in the war re-formed as the 7th and 8th Battalions The King's Royal Rifle Corps.

In 1803 The Queen's Westminsters was formed and in 1922 amalgamated with the Civil Service Rifles. In 1940 the Regiment formed the 11th and 12th Battalions The King's Royal Rifle Corps. The London Rifle Brigade had been a City of London Regiment since 1859, and many of the present-day links with the City are traced back to this Battalion. In 1940 they became the 7th and 8th Battalions The Rifle Brigade and the Rangers, another London Rifle unit became the 9th and 10th Battalions The King's Royal Rifle Corps. The successors to the London Rifle Brigade and the Rangers amalgamated in 1950. The latest addition came in 1988 when the Battalion raised a new Home Service Force Company.

General

The Battalion's wartime role is in support of BAOR and as part of its equipment has the Milan, Law 80 and the 66mm anti-tank weapons. It is able to deploy by foot, wheeled vehicles or helicopter. The Battalion has the freedom of the City of Westminster with the right to march through the City with swords fixed and bugles sounding. The strong links with the City of London are maintained, and each year it takes part in the Lord Mayor's Show. There are also strong links with five of the great Livery Companies, the Grocers', Goldsmiths', Haberdashers', Salters' and Clothworkers'. This is recognized each year by the provision of Guards of Honour for Livery functions. Because of this and other City and ceremonial duties, the Battalion has, uniquely, the establishment of No. 1 Dress ceremonial uniform for certain of its Riflemen.

As befits a regiment that recruits from the Cities of London and Westminster, many well-known people have served in its ranks. The Battalion Magazine of 1987 to 1988 reported in its obituaries the passing of Henry Spencer Moore, who had been a Civil Service Rifleman during the First World War, and, of course, later became the world-famous sculptor and artist, and an official war artist in the Second World War. At the village of Zillebeke in Belgium there is a monument to the Queen Victoria Rifles and their dead of two world wars.

5th (V) Battalion

Companies

A at High Wycombe;
D at Aylesbury;
E at Milton Keynes;
HQ at Oxford.

History

The Battalion was raised on 1 December 1986, and has grown out of the two Oxfordshire and Buckinghamshire rifle companies of the 4th Battalion in London. It is the direct descendent of three regiments. The 43rd Regiment was raised in 1741 and the 52nd in 1755, the 43rd gaining an early battle honour as part of the 60th Rifles under General Wolfe at Quebec.

These two regiments won immortal fame when fighting against Napoleon in the Peninsula. They later formed The Oxfordshire and Buckinghamshire Light Infantry. The King's Royal Rifle Corps (60th Rifles) was raised in 1755 from British settlers in North America, and fought against the Red Indians and the French. In 1797 a new Battalion formed in England to act as skirmishers in the later battles against Napoleon.

It is interesting to look back at the Volunteer movement in Buckinghamshire at the beginning of the last century. Between 1803 and 1808 the Loyal Volunteer Infantry for the county were the Buckingham Infantry Volunteers. They were formed on 27 August 1803 and their Colonel was Colonel George, Marquis of Buckingham. They consisted of the Buckingham (1st

The Lord Mayor of London visits the Royal Green Jackets. Looking on is Lt.-Col. Neil Johnson, the volunteer commanding the Battalion (4 RGJ).

or Southern Regiment), the Buckingham (2nd or Middle Regiment) and the Buckingham (3rd or Northern Regiment).

The Volunteers were replaced by the Local Militia between 1808 and 1816. (These are not to be confused with the Regular Militia, the locals being part-time volunteers.) There was nothing then until 1859, when the Infantry Volunteers were raised again, and in December the first sub-division of Bucks Rifle Volunteers formed.

General

As this is a new Battalion, initially its role is home defence, but it is likely to change to being in support of NATO from about 1990.

The modern infantry soldier will wear the fully protective camouflage-pattern Nuclear, Biological and Chemical suit with the S10 respirator. He will have new personal load-carrying equipment (PLCE) which will take the place of the existing webbing, and he will be equipped with the SA 80 rifle.

SA 80 5.56 mm Weapon

There are two 5.56 mm weapon systems. The Individual Weapon (IW) is a rifle with an automatic fire capability. The Light Support Weapon (LSW) is a light machine-gun. They are very similar, one being a variation on the other. The IW is replacing the SLR and SMG. When issued to infantry it is equipped with a times 4 magnification Sight Unit, Small Arms, Trilux (SUSAT) optical sight. The LSW replaces the GPMG in the light role as the section light machine-gun. As a variation of the IW it has a heavier, longer barrel and at least 80 per cent of the parts are interchangeable. They both take the SS109 5.56 NATO standard cartridge. The method of operation is the same, gas, selective fire of single shot or fully automatic. Both systems have the 30 round magazine. The IW weighs 4.98 Kg, with optical sight and loaded magazine, whereas the LSW is heavier, at 6.88 Kg. The IW has a range of 500 metres with a rate of fire being 610 to 770 rounds per minute, whereas the LSW reaches 600 metres with a rate of fire of 675 to 725 rounds per minute.

Milan portable anti tank guided weapon

MILAN, (Missile d'Infantrie Leger Anti-Char) was originally produced by a West German and French consortium, with issue to the French and German services in 1975. The weapon was not issued in any quantities to the British Army until 1980. It is a second-generation anti-tank missile. The operator keeps the sight on the target and the missile is automatically locked-on and guided to it by a wire less than 0.4mm thick. When it first fires, it is propelled out of its tube by a gas generator, which also discharges the empty tube backwards. When the missile is far enough away not to injure the operator, the rocket fires and four in-flight fins spring outwards. This delayed firing also helps conceal the firer, by not giving away an exhaust 'signature' at the firer's location. MILAN is now the basic infantry medium-range anti-tank guided weapon and used mainly in the ground role, but it can be mounted on a Spartan. It can also be fired at night using the MIRA thermal imaging sight.

The missile, which has a calibre of 115mm, is 1.26 metres long and weighs 11.8 kg. Its range is from 25 to 2,000 metres and its maximum range takes 13 secs of flight. The warhead is a shaped charge.

Left *Loading the 51 mm Mortar with an HE bomb; note the ammunition satchel* (Royal Ordnance).

Opposite *Ordnance Muzzle-Loading 81 mm L16* (Royal Ordnance).

7.62mm Weapons

L1A1 Rifle (self-loading rifle-SLR) and L7A2 GPMG. The SLR has been the basic infantry personal weapon for some years now, but is being replaced by the SA 80. It takes the 7.62 NATO standard cartridge and is gas-operated single shot only. There is a 20 round magazine, and empty it weighs 4.55 Kg. It is semi-automatic with an effective range of 300 metres.

The GPMG infantry version is used as a light machine-gun at section level. Its main use is in a sustained fire role, mounted on a tripod with the C2 sight unit. In the light role it is being replaced by the LSW. It is belt fed and weighs 11.77 Kg. The cyclic rate of fire is 625 to 750 rounds a minute. Its effective range in the light role is 800 metres; in sustained fire (SF) role with tracer, 1,100 metres; with observed strike, 1,800 metres.

9mm L2A3 Sub-machine-gun (SMG)

This is a short-range, self-protection weapon used by crews such as signallers, drivers, etc whose primary duty precludes carrying a rifle. It is also being replaced by the SA 80. It fires the 9mm parabellum cartridge. It is blowback-operated, selective fire with a cyclic rate of 550 rounds per minute. It weighs 2.72 kg empty.

51mm Mortar L9A1

A mortar is issued to each infantry platoon and provides short-range indirect fire of HE, smoke or illumination bombs. It has a calibre of 51 mm, is 750 mm long and weighs 6.28 Kg. It has a range of between 50 to 800 metres and can fire at a rate of eight rounds per minute.

81mm Mortar L16A2

This provides the infantry with an indirect fire weapon system to provide high explosive, smoke and illumination rounds at battalion level.

It is of 81mm calibre, and 1.27 metres long. The weight of its barrel is 12.28 kg, its bipod is 11.36 kg and the base plate is 11.36 kg. It has a range of between 200 and 5,660 metres.

The Escape of 2/Lt L. Lucas

Second Lieutenant Lucas was a platoon commander in 'C' Company during the withdrawal from Calais in 1940. The piece that follows is taken from a letter by Major R.H. Sampson to Major H. Morgan, dated 16 June 1940, and reproduced by kind permission of Lieutenant-Colonel Neil Johnson, CO of 4th Battalion The Royal Green Jackets.

I saw 2/Lt L. Lucas and got his account at some length; perhaps your troops had better have it in full. 2/Lt Lucas was attacked from his left and right fronts and his right rear and he was cut off from the harbour wall. He saw many British and French soldiers scrambling over the wall, and by some railway trucks at the end of the jetty, but who was who he did not know. Firing went on by the harbour for another half hour or more, and in the town longer still. What was happening he had no idea.

He was marched round Calais to a church at the rear. There were many prisoners but he did not notice individuals as closely as he might, as he saw no point, and besides was kept away from all other ranks. He spend most of the time talking to 2/Lt E. Hamilton as to how they should spend the next five years. He saw Capt. G. Bowring with a slight wound in his leg, the bullet went in and out, being driven off in an ambulance. He also saw 2/Lt. F. Banbury and 2/Lt Courtenay and Sgt. Brett, also from his description of a D.R. who ought to have been with 'D' Coy, but was with HQ — tall, with a small moustache, played Rugby, also a signaller who might, from his description be Knowles or Lawrence, small, leering expression and wore glasses. He also saw, as prisoners, from all the units, 20 Officers and some hundred men.

About 8 pm, or later, they were all marched out down the St Omer Road. Some Frenchmen in front went too fast and the Column straggled. The crossroads had a sentry on but he finally found himself alone owing to the straggling, on a forked road. Taking the view that anyone can be a bloody fool once he went down the track which he knew to be wrong. About 20 yards down he slipped through a hedge and made his way back, intending to whisper to the others to do the same. However, he heard a German Officer telling the Column not to straggle, so he hid under a bush and waited and promptly went fast asleep. Not surprising when you remember that they had hardly slept for 6 days. When it was light he discarded his overcoat, took some sacking off a scarecrow and put it round his shoulders, thus hoping that he looked like a French peasant. Cautiously he made his way to the shore, especially when he had to cross roads which were being used by the Germans. He reached the coast in the early afternoon between Calais and Cap Gris Nez, i.e. the Boulogne side. He spotted a small boat on the shore, hid in the dunes, waited and slept. In the early evening he attracted an old Frenchman and a woman and asked for bread and water. He had some food on him — British M. and V. ration issued to him by the Germans, but he had forgotten to eat it all day, as he had got out of the practice of eating. The Frenchwomen — well, in 2/Lt. Lucas' words 'I don't want to upset International goodwill and I am sure it was a kind thought, but she brought me the worst bottle of beer I have ever tasted.' Fortified by this he was pushed off at 11 pm by the Frenchman. He had found some oars and a rowlock, and improvised another of rope. The boat was about 10 feet long, painted white, and when a searchlight was turned on it, which happened every half hour, 'Felt like the Queen Mary'.

The Navy picked him up half a mile outside Dover Harbour, and said 'Must you row through a minefield?' He says he rowed 'Like a Brighton Boatman on Saturday Afternoon'

but admits that the searchlight 'Was a powerful aid to rowing'. Early that afternoon the Navy sent him, after giving him a good lunch, I am glad to say, to have his arm dressed. It was, I gather, quite a minor scratch, but he did not mention it until this point in his story. Incautiously he went in to a Hospital Train and sat down. He instantly went to sleep, woke up to find the train going through Oxford next stop Middlesbrough. It took him two days to get back from there.

The Second Infantry Division

The Second Division was born in Portugal during the Peninsular War (1808 to 1814). The Commander of the British Army, General Sir Arthur Wellesley, later Field Marshal The Duke of Wellington, recognized the need for a chain of command between his Army headquarters and the Brigades. As a result, on 18 June 1809 a General Order of the Day was issued from the Adjutant-General's office at Atranches forming the Divisions. Lieutenant-General Rowland Hill was the first General Officer Commanding (GOC) of the Division, which first saw action at the Battle of Talavera in 1809. Initially the Division had consisted of six battalions, but this was increased to ten, and it took part in all the major actions throughout the Peninsular War. It gained for itself the title of 'The Observing Division' because it was often detached from the Army to shadow the enemy or make a reconnaissance.

Following this war, it acted as an Army of Occupation in the South of France, before returning home. When Napoleon escaped from Elba it moved to the Low Countries. It took its place on the right of the Allied line at the Battle of Waterloo.

Its next active service was in the Crimean War between 1854 and 1856 and it took part in the Battles of the Alma, Inkerman and the Siege of Sebastapol. It defeated the Russian Army alongside the Light Division in the crossing of the River Alma.

During the last part of the nineteenth century, 2 Division took part in three conflicts. It was in the punitive expedition mounted from India against China, and it occupied Peking in 1860. In 1879 it took part in the suppression of the Zulu Kingdom and was a major part of the army that finally brought about the destruction of Shaka's Empire at Ulundi on 4 July 1879. The third conflict was in Egypt in 1882, when it formed part of the force commanded by Sir Garnet Wolseley which crushed the revolt led by Arabi Pasha at Tel el Kebir. During the Boer War, the Divisional HQ was in South Africa but took no part in the major engagements and was withdrawn home to re-form at Aldershot on 1 April 1902.

Aldershot was the Divisional home before and after the First World War. Mobilized on 3 August 1914, it was part of the BEF in France and between 28 August and 9 September was part of the retreat from Mons, a fighting withdrawal of 200 miles in 13 days. It fought at Vimy Ridge and in the last year of the war was in the advance into Germany, reaching Cologne on 27 December 1918 Among its between-wars GOCs was Major-General A.P. Wavell, who introduced Divisional Exercises, which prepared it for its second journey to France, this time on 15th September 1939.

Until 10 May 1940 it was occupied digging trenches and patrolling, during which time the Wehrmacht invaded the Netherlands, Belgium and France, but for the next to weeks, 2 Division was in constant contact with the enemy. It conducted a series of fighting withdrawals to safety from the Dyle to Dunkirk. Most of the Division was evacuated by the Royal Navy. Back home it moved to the East Riding of Yorkshire to re-equip. This was to counter the expected invasion, and units manned the defended coast from Spurn Head to Filey. The next move was in April 1942 when the Division left England for India and trained alongside 36 Division to counter the threat to India and Burma by the Japanese. 6 Infantry Brigade from the Division was in the 1943 Arakan Campaign, but in April 1944 all the Division was rushed to Kohima to relieve the pressure on the Garrison. This lasted from 4 to 16 May. After success there, it's next job was to open the road to Imphal and from 16 May until 22 June they cleared the road, destroying the entire 31st Japanese Division as well as helping to relieve Imphal. 4 and 5 Infantry Brigades advanced into Burma to capture Mandalay, advancing 150 miles in 20 days through Japanese-infested territory. The Division marched south and crossed the Irrawaddy on 15 February 1945, and Mandalay was captured in March.

After the War, the Division first of all did duty in Malaya and Singapore, restoring law and order. In February 1947 it was moved to Germany to join BAOR. The Divisional HQ eventually was established at Lubbecke where it remained for 25 years. Among the new equip-

ment it pioneered into use was the first battlefield computer and a system of command, named WAVELL, after the former GOC. In 1977 the Divisional HQ was granted the Freedom of the town of Lubbecke, and on 12 November 1983 it took formal leave of the town, and returned to York after an absence of over 40 years.

In its modern role in 1 Corps rear area, the Division would move to Germany in time of war. Of its three Brigades, two are almost entirely found from the TA and amongst the Divisional Troops there are two TA Engineer Regiments. The two TA Infantry Brigades are 15 at Topcliffe and 49 at Chilwell. 15 Infantry Brigade started life in 1905 at Fermoy, and served in Ireland and France with the BEF. It returned to Belfast in 1918 but from 1924 to 1929 was in Germany. On re-forming in October 1929 it moved to York. The Second World War saw it once more with the BEF in France. In April 1940 it was sent to Norway, but one year later it was in Northern Ireland. After a spell in England it sailed to India, then by way of the North West Frontier into Persia. From July 1943 to June 1944 it saw action in Sicily and Italy, finally entering North-West Europe in 1945 taking part in Operation Enterprise, the crossing of the River Elbe. It was disbanded on 31 March 1948 in Hanover. 1 January 1982 saw the Brigade's rebirth at Topcliffe. Its symbol is a male merlin on a scarlet infantry background.

49th Infantry Brigade commemorates the 49th West Riding and Midland Infantry Division, a Territorial Force Division raised in 1908. It saw extensive action during the First World War, firstly at Ypres and then the Somme. In 1917 it was at Arras, followed by operations on the Flanders Coast and finally the third Battle of Ypres. Back in action for the Second World War, it was part of 'AVONFORCE' in Norway before moving to occupy Iceland in May 1940. It was here that the Divisional Polar Bear insignia was introduced. 49th Division fought across Northern France and Belgium and was at the capture of Arnhem in April 1945. It returned to Nottingham in April 1947 as an Armoured Division, but reverted to the infantry role in 1956. It was disbanded in 1967.

Both these Brigades consist of four or five TA Infantry Battalions, a Yeomanry Reconnaissance Regiment, and TA Royal Artillery. Many of the supporting corps for the Division are also TA.

8 Airborne Units

The TA plays a full part in the Army's airborne role, with three battalions of the Parachute Regiment, two Regiments of Special Air Service and a Squadron of the Army Air Corps. Many of the support services also have their airborne elements.

The Parachute Regiment

Regimental badge
Upon a spread of wings, an open parachute with the royal crown and lion above.

Motto
Utrinque Paratus.

Regimental marches
The quick march is *The Ride of The Valkyries*, and the slow march is, *Pomp and Circumstance, No. 4.*

Colonel in Chief
HRH The Prince of Wales KG.

Stable belt
Maroon, with a silver buckle embossed with a cap badge.

4th Battalion

Companies
A at Liverpool;
B in Oldham;
C at Gateshead;
D at Stockton on Tees;
16 (Lincoln), in Lincoln and Leicester;
HQ at Pudsey.

Regimental dress
The 4th Battalion wears the black DZ flash and lanyard.

History
The Battalion was formed in 1967 by the amalgamation of the 12th/13th (Yorkshire and Lancashire) and the 17th (9th Durham Light Infantry) Battalions of the Parachute Regiment. The 17th had been formed in 1943, as the name suggests from the 9th (Durham) Light Infantry. The 12th (Yorkshire) Battalion also formed in 1943, from the 10th Battalion the Green Howards, which had itself been formed in 1939 out of the 2nd East Riding Yeomanry. The 13th (Lancashire) Battalion formed from the 2/4th Battalion the South Lancashire Regiment.

16 Company has an unusual history, having been formed in 1950 as an independent Parachute Company. For its first six years it had the title 16th Airborne Divisional (Lincoln) Independent Company, with a role of a pathfinder force for the Division. Historically, it could be said that it was derived from the 21st Independent Parachute Company of the 1st Airborne Division at Arnhem. In 1956 the 16th Airborne Division (TA) was disbanded and the Company changed its name to 16 (Lincoln) Company, remaining an independent pathfinder unit.

In 1967 it moved to Newport in Lincoln and in 1968 became part of the Strategic Command (STRATCO), changing its name yet again to 16(V) Independent Company. It kept this name and its role as a patrol and recce Company until 1978, when it became part of 15 (Scottish Volunteer) Battalion, but on 11 July 1984 it was transferred to 4 PARA.

General
In common with all TA Parachute Units, the Battalion has a role in support of BAOR in time of war.

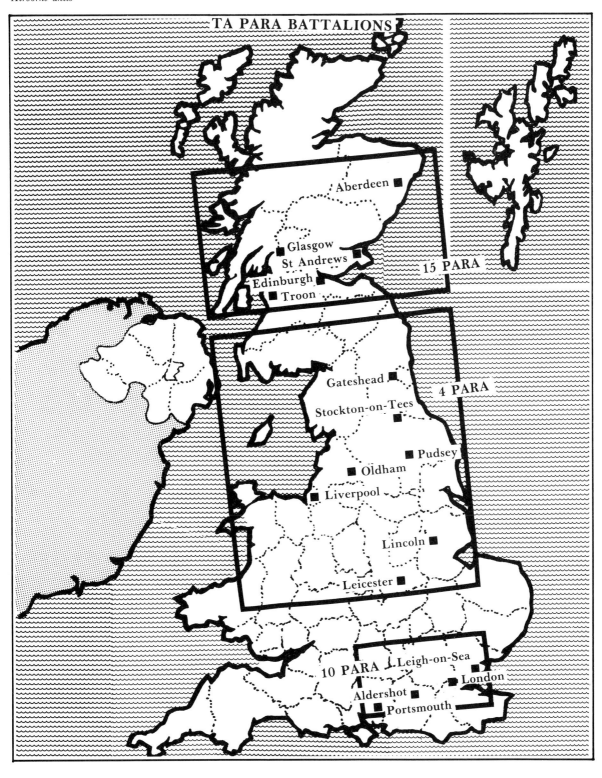

Men of the 4th Battalion leave the DZ to take up their exercise positions.

Its unique means of getting to war, however, makes it a very flexible organization, capable of being re-roled at short notice to wherever it is needed. Training for the role includes the full range of infantry skills, together with parachuting. They are specialists in the role of fighting in built-up areas (FIBUA).

10th Battalion

Companies

1 at White City, West London;
2 at Croydon, Blackheath and St Mary Cray;
3 at Finchley;
4 at Chelsea;
Support Company at Aldershot and Portsmouth;
Mortar Platoon at Leigh on Sea;
HQ and HSF at Chelsea.

Regimental dress

This Battalion wears a black DZ flash on the right arm with a red roman 'X' in the centre.

History

The Battalion traces its history back to December 1942, when it was raised at Kabrit in the Suez Canal Zone. It formed from a nucleas of 200 officers and men who had volunteered for parachute duty from the 2nd Battalion The Royal Sussex Regiment. In March 1943 it moved to Palestine, where better training facilities existed, but two months later it moved to Tunisia to join the 1st Airborne Division. Despite training for the invasion of Sicily, it was not required for the operation. Early in September the Battalion sailed with 2 Parachute Brigade to Italy, and landed at Taranto. After securing the bridgehead, it was released to pursue the withdrawing German forces, and found itself against the German 1st Parachute Division at Castellaneta. A fighting patrol from the Battalion made a superior force of enemy withdraw from an important airfield, Gioia Del Colle, thus allowing its use by the RAF to provide urgently-needed fighter cover for the Salerno landings.

The Battalion was withdrawn from Italy and returned to the UK. In September 1944, 10 PARA were dropped for the Battle of Arnhem. In common with all the airborne forces in that battle, heavy casualties were suffered, and on 25 September the 36 survivors crossed the lower Rhine to safety. During this battle, one of the original Royal Sussex volunteers, Captain Lionel Quiripel, gained the VC for his valour on 19 September.

After the War 10 PARA re-formed, on 1 May 1947, as a TA unit. It is the only TA parachute battalion that can claim direct association with its wartime counterparts, and because of this there are still very strong links with the people of Arnhem, who warmly host them each year on the occasion of the annual memorial visit and exercise.

General

To train for its wartime role, the Battalion often goes abroad. To remain qualified for his wings, a para-trooper needs to make at least one descent each year, although four descents is the average. A recruit on joining his company spends six to ten weeks improv-ing his fitness and basic skills. He then attends a weekend to be familiarized with tests that he will have to pass. On four successive weekends, he attends for training, culminating in the 'P' Company training at Aldershot where he undergoes the same tests as a Regular soldier. After passing P Company, he attends a two-week recruits' cadre at the Parachute Regiment depot. He is then posted back to his com-pany, but does not go on his parachute course until he has attended regularly for a minimum of six months. The Battalion is proud of its skill at arms, having won the London District Rifle Association Competition 12 years in succession.

15th (Scottish Volunteer) Battalion

Companies

A in Glasgow;
B at Aberdeen and St Andrews;
C in Edinburgh;
D (Fire Support) at Troon;
HQ in Glasgow.

Regimental dress

A patch of Hunting Stewart tartan is worn behind the cap badge, an honour conferred by the late King George VI. The Pipes and Drums of the Battalion wear the MacKenzie tartan.

History

The Battalion was raised in 1947, and to start with

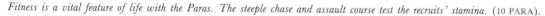

Fitness is a vital feature of life with the Paras. The steeple chase and assault course test the recruits' stamina. (10 PARA).

Helicopter abseiling (10 PARA).

A part of training is the stretcher race, eight miles across country in 1½ hours. Teams of eight carry a 180 lb stretcher, wearing fighting order (10 PARA).

contained mainly the reservist officers and soldiers who had served in the 1st and 5th (Scottish) Battalions in the Second World War. On 1 April 1967 it was renamed and took its present title. It acquired a fourth rifle company, 16 (Lincoln) in April 1978. In 1983 it was given a new role of FIBUA, and on 11 July 1984, 16 (Lincoln) Company transferred to 4 PARA.

General

The Battalion has a role in support of BAOR in time of war.

Special Air Service Regiment

Regimental badge
A winged dagger striking downwards with the motto *'Who Dares Wins'*.

Regimental march
March du Regiment Parachutiste Belge.

Stable belt
Plain blue.

Regimental history
The SAS was born in the Western Desert in 1941. It was designed for long-range raiding and reconaissance, especially for attacking communications, airfield and enemy headquarters. It first went into action on November 16 1941, and destroyed more than 350 enemy aircraft on the ground at Gazala and Tmimi. Hitler issued the following order: 'Captured Special Air Service troops must be handed over at once to the nearest Gestapo unit . . . these men are very dangerous . . . they must be ruthlessly exterminated.' This resulted in many being shot on capture as the war took the SAS into Italy and Europe.

Right and above right *Members of the TA's crack SAS in training* (SAS).

SAS training can be some of the toughest in the world, and the TA volunteers get no privileges and need to be as fit and self-reliant as their regular colleagues (SAS).

From the mid 1970s, the Regiment has specialized in counter-terrorist techniques, as well as maintaining their traditional covert wartime role.

21st SAS Regiment (Artists) Volunteers

History
21 SAS formed in 1947 and it embodied The Artists' Rifles, an old and famous TA Regiment. The Regular Army did not re-form the SAS until three years later, when 22nd SAS Regiment was born, so perhaps 21 SAS is the only TA unit to be 'parent' to a Regular Army unit.

The Artists have their origins in the middle of the last century when in 1860 it was decided to form a Corps of Artists, consisting of painters, sculptors, engravers, musicians, architects and actors. The badge chosen was of two heads, one of Mars and the other of Minerva, the Goddess of Wisdom, thus representing both war and arts. The Corps was officially named the 38th Middlesex (Artists) Rifle Volunteers,

which changed in 1881 to The 20th Middlesex (Artists) Rifle Volunteers, and again in 1908 to the 28th Battalion London Regiment (Artists' Rifles). In 1939 when the Regiment was posted to the Officer Producing Group, it was officially simplified to The Artists' Rifles.

In the Boer War, the Artists contributed the largest detachment to the City Imperial Volunteers.

In 1914 they were mobilized and sailed for France. To make up for the colossal losses of officers in the 7th Division, 52 privates from the Regiment were selected, and made officers the same day, the Commanding Officer fixing an officer's star to each shoulder strap of their privates' uniforms, and so dressed they joined their new Companies with other battalions and regiments in 7th Division, many finding they were the only officer in the company, and therefore its commander.

Following the 'First Fifty', a stream of 10,256 officers were provided for the Army from the Artists during the War. As a regiment, it was in the thick of the fighting at Passchendaele, as part of the Royal Naval Division.

Brigadier Alastair Stevenson Pearson, CB DSO OBE MC TD HML

Brigadier Pearson has a distinguished military career spanning 45 years, and still continuing as the Honorary Colonel of 15th (Scottish Volunteer) Battalion, The Parachute Regiment. His name is a byword for courage, example and leadership within the Parachute Regiment and Airborne Forces, where he was awarded the Military Cross and the Distinguished Service Order with three bars for his gallantry and brilliantly-executed offensive operations against the enemy during 18 short months in North Africa, Sicily and then the Normandy landings.

He has been involved with the TA for much of his adult life. He raised and commanded the Battalion from 1947 until 1953 and he directed the affairs of the Army Cadet Force in Scotland from 1967 until 1981. He was the most decorated wartime officer in the Airborne Forces.

He started with 6 Highland Light Infantry from 1939 until 1940, then became a Company Commander in 2 PARA in 1941. The following year he was a Company Commander and then Second in Command of 1 PARA. In November 1942 he took command of 1 PARA at the age of 27 when the CO was wounded, and remained until July 1943, when he was incapacitated by malaria. In December that year he commanded 8 PARA and led them into Normandy. At the end of the War he commanded the Reserve Battalion at York, until he returned to civilian life in 1947. As a TA officer he commanded 15 PARA from 1 May 1947 until 10 November 1953. From then until 1959, as a Colonel, he was Deputy Commander of 44 PARA Bde TA. He was an ADC to HM The Queen from 1956 to 1961. From 1960 until 1963 he became Deputy Commander (North) of 44 Independent PARA Bde TA. He became the Honorary Colonel to 15 PARA from 1963 until 1967, and again from 1983. In the rank of Brigadier he commanded Scotland Army Cadet Force from 1967 until 1981.

Since the Second World War for his services to the TA and Cadets he has gained the OBE, 1953, the CB 1958, the TD and a Knighthood of the Order of St John. He was also made a Deputy-Lieutenant and subsequently Her Majesty's Lord-Lieutenant for Dumbartonshire in 1979.

In the First World War, 15,022 men passed through the Regiment, and of these 2,003 were killed, 3,250 wounded, 532 posted as missing and 286 taken prisoner. A most impressive list of awards for gallantry was made to Artists, including 8 VCs. The Regiment did not see action in the Second World War as a unit, but remained an Officer Training Unit.

General

The Regiment has its headquarters in London, with detachments throughout the south of England and Wales. The old tradition of mounting a guard of honour at the annual opening of the Royal Academy Summer Exhibition was inherited from the Artists, and is carried on today. The Regiment also enjoys a relationship with the City of London through its adoption by The Worshipful Company of Glovers in 1955.

23 SAS Regiment

History

The Regiment was formed in 1967 and can trace its history back to the Intelligence School 9 (TA). It had been found during the Second World War that aircrews shot down over enemy-occupied territory were rescued wherever possible by organizations within the local population. After the war the RAF believed that in the event of another war, shot-down aircrews could not necessarily rely on the locals for help to escape, so some other method was needed. In May 1947, the Director of Military Intelligence formed Intelligence School 9 (TA) in conjunction with Air Intelligence Unit 9 in order to train teams who could establish cells in hostile territory to rescue shot down aircrew and get them safely home. This was a combined service unit consisting of officers and men from all three services, training in small groups specializing in signalling, field craft, first aid and navigation. Training emphasis was placed on escape and evasion techniques in those early days. The seriousness of the role can be emphasized by the quality of the various Commanding-Officers, including the late Lieutenant-Colonel Airey Neave DSO OBE MC, of Colditz fame. The security of this unit was so high that its designation was changed a number of times, so as to confuse any potential enemy studying its formation. Because of its excellent network of cells and communications links, it would have been of value for the other intelligence agencies as well. In 1967 all this changed, and the unit took on its current role and form as a standard SAS unit.

General

The Regiment has its headquarters in Birmingham, with detachments in the North of England and Scotland.

Army Air Corps

Regimental badge
A laurel wreath surmounted by the crown; within a wreath, an eagle.

Regimental marches
The quick march is *Recce Flight*, and the slow march is *The Thieving Magpie*.

Stable belt
Dark blue with a central light blue band. The beret is also light blue.

General
The TA complement of the Corps is only small and consists of two organizations. The AAC TA Pool at Central Volunteer HQ at the Army Air Corps Centre at Middle Wallop administers a specialist pool of pilots and aircrewmen who are allocated to units in UKLF and BAOR for annual training.

Formed on 1 April 1986 as an independent TA unit, 666 Squadron attached to 7 Regiment AAC at Netheravon Airfield, carries out tasks in both peace and war for HQ UKLF. It takes its number from a previously-disbanded Regular Army squadron.

Scout AH Mark 1 Helicopter

The first prototype Scout flew in 1958, and in 1962 the first production models were taken into service for trials. It became operational a few years later. The original design had been called the P531 by Saunders Roe, but the aircraft was eventually produced at Yeovil in Somerset by Westland Aircraft. In its Regular Army service it had two main roles, the first a utility or workhorse role of casevac, carriage of loads both internal and underslung, passenger carrying, communications and liaison work as well as ground support. Its other role had been as anti-armour, equipped with four SS11 ATGM and the AF 120 stabilized magnifying roof sight. It proved a very rugged and robust aircraft, but is now replaced in Regular units by the Lynx.

The Scout is still ideal for the role of the TA Squadron of the Army Air Corps, however.
Data: Rotor diameter is 9.83 metres; length of rotors turning is 12.39 metres; height to rotor hub is 2.72 metres, height of rotors turning is 3.43 metres; length of fuselage is 9.30 metres; width of fuselage is 2.59 metres; weight is 1,608 kg unladen and 2,428 kg maximum; range is 200 nautical miles, but in the anti-armour role this is reduced to 80 nautical miles; speed is 100 knots, cruising; crew is 2; passengers 5, including one crewman.
Weapons: The Scout may be fitted with SS11 ATGM, wire-guided CLOS, range 3,000 metres; GPMGs, 7.62 mm; and rockets, MATRA or SNEB 68mm, AP or anti-personnel in two seven tube launchers, range 1,500 metres.

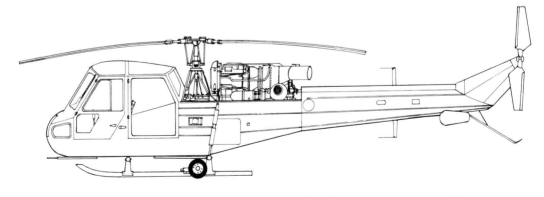

9 The Corps and Services

The fighting, teeth arms of the Army always seem to get the glamour, and sometimes those of us serving in support in the various corps and services feel we are somewhat looked down on by the cavalry and infantry. In reality these days, it is not so. The vital tasks that members of all corps undertake are more than ever deciding factors in the success or otherwise of an exercise or operation. In dealing with the TA element of each corps I have tried to indicate its role in the larger scheme of things. The pride that each member of each corps feels is manifest in that he or she feels that the Army would grind to a halt if it were not for them. In many cases, this is true; for instance, without the Ordnance Corps, there would be no petroleum for the fighting vehicles and no ammunition for the teeth arms to fire, and their range of skills and stores takes them far beyond the derogatory term of 'blanket stackers'. The movers of the Royal Corps of Transport operate a transport system without which neither the men nor the stores would reach the front line in a fit state to fight.

Whatever a man's cap badge, with the possible exception of the Chaplains, he has to be able to operate as an infantry man, and all ranks have to be able to survive in battlefield conditions, especially NBC.

Royal Army Chaplains' Department

Regimental badge
Upon a wreath of laurel and oak, a Maltese Cross.

In the centre a quatrefoil voided with a circule inscribed with the motto *In this Sign Conquer*. The whole ensigned with the crown.

For Jewish Chaplains: Upon a wreath of laurel and oak, a Star of David. In the centre of the Star, a circle containing a quatrefoil voided. The whole ensigned with the crown.

Regimental marches
Both the quick and slow marches are the *Trumpet Voluntary*.

Stable belt
Black with a purple band in the centre, fastened by two leather straps.

History
There is not much information about the history of the TA element of their Department. The Army List for 1919 shows Chaplains Department, Territorial Force and records Chaplains attached to Royal Artillery, Royal Engineers (Field), Royal Engineers (Signal Service), Royal Engineers (Fortress), Royal Army Service Corps and Royal Army Medical Corps. In each case they were attached to the Territorial Force of the regiment or corps. Some of these Chaplains had been attached for some time: as early as 1896 in one case, with many more from 1902, so there was obviously a Volunteer element of the Department before the First World War.

The three Army Chaplains who received the VC for their valour during the First World War were all Temporary Chaplains rather than TA men. The first clergyman to receive the VC was the Revd. J.W. Adams. He was a volunteer, but not a member of a UK Volunteer Force. He was with the Bengal Ecclesiastical Department and went with the Kabul Field Force as a Chaplain. During an action at Killa Kazi, some men of the 9th Lancers fell into a wide nullah or ditch. The Afghans were nearby, but Mr Adams rushed into the water and extricated the men. There was doubt as to whether or not he was eligible for the VC, as he was not actually in the Army, but as the Queen wanted him to have it, the regulations were amended. He was recommended for the VC in 1879, but it was not gazetted until 26 August 1881.

General

The Department is multi-denominational, and each Regimental Chaplain has men under his spiritual care whose allegiance is not necessarily to his particular branch of the Church. The role of the Chaplain is very similar to that undertaken in a civilian parish, including the administration of the Sacraments and conduct of Public Worship. In peace time, the Chaplain will join in with training of the unit, so as to be prepared for time of war when he would take on the full role with his Army 'parish'.

Chaplains are appointed by the Parliamentary Under-Secretary of State for the Armed Forces, on the nomination of the accredited representatives of the various denominations. These include the Church of England, Roman Catholic Church, the Baptists, United Reformed Church and Jews, as well as the Presbyterian Churches, that is the Church of Scotland, the Free Church of Scotland, the Presbyterian Church in Ireland and the Presbyterian Church of Wales. Members of the Department do not hold military ranks: however, the grades of Chaplains to the Forces equate to ranks, so 3rd Class are as Majors and 4th Class as Captains. They wear the appropriate badges of rank, but are not referred to by a military title.

This is the only branch of the army where personnel do not undergo weapon training, nor do they carry weapons. They do, however, have to assimilate the various military skills because of the need to conduct themselves safely in battle conditions, and to be able to live in the field alongside the soldiers. They need to appreciate the role of the unit they are attached to. For example, if that is a parachute unit, then they too would undertake parachute training and qualify for their wings.

Royal Corps of Transport

Regimental badge

On a star of eight points in silver within a scroll terminating in sprigs of laurel and inscribed *Royal Corps of Transport* all in gold encircling the garter proper on a crimson ground the royal cypher also in gold ensigned with the crown also in silver.

Regimental marches

The quick march is *Wait for the Wagon.*

Colonel-in-chief

HRH Princess Alice, Duchess of Gloucester.

Stable belt

Blue, white and red.

History

During his term of office as Quartermaster General, Sir Redvers Buller used his experience in the Zulu Wars to reorganize the logistic corps. He much appreciated the importance of proper logistic support for the Army, and was responsible for the formation of the second Army Service Corps. In 1888, the two functions of supply and transport were linked, and the Corps became a combatant regiment, with terms of service of officers and soldiers similar to the rest of the Army. From its experiences in the Boer War, the Army Service Corps was able to develop into an organization which could cope with the needs of an army in a European war against sophisticated opponents.

The First World War saw the emphasis change from animal to mechanical transport. On 27 November 1918, the Corps received its Royal prefix.

In 1965 the responsibility for the provision of ammunition and petrol, oil and lubricants was transferred to the Royal Army Ordnance Corps, and the operation of railways and docks, as well as responsibility for movement control, was taken over from the Royal Engineers. That same year, the Royal Army Service Corps was retitled Royal Corps of Transport.

General

The official description of the work of the Corps is: 'The chief responsibility. . .is to organize and operate the means of transport which support the British Army in war and peace. In addition the Corps executes the movement of men and material worldwide, operates ports and performs certain functions in connection with air movement and air logistic support.' This states clearly the job of the Corps, and to support the Army the TA provides a number of regiments to undertake a variety of roles from general driving and transporting, ambulances for the medical services, ammunition transport for the artillery, and railway specialists.

The Headquarters and Depot for the RCT TA is at Grantham in Lincolnshire. Specialist units of the Corps are based there, including four regiments, eight

Above *Drivers of the RCT need to take their vehicles over any kind of terrain, and their training goes far beyond the normal required for the HGV licence* (151 Transport Regt).

The RCT need to operate under NBC conditions (151 Transport Regt).

Left *Considerable driving skill is demanded from the RCT volunteers, and loading one vehicle onto the back of another is not as easy as it looks* (151 Transport Regt).

Below left *Being bogged down is a hazard of driving overland* (151 Transport Regt).

Right *Essential supplies of ammunition are moved in to the battle area to maintain the fighting strength of the troops* (216 Sqn RCT(V)).

Below *The RCT also have their HSF Squadron, seen here guarding a key point.*

independent squadrons and two large staff units, the latter providing liaison officers and movements staff officers to 50 British and NATO headquarters and units throughout the Continent and UK.

All the movement control elements of the Corps, together with Port and Railway Squadrons, are specialist units. HQ TA RCT runs all recruit and trade-training courses for the RCT TA, and provides all administration and training support for the specialist units.

RCT Independent units

Rather more than half the TA units of the Corps are Independent. These include:

150 (Northumbrian) Regiment, with its RHQ at Hull where it also has a band. Squadrons are 218 (East Riding) at Hull; 217 (Yorks) in Leeds, and 216 (Tyne Tees) at Tynemouth.

151 (Greater London) Regiment, with Squadrons 210 at Croydon, Clapham, Redhill and Sutton; 240 at Barnet, Slough and Hitchin; 562 at Southall, Bow and East Dulwich; and 215 (Essex) at Grays and Leigh-on-Sea.

152 (Ulster) Regiment, with Squadrons in Belfast and Londonderry.

153 (Highland) Artillery Support Regiment, with Squadrons 230 in Edinburgh; 231 at Dunfermline; 239 (Highland Yeomanry) at Cupar, Leven and Glenrothes, and 212 Ambulance at Aberdeen and Dunblane. The Regiment has Pipes and Drums as well as a motorcycle display team called the Blue Arrows.

154 (Lowland) Regiment, with Squadrons 221 in Glasgow; 222 at East Kilbride; 251 in Irvine; and 225 (QOLY) at Grangemouth and Edinburgh. 225 Squadron was formed from former members of The Queen's Own Lowland Yeomanry, which had been a reconnaissance regiment with The Royal Armoured Corps, disbanded in 1967. The old Regiment had three distinguished antecedents, The Lanarkshire Yeomanry, The Lothians and Border Horse and The Queen's Own Royal Glasgow Yeomanry. An eminent member of The Lothians and Border Horse was Sir Walter Scott, who was its Regimental Quartermaster at one time. All three regiments were equipped with tanks during the Second World War. A peculiarity of 225 Squadron is that its members retain the QOLY collar badges on their service dress uniforms.

155 (Wessex) Transport Regiment from Taunton has 232 Squadron at Tavistock and Plymouth, and 245 at Bristol. The Regiment traces its history back to 1904 when an Army Service Corps Company was formed from existing soldiers of the 2nd (Prince of Wales's) Volunteer Battalion, the Devonshire Regiment, which was the foundation for the 43rd (Wessex) Divisional Column RASC TA. In the First World War it took part in the Gallipoli Campaign, and after evacuation to Egypt in January 1916, the supply personnel went to France and the rest joined other formations. In the next war, the Column landed in France after D-Day, supporting the Army's move into Germany. In 1965 the Column took its present title.

156 (Merseyside and Greater Manchester) Transport Regiment has its HQ in Liverpool with the following four Squadrons: 234 (Wirral), 235 (Liverpool), 236 (Greater Manchester) and 238 (Sefton). Each Squadron's location is indicated by its title. The Regiment formed on 7 June 1980 from 156 (Lancashire and Cheshire) Transport Regiment, but its history goes back to the formation of the Territorial Force in 1908 and the raising of two Divisional Supply and Transport Columns in Lancashire from the volunteer companies of the Army Service Corps and Infantry volunteer units. Among the antecedents of the Squadrons, 234 was originally 102 Armoured Transport Regiment RASC, which became an amphibious unit from 1948 until 1957. 238 Squadron, the newest part of the Regiment has its origins with the 40th (King's) Royal Tank Regiment, which amalgamated with the 41 RTR in 1956, and in 1967 became C Squadron of The Duke of Lancaster's Own Yeomanry. In 1968 some of that unit's members rebadged to RCT. The 40th Tanks saw action in North Africa and Italy during the Second World War. The Regiment enjoys the freedom of Birkenhead through 234 Squadron, and of Southport through 235 Squadron. 238 Squadron received the Freedom of the Borough of Sefton in March 1982. In order to support 1 (BR) Corps in Germany in time of war, it is equipped with 16 tonne Fodens, 4 tonne Bedfords, Armstrong motorcycles, and Land Rovers.

157 (Wales and Midlands) Transport Regiment has its HQ at Cardiff, and its Squadrons are: 223 (South Wales) at Swansea; 224 (West Wales) at Carmarthen, Haverfordwest and Lampeter; and 237 (Midlands) at West Bromwich and Stoke-on-Trent. 233 Squadron traces it history to 53 Divisional Train ASC formed in 1909, and in 1966 they were granted the Freedom of the Borough of Port Talbot. 237 Squadron was formed at West Bromwich in May 1967 from four companies of 48 Divisional Regiment RCT. A (Pembroke Yeomanry) Troop of 224 Squadron has a rare distinction, tracing its history back through the Pembroke Yeomanry to the Castlemartin Yeomanry who gained the only volunteer battle honour on British soil when they helped to round up invading French forces on 22 February 1797.

216 (Tyne Tees) Squadron is part of a Regular Army

regiment, 2 Infantry Division Transport Regiment. As such, much of its training is carried out alongside regular soldiers. To equip it for its war role it has a wide range of vehicles, from Land Rovers to tankers. It traces its history to November 1938 when 30 (AA) Brigade Company RASC was formed at Darlington. It served through the Second World War, despite a number of title and number changes, until it was re-formed as 923 Company RASC in May 1947. It took up its present role in 1983 when 2nd Infantry Division returned to York, and the Divisional Transport Regiment was re-formed.

395 Air Despatch Troop is one of the smallest independent units, and is located at RAF Lyneham at Chippenham.

Bedford MK (4 × 4) 4 tonne truck

This has replaced the familiar Bedford RL Truck that served the British Forces so well from the early 1950s. The new one was introduced during the 1970s and has been produced in many variations. There are two main versions, the cargo truck and the cargo truck with a winch. Both of these are capable of being converted to a variety of uses. The Bedford MK (4 × 2) is also used throughout the Army for general stores carrying and driver training. The truck has a crew of one or two depending on its task.

Data: loaded weight is 9,650 kg, length is 6.579 metres, with a height to top of tarpaulin of 3.404 metres. The width is 2.489 metres. It has a maximum road speed of 73 km/h and on roads has a range of 560 km. The engine is a Bedford six cylinder, giving 106 brake horse power with a capacity of 5.42 litres.

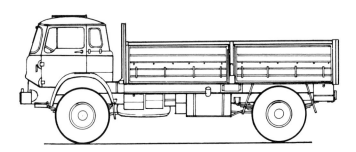

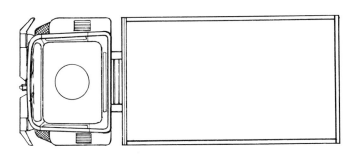
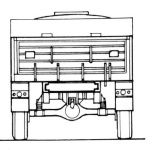

Foden 16 tonne 8 × 4 commercial pattern low mobility cargo truck

This series of vehicles is based on an ordinary commercial design, adapted for military load-carrying work along the lines of communication, with limited off-road work at terminals. Within the UK it has a maximum capacity of 18.27 tonnes and the military pattern body is 8.077 metres long, therefore able to accommodate up to 12 pallets or unit load containers of standard NATO sizes. It has a steel body with a timber floor, and the tailboards and dropsides are removable and interchangeable. Variations in service include the 12,000 litre Fuel Tanker, the 22,500 litre Fuel Tanker, and an eleven cubic metre tipper truck. These are in use with the RCT and RAOC. Being based on ordinary commercial models gives lower procurement costs and easier provision of spare parts. Production of this range of vehicles started in 1976 and was virtually completed two years later. Ease of accessibility is a virtue retained from the commercial models, and the cab can be tilted forward to expose the engine.

Data: The gross weight is 30.48 tonnes. It has a range of 500 km and a maximum road speed of 77 km/h. It is 10.278 metres long, 3.137 metres high and 2.497 metres wide. The engine is a Rolls-Royce Eagle 220 mark III with a capacity of 12.17 litres, developing 220 brake horse power.

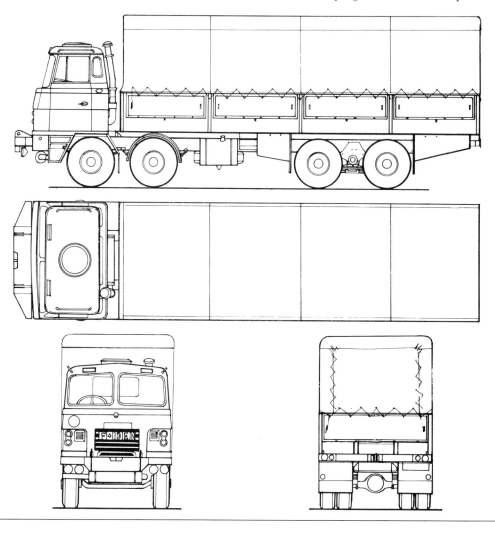

Armstrong MT 500 Military Motorcycle

This is now the general purpose motorcycle in the Army, and has replaced the earlier Canam machine in all arms.

Data: The dry unladen weight is 161 kg, the unladen seat height is 885 mm maximum, and the minimum laden ground clearance is 185 mm. The engine is an air-cooled single cylinder four stroke of 485 cc capacity, giving 32 brake horse power at 6,200 rpm. It has a five-speed integral with engine gearbox operating through a multiplate wet clutch. The maximum road speed is 167 km/h with an approximate range of 329 km. It can accelerate from nought to 106 km/h in 9.5 seconds.

Territorial Army Medical Services

The Army's medical services, staffed by both Regular and Territorial officers and soldiers, are formed by the Royal Army Medical Corps (RAMC), the Royal Army Dental Corps (RADC) and the Queen Alexandra's Royal Army Nursing Corps (QARANC). The Army needs a relatively small Regular service to maintain its peace-time requirements for hospital and routine health care of its soldiers and families. In time of war, however, this service has to more than double to cope with the much larger Army and expected battle casualties. Some of the additional service men and women will come from the reserves, but the most significant portion will come from the TA.

The three Corps manage a system which starts where there is a battle and stretches back to the UK. Casualties from the 'teeth arm' will receive their first medical aid from a doctor at the Regimental Aid Post (RAP), which is as close to the battle as possible. His job is to provide the essential life-saving treatment and to prepare a casualty for evacuation. From the RAP, the casualty goes back to the field ambulance. This is a mobile RAMC unit, which uses armoured, tracked and wheeled ambulances. Treatment is given at the two dressing stations that form part of the unit. This is aimed at continuing and reinforcing where necessary the first aid and resuscitative measures started in the RAP. Further back from the front are the field hospitals, where life-saving surgery is given, making casualties fit to be moved even further back.

To the rear are the general hospitals. These are large static units that provide treatment for the less seriously wounded, and the longer-term care of the sick and convalescent. Some of these hospitals will have specialist teams for neuro-surgery, burns, ophthalmic and maxillo-facial surgery. The Army Medical Services also provide field surgical teams (FSTs), consisting of surgeons, anaesthetists, theatre sisters and technicians.

Royal Army Medical Corps

Regimental badge
The Rod of Aesculapius the Serpent in silver within a wreath of laurel all gold thereunder a scroll inscribed *In Arduis Fidelis* in silver the whole ensigned with the crown in gold.

Regimental marches
The quick march is *Here's a Health unto His Majesty* and the slow march *Her Bright Smile Haunts Me Still.*

Colonel-in-Chief
HM Queen Elizabeth the Queen Mother.

Stable belt
Old Gold, Royal Blue and Cherry Red.

Regimental dress
Warrant Officers and Officers wear a Cherry Red jersey heavyweight with barrack dress.

Royal Army Dental Corps

Regimental badge
Within a laurel wreath a dragon's head and sword;

beneath, a scroll bearing the motto *Ex Dentibus Ensis*. The whole surmounted by a crown.

Regimental march

The quick march is *Green Facings*.

Stable belt

Green, red and blue.

Regimental dress

Warrant Officers and Officers wear a green jersey heavyweight in barrack dress.

Queen Alexandra's Royal Army Nursing Corps

Regimental badge

The cypher of HM the late Queen Alexandra combined with the Dannebrog, the whole within a laurel wreath inscribed with the Corps motto *Sub Cruce Candida* surmounted by a crown. On the lower portion of the wreath a scroll inscribed QARANC.

Regimental march

The quick march is *Grey and Scarlet*.

Colonel-in-Chief

HRH Princess Margaret, Countess of Snowdon.

Stable belt

White, red and blue.

History

There have been military medical services since the Regular Army was founded following King Charles II's restoration in 1660. It was not until 23 June 1898, however, that the medical officers and soldiers were incorporated into one body, The Royal Army Medical Corps. They have been needed in every campaign fought by the Army, and to testify to their gallantry, members of the Corps have been awarded 31 VCs including two double VCs. The QARANC was formed at the same time as the WRAC, on 1 February 1949. It replaced The Queen Alexandra's Imperial Military Nursing Service, which could trace its origins back to a group of nurses who took the

name of the third daughter of Queen Victoria in 1897, The Princess Christian's Army Nursing Service Reservists. In the Boer War it sent some 1,300 nursing officers overseas. Another predecessor was the Territorial Force Nursing Service, which was firmly established by the outbreak of the First World War, and supplied 8,000 nurses during the war years.

Individual units of the Army's Medical Services (TA) have impressive histories. 144 Parachute Field Ambulance goes back to April 1942 when, as 16 Para Field Ambulance, it was formed as part of 1st Airborne Division. 211 (Wessex) Field Hospital, although only formed on 1 April 1967, claims ancestry through 128 Field Ambulance to 1907. In the First World War this unit was awarded the French Croix de Guerre. This gives members of the unit the right to wear the ribbon of the medal on the left upper arm.

This was awarded for the unit's efforts between 22 and 25 October 1918 when the town of St Amand was heavily bombarded and 2,000 wounded, sick and disabled civilians were treated.

Although many of the medical units go back to the end of the last century, 220 (1st Home Counties) Field Ambulance is unique. Formed in 1886 as Volunteer Medical Staff Corps, 5th Division, it was just eleven years later when a severe typhoid epidemic swept through Maidstone in Kent. The unit volunteered for nursing and 'soup kitchen' duties, and as many as 30 men each night were caring for and nursing the victims. In 1900 the unit sent a detachment to the Boer War. In 1908, with the formation of the Territorial Force, it became the 1st Home Counties Field Ambulance. Its members were fully tested in the First World War, dealing with over 200 casualties a day soon after their arrival at the front line in January 1915. During the war three DSOs and five MCs were among the many honours awarded. In the Second World War the unit was on the Belgian front in time for the retreat to Dunkirk. Half the unit spent the rest of the war as prisoners, but the rest re-formed and served in North Africa and Italy, then on D-Day plus 4 landing in Normandy.

222 (East Midland) Field Ambulance stems from two sources. In 1902 the Sherwood Foresters Volunteer Infantry Brigade Bearer Company RAMC was formed, and on the formation of the TF in 1908 became the 1st North Midland Field Ambulance (TF). During the First World War it went to France with 46 (North Midland) Division, and it formed into four separate Field Ambulances. In 1920 it re-formed in its pre-war title and role. Two years later it took the number of its Brigade, 137 North Midland Field Ambulance (TA). In the Second World War it changed its role and title to 137 (Northern Midland) Field Dressing Station, a title it retained in 1947 when it re-formed as a TA unit.

1912: members of 88 Field Ambulance at their Woodbridge Road Drill Hall.

The other source also originated in 1902 with the formation of the Leicestershire and Lincolnshire Volunteer Infantry Brigade Bearer Company RAMC. In 1908 this became the 2nd North Midland Field Ambulance (TF). It also went to France with 46 Division and it too grew into four Field Ambulances. It re-formed in 1920 as 2nd North Midland Field Ambulance (TA), but two years later was disbanded as an economy. It was raised again for the Second World War as 3rd (2nd Northern) Casualty Clearing Station, its title altering during the War to 9 (Northern) CCS. This was the title it retained in 1946 as a TA unit, but the following year it changed to 149 (Leicestershire) Field Ambulance. On 31 January 1967 these two units merged to form 222 (East Midlands) Field Ambulance RAMC (V).

257 (Southern) General Hospital formed in April 1967, from five separate units. These were 10 (London) General Hospital, 57 (Middlesex) General Hospital, 161 (Ipswich) Field Ambulance, 162 (Cambridge) Field Ambulance and 163 (Norwich) Field Ambulance. On 1 December 1969 the 'Eastern' in the title was changed to 'Southern'.

10 (London) started life as 10 Field Dressing Sta-tion, raised and based at the Duke of York's HQ at Chelsea before the Second World War. The unit was at Dunkirk, where it was largely captured. In 1947, it was re-formed at Chelsea as a General Hospital.

57's history is similar to that of 161, 162 and 163. A Volunteer Medical Company existed before the 1908 formation of the TF, when it became 167 and 168 Field Ambulances. 167 split off a cadre which became 162 Field Ambulance, and this unit shared accommodation with a Company of the Middlesex Regiment (57th of Foot, the 'Diehards'). 162 Field Ambulance was in 54 Division in 1914 and served in France, moving to Palestine in 1917 to take part in the third battle of Gaza. During the Second World War it became a training unit, before going to France after D-Day as a Field Ambulance on the lines of communications. After the War, 2 (London) General Hospital was raised, but the title was changed to 57 (Middlesex) in 1948 to avoid confusion with 2 (Scottish) General Hospital. 57 was chosen because of the historic association with the 57th of Foot.

161 had been with 21 Army Group in North-West Europe at the latter part of the Second World War and was responsible for much of the relief work when

Medics under training need to know about weapons, either to defend themselves and their patients, or to fight to recover a casualty.

Belsen was liberated. Re-formed in 1947 it became part of 161 Brigade and 54 East Anglia Division at Ipswich until 1967. 162 was re-formed at Cambridge in 1948, sharing accommodation with 6 General Hospital. Little is known of 163 prior to 1951, when it had been a Field Dressing Station, but in 1957 it became a Field Ambulance at Norwich.

257 are also the hosts for the Army Medical Services Band. A pipe band had been formed by 57 (Middlesex) General Hospital in 1953 and this was continued with varied fortunes in 1967, but in April 1984 all the assets of the RAMC Staff Band were transferred to 257 and the band was re-formed as a TA Band.

General

Today a large number of volunteers are members of specialists units attached to the TA HQ at Keogh Barracks in Aldershot. Among the independent Field Ambulance Units are 144 (Parachute) at Chelsea, Bilborough and Cardiff; 220 (1st Home Counties) at Maidstone and Tunbridge Wells; 221 at Kingston upon Thames, and Clapham; 222 (East Midlands) at Leicester, Derby and Bulwell; 223 (Durham) at Newton Aycliffe, Barnard Castle and Stockton on Tees; 224 at Stoke-on-Trent; 225 (Highland) at Forfar; 250 at Hull and Grimsby; 251 (Sunderland) in Sunderland; 252 (Highland) at Aberdeen and Montrose; 253 (Northern Ireland) at Belfast and Londonderry; and 254 at Cambridge. The Field Hospitals include 211 (Wessex) at Barnstaple, Truro, Plymouth and Exeter; 212 (Sheffield) in Sheffield; and 219 (Wessex) at Keynsham near Bristol, and Portsmouth, Weymouth and Oxford. The General Hospitals are 201 (Northern) at Newcastle upon Tyne, and Cramlington; 202 at Birmingham and Coventry; 203 (Wales) at Cardiff, Newport and Swansea; 204 (North Irish) at Belfast, Carryduff, Dungannon and Holywood; 205 (Scottish) at Glasgow, Edinburgh, Dunoon and Inverness; 207 (Manchester) at Old Trafford, Halton and Blackburn; 208 (Merseyside) at Liverpool and Ellesmere Port; 217 at Walworth and Blackheath in South London, and Brighton; and 257 at Chelsea, Harrow, Ipswich and Norwich.

Hygiene is an essential skill for the medics.

TA members of the QARANC and RAMC train at first aid.

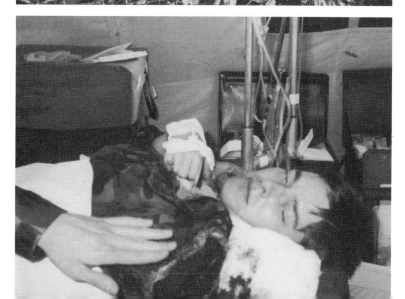

A simulated casualty (217 General Hospital).

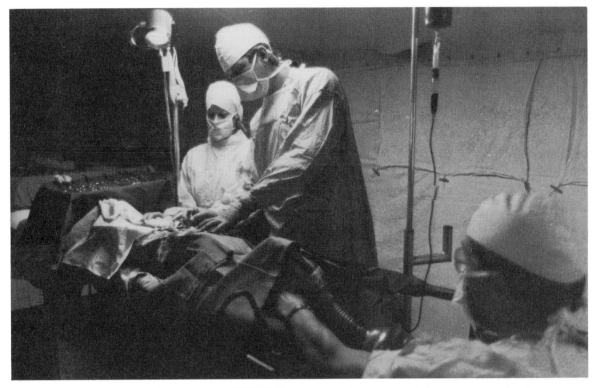

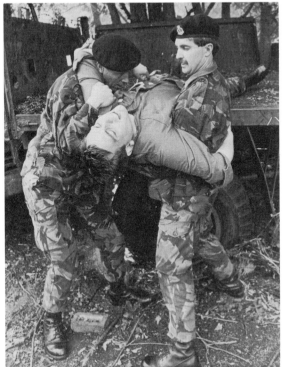

Above *Surgeons at work in a canvas operating theatre.*

Left *The Combat Medical Technician is the linchpin of the RAMC and needs to be able to turn his hand to anything.*

Below *Two Combat Medical Technicians under training at Aldershot, prepared to defend their Field Hospital.*

Operating Theatre Technician

The operating theatre technician (OTT) has to prepare the operating rooms and anaesthetic for use in the various hospitals and in the field. An OTT needs a detailed knowledge of drugs, instruments and equipment used, as well as the hazards and complications that could arise during and after surgery. A most exacting task is the proper sterilization of all equipment and the cleaning of the operating theatres. This calls for a high degree of skill. The recruit OTT needs a good all-round education. The aim of training is to get each OTT to the high standard where he can take subordinate charge of an operating theatre under all circumstances, and the top OTTs can be eligible for a commission.

Royal Army Ordnance Corps

Regimental badge
The Arms of the Board of Ordnance within the Garter surmounted by the Crown. Motto *Sua tela tonanti* (normal translation 'To the Warrior his Arms').

Colonel-in-Chief
THE QUEEN.

Regimental march
The quick march is *The Village Blacksmith*.

Stable belt
Blue with two red horizontal stripes.

History
The RAOC has been heavily dependent on TA units since 1920, when Divisional Ordnance Companies were formed for each TA Division. Former officers and men who had served with the Corps during the war, including a number of civilians in the depots, were quick to respond. Pride of place is given to Major E. Williams, who is the first recorded RAOC

TA officer in the Army List, and he served with the Northumbrian Ordnance Company from 31 May 1920. He was quickly followed by others joining the 1st and 2nd London, Highland, Welsh, Essex and West Riding Companies. Great energy and enthusiasm, characteristics of the TA, brought most companies quickly up to strength, but as part of the national economy drive the establishments were later

Combat Medical Technician
The linchpin of the RAMC is the Combat Medical Technician (CMT). He works right up in the battle area, treating the wounded and getting them back to the field ambulance. This means that a CMT has to be a very efficient soldier, able to survive, fight if necessary and stay alive in the battlefield: all this as well as being very adept at first aid. This job requires no special qualifications for a recruit, only a good all-round education and a good level of fitness.

The initial recruit training leads to CMT Class 3 with the basic training in first-aid techniques and theory. At this stage a CMT will know as much about camouflage, map reading and staying alive as any TA infantryman, as well as being proficient at the sub-machine-gun. A good knowledge is needed also about the types of weapon used by infantry and armour, so as to be able at least to make them safe when dealing with casualties. Driving skills are necessary, as is the ability to use radio communications effectively, so as to report back to the field ambulance and radio for help when needed. An important part of the work is to be able to set up tented units and instal the vital equipment needed to operate them. Once a CMT is adequately experienced as a Class 3 technician, more training and experience will advance him eventually to CMT Class 1.

With increased qualifications, promotion is open to a CMT. As a Sergeant, for example, a CMT will be in charge of a section of a field ambulance, and perhaps co-ordinate the collection, treatment and evacuation of casualties in a designated area of the battlefield. The Sergeant would also have responsibility for feeding, re-supplying, defending and transporting his soldiers and the wounded in his charge. Experienced CMT may become Warrant Officers or be commissioned either as Administrative Officers or in the Quartermaster category.

Ammunition on its way up to the front.

cut. Many keen and able men were discharged, but those who were left carried on the training, giving valuable assistance to the Regulars of the Corps at the annual manoeuvres.

By 1923, the companies were in an operational state, well trained to assist in the issue of stores to their formations. The Company with 56 London Division, with a strength of only 27 other ranks, trained for a camp period over four weeks, during which time they handled over 200 tons of stores. In the first weekend of the camp they drew the stores from Hilsea and set up a divisional dump at East Boldre in the New Forest, and the next week the issue and return of surpluses occupied their time. During the last week they received all their stores back, checked, sorted and loaded them on to railway wagons for return to Hilsea by the Friday night. In 1924, the 49th (West Riding) Company had the unusual experience of receiving over 400 tons of stores in the docks at Douglas, Isle of Man, for the divisional camp at Ramsey. Persistent rain fell, but they stuck to their timetable, and all stores were transferred in good order, and this with a strength of only 17 men. In the Second World War, RAOC TA units operated and fought in every theatre of battle, and specialist RAOC TA personnel in the Army Emergency Reserve fought in Korea and Suez. During the 1960s, RAOC TA suffered, as did the rest of the TA, with reorganization, but they have expanded again during the 1980s.

General

The RAOC is the Army's principal supply Corps, providing all the weapons, missiles, ammunition, vehicles, technical equipment, fuel and food required by a modern army. To carry out these tasks, the most up-to-date equipment is used to account, hold and handle the vast quantities of stores involved.

The Independent Ordnance Companies (V) are 22 at Middlesborough, 23 in Leeds, 55 for Middlesex, 72 at Telford, 73 at Romford and Colchester, 93 at Portsmouth, 94 (Scottish) in Glasgow, and the latest addition, 95 in Bristol. The tasks for these companies vary from holding general stores, to handling combat supplies and the storage and issue of bulk supplies of fuel. There are also a number of independent stores sections supporting REME Workshops and 383 Commando Petroleum Troop, based in Southampton, which is a part of the Ordnance Squadron of the Commando Logistic Regiment, Royal Marines.

There are 48 Specialist Units, commanded and administered by the TA HQ RAOC at Camberley in Surrey. These are trained to carry out tasks covering the whole spectrum of the Corp's duties. These include the operation of laundry equipment in support of RAMC field and general hospitals, and this job is unique to these specialist units. RAOC TA specialists worked full-time with the Army in the immediate aftermath of the Falklands War to assist in fuel handling and laundry operations.

An interesting tradition in the Corps is that, on posting, senior officers serving in Ordnance depots are expected to plant a walnut tree. This dates back to the Napoleonic wars, 1792 to 1815, when there was an acute shortage of walnut for the manufacture of gun stocks. The modern somewhat derogatory nickname for the Corps is 'blanket stackers'; however, a much earlier name was 'The Sugar Stick Brigade', and this stemmed for the red and white pattern on the uniform braid. An unusual Warrant Officer Class One appointment in the Corps is that of Conductor. It can be traced back to 1327 when Edward III appointed Conductors to convey stores. Today's appointment is considered the senior Army Warrant Officer appointment. The patron saint of the Corps is St Barbara.

Eager Beaver

The Eager Beaver is a rough terrain fork-lift tractor. It can go almost anywhere, and carry a very wide range of loads including ammunition, engine packs, spares and fuel pallets. The tractor, wheeled, fork lift 4,000 lb, Eager Beaver Mark 2, to give it its full title, was produced by Royal Ordnance plc at Nottingham. It is used throughout the services for loading and unloading. It can be either a 4 × 2 or a 4 × 4 vehicle, and is capable of fording up to .76 of a metre depth of water. **Data:** weight complete 2,961 kg, reducing to 2,560 kg for transport by air; it is 5.461 metres long and with the fork raised to its maximum its height is 3.708 metres, but to the top of the mast it is 2.388 metres, reduceable to 1.829 metres for transport by air. It is 1.854 metres wide. On roads it has a range of 644 km, but half that when used across country. It has a Perkins 4236 diesel of 3.8 litres, giving 78 brake horse power. Its maximum lift capability is 1,814 kg.

The fork-lift tilt is 13 degrees forward and 20 degrees backwards. Extras are available, including a small crane and an enclosed driver's cab.

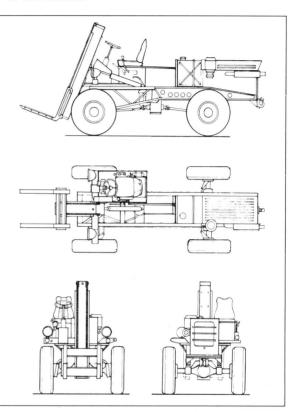

Corps of Royal Electrical and Mechanical Engineers

Regimental badge

Upon a lightning flash, a horse forcene gorged with a coronet of four fleur de lys, a chain reflexed over its back, and standing on a globe. Above a crown upon a scroll bearing the letters *REME*. Motto *Arte et Marte*.

Regimental Marches

The quick march is *Lillibulero* and *Aupres de ma Blonde*, and the slow march is *Duchess of Kent*.

Colonel-in-Chief

Field Marshall HRH Prince Philip, Duke of Edinburgh KG.

Stable belt

Dark blue, red and yellow.

General

The role of the Corps is to keep the Army's wide

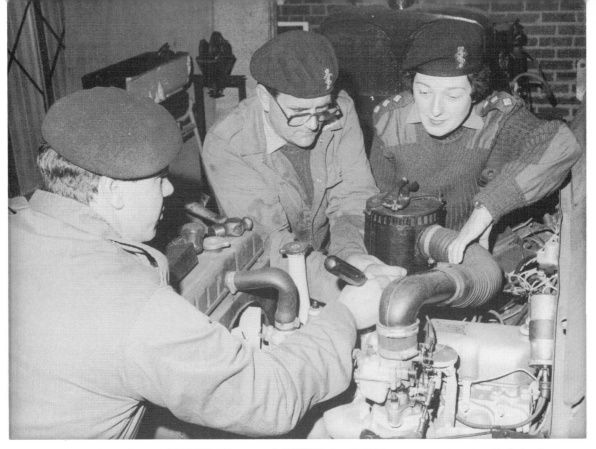

Above *Captain Elizabeth Warren commands a NATO workshop* (Roger Tutt).

REME are not only craftsmen, but have to be soldiers as well: **Left** *a REME volunteer leads a patrol* (151 Transport Regt.); **Above right** *Staff Sgt. Williams serving with* 10 PARA *heads the Battalion's rifle team* (10 PARA).

Right *REME fitter works on a motor cycle.*

range of vehicles and equipment in a state fit for operational use in time of war. A relatively new corps, only being established in 1942, it now provides skilled technicians and tradesmen to all major units. Many TA REME members are part of LADs, that is Light Aid Detachments, or Workshops. The LADs accompany their parent unit into battle, be it front-line infantry, the Yeomanry or a Signals Regiment in the rear area. The range of trades in the Corps includes electronic, aircraft, maritime, vehicle, weapons, driving and administrative.

There are three TA Recovery Companies of the Corps. 118 is at Leicester, Northampton and Corby; 119 (Holywell) is at Prestatyn, and 124 (Tyne Electrical Engineers) at Newcastle upon Tyne and Newton Aycliffe. The major role of these units is the recovery of broken down or damaged equipment. 118 Recovery Company was formed in 1967 from several disbanded units, and has amongst its roles the recovery of vehicles and equipment, and the clearance of the main supply routes, as well as returning vehicles and equipment from the forward battle areas to REME Workshops for repair. With a total strength of over 200 officers and men, it comprises a Headquarters platoon, four light Recovery Platoons and a General Service Platoon. Each Recovery Platoon is fully self-supporting.

The REME task

The tasks of REME can be summarized as follows:

1. Promotion of reliability and ease of maintenance of Army equipment from its inception to the end of its useful life.
2. Advice to other arms and services on professional engineering and matters affecting the reliability and maintenance of equipment.
3. Preparation of procedures and instructions concerning the repair and maintenance of equipment.
4. Maintenance of equipment in a fit state for operational and training use by periodic inspections, defects investigations, modification and repair.
5. Recovery of broken down or damaged equipment.

Above *Running repairs to keep the army on the move.*

Below *REME stores need to be extensive to cope with the wide range of vehicles and equipment* (COI).

133 Corps Troops Workshop is located at Maidstone and Deal in Kent. Not for them the centrally-heated workshops and a set time for each job. They have to put the Army back on its wheels and tracks in double-quick time in the field. 9 Field Workshop at Portsmouth provides technical repair support to units of the Logistic Support Group (LSG). This means keeping roadworthy a complete range of wheeled vehicles from motorcycles to 16 tonne cargo trucks vital to the chain of resupply. They also repair the complete range of small arms, machine-guns,

anti-tank weapons, radios and associated equipment. This workshop is divided into four platoons. Number 1 Platoon deals with vehicles. Number 2 Platoon has the armourers as well as metalsmiths and telecommunications experts. Number 3 Platoon holds the stores, the HQ Platoon provides the command and control as well as administrative back-up.

Unique in the Corps is 126 Reclamation Unit at Coventry which has a headquarters and two platoons of independent TA members, and one platoon of specialist TA. This unit's skill is to be able to can-nibalize vehicles written off by either accident or enemy action, and not only provide a supply of spare parts, but also build completely new vehicles from the bits and pieces of others.

There are 24 specialist units under the direct command of the TA HQ at Bordon in Hampshire. The Corps is also unusual in that there are three specialists units that form permanent parts of Regular Army units. These are 3 Field Workshop at Tidworth, 15 Field Workshop at Catterick and 17 Port and Maritime Workshop at Marchwood.

Recovery Vehicle Wheeled

The Foden (6 × 6) Recovery Vehicle, Wheeled (GS) is a Foden Truck 6 × 6 wheeled drive chassis fitted with the EKA Compact Recovery unit. This includes powered winches and crane facilities for lifting vehicles, and for supported or suspended tow. It was ordered for the Army in September 1984 and is a development of the Foden FH70 tractor and limber vehicle. With its power and equipment, it can recover all of the Army's logistic support vehicles, up to and including the 16 tonne, and can recover wheeled tracked and plant and equipment vehicles up to its capacity.
Data: It has a Rolls-Royce 350 Mark III engine of 12.7 litres, four-stroke diesel straight six turbocharged giving 290 brake horse power at 1,950 rpm. This gives a maximum road speed of about 100 km/hr (62 mph).

The main winch is a Rotzler with a 25-tonne capacity, and 80 metres of wire rope; the front winch is a Hudson Wharton with a 10-tonne capacity.

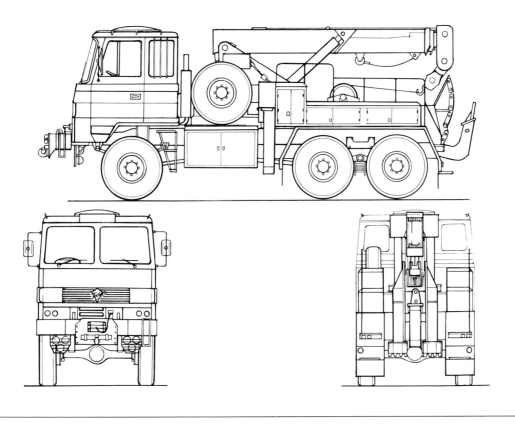

Corps of Royal Military Police

Regimental Badge
Within a laurel wreath, the royal cypher with crown above. Beneath, a scroll inscribed *Royal Military Police*. Motto: *Exemplo Ducemus.*

Regimental march
The quick march is *The Watchtower.*

Colonel-in-Chief
THE QUEEN

Stable belt
Red.

Regimental dress
The red beret is worn with combat, working and bar-

Giving accurate directions is just one of a TA RMP's duties (Roger Tutt).

rack dress, and a red lanyard is worn by Officers and Warrant Officers (Class 1) in service dress, and barrack dress shirt-sleeve order. The number one dress hat has a red top. When on provost duties, members of the Corps wear a red armband marked 'MP'. NCOs also wear a whistle and chain.

History
The early civilian title of 'Provost' was in the 16th century joined to the military term 'Marshal', to denote the earliest form of military policeman. Although a similar office to that of Provost Marshal existed before that, the first positively identified as such was Henry Guyleford, Provost Marshal of the 1511 Cadiz Expedition, and at the 1520 meeting between French and English Kings, known as the 'Field of the Cloth of Gold'. In 1813, Wellington raised the Staff Corps of Cavalry for Police duties, copying the then continental practice of having a permanent Military Police establishment. Members of this Corps wore a red scarf round the right arm for identification.

It was disbanded, but during 1854, a Mounted Staff Corps was raised from the Royal Irish Constabulary for duty in the Crimea, although after that war, they also were disbanded. A Mounted Military Police Corps was formed on 13 June 1855 for duty in Aldershot, from cavalry volunteers. Military Foot Police were formed in Egypt in 1882. Both mounted and foot police served in the Boer War.

Following the setting up of the Territorial Force in 1908, the establishment included an Assistant Provost Marshal and the Military Mounted Police. In 1938 a CMP Supplementary Reserve was formed into which 850 Automobile Association patrolmen were enlisted, and in the Spring of 1939, TA Provost Companies were raised with a strength of just over 1,000 all ranks, all of which saw service during the Second World War.

During the First World War, the Police had to learn new tactics, having to relearn its role under the altered conditions of battle. A major effort had to be made to control traffic and an efficient organization was soon in being. One Assistant Provost Marshal (Captain Straughan) produced the first traffic lights, in Poperinghe in 1916, using coloured flags by day and lamps by night. Their efforts resulted in the elimination of pre-battle casualties and of stagnation of men and supplies. In his final despatch, Earl Haig said: 'In the battle zone, where they frequently had to do duty in exposed position under heavy fire and suffered heavy casualties, the Military Police solved an important part of the problems of Traffic control by preventing the unavoidable congestion of troops and transport on the roads in the vicinity of active operations from degenerating into confusion.'

In the Second World War, Regular and Territorial military policemen served in all theatres of the war, and this service was recognized on 28 November 1946 when the 'Royal' prefix was awarded.

General

For many years, the TA RMP Companies took the name and number of the Division or Brigade for which it provided provost services, for example among the five units that came together to form 243 Company in 1967 were 51 Highland Division and 52 Lowland Division Provost Companies. Today there are five independent companies: 116 at West Bromwich, Coventry, Old Trafford and Cardiff; 243 at Edinburgh, Glenrothes and Stranraer; 252 at Stockton on Tees, Hull and Gateshead; 253 in South London, Brighton and Southampton; and 254 in Northern Ireland. In addition, under command of TA HQ at Chichester are two specialist companies, 163 and 164 Provost Companies and an SIB detachment. These draw their members from the civilian police service and the AA.

The wartime role of the Provost Units remains mainly traffic control, but they have to take on the additional tasks of NBC reconnaissance, military discipline and the maintenance of routes from such as sabotage, subversive or special forces attacks. Deserters and lost servicemen, prisoner of war control and refugees will also be problems they will have to tackle.

The standards demanded of the volunteer in the Corps are probably higher than in other arms, and the man or woman is expected to take on responsibility at an early stage. The basic rank in the Corps is Lance Corporal, and often they work alone or in small groups. Platoons in the Corps are commanded by Staff Sergeants, and Provost Companies are unusual in that they normally have a Warrant Officer Class One, a Regimental Sergeant Major as the Senior Warrant Officer.

Royal Army Pay Corps

Regimental badge

The royal crest in gold thereunder a scroll inscribed *Fide Et Fiducia* in silver (Faith and Confidence).

Regimental march

The quick march is *Imperial Echoes.*

Stable belt

A broad blue stripe, a double width primrose stripe, a single width white stripe and a broad red stripe.

General

Each Independent Unit of the TA has a small section of RAPC volunteers who provide the pay and financial support for that unit in conjunction with the permanent civilian administrative staff. Major units have a Paymaster, who is an officer whose rank will be from Second Lieutenant to Major, who is normally the imprest holder as well as the financial adviser to the Commanding Officer. He is supported by a small team of military accountants from Private to Warrant Officer, Class 2. These deal with the individual accounts of the soldiers of that unit on all matters relating to an individual's pay and allowances. Minor units normally have a senior NCO of the RAPC(V) who carries out the same functions for the individual soldiers, but is not the imprest holder.

At Worthy Down near Winchester, there is a Central Volunteer HQ where there is a specialist pool of Paymasters and military accountants, from Private to Major in rank and recruited nationally. These individuals form Unit Administrative Offices based upon similar lines to Independent Pay Teams and providing similar support to a large variety of Headquarters in the event of mobilization. The other tasks of CVHQ volunteers are to provide specialist pay units for particular operational tasks as well as individuals to act as reinforcement for the Fixed Centre pay Offices, according to their skills.

As well as the need to be the financial experts to the Army, each member of the RAPC has to master and maintain the basic military skills as an infantry soldier, to be able to take a full part in the role of the unit in which they serve.

Royal Army Veterinary Corps

Regimental badge

The figure of Chiron in silver within a wreath of

laurel thereunder a scroll inscribed *Royal Army Veterinary Corps*, the whole ensigned with the crown all gold.

Regimental marches
The quick march is an arrangement of *Drink Puppy Drink* and *A Hunting We Will Go*, and the slow march is *Golden Spurs*.

Stable belt
The belt is in stripes of a broad one in navy, a narrow one in yellow, a broad one in maroon, a narrow one in yellow and a broad one in navy.

Regimental dress
Members of the Corps wear a round-necked maroon jersey heavyweight with barrack dress.

General
There are two TA units with the Corps. One is based in BAOR and consists of one officer and thirty other ranks, all of whom are dog-handlers. The other unit is the RAVC TA Officers' Pool of veterinary officers. The Corps also trains members of the TA and HSF as dog-handlers.

Royal Pioneer Corps

Regimental badge
Two Pioneer axes crossed in saltire beneath their heads and surmounted on a Pioneer sword and laurel wreath below the same a scroll inscribed *Royal Pioneers* and the whole ensigned by a royal crown all argent.

Regimental march
The quick march is *The Pioneer Corps.*

Colonel-in-Chief
HRH The Duke of Gloucester.

Stable belt
Dark blue with red and green horizontal stripes. The buckle is silver with the regimental badge thereon.

Regimental dress
The beret is Khaki. Officers wear a black patch behind the badge on the beret.

General
Versatility sums up the task of the Corps today. Things have changed since its members were the Army's labourers, although still wherever the Army has a task that does not readily fit into the role of another corps or organization, the Corps is likely to find itself on the receiving end. They are fighting soldiers, but specialize in many security duties, including that of dog handling as well as assisting in moving stores, loading and unloading vehicles, ships and aircraft. The TA is represented in the Corps by three specialist Companies attached to the CV HQ at Wooton, as well as a Civil Labour Unit.

Intelligence Corps

Regimental badge
A Union rose within two branches of laurel surmounted by a crown; below the laurel, a scroll inscribed *Intelligence Corps.*

Motto
Manui Dat Cognitio Vires (Knowledge gives strength to the arm).

Regimental marches
The quick march is *The Rose and the Laurel* and the slow march *Trumpet Tune (and Ayre).*

Colonel-in-Chief
Field Marshal HRH Prince Philip, Duke of Edinburgh KG.

Stable belt
Green, with a centre grey band edged in red, top and bottom.

Regimental dress

Members of the Corps wear the cypress green beret.

General

The Intelligence Corps first existed between 5 August 1914 and 12 December 1929, but it was re-formed for the Second World War, the approval of King George VI being given on 15 July 1940, and announced in Army Order 112, four days later.

The TA element of the Corps is the Intelligence and Security Group (Volunteers), which has its headquarters in London and sub-units throughout the United Kingdom. Recruits have high academic qualifications with a good grounding in modern languages. The Group is affiliated to the Worshipful Company of Painter Stainers, a City of London Livery Company.

Members of the Corps have two basic duties: security and combat intelligence. These two often overlap, especially in wartime. All members are trained in the basic arts of both disciplines as well as additional skills, such as languages or photography.

To illustrate the work of the Corps, let us look at them on exercise.

Combat Intelligence

A British Division has deployed and waits in defensive positions for the advance of a force representing the enemy. The attack comes in the early hours one morning. In his tactical headquarters, the Major-General commanding the Division receives his briefing from the G2, Intelligence Staff on the current situation. Before he can plan his defensive operations he needs to know more about the enemy, and looks to his staff to find the answers:

What is the enemy strength and composition?

What are the enemy's objectives, his weaknesses and his headquarters?

When will he commit his immediate reserves?

Anticipating this briefing, the staff would have gathered in reports from the various armoured reconnaissance units, who are watching and reporting; refugees will have been questioned on what they have seen or heard; photographic reconnaissance crews will have been briefed; radar has monitored the enemy; helicopter pilots will have made visual observations and reported back; and information from other front-line troops on the Divisional flanks will have been collated. All sources of information will have been studied, along with the results of photo reconnaissance. As prisoners come in, they are questioned in their own language by Intelligence staff, and captured documents and maps are analysed. This vital briefing to the Divisional Commander is given using battle maps and photographs. The better his knowledge of the enemy, the better he can fight the battle.

Once the briefing is over, it is then a continuous process to keep that vital information up to date, constantly analysing new data as it comes in from whatever source.

Army Catering Corps

Regimental badge

Within a circle inscribed *Army Catering Corps* an ancient Grecian brazier set upon a scroll bearing the motto *We sustain*. The whole surmounted by a crown. The brazier in silver, the remainder in gold.

Regimental march

The quick march is *Sugar and Spice*.

Colonel-in-Chief

Honorary Major-General HRH The Duchess of Kent.

Stable belt

Grebe grey, bunting yellow and navy blue, with a central buckle and mounted Corps badge.

General

Only established in 1941, the Army Catering Corps provides feeding for all levels of the Army. The Corps is represented in most TA units, feeding the officers and men whenever the unit gets together. A large group of specialist caterers is maintained at the Central Volunteer HQ at Aldershot. Many TA members of the Corps in civilian life are in the hotel and catering profession, thus bringing to the Army some very well qualified and experienced caterers. As well as being skilled at catering, each member of the Corps has to be trained as a soldier, capable of taking his or her place alongside the members of the regiment or battalion to whom they are attached in the fighting role. It is not unusual for TA members of the Corps to win the various competitions open to both Regular and TA in 'combat catering', which tests everything from weapons to pastry.

Women's Royal Army Corps

Regimental badge
A laurel wreath surmounted by a crown; within the wreath a lioness rampant. *Sauviter in modo, fortiter in re.*

Regimental marches
The quick march is an arrangement of *Lass of Richmond Hill* and *Early One Morning*, the pipe air is *The Nut Brown Maiden* and the slow march is *Greensleeves.*

Commandant-in-Chief
HM Queen Elizabeth the Queen Mother.

Controller Commandant
Honorary Major-General HRH The Duchess of Kent.

General
The WRAC is organized and trained as an integral part of the Army. As its TA members are employed in jobs within the regiments, battalions or other corps, they have a wide range of trades. Their role is non-combatant, but they need to know something of the weapons available in the unit to which they are attached. In many cases, the Royal Signals for example, some of the operational, as well as support posts can be undertaken by either a man or woman, including command tasks. It is now not unusual for a member of the WRAC to command a troop or squadron, and some have risen higher.

History
The first definitive work on the history of women in

WRAC best young shot receives her trophy (38 Signal Regiment).

the Territorial Army was that of Major Pam Huggett, a TA Public Information Officer. She produced an article for the Territorial Army Magazine (which is no longer in publication) which appeared in their 75th anniversary souvenir issue in 1983. She had joined 39 (City of London) Signals Regiment in 1972, and as a Corporal in 1975 was commissioned, moving to the TA Pool of Public Information Officers two years later. The WRAC and QARANC are unique in that they are corps of both the Regular Army and TA whose pedigrees are only from the volunteers, the first women in uniform being members of volunteer bodies.

The Girls in Green and Grey

Soon after the formation of the Territorials it was realized that this new force, most of which were field forces, needed, or could need, nursing cover, and a circular was sent to all Territorial Association Secretaries in August 1908 requiring them to 'staff' 23 hospitals around the country.

The Associations were expected to get, and hold, a list of nurses who were prepared to put their skills to military use in the event of an invasion. Priority was given to members of the Princess Christian's Army Nursing Service reservists, probably the forerunner of women's service in this country, which had already proved itself in the Boer War by sending some 1,300 nursing officers overseas. By 1908 there was a second nursing reserve set up by the Princess of Wales, later to become Queen Alexandra, which become the Queen Alexandra's Imperial Military Nursing Service and eventually Queen Alexandra's Royal Army Nursing Corps. But many new names were needed, names of nurses who had at least three years' nursing service and were between 25 (this was later lowered to 23) and 50. The most important people to recruit were the matrons, especially as these were the only members of the new Territorial Force Nursing Service who were expected to give any time, during peace, to the new service. The nurses were expected to report once a year to confirm they were still nursing, to give their current address and working establishment, whereas the matrons had to attend for one week a year to be instructed in the Army's way of doing things and to test their efficiency. To show how little things change, the required attendance for a nursing officer today is still only eight days.

These matrons were expected not only to run their own civilian hospitals (it was a requirement of their service that they held such a post), but were also expected to administer their TFNS hospital and attend the training week as a true volunteer, a small honorarium being paid if they were acceptable.

By the outbreak of the First World War the TFNS was firmly established and supplied over 8,000 nurses during the war years, the first General Hospital landing in France on 12 August 1914, six years almost to the day after the force was started.

Meanwhile, the non-nursing ladies had not been idle. Realizing that there were still gaping holes in the system, a group of horsewomen got together, called themselves the First Aid Nursing Yeomanry, and prepared themselves to ride into the field of battle to retrieve the injured and return them to the safety of the military hospitals which were accommodated in large houses or tents, a situation which had existed in Roman times and still exists today.

Luckily by the time the First World War broke out, the horse had already been overtaken by the motor vehicle and the girls had been trained as motor mechanics and drivers. Maybe it was an indication of the Englishman's distaste of women in uniform, or perhaps he was just protecting his women; either way their services were initially rejected by England, although they were readily accepted by Belgium and France.

In 1914 another service emerged. The Women's Legion employed cooks and drivers and it aimed to be 'a capable and efficient body of women whose services could be offered to the state to take the place of men needed in the firing line or in other capacities'.

Another formation of drivers was also in the field, the Volunteer Aid Detachment, formed in 1910, who were ambulance-driving nursing auxiliaries.

In an effort to integrate all these separate agencies, the War Department authorized the Women's Army Auxiliary Corps in 1917. The Corps was paid and controlled by the War Department and the girls, other than nurses, were initially employed only overseas, but later they were accepted at home and many were employed as clerks and in signals, where they were known as the Hushwaacs. Queen Mary was very impressed by this service and in 1918 gave it her name and became Commandant-in-Chief.

In the period after the War, when everyone was taking note of the lessons learned and working towards greater efficiency and better administration, the traditional ploy of change the name and change the image was used, and the Territorial Force became the Territorial Army. The TFNS became the TANS and the Queen Mary's Army Auxiliary Corps was disbanded in 1921, leaving the original organizations still in the field; they had been reluctant to relinquish their individuality, anyway.

Although the nurses had been accepted by all as having officer status, there was no rank structure among them, except for the normal hospital hierarchy. As a result it was not possible to award them the Military Cross. They were therefore awarded the

Military Medal, which was instituted by King George V 'for bravery in the field or, as in the case of women, for devotion to duty under fire'.

Nothing more was done until the rumblings of war began to echo across Europe again. After much discussion between the Territorial Army, the Air Force Associations and the existing voluntary women's organizations a scheme was formulated and Royal Assent given for non-nursing women to be affiliated with the TA, on 9 September 1938. This gave the go ahead for the recruitment of 20,000 women between the ages of 18 and 50 into companies of varying sizes, each to be commanded by a woman officer and attached to a Territorial Army unit in peace-time. The organization would be called the Auxiliary Territorial Service. The ATS was born.

Details of the organization were sent to TA Associations ten days later, with the instruction to take no action other than to accept nominations from the recognized groups, i.e. FANY, Women's Legion, VAD and the new Emergency Reserve which had fairly recently been set up to train potential officers. The reasoning behind this was to select a few officers and give them some training prior to general recruitment.

Each county was to appoint a female County Commandant and she would fill the appointments of junior officers. The status of the volunteers, both officers and members, was that of camp followers: civilians in the eyes of the law, and subject to military law only in the same way as all other civilians attached to the military.

It is true that one of the terms of enrolment was that every member would agree, if necessary, to accept minor punishments from her officers, but as the officers held no commissions, there was no vestige of authority by which these punishments could be enforced. Well before all the details of service could be sorted out the Munich crisis was upon the country and the hurried public announcement of the new service was made on 27 September 1938. The TA Associations had had their instructions for less than ten days. The local TA units had received no communication at all and adjutants of TA units all over the country, already busy checking their own mobilization procedures, were suddenly besieged by women eager for information as to how, when and where they could join.

When the panic of that autumn was over and the original volunteers received notification of this new service they discovered there were two types of service, local and general. Local service meant that on mobilization the volunteer could only be called upon to serve within daily reach of her home, whilst general service volunteers undertook to serve anywhere in the United Kingdom or overseas.

Annual camps would be held, and weekly training evenings, on the same lines as the men's Territorial Army. A uniform was issued for camp and training, but not bought from Selfridges as the non-affiliated ones had been. No one had decided what to pay the women, but all ranks received ten shillings for attending ten drill nights, while junior ranks received £1 for a 15 day camp and officers £2 for the same period. When mobilization came in 1939, the first ATS companies were called up, still not knowing what their rates of pay would be.

Uniform was one of the issues that convinced the War Office of the need for a lady Director. The Director General of the TA and his all-male staff found that Staff College training had not equipped them to deal with this new force of women. The last straw came when they were expected to decide whether to issue brassières and suspender belts or corsets. Officers and instructors of the TA units around the country were suffering from the same problem. Although the new companies of ATS were supposed to have their own officers, they were often chosen because they were geographically available, and not for any military knowledge. So it fell to the warrant officers in the first TA units to give the girls their first basic training in drill, first aid, field hygiene and military law as it applied to them. To say the least, the duties of these new girls were still very ill-defined. It came as no surprise to those connected with the original women's services when Dame Helen Gwynne-Vaughan was selected as the first Director. Although officially 'over age', she already had some 20 years experience of women's service connected with the military. In 1917, at the age of 38, and recently widowed, she had been head of the Department of Botany at Birkbeck College when she was asked if she would be interested in the WAAC. She became its Chief Controller overseas, planning and preparing the way for women to go to France.

In 1918 she had become head of the Women's Royal Air Force, and after demobilization had been largely instrumental in the formation of the Emergency Service. As a result she had been consulted repeatedly during the planning stages of the ATS.

The TANS merged with the AWIMNS under one Matron-in-Chief, and once again at the outbreak of the war the reserve was ready, each member holding secret mobilization papers waiting for the announcement by the BBC or in the Press, and on 10 September 1939 the first QAs went to France under the same conditions as they had done 25 years earlier. They were still camp followers, still had no rank structure, and neither were they protected by the Geneva Convention.

After Dunkirk the 'replacement of men by women' policy needed to be maximized. No longer could they accept ATS volunteers on a local service agreement,

WRAC recruits in barracks.

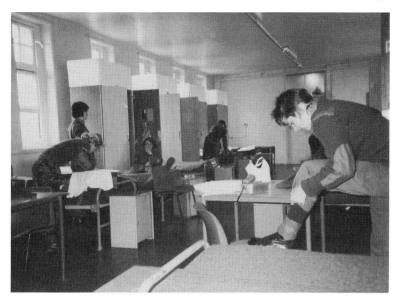

it was all or nothing. In late April 1941 the Defence (Women's Forces) Regulations were passed and at the end of May officers received commissions. On 1 July of the same year the Army Act was applied in modified form to the ATS. Shortly afterwards Dame Helen was replaced by Controller Jean Knox. The establishment of the ATS went from 40,000 to 200,000. Dame Helen wrote 'At last our women have ceased to be camp followers. At last the preliminaries have been achieved and the stage is set for them and for their power to serve'. The order permitting conscription of women was signed 5 March 1942.

The country found that six years of war had disrupted more than just social attitudes, but everyone was agreed on one thing, they would not let the ATS go as they had the QMAAC after the First World War. By the end of 1946, 403,000 ATSs and QAs had been demobilized and the TA was re-formed again on 1 January 1947. Although the title of the women's service remained the Auxiliary Territorial Service, a number of girls stayed on to become Regulars, many of whom had joined in 1938 as Territorials, been through the war years and then decided to stay in uniform. Alternatively, people rejoined the TA and helped to build the new battalions which were being formed all over the country, mostly on a county basis. They were attached to brigades and were usually about 300 strong, although size did vary, the largest being the West Lancashire, which covered Manchester, Cumbria and Westmoreland. Battalion training was given to cooks, clerks and drivers, stewardesses, medical orderlies and telephonists, but in the early days there was likely to be more officers than other ranks. There were some openings in mixed

signals and transport regiments where the girls could train with the men because their training was the same.

After a short time the newly established regular women's services became a Corps of the British Army. The ATS title certainly did have territorial connotations: the Women's Royal Army Corps replaced the ATS on 1 February 1949 and the Queen Alexandra's Royal Army Nursing Corps replaced the QAIMNS.

The ATS was not formally disbanded until 1954, but all the women in the TA who wished to transfer to the new Corps had to have their applications countersigned by a member of the Regular Corps. Many of the ATS Territorials who remained with the Regular Corps found that their post-war careers took them back to work very closely with TA units as training majors and adjutants. The strength of the women's TA was at its height at this time. The women's battalions, which were to be completely disbanded in the next ten years, accounted for ninety per cent of the 4,000 officers and servicewomen on the books in 1957. Conversely, the Territorial Army Nursing Service, which was now QARANC(TA), was at its lowest ebb, there being only 150 officers and servicewomen. The nursing service, however, did not suffer the same tremendous cutback as the WRAC and increased its numbers tenfold in the next ten years, while to belong to the WRAC(V) after the reorganization of 1967 was akin to belonging to a select club, there being only 370 on recorded strength, and all attached to mixed units. It was no wonder that the public did not realize there were openings in the Territorial Army for women, when so much publicity had been given to the reductions. It took fifteen years of hard recruiting and positive publicity to re-educate young women into joining, and only now have the numbers been recovered that were lost in the sixties.

Dual manning has been a mixed blessing for both Corps. In the Signals regiments there are many trades which are open to both men and women, and certain establishments have traditionally appealed more to the girls than the men.

As a result, mixed signals regiments find that most of their data telegraphists posts are filled by women, maybe because of the typing and paperwork, while the General Hospitals are finding more and more trained male nurses are taking the places that used to be filled by QAs. The openings for WRACs have increased gradually from Signals and RCT to include some Infantry units and REME, while to the girls in the University Officer Training Corps, the world is their oyster. The UOTCs opened to girls in the early fifties, with the aim not necessarily to recruit them into the Regular Army or the TA, but to give them an insight into the way the Army works and what it has to offer. From the very beginning, girls joined their UOTCs on attachments that were not generally open to girls in the TA. As a result they joined whichever corps or regiment had a unit at their University and, because they were doing the same training as the men, they learned very early in their careers to handle weapons.

The handling of weapons has been one of the biggest changes to affect the WRAC in recent years. For a long time the girls have been allowed sporting shooting only, but without altering their role, which remains non-combatant, they were at last allowed to train with hand guns, for self-defence purposes. They are still not issued with a personal weapon, but those who parade with a combatant unit are taught to handle a weapon when their Commanding Officer thinks there is a requirement.

The other major change recently has been in discipline. No longer does a unit employing women need to have a senior WRAC officer on its strength. Male senior officers have the right now to discipline the girls. The 'Queen Bees', as they were affectionately known, safeguarded the interests of the girls in their units and often had a very tough time doing it. On the other hand they were very strict with the girls themselves, maintaining and expecting very high standards from a small number of girls that could be outnumbered ten to one by the men.

The Pool of TA Public Information Officers

This is a pool of officers from all arms, including the WRAC, who have media and public relations skills

and experience in their civilian lives. Its members consist of journalists and editors, broadcasters and script writers, as well as public relations personnel.

The public needs to know about the Army, so TAPIOs are tasked to support the overall public relations policy objectives of the Army. The pool traces its origins back to the journalists who became specialist PR officers in the Second World War, and to the later TA Observers Pool. It is now established as a part of the Headquarters UKLF, and in peacetime it supports the Army's Public Information staff and the TAVRA staff. In war the Pool provides immediate reinforcement for the regular P Info staff in the UK, BAOR and elsewhere.

On exercise in the UK or abroad, TAPIOs will be found as part of a headquarters staff, assisting to operate a Press Information Centre or facilitating members of the Press with a project in the field.

The Music of the Territorial Army

Bands are a part of British military life, and despite the sophistication of the modern Army, they still have a place. Their role in the ceremonial life of the Army is essential, as their music not only provides entertainment for spectators but provides a vital aid to the marching in a parade, as well as helping to generate pride in the regimental family. Bands have considerable public relations impact, not only the sound of their music, but the appeal of their uniforms, many of which are ceremonial, rarely seen in other parts of the Army.

Bandsmen have nearly always had a secondary duty as stretcher bearers, and in today's Army they are now trained up as basic combat medical technicians. One of their roles will be to help staff the Army's hospitals.

The Territorial Army has twenty four bands throughout the country, and some of them have interesting antecedents.

Inns of Court and City Yeomanry Band

This is the band of the Royal Yeomanry, and like all other units of the Regiment it wears the uniform and badges of the Regiment of which it previously formed part. In this case the band carries on the TA traditions of the Inns of Court and City Yeomanry.

The band has its base in the traditional headquarters of the old Regiment in Lincoln's Inn, in the City of London, just north of Fleet Street. The records of that Regiment and its predecessors show that in the middle of the last century the officers hired five Italian musicians to provide them with music. The present band dates from about 1960 when musicians were recruited from the then Maidenhead Town Band. It flourished, and in 1967, when the Royal Yeomanry was formed, it became the new Regiment's band. The present Bandmaster is Mr Richard Walthew, recently retired from the Regular Army, having being the Band Corporal Major of the Band of the Life Guards. The band has an established size of 38 musicians, and it is growing into a concert band of a high standard. It attracts many former Regular Army musicians, especially from the Brigade of Guards, and has also been joined by students and graduates from the London Colleges of Music. Some members are professional or semi-professional musicians in their civilian lives. The high standard that has been reached is indicated by the gradings it has received when inspected by the Kneller Hall School of Military Music. In 1973 the grade was Excellent, the second highest grade, and in 1987 this was surpassed by the highest grade, Outstanding.

There are two uniforms for the band. Blues as worn by Cavalry and Yeomanry Regiments, and the full dress of one of its predecessor Regiments, the City of London Yeomanry (The Rough Riders). The full dress consists of a Lancer Cap with purple plume, a light blue tunic with purple facings and light blue overalls.

The band has engagements at home and abroad, in addition to its regimental duties. There have been several trips to Germany and twice it has toured Switzerland, where it has been twinned with Stadtmusic Zurich, the band of the City of Zurich. Each year it can be seen marching as part of the Lord Mayor's Show in London, but it also plays at concerts, both private and public. A favourite venue for the Band is the Fairfield Hall in Croydon. It has had several BBC engagements as well as having broadcast on Swiss radio. It has recorded the six regimental marches of the Royal Yeomanry, and there are plans to undertake further recordings.

The Royal Gloucestershire Hussars Band

In May 1984 the band celebrated its one hundred and fiftieth anniversary. A month after the Gloucestershire Yeomanry Cavalry had been formed, a meeting was held on 16 May 1834, where 'it was resolved to establish a Band, each troop to provide four musicians'. There are not many records of its early activities, but in 1871 it played the Yeomanry to the ranges and back, and in 1880 there is a record that at an Officers Mess Meeting, £20 was sanctioned to pay on account of the Band. From 1885, however, the Band served on a more businesslike footing. In 1890 the regimental march *D'ye ken John Peel* was first adopted, which was very appropriate as among the officers serving in the Regiment were four Masters of Hounds and a Field Master, as well as the fact that most members rode to hounds.

In 1891, it is recorded:

> The Band was now given a more suitable uniform than the one they had previously been wearing — pantaloons and boots being substituted for overalls, and scarlet hussar forage caps issued in place of old-fashioned peak caps. Pains were also taken to engage a number of old cavalry soldiers in the ranks of the Band in order to improve its equestrian powers as far as possible, which up to the present could not be said to have shown a high standard of excellence.

The band was disbanded shortly before the outbreak of the First World War, but re-formed in 1918 by Bandmaster, Mr Frank Dawes. He ran a hardware shop in London Road, Gloucester, and at the back had rehearsal rooms. All his employees were in the band, as well as a few professional musicians. It had a good reputation locally, playing in concerts and events in the county, as well as at regimental occasions. It was disbanded on the outbreak of the Second World War, and during the war Mr Dawes' house was destroyed, and with it the instruments, music and band uniforms. It was not re-formed again until 1959.

Since its re-forming it has had an unbroken existence, but there have been two distinct periods: from 1959 to 1967 as a brass band under Bandmaster Hopkins, and from 1967 when it has been a military band, the principal difference being the addition of woodwind in the latter.

Between 1961 and 1966 the Band entered 36 brass-band contests, both locally and nationally, winning 10 and being placed on 11 other occasions, moving to Section 1 in so doing. An early bandmaster, Mr Eric Hopkins, when recruited promised that the strength of the band would reach twenty five within six months and would broadcast within two years. Both these were achieved, the band appearing on the radio on 24 December 1962. When fully recruited, no fewer than four of the Bandsmen had sons also in the band.

In 1967, the bombshell of the savage cuts in the TA came, with the Regiment being disbanded. On 31 March the Regiment's brass band was disbanded, to be re-formed the following day with the band of the 5th Gloucesters, as a military band, and moved to Eastern Avenue at Gloucester, where it remains today. All the Hussars' kit, uniforms and the like, however, were removed to a private house, and the band survived. In the cuts of that year, somehow the band seems to have come through unscathed. The Band Secretary, Staff Sergeant Jack Thomas, took over the administration, including the pay, because the old Regiment had ceased to exist, being re-formed only as a cadre in 1969. They were administered for a while by 37 Signal Regiment at Bristol. Although the Wessex Yeomanry formed in 1971, it was not until 1 April the following year that the band rejoined the Regiment, administered once again from its base at Cirencester. Since then the Band has flourished.

34 (Northern) Signal Regiment (Volunteer) Band

This band has its headquarters at Brambles Farm in Middlesbrough and consists of 33 musicians, two of whom are WRAC and 20 of whom are former Regular Army musicians. The ceremonial dress is exactly the same as that for the Royal Corps of Signals Staff Band, consisting of scarlet tunics, blue cavalry-style trousers with a two and a half inch red stripe, George boots and spurs, amber dress cords, and a short busby with badge and red plume. They are able to perform as a concert or marching band, and have a fanfare team. There is also a 16-piece dance band and a 10-piece German-style 'Oompah' band. They average about 60 engagements a year, mostly in the North East, but sometimes to London or elsewhere in the UK. In 1983 they travelled to Mulheim in Germany to help celebrate the twinning of the towns of Darlington and Mulheim.

The Band was formed on 1 April 1967 when 49 and 50 Divisional Signals Regiments amalgamated, and it is the only Royal Signals TA Band. In common with other TA bands, they have a NRPS Staff Sergeant to co-ordinate the training.

The marching and concert bands of 34 (Northern) Signal Regiment.

The Band, which plays the Royal Corps of Signals Regimental March at the conclusion of all performances, was graded as very good on their last quinennial inspection by the Inspector of Army Bands in 1987.

The Volunteer (Northumbria) Band of The Royal Regiment of Fusiliers (6RRF)

The Band, with its headquarters in Newcastle upon Tyne, had orginally formed in 1951 as part of the 43rd Royal Tank Regiment, which became the 6th Battalion Royal Northumberland Fusiliers (TA) in 1956. Following the reorganization of the TA, the band was retitled Number 9 Staff Band in 1968, but took its present title in 1977.

There are 35 members in the Band, and it regularly turns out with 25 on parade. The uniform for band events is dress blues, cords and beret with hackle, and a cape and white mits during winter months. It is a marching band and has a full drum corps, who wear a scarlet uniform.

It is a family-type of band, with fathers and sons in its ranks. The present Sergeant-Major, Mr C.G. Collins, has three sons serving with him. Members have taken part in some major engagements, including appearing at the Royal Tournament and Beating the Retreat on Horse Guards in London.

The Fusiliers Volunteer Band

This band has been going in one form or another for up to 57 years, and has its base at Coventry in Warwickshire, administered by 5RRF. It was previously the band of the 7th Battalion, Warwickshire Fusiliers. In its present strength of 29 musicians there are six WRAC. It recently was required to form a fanfare team for a visit to Leamington Spa by the Queen, and the fanfare team has now become a permanent feature of the band. They have also played at such regular events as the Royal International Horse Show at the Birmingham National Exhibition Centre, and at the Ryder Cup.

The Royal Anglian Regiment Band (TA)

The Band took its present form and role on the reorganization of the TA in 1967. Before then it had been part of the 4th/5th Battalion, The Northamptonshire Regiment, with some elements from the Suffolk, Cambridgeshire, Bedfordshire and Hertfordshire Regiments included. During the Second World War many of the Band went with the BEF to France as medical assistants. It was during the period 1939 to 1940 that Sergeant Horace Rayment, a clarinet player, was awarded the Military Medal and bar, dispelling the popular image that Bandsmen are rear-area soldiers.

Those members of the Band who were in reserved occupations or too old for active service remained at home and formed a Home Guard Band based at the depot in Northampton.

Between 1967 and the time the Band took its present title, on 1 August 1968, the Band was called Number 4 Area Band. Although it is administered by the 5th Battalion The Royal Anglian Regiment, it serves all three TA Battalions of the Regiment. Of its 37 musicians, there are a number of WRAC and some Junior Bandsmen, so the age range is from 17 to 57 and there is one father and son combination serving. Among the honorary members of the band, who play with them at times for their own enjoyment, is Mr James Stallerbrass BEM, who has over 50 years of military music experience. The current Bandmaster is a former Regular Bandmaster, having served in that capacity with the Queen's Regiment, but who started with the Army in the 3rd Battalion The Royal Anglian Regiment.

The uniform worn by the band for its events is ceremonial scarlet tunics of the Royal Anglian pattern, with black epaulettes and cuffs and piped in white on the front, reverse and cuffs. The buttons are Royal Anglian pattern, showing the Leicestershire Tiger surmounted by a Laurel Wreath. There are six large buttons at the front, two small on the epaulettes, and six large on the skirt at the back of the tunic. Senior NCOs wear sashes, and badges of rank are gold on red. The trousers are standard Number One dress issue, with a one-inch red traditional infantry pattern stripe. The uniform is complemented by a Home Service Helmet in black, with brass fittings and a curb chain. For less prestigious events, at the Bandmaster's discretion members wear the Number One dress Blues uniform with a red cloth belt. This is worn without dress cords or wings. In both blues and ceremonial style uniforms medals are worn. The Number One dress forage cap with chin strap is worn with Blues. WRAC Bandswomen wear the standard WRAC dress uniform, with dress cords and cloth cap.

The band has many engagements, and as there are a number of RAF Stations in the area, is in great demand at their mess functions. It has a military band combination of brass, reed and percussion instruments. The band has a shortfall of french horns, saxophones, trombones and clarinets, and this presents a problem sometimes when selecting music; however, they are able to muster a very reasonable repertoire, as well as having the ability to change style. These styles include the full military band, a

16-piece dance or swing band, and a smaller jazz band combo. The last two are mainly used for events when a sponsor is paying the fees, with no cost to the public funds.

Regimental Band Royal Highland Fusiliers (TA)

This band is administered by the 1st Battalion 52nd Lowland Volunteers, and has its headquarters in Glasgow. It has about 28 members, six of whom are WRAC. The dress for band events is Number One Dress, Archer Green, in common with all Scottish Division Bands. The accoutrements are the same as for the Regular Army RHF Band, expect that plaids or Feather Bonnets are not worn.

It has the ability to provide marching and concert programmes, as well as dixieland, brass and wood-wind ensembles, and has many engagements at regimental functions as well as at fetes, festivals and parades.

The band formed in its present state in 1967, when all other TA bands in the Lowlands were disbanded.

The Volunteer Band of the Staffordshire Regiment (The Prince of Wales's)

This band, which changed its name in 1988 from the Band of the Mercian Volunteers, has its headquarters in Wolverhampton, and consists of 37 musicians, eight of whom are WRACs.

The ceremonial dress for male musicians is Number One Dress, consisting of forage caps, white belt with square silver buckle and regimental cap badge, shoes, shoulder wings and yellow dress cords. The Corps of Drums wear scarlet tunics with wings, embroidered with crown lace, infantry pattern, and infantry helmets of the Wolseley pattern.

The band's engagements include marching displays, processions, parades and concerts. In 1988 the band led the Lord Mayor's procession in Birmingham, gave a concert in the Wolverhampton Civic Centre, played at a One-Day International Cricket Match at Edgbaston, as well as the usual regimental and mess events and parades of Royal British Legion, Normandy, Korean, and Dunkirk Veterans.

The Band was formed in 1967 as the Band of the Mercian Volunteers, raised on the reorganization of the TA, and the original musicians came mainly from the 5th/6th Battalion The North Staffordshire Regiment, based in Burton-on-Trent. Today the Band is administered by the 3rd (V) Battalion The Staffordshire Regiment.

The Royal Regiment of Wales (TA) Band

The Band was formed in 1967, when the Monmouthshire Regiment and the Welch Regiments were disbanded and in their place The Welsh Volunteers were raised. In 1971 the elements of TA Infantry in South Wales were incorporated into the 3rd (V) Battalion The Royal Regiment of Wales. It is based at Newport in Gwent and made up of musicians originally from local brass bands or former Regulars from Army bands. The 3rd Battalion Corps of Drums, also based at Newport, accompany the Band on many of its parades and marching displays, as does the regimental mascot 'Dewi', a Kashmir goat from the royal herd.

The Band is a brass band, and does not have a woodwind section. Its present Bandmaster, Mr D.A. McCarthy, has served in the Band since 1968, and has played principal cornet with many famous brass bands.

At its many functions, including honorary degree ceremonies, inaugurations of High Sheriffs, as well as military and sporting events, the band wears its Number One dress, which is scarlet tunics and spiked helmet. There is a special mess uniform for playing at dinners.

North West Infantry Band (TA) (King's)

The present Band originated in 1959 with eight members of the 102 (Cheshire) Transport Column, RASC. Within 12 months it had reached full strength, with more members coming from the Royal Tank Regiment, Parachute Regiment, Artillery and the King's Regiment. In July 1965, when the RASC became RCT, the Band became part of 102 (Cheshire) Regiment RCT. For many years it was the champion North West Band, and it won the National Military Band contest at Reading in 1965. In 1966 the Band transferred to the Lancastrian Volunteers, with headquarters at Peninsula Barracks in Warrington. It had the honour to form part of a guard of honour for Her Majesty The Queen in 1971, when she opened the new Mersey Tunnel. In 1975, the Band rebadged to the 5th/8th Battalion the King's Regiment (V), and was designated an Area Band administered by that Battalion. The uniform worn is the same as that for the 1st Battalion King's Regiment, with whom they have close links.

This band is one of only two in the TA with a Director of Music, the other being the HAC. A Director of Music is a commissioned officer, whereas a Bandmaster is usually a Warrant Officer.

Band of the Yorkshire Volunteers

This band has its headquarters at Pontefract in the West Riding of Yorkshire, and it provides musical support for all battalions of the Regiment.

The Yorkshire Volunteers were formed on 1 April 1967 from a number of older Yorkshire TA Regiments. None of the six post-1967 Yorkshire battalions were authorized to retain or form a Regimental Band, so all the bands of the former TA battalions were disbanded, except The Leeds Rifle Band. This was retained, and redesignated The Yorkshire Brigade (Leeds Rifles) Band T&AVR. This lasted only eighteen months, as the Yorkshire Brigade was disbanded in July 1969, when the Band was renamed the Band of the Yorkshire Volunteers. The origins of The Leeds Rifles Band go back to 1859 when the 7th Yorkshire (West Riding) Rifle Volunteer Corps, popularly called 'The Leeds Rifles' was formed at the Town Hall in Leeds. It is not known exactly when the Band formed, but very early photographs show the Band formed up within a battalion square. In 1887, The Leeds Rifles Battalion was affiliated to The West Yorkshire Regiment (PWO), but they retained their original Rifle Green uniform and distinctive Leeds Rifles badges. These were maintained until 1968 when, as the Yorkshire Volunteers, the Band was dressed in regimental scarlet.

Army Medical Services TA Band

The Band was formed in 1984 as a TA band when the RAMC Staff Band was disbanded in April of that year. It is administered by 257 (Southern) General Hospital RAMC(V). Not only was the property of the former Regular Band invested in the new TA band, but the Band Sergeant-Major, Mr M.P. Feehily, came over as the Bandmaster, and a Regular Army Corporal from the Staff Band came across to help deal with the administration. The Regular Band had been based at Keogh Barracks at Ash Vale near Aldershot, the home of the RAMC, but the new TA Band has it headquarters at the Duke of York's HQ at Chelsea in London. Although there were many difficulties in forming the new band, in the November of the year it formed it was able to perform at a regimental dinner at the HQ mess of the Royal Army Medical College, and this was six months ahead of schedule.

Although now part of the TA, its origins are all Regular Army, and it is the true successor to the band formed in the 1880s for the Medical Staff Corps. The present Band is not just RAMC, but has WRAC and QARANC members as well, so can be said to truly represent most aspects of the Army's medical services.

The original Corps March *Her Bright Smile Haunts*

Me Still was reputed to be a tribute to Florence Nightingale, and this had been followed by *Washington Post* and *Bonnie Nell*, which remained the Corps March until 1948. In order to commemorate the Golden Jubilee of the Corps, and as a tribute to Her Majesty The Queen, now The Queen Mother, Colonel-in-Chief of the Corps, *Here's A Health Unto His Majesty* was officially adopted as the Corps march, and *Her Bright Smile Haunts Me Still* is retained as the slow march.

The Honourable Artillery Company Band

Lost in the mists of time as the origins of the HAC are, so are those of the Band. They have no doubt that there were bandsmen with the Company at the very beginning, but little has been written about them. In 1711, it is recorded that the sum of £4 was allowed for drums, music and grenades, and in order of march before His Majesty The King on 2 March 1727, 'The Grenadier Music, in a Rank' came seventh in precedence. Because of financial considerations in 1754, it was considered that the 'Grenadier's Music' was an unnecessary expense at breakfasts provided after public marches. In 1782, the Company marched through the City to Hyde Park, headed by the Regimental Band to celebrate the King's birthday. It consisted of four clarionets, two horns, one trumpet and two bassoons. There were also a Drum Major, eleven drummers and ten fifers. The history of the band is one of the history of ceremony of the Company, and many such duties are still carried out today. Traditionally it leads the Guard of Honour to and from the Guildhall for Heads of State and other distinguished visitors, and always has a part to play in the Lord Mayor's show, marching close to the gilded coach.

The Band also forms an orchestra to play for the Company and Ceremonial Dinners in the Long Room at Armoury House, Mansion House, Guildhall and various livery halls in the City.

Up to the First World War, the Band had been maintained and paid for out of the Company's funds, but when the TA was formed in 1920, the bandsmen became TA soldiers. The Band has maintained close links with both the Guards Regiments and the Royal Artillery, and many of the TA musicians are former Guards or Gunner bandsmen. In July 1968, the Band was inspected by the Inspector of Army Bands and the Chief Instructor of the Royal Military School of Music, Kneller Hall. The result was a splendid report and the Band was upgraded to a 'Staff Band', and this meant it then had the right to a commissioned officer as a Director of Music. Today the band consists of 45 musicians and is under the direction of

The pipes of the 4th (V) Battalion The Royal Irish Rangers.

Major Don Pryce, a former Regular Army Director of Music.

The Bands of The Territorial Army

Most bands are available for functions, but there are certain rules governing their use. Functions are in categories, such as official; service commerations; charities; unit functions; fee-paying engagements; and community relations. Before deciding whether or not an engagement can be accepted, the first priority is to decide whether or not it is suitable for the type of music the band can perform and the instruments it possesses. The next question is, are sufficient musicians with the correct combination of instrument capability available on the day? Like all TA soldiers, the musicians must put their families and civilian job first. All things being equal, the decision is usually made by the Band President, either the Training Major or Adjutant of the parent unit, in conjunction with the Director of Music or Bandmaster. Details of the units and bands should be found in the telephone book under 'Army', or details can be obtained by way of the local TAVRA office.

The twenty four bands of the TA are:

The Honourable Artillery Company Band, stationed at Armoury House in London, EC1;
The South Nottingham Hussars Yeomanry (RHA) Band, at Bulwell in Nottinghamshire;
The Royal Yeomanry Band (Inns of Court and City Yeomanry) in London, WC2;
The Royal Gloucestershire Hussar Band of The Wessex Yeomanry in Gloucester;

The Lancashire Artillery Volunteers Band at Bolton in Lancashire;
34 (Northern) Signal Regiment (Volunteer) Band, Royal Corps of Signals, at Middlesbrough;
The Royal Scots Territorial Band in Edinburgh;
The Queen's Regiment Band (TA) (5 QUEENS) at Canterbury in Kent;
The Volunteer (Northumbria) Band of The Royal Regiment of Fusiliers (6RRF) at Newcastle upon Tyne;
The Warwickshire (Volunteer) Band (5RRF) at Coventry;
The Royal Anglian Regiment Band (TA) at Peterborough;
The Band of The Devonshire and Dorset (1st Rifle Volunteers) Regiment at Exeter in Devon;
Regimental Band The Royal Highland Fusiliers (TA) in Glasgow;
The Volunteer Band of The Staffordshire Regiment (The Prince of Wales's) in Wolverhampton;
The Royal Regiment of Wales (TA) Band at Newport in Gwent;
The North Irish Staff Band (TA) in Belfast;
North West Infantry Band (TA) (KING'S) at Warrington in Cheshire;
The Hampshire and Dorset (Wessex) Band (TA) in Winchester;
51st Highland Volunteers Band in Perth;
Band of The Yorkshire Volunteers in Pontefract, West Yorkshire;
150th (Northumbrian) Regiment Royal Corps of Transport (Volunteers) Band in Hull;
The Berkshire, Buckinghamshire and Oxfordshire (Wessex) Band at Reading in Berkshire;
Light Infantry Burma Band (7 LI) in Durham;
Army Medical Services TA Band at Duke of York's HQ at Chelsea in London.

Appendices

Appendix 1 Chronological table of significant dates

1537 Honourable Artillery Company granted a charter by Henry VIII to its predecessor, the 'Fraternitie or Guylde of St. George, Maisters and Rulars of the Science of Artilleri as afforesaid rehearsed for long bowes, cross bowes and hand gunnes.'

1577 Foundation of the Royal Monmouthshire Royal Engineers (Militia).

1638 to **1651** The Civil Wars.

1794 The volunteer associations regulated nationally, and many of the Yeomanry regiments founded.

1795 to **1847** A period of civil unrest with bread riots and later the Chartists. Yeomanry called out on many occasions to keep the peace.

1844 The first of the 'Three Panics', the public alarm about inadequate defence of the country.

1851 In December, apprehension of a French invasion, so the Militia reintroduced the following year.

1852 Militia become a voluntary organization.

1859 The third and most serious panic of fear of invasion by another Emperor Napoleon. As a result the Volunteer Force took root as an auxiliary to the Regular Army and Militia.

1871 Control of the auxiliary forces taken over by the Crown from the Lord-Lieutenants of the counties.

1881 The Regular Army underwent reorganization, known as the Cardwell reforms, and a new system of territorial groupings improved contact with volunteers.

1882 Members of the Post Officer Volunteers went on active service to Egypt.

1897 The formation of Princess Christian's Army Nursing Service Reservists.

1899 In December, the Lord Mayor of London, on Government authorization, raised the City Imperial Volunteers for the Boer War.

1900 The Boer War in South Africa meant active service companies of volunteers joined the Regular Army. 18,000 volunteers went to South Africa.

1904 In May, the Royal Commission of the Militia and Volunteers reported that the Militia was unfit to take the field for the defence of the country, and as for the volunteers, 'neither the musketry nor the tactical training of the rank and file would enable it to face the troops of a continental army.'

1907 The Territorial and Reserve Forces Act.

1908 In April the Territorial Force formed. In the same year the Queen Alexandra's Imperial Military Nursing Service formed and in August the Territorial Force Nursing Service was envisaged.

1908 On 17 August, the Territorial Decoration (TD) replaced the Volunteer Decoration (VD) as the reward for long officer service.

1909 The term 'Imperial' dropped from the titles of Yeomanry Regiments.

1910 Volunteer Aid Detachment (VAD) formed for women to act as ambulance-driving nursing auxiliaries.

1914 The First Aid and Nursing Yeomanry (FANY) had been formed by this year and trained as motor mechanics and drivers.

1914 In October the first Territorials in action were The Queen's Own Oxfordshire Hussars in a fight with a group of German cyclists.

1914 On October 30, the London Scotttish in action, with 640 casualties.

1917 Women's Army Auxiliary Corps authorized.

1918 WAACs became the Queen Mary's Army Auxiliary Corps.

1918 The end of the First World War on 11 November meant that 129,806 territorial soldiers had been killed in action.

1920 March: volunteers reconstituted as the Territorial Army. The bounty was £4 for a recruit and £5 for a trained soldier each year.

1921 QMAAC disbanded and the TFNS became the TANS.

1926 The General Strike: TA embodied for 90 days.

1939 The Militia reintroduced for six months, but absorbed by wartime Army in September.

1939 In April the TA establishment doubled.

1939 In August the TA Anti-Aircraft Command soldiers in uniform at their guns.

1939 September 1, the TA embodied for war, which was declared two days later.

1939 September, the Armed Forces Act made every soldier full-time and suspended TA status.

1939 September 9, the Auxiliary Territorial Service (ATS) born.

1940 Local Defence Volunteers, later the Home Guard, formed.

1947 January 1, the post-war TA reconstituted and recruiting started on 1 May.

1950 National Servicemen joined TA units for three and a half years, following their two years' service with the Army.

1952 At the end of the year, the TA strength was 198,500.

1955 Anti-Aircraft command disbanded.

1956 The TA was reorganized. Annual bounty was £20.

1958 The Golden Jubilee of the TA.

May 10, review by HM the Queen Mother of the TA in Northern Ireland.

June 21 a thanksgiving service in Westminster Abbey and Westminster Cathedral.

June 22 the Queen reviews 8,000 TA in Hyde Park.

July 5, the Queen reviews 3,000 TA in Edinburgh.

1961 The last intake of National Servicemen.

1962 April 1, the TA Emergency Reserve, the 'Ever Readies' started. Bounty now £150.

1964 In December, the TA strength 116,500.

1965 April, some Ever Readies called out to reinforce the Royal Sussex Regiment being sent to Aden, and some for the various corps.

1967 The TA cut, divisions and brigades as well as many regiments disbanded or reduced to cadres. New units were formed by amalgamation.

1967 TA became TAVR.

1968 In March the strength of the TAVR was 54,800.

1970 In March the strength was down to 47,589.

1971 An expansion of the TA, new regiments including four new Yeomanry regiments formed.

1978 The Shapland committee.

1982 The title of Territorial Army restored to replace the cumbersome TAVR.

1983 The TA 75 years old.

1986 to **1990** Further expansion of the TA, aiming for an establishment of 90,000 including the new Home Service Force.

1986 National Employers' Liaison Committee started work.

Appendix 2 Sandhurst

Captain G. Bartlett, JP, QUEENS, a journalist with the Daily Telegraph, is a TA officer and a member of the Territorial Army Public Information Officers' Pool. In order to widen his knowledge of the Army, he managed to get himself a place on the Regular Army course for newly-commissioned specialist officers. This is his account of those weeks.

There are those who will seriously question the sanity of a 45-year old national newspaper man who volunteered to be beasted around Sandhurst for a month with Regular officers half his age, marched, double-marched and endurance tested to the point of collapse and profanely abused by pace-stick wielding martinets.

'Captain Bartlett Sir, you're bloody idle...swing those arms shoulder high... I'm watching you' stands out in my memory, as does 'Stop fidgeting you dumpling...' and to an Army lawyer in my platoon: 'Captain Binks Sir, you look like a p**** with a cap and belt on.'

All good humility-inducing stuff for sensitive Army doctors and dentists, a vet, lawyer, pharmacist, nurses and a Roman Catholic Padre, already commissioned for their professional expertise, taking part in the Service Familiarization CMDVLP course — known colloquially as 'The Tarts and Vicars'.

A colloquialism which suggests a doddle, yet belies the hard reality of a course which left resilient 22-year olds wondering aloud how much more hassle they were expected to take. But despite the legendary Sandhurst 'buggerance factor', the abuse, the physical and psychological pressures subtly applied, it was, for the majority of us, an intensive Army training experience of a lifetime.

For me, the oldest course officer and only Territorial Army Public Information Officer (TAPIO), it was something more: fulfilment of a lifetime's ambition to 'go to Sandhurst', which began with a peremptory tap on my Redoubt Lines study-cum-bedroom door with a Colour Sgt's pace stick — and ended in driving snow 'Passing Out' on the hallowed Academy parade ground.

The intervening weeks had been taxing and obsessively busy, our long days crammed full of lectures and demonstrations, map reading and drill, rapid and frequent changes of uniform, section attacks and patrols, skill at arms training, laid-back periods in the Signals Wing ... PT and punishment press-ups.

Oh yes, and shining parades — few of us will ever forget the long arduous hours spent after busy working days, in our halls of study, burning the bumps off our service brown shoes with hot knives and spoons and then bulling them to a mirror shine.

Neither will we forget shrinking berets to acceptable proportions after Colour Sergeant David Gregson, 29, asked Captain John Kay — a young RAMC officer with the biggest appetite I have ever known — in his inimitable way, 'Tell me Sir, do you have a pair of knickers to match that beret?'

Service dress ties will never be the same either, after Colour Sergeant Gregson told us you could always spot a 'sprog officer' by his tie width. We soaked them, stretched them for nights, steam ironed them — they are no longer 'sprog-width', but measured at least eight-feet long.

'Your room is in bog order, Sir', came the frequent NCOs' cry during early morning room inspection in One Platoon's accommodation block. I remember standing rigidly to attention while my lockers and drawers were inspected for correct arrangement, when into the corridor sailed both my mess tins accompanied by a mock scream. 'You're a knob Sir — you're not seriously telling me you cleaned those are you?' grinned Staff Gregson. 'Show parade unless you do so ASAP'.

We thought of collecting money for the first man put on show parade. Mine was for fidgeting on the parade ground: 'Show parade you bloody doughbag, showing yourself standing still', which was subsequently inexplicably cancelled. But Welsh Nursing Officer, Lieutenant Martin Thomas, was not so fortunate, his came to fruition with a long wait outside the CSM's office in No 2 dress.

From day one, we were injected at an incredible rate of knots with as much information as our Directing Staff could muster, on everything from the role of the padre, officer behaviour, soldiers' pay and radio voice procedure, to military law, service writing, principles of leadership, pistol familiarization, CEPO/CEMO and 'O' groups.

There were personal triumphs, such as passing one's battle fitness test in Army boots and denims over a three-mile circuit, successfully hosting a member of the Directing Staff on Dinner night, and giving a passable set order.

And there was the ignominy too, when it became patently obvious that you couldn't 'map read your way out of a paper bag', when your BATCO instructions refused to translate, when you had to be nudged awake during another dreadful vufoil lecture, or when the CSM ordered 'left wheel' you turned right and you were offered a 'pace stick stuffed up your nose. . .Sir'.

Interviews 'without coffee' came fast and furious to some who were adjudged to have given 'a pretty crappy set of orders that would have meant certain death for your patrol', slept through early morning parade in drill order, accidentally fired an SLR during 'For Inspection, Port Arms' or drunkenly demolished a fellow officer's door.

The coffee-less beratings were given with aplomb by our Platoon Commander, Major Alastair Goulden, a QUEENS officer with a natural and enthusiastic talent for teaching military skills, and who is a stickler for correct dress and general propriety.

A man of boundless energy who leads from the front covering every inch of the ground with us, Major Goulden — whose guidance and kindness steered a fellow QUEENS officer through many sticky patches — has three prime fixations: coasters, who give less than their all; smokers 'as a reformed 60-a-day man I loathe the weed'; and headovers.

'Headovers are worn on your head' he told us reasonably enough: 'Don't let me ever see any of you wearing them up over your ears, it looks quite appalling.'

There were times when some felt like opting out of a course which occasionally seemed set to break our spirits, or when the requirement to balance precariously on a metal climbing frame 30 feet above the ground or career hell for leather on the 'death slide' across a lake, turned some into ashen, shaking wrecks.

Then, like the gorgeous little brunette who sobbed herself to sleep one night after being roundly abused by her platoon Colour Sergeant, you realize that the pressures are quite deliberate, that as officers you must function — and function well — despite them, and that you are singularly useless to your soldiers if you cannot.

Suddenly the physical and mental pain, the anguish, the disorientation, yes the sheer 'buggerance' ladelled out in liberal doses by our Directing Staff, begins to make a lot of sense and you determine to endure and survive it, come what may.

The culmination of our training was Exercise Terrier, weighed down by Complete Equipment Marching Order (CEMO) and rifle, involving nearly three days in the field on compo rations cooked on hexistoves, practising section attacks, recce patrols, setting up patrol group bases — with scant protection by night of basher or slit trench only.

Stand-to at dusk on day one of Exercise Terrier, and there are no lights, no cigarettes, no unnecessary sounds — your claustrophobic world closes in and you are an extension of your rifle, lying prone at two o'clock, getting damp, cold and more and more uncomfortable.

'Put that bloody cigarette out Captain Bartlett' snaps the Platoon Commander, looming large and unexpectedly, 'You're inviting a bullet through the brain — that glow can be seen for miles, for ***** sake man.'

More ignominy, but I say 'Yes Sir, I'm sorry. . .' in the most chastened voice I can muster, and think of the joy of dining with my wife Jean at a hotel near our Kent home in just a few days' time. 'And by the way' snaps Major Goulden, 'Undo the top button of your combat jacket — Queen's officers never have that button done up.'

Several hours later I am heading out of our patrol base on a recce patrol, led by a likeable young Royal Army Dental Corps Officer, Captain Matthew Pendle, whose ready wit and sardonic observations over the gruelling weeks have given Platoon One much solace and pleasure.

Within a couple of hours we are back at patrol base, mission accomplished, and I crawl under my basher, zip myself up in my 'green army maggot' and sleep soundly for two hours, until shaken awake for sentry duty at 3.30 a.m. It's bitterly cold and excruciatingly boring — my hip flask of whisky mac suddenly assumes a new importance. Distinct shapes of enemy soldiers loom ahead but there is nothing there. Five minutes seem like an hour and your limbs stiffen painfully as the patrol base slumbers. 'What the hell are we doing this for', I ask idly of John Binks lying next to me on a dew-sodden ground sheet. 'Don't ask me mate', says the personable young lawyer with instant recall on how long it takes a man to hang, 'But it marginally beats shining parade.'

As on a previous 'stag duty' on this course, my mind conjures up the horror of the First World War trenches and I wonder how on earth our troops at places like Ypres, Verdun, and on the Somme endured it year after year — and a Surrey Common with an enemy firing blanks becomes very cosy indeed.

Stand to at 6 a.m. and then breakfast, during which a newspaper man used to hotel meals and facilities when 'out in the field' can only find time to cook his packet of rolled oats by mixing it with cold water and eating 'biscuits brown', if he is going to be packed and ready to march in time.

Major Nigel Corner, an Army surgeon clearly sceptical of anything Territorial Army, neatly slices his tin of bacon burgers and cooks them on his natty Gaz stove. He kindly offers to heat my mess tin of water and I have a 'brew' of hot chocolate without as much as removing my hexi block from my webbing.

Nigel is a natural leader. 'Garry Gortex' is an equally natural survivor. 'The way to get through this' he once told me after being berated for arrogance by our DS staff 'Is to think purely and simply of No. 1.'

Day Two of the final exercise is devoted to siting a defensive position, digging slit trenches, marching for miles with a full pack and then living in your six feet-by-two hole in the ground.

Feeling very jaded as I dig our main GPMG trench with John Binks, I notice the Academy Assistant Commandant, Brigadier Pat Hargrave, striding towards us with the Old College Commander, Colonel Mike Holroyd Smith, and our popular Company Commander, Major Archie MacKenzie who,

just like Major Goulden, believes in leading from the front.

'My God, what a combination — an Army lawyer and a national newspaper reporter' says Major MacKenzie. 'Are you both OK?' Earlier Colonel Holroyd Smith, with commendable honesty, had told me that a directly-commissioned Captain with zero experience was 'Nothing more than a load of balls', so I tucked my arms in, stood to attention minus steel helmet, and said nervously 'Yes Sir'.

Colonel Mike grinned wryly as I was despatched to relieve Geordie Male Nursing Officer, Lieutenant Chris Wynn, doing look-out patrol in a patch of scrubland on a hill. Since it was close to main meal time, I mercifully escaped the indignity of actually trying to cook my main meal. I was going to salvage what I could — and cold — from my webbing pouches, but a beautiful, petite little pharmacist, Lieutenant Angela Haste of the RAMC took pity on a gnarled old journalist and cooked a wonderful hot meal for me. 'Now you just make sure you eat it all up' she told me, 'I am making you a brew of coffee and you have biscuits with it — incidentally, make sure you eat your orange for necessary vitamin C.' Angela, what can I say, except let me buy you dinner in Fleet Street — and soon.

Major Goulden appeared at this stage: 'Ah Gerry, how's your sense of humour?' he asked enigmatically. With considerable foreboding I kept (hopefully) a stiff upper lip and replied: 'Fine Sir, absolutely fine.' 'Good', he said, 'I'm going to test it later on.'

And test it he did, with a ten-mile recce patrol from 9p.m. until about 1.30 a.m. on day three of Exercise Terrier, after 48 hours with less than two hours' sleep. 'A mere stroll' he said. 'I was going to order you to command it, but I didn't fancy chasing you all over the countryside in ever-decreasing circles.'

Sentry duty on return, then 30 minutes' unsatisfactory sleep, stand-to at first light in heavy snow — and we were routed by the excellent Gurkhas, who overran our positions in a matter of seconds.

I will never forget the most wonderful sight in the world — an Army 4 ton truck trundling towards us to take us back to Sandhurst. And I now understand the true pathos of three words often heard in the Army — PBI — poor bloody infantry.

Appendix 3 Council of Territorial Auxiliary and Volunteer Reserve Associations
(as at August 1989)

Patron
Major General Lord Michael Fitzalan Howard, GCVO, CB, CBE, MC, DL.

President
Colonel The Rt. Hon. The Viscount Ridley, TD.

Chairman
Lieut-General Sir Peter Hudson KCB, CBE, DL.

Vice Chairmen
Colonel M.S. Lee-Browne, OBE, TD, DL.
Colonel R.M. Stewart, OBE, TD, DL.
Commodore J.W. Wightman, CBE, RD, RNR.
Colonel R.A. MacTaggart, TD, RD, ADC.
Air Vice-Marshal W.J. Herrington, CB.

Council Secretariat
Secretary: Major-General M. Matthews, CB.
Deputy Secretary: Brigadier T.S. Sneyd.
Secretary Pension Plan: Captain R.C. Barnes, ERD.
Address: Centre Block, Duke of York's Headquarters, Chelsea, London, SW3 4SG telephone 01 730 6122.
Note: Each Territorial Auxiliary and Volunteer Reserve Association is represented on this Council by its President, Vice Presidents, Chairman, Vice Chairmen and Secretary.

TA & VR Associations

1 Highland Association, for Highlands, Grampian, Tayside, Fife and Central Regions and part of the Strathclyde Region (The Districts of Dumbarton, Clydebank, Bearsden and Milngavie, Strathkelvin, Cumbernauld and Argyll) and the island areas of Shetland, Orkney and Western Isles. HQ address is 365 Perth Road, Dundee, DD2 1LX, phone 0382 68283/4.

2 Lowland Association, for Lothian, Borders, Dumfries and Galloway Regions, and part of the Strathclyde Region (the Districts of the City of Glasgow, Monklands, Motherwell, Hamilton, East Kilbride, Eastwood, Lanark, Renfrew, Inverclyde, Cunningham, Kilmarnock and Loudoun, Kyle and Carrick and Cumnock and Doon Valley). HQ address is 75 Berkeley Street, Glasgow, G3 7EA, phone 041 221 2273.

3 North of England Association, for Northumberland, Durham, Tyne and Wear and Cleveland. HQ address is 53, Old Elvet, Durham, DH1 3JJ, phone 091 3847202.

4 Yorkshire and Humberside Association for North Yorkshire, West Yorkshire, South Yorkshire and Humberside. HQ address is 20 St George's Place, York, YO2 2DS, phone 0904 623081.

5 North West of England and Isle of Man Association for Cumbria, Lancashire, Merseyside, Greater Manchester, Cheshire and the Isle of Man. HQ address is Alexandra Court, 28 Alexandra Drive, Liverpool L17 8YE, phone 051 727 4552.

6 Wales Association for the Counties of Wales, HQ address is Centre Block, Maindy Barracks, Cardiff, CF4 3YE, phone 0222 220251/23.

7 West Midlands Association for Hereford and Worcester, Shropshire, Staffordshire, Warwickshire and West Midland Metropolitan. HQ address is Tennel Grange, Tennal Road, Harborne, Birmingham B32 2HX, phone 021 427 5221.

8 East Midlands Association, for Derbyshire, Leicestershire, Lincolnshire, Northamptonshire and Nottinghamshire. HQ address is 6 Clinton Terrace, Derby Road, Nottingham, NG7 1LZ, phone 0602 476508.

9 Western Wessex Association for Avon, Cornwall, Devon, Gloucester, Somerset and Wiltshire. HQ address is 2 Beaufort Road, Clifton, Bristol, BS8 2JS, phone 0272 734045.

10 Eastern Wessex Association for Berkshire, Buckinghamshire, Dorset, Hampshire, Isle of Wight and Oxfordshire. HQ address is 30 Carlton Place, Southampton, SO1 2DX, phone 0703 228661.

11 East Anglia Association, for Bedfordshire, Cambridgeshire, Essex, Hertfordshire, Norfolk and Suffolk. HQ address is 'Springfield Tyrells', 250 Springfield Road, Chelmsford, CM2 6BU, phone 0245 354262.

12 Greater London Association, for the area of the Metropolitan Police District, including the City of London, the boundaries of London and Middlesex, and parts of Kent, Surrey, Essex and Hertfordshire. HQ address is Duke of York's HQ, Chelsea, London, SW3 4RY, phone 01 730 8131.

13 South East Association for Kent, East Sussex, West Sussex and the County of Surrey (excluding the part of that County within the Metropolitan Police District). HQ address is Sandling Place, Chatham Road, Maidstone, Kent, ME14 2NJ, phone 0622 691 888.

14 Northern Ireland Association for the six counties of Ulster, HQ address is 25 Windsor Park, Belfast BT9 6FR, phone 0232 665024.

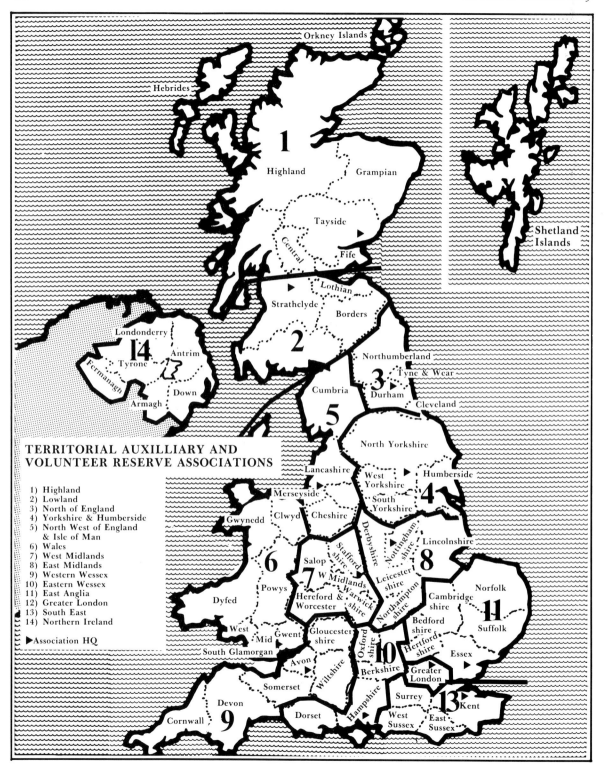

Orkney Islands

Hebrides

1

Highland   Grampian

Shetland
Islands

Tayside

Central

Fife

Lothian

Strathclyde

Borders

Londonderry

14

Antrim

Fermanagh

Tyrone

Down

Armagh

Northumberland

3

Tyne & Wear

Durham

Cleveland

Cumbria

5

North Yorkshire

Lancashire

West
Yorkshire

Humberside

4

Merseyside

South
Yorkshire

Clwyd   Cheshire

Gwynedd

Derbyshire

Nottingham
shire

Lincolnshire

Salop

Stafford
shire

8

Powys

7

W Midlands

Leicester
shire

Northampton
shire

Norfolk

6

Dyfed

Hereford &
Worcester

Warwick
shire

Cambridge
shire

11

Bedford
shire

Suffolk

West

Mid

Gwent

Gloucester
shire

Oxford
shire

Hertford
shire

Essex

South Glamorgan

Avon

10

Berkshire

Greater
London

Wiltshire

Somerset

Hampshire

Surrey

13 Kent

Devon

9

Dorset

West
Sussex

East
Sussex

Cornwall

**TERRITORIAL AUXILLIARY AND
VOLUNTEER RESERVE ASSOCIATIONS**

1) Highland
2) Lowland
3) North of England
4) Yorkshire & Humberside
5) North West of England
   & Isle of Man
6) Wales
7) West Midlands
8) East Midlands
9) Western Wessex
10) Eastern Wessex
11) East Anglia
12) Greater London
13) South East
14) Northern Ireland

▶Association HQ

Appendix 4 Some Victoria Crosses of the Territorial Army

I am most grateful for the kind help of The Victoria Cross and George Cross Association and in particular their archivist, Miss Rose Coombs MBE whose guidance and advice has been invaluable.

It would appear that it is not possible to arrive at a definitive list of VCs awarded to the Territorial Force or the Territorial Army. The reason is the tremendous amount of cross-posting that goes on in war, with TA officers and men serving in non-TA units, and Regular or war-time conscripts and non-TA volunteers serving in units that started the war as TA or TF, and were re-formed as TA after the war. The contents of this appendix can only therefore be taken as a guide and it is inevitable that some are included who are not TA or TF and some will have been regrettably missed out.

First World War

AMEY, Lance Corporal, (later Corporal) William, 1/8 Royal Warwickshire Regiment, at Landrecies on 4 November 1918. He was born at Duddeston on 5 March 1881 and died at Leamington Spa on 28 May 1940. Also awarded the Military Medal.

ANGUS, Lance Corporal, William, 8 Highland Light Infantry, at Chivenchy on 12 June 1916. He was born at Armadale, Linlithgow on 28 February 1888 at died at Carluke, Lanark on 14 June 1959.

BALL, Captain Albert, 7th Nottinghamshire and Derbyshire Regiment, attached to Royal Flying Corps. In France between June 1916 and May 1917. He was born at Lenton in Nottinghamshire on 14 August 1896 and died at Annoeullin, France on 7 May 1917. He is buried in the German Cemetery at Annoeullin. Also awarded the Distinguished Service Order and two bars, the Military Cross, the French Legion D'Honneur, and the Russian Order of St George Fourth Class.

BARRETT, Colonel John Cridlan, 1/5 Royal Leicester Regiment, at Pontruet, France, on 24 September 1918. He was born at Leamington Spa on 10 August 1897 and died in Leicester on 7 March 1977. Also awarded the Territorial Decoration and made a Deputy Lord-Lieutenant.

BAXTER, Second Lieutenant Edward Felix, 1/8 (Irish) King's Liverpool Regiment, at Blairville, France on 17 and 18 April 1916 - posthumous. Born at Old Swinford, Stourbridge, Worcestershire on 18 September 1885. He is buried in the Fillievres British Cemetery.

BELCHER, Lance Sergeant, (later Captain) Douglas Walter, 1/5 (LRB) London Regiment at Wieltje-St Julien, Belgium on 13 May 1915. He was born at Surbiton in Surrey on 15 July 1889.

BISSETT, Lieutenant (later Major) William Davidson, of 1/6 Argyll and Sutherland Highlanders at Maing in France on 25 October 1918. He was born at St Martin's, Crieff, Perthshire, and died at Wrexham in Flint on 12 May 1971. He is buried in the Aldershot Military Cemetery.

BORTON, Lieutenant-Colonel Arthur Drummond, 2/22 London Regiment, at Sheria, Palestine on 7 November 1917. He was born at Chevening in Kent on 1 July 1883 and died at Hinton in Kent on 5 January 1933. Also awarded the Distinguished Service Order and made a Commander of the Order of St Michael and St George.

BOUGHEY, Second Lieutenant Stanley Henry Parry, 1/4 Royal Scots Fusiliers, at El Burf, Palestine on 1 December 1917. He was born in Ayrshire on 9 April 1896 and died near Ramleh, Palestine on 4 December 1917 and was buried in the Gaza War Cemetery.

BRADFORD, Lieutenant-Colonel (later Brigadier-General) Roland Boys, 9 Durham Light Infantry at Eaucourt l'Abbaye on 1 October 1916. He was born at Etherley, County Durham on 22 February 1892 and died at Cambrai in France on 30 November 1917 and is buried in the Hermies British Cemetery. Also awarded the Military Cross, and brother of Lt.-Col. G.N. Bradford, also a VC.

BROOKS, Company Sergeant Major Edward, 2/4 Oxfordshire and Buckinghamshire Light Infantry, at Fayet, near St Quentin on 28 April 1917. He was born at Oakley in Buckinghamshire on 11 April 1883 and died at Oxford on 26 June 1944.

BUCHAN, Second Lieutenant John Crawford, 1/7 Argyl and Sutherland Highlanders, at Marteville, France on 31 March 1918, posthumous. He was born at Alloa on 10 October 1892. He is buried in the Roisel Commonwealth Cemetery.

BURT, Corporal (later Sergeant) Alfred Alexander, Hertfordshire Regiment, at Cuinchy in France on 27 September 1915. He was born at Port Vale in Hertfordshire on 3 March 1895 and died at Chesham in Buckinghamshire on 9 June 1962.

CALDWELL, Sergeant (later Company Sergeant Major) Thomas, 12 Royal Scots Fusiliers at Audenarde, Belgium, on 31 October 1918. He was born at Carluke in Lanarkshire on 10 February 1894 and died at Adelaide in Australia on 7 June 1969.

CHAVASSE, Captain Noel Godfrey, RAMC attached to 1/10 Kings Liverpool Regiment (Liverpool Scottish), FIRST at Guillemont on 9 August 1916, and A BAR at Wieltje in Belgium between 31 July and 2 August 1917. He was born at Oxford on 9 November 1884 and died at Brandhoek in Belgium on 4 August 1917. He is buried in the Brandhoek New

Military Cemetery, and there is a plaque in the Liverpool Scottish Headquarters and a window in Liverpool Cathedral. He was also awarded the Military Cross.

CHRISTIE, Lance Corporal John Alex. 1/4 London Regiment, at Fejja in Palestine on 21 and 22 December 1917. He was born at Edmonton in North London on 14 May 1895 and died at Stockport in Cheshire on 10 September 1967.

CLAMP, Corporal William, 6 Yorkshire Regiment, at Poelcapelle, in Belgium on 9 October 1917, posthumous. He was born at Motherwell in Lanarkshire on 28 October 1891.

CLOUTMAN, Major Brett McKay, Royal Engineers at Pont Sur Sambre on 6 November 1918. He was born in London on 7 November 1891 and died on 15 August 1971 and is buried at Highgate. His was the last VC awarded during the First World War. He was also awarded the Military Cross. He was in the London University OTC from 1909 to 1912, with 12 County of London Regiment (Rangers) from 1914 and commissioned into the Kent (Fortress) RE March 1915. After the war he was called to the Bar, and was knighted in 1952.

COLLIN, Second Lieutenant Joseph Henry, 1/4 King's Own (Lancaster) at Givenchy, France on 9 April 1918, posthumous. He was born on 11 April 1893 and is buried in the Vieille Chapelle New British Cemetery, and there is a plaque in his memory in Lancaster Priory.

COLLINS, Acting Corporal (later Sergeant) John, 25 Royal Welch Fusiliers in Palestine on 31 October 1917. He was born at West Hatch in Somerset on 10 September 1877 and died at Merthyr Tydfil on 8 September 1951. Also awarded the Distinguished Conduct Medal and Military Medal.

COLTMAN, Lance Corporal William Harold, 1/6 North Staffordshire Regiment, at Mannequin Hill near Sequehart, France 3 and 4 October 1918. He was born at Rangemore in Staffordshire on 17 November 1891 and died at Burton-on-Trent on 19 June 1974. There is a plaque in his memory in the Regimental Chapel in Lichfield. Also awarded the Distinguished Conduct Medal and bar, and the Military Medal and bar, which made him the most decorated non-commissioned officer in the First World War.

COURY, Second Lieutenant, (later Captain) Gabriel George, 3rd attached to 1/4 South Lancashire Regiment at Arrowhead Copse on the Somme on 8 August 1916. He was born in Liverpool on 13 June 1896, where he died on 23 February 1956.

CRAIG, Second Lieutenant John Manson, 1/4 attached to 4/5 Royal Scots Fusiliers in Palestine on 5 June 1917. He was born in Comrie, Perthshire on 5 March 1896 and died at Crieff, on 19 February

1970. During the Second World War he served as a Wing Commander in the RAF.

CRUICKSHANK, Private (later Major) Robert Edward, 2/14 London Regiment (London Scottish), east of Jordan on 1 May 1918. Born at Winnipeg in Canada on 17 June 1888 and died at Blaby in Leicestershire on 30 August 1961.

DAYKINS, Corporal (later Sergeant) John Bruton, 2/4 (Hallamshire) Yorkshire and Lancashire Regiment at Solesmes, France on 20 October 1918. He was born at Ormiston on 26 March 1883 and died at Jedburgh on 24 January 1933.

DEAN, Lieutenant (later Colonel) Donald John, 8 Royal West Kents. North West of Lens, from 24 to 26 September 1918. Born in London on 19 April 1897 and died at Sittingbourne in Kent on 9 December 1985. Also awarded the Territorial Decoration and was a Commander in the Royal Danish Order Dannebrog. He was also a Deputy Lord-Lieutenant and Justice of the Peace.

DUNKLEY, Lieutenant-Colonel, Bertram Best, 2/5 Lancashire Fusiliers at Wieltje, Belgium, on 31 July 1917. He was born in York on 3 August 1890 and died near Ypres on 5 August 1917, and is buried in the Mendinghem British Cemetery.

EDWARDS, Sergeant Alexander, 1/6 Seaforth Highlanders. North of Ypres on 31 July and 1 August 1917. He was born at Lossiemouth on 4 November 1885 and died near Arras on 24 March 1918. His name is recorded on the Arras Memorial to the missing.

ERSKINE, Sergeant John, 5 Cameronians (Scottish Rifles) at Givenchy on 22 June 1916. He was born in Dunfirmline on 13 January 1894 and died at Arras on 14 April 1917. His name is recorded on the Arras Memorial to the missing.

FINDLAY, Major George De Cardonnel Elmsall, Royal Engineers, a Regular officer serving with a Territorial Force Unit, 409 (Lowland) Field Company, at Catillon in France on 4 November 1918. He was also awarded a Military Cross and bar.

FORSHAW, Lieutenant (later Major) William Thomas, 1/9 Manchester Regiment, at Gallipoli from 7 to 9 August 1915. He was born at Barrow-in-Furness on 20 April 1890 and died at Holyport, in Berkshire on 26 May 1943.

GRAHAM, Lieutenant (later Lieutenant-Colonel) John Reg Noble, 9 Argyll and Sutherland Highlanders attached to 136 Company Machine Gun Corps, at Istabulat, Mesopotamia, on 22 April 1917. He was born at Calcutta in India on 17 September 1892 and died in Edinburgh on 6 December 1980. He was also awarded the OBE and later knighted, and also served in the Second World War.

GREAVES, Corporal (later Sergeant) Frederick, 9 Nottinghamshire and Derbyshire Regiment at

Poelcapelle on 4 October 1917. Born at Killamarsh in Derbyshire on 16 May 1890 and died in Chesterfield on 11 June 1973. His name is recorded on a memorial in Birmingham.

GREEN, Captain John Leslie, Royal Army Medical Corps attached to 1/5 Nottinghamshire and Derbyshire Regiment at Foncquevillers on 1 July 1916, posthumous. Born at St Neots in Huntingdonshire on 4 December 1888 and is buried in the Foncquevillers British Cemetery.

HAINE, Second Lieutenant (later Lieutenant-Colonel) Reginald Leonard, 1 Honourable Artillery Company, at Gavrelle in France on 28 and 29 April 1917. He was born at Wandsworth in London on 10 July 1896 and died in London on 12 June 1982. He served in the Second World War with the Home Guard.

HARVEY, Private (later Corporal) Jack, 1/22 London Regiment at Peronne on 2 September 1918. Born at Peckham in South London on 24 August 1891 and died at Redhill in Surrey on 15 August 1940.

HEWITSON, Lance Corporal (later Corporal) James, 1/4 King's Own (Royal Lancashires), at Givenchy on 26 April 1918. Born at Coniston in Lancashire on 15 October 1892 he died at Ulverston on 2 March 1963.

HIRSCH, Captain David Philip, 4 Yorkshire Regiment, at Wancourt in France on 23 April 1917, posthumous. He was born in Leeds on 28 December 1896 and is recorded on the Arras Memorial to the Missing.

HUFFAM, Second Lieutenant (later Major) 5 Duke of Wellington's (WR) Regiment at St Servin's Farm, France, on 31 August 1918. He was born in Dunblane on 31 March 1897 and died at Stanmore in Middlesex on 16 February 1968. During the Second World War he was an Assistant Provost Marshal in France in 1940.

HUNTER, Corporal (later Sergeant) David Ferguson, 1/5 Highland Light Infantry at Moeuvres on 16 and 17 September 1918. Born at Kingseat in Dunfirmline on 28 November 1891 and died in Dunfirmline on 14 February 1965.

HUTCHINSON, Private (later Corporal) James, 2/5 Lancashire Fusiliers, at Ficheux, France on 28 June 1916. Born at Bank Top, Radcliffe, Lancashire on 9 July 1895 and died at Torquay in Devon on 22 January 1972.

HUTT, Private (later Corporal) Arthur, 1/7 Royal Warwickshire Regiment, at Terrier Farm, Poelcapelle 4 October 1917. He was born at Earlesden, Coventry on 12 February 1889 and died in Coventry in 14 April 1954. He is commemorated at the War Memorial Park in Coventry.

JOHNSON, Lieutenant James, 36 Northumberland Fusiliers, in 1918.

JOHNSON, Sergeant William Henry, 1/5 Nottinghamshire and Derbyshire Regiment at Ramicourt in France on 3 October 1918. Born at Worksop in Nottinghamshire on 15 October 1890 and died at Arnold in Nottinghamshire on 25 April 1945.

JOHNSON, Temporary Major Frederick, Royal Engineers, at Hill 70, France on 25 September 1915. Born on 15 August 1890 at Streatham in South London, died on 26 November 1917 and is remembered on the Cambrai memorial. Also awarded the Distinguished Service Order and had been a member of the London University OTC.

KEYWORTH, Lance Corporal (later Corporal) Leonard James, 1/24 London Regiment, at Givenchy on 26 May 1915. Born in Lincoln on 12 August 1893 and died at Abbeville on 19 October 1915. Buried in the Abbeville Commonwealth Cemetry.

KNIGHT, Sergeant (later Second Lieutenant) Alfred Joseph, 2/8 London Regiment (POR), at the Alberta Sector, Ypres, on 20 September 1917. Born at Ladywood in Birmingham on 24 August 1888 and died at Birmingham on 4 December 1960.

LAFONE, Major A.M. Middlesex Yeomanry, at Gaza, on 27 October 1917.

LAUDER, Private David Ross, 4 Royal Scots Fusiliers at Cape Helles, Gallipoli on 13 August 1915. Born in East Glentire on 21 January 1894 and died in Glasgow on 4 June 1972.

McBEATH, Lance Corporal, Robert, 1/5 Seaforth Highlanders, at Cambrai on 20 November 1917. Born at Kinlochbervie, Lairg in Sutherland on 22 December 1897 and died at Vancouver, British Columbia, on 9 October 1922.

McGREGOR, Lieutenant David Stuart, 6 Royal Scots attached to 29 Machine Gun Corps, at Hoogemolen on 22 October 1918, posthumous. He was born in Edinburgh on 16 October 1895 and is buried in the Staceghem Commonwealth Cemetery.

McGUFFIE, Sergeant Louis, 1/5 King's Own Scottish Borderers, at Wytchaet 28 September 1918. Born at Wigtown on 15 March 1893 and died at Wytchaete on 4 October 1918, buried in Zantvoorde British Cemetery.

McINTOSH, Private, George Imlach, 1/6 Gordon Highlanders, at Ypres on 31 July 1917. Born at Buckie, Banff, on 24 April 1897 and died in Aberdeen on 20 June 1960. During the Second World War served in the RAF as a Flight Sergeant.

McPHIE, Corporal James, 416 Field Company, Royal Engineers, at Canal de la Sensee, Aubensheul, France on 14 October 1918, posthumous. He was born at Edinburgh on 18 December 1894 and is buried in the Naves Commonwealth Cemetery.

MARTIN-LEAKE, Captain (later Lieutenant-Colonel) Arthur, the FIRST whilst serving with the South African Constabulary at Vlakfontein, in the

Boer War, on 8 February 1902 and a BAR when serving with the Royal Army Medical Corps attached to 5th Field Ambulance from 29 October to 3 November 1914 near Zonnebeke. He was born at Standen, near Ware in Hertfordshire on 4 April 1874 and died at Ware on 22 June 1953. He is buried in the High Cross Churchyard at Ware. This was the first case of a bar being awarded to the VC.

MAYSON, Lance Sergeant Tom Fletcher, 1/4 King's Own (Royal Lancashire) Regiment, at Wieltje on 31 July 1917. Born at Silecroft, Cumberland on 3 November 1893 and died at Barrow in Furness on 21 February 1958, buried in St Mary's Churchyard at Whicham and there is a plaque in his honour in Lancaster Priory.

MEEKOSHA, Corporal (later Captain) Samuel (later changed name to Ingham), 1/6 West Yorkshire Regiment, at River Yser, 19 November 1915. Born in Leeds on 16 September 1893 and died at Blackwood, Mons, on 8 December 1950.

MEIKLE, Sergeant John, 4 Seaforth Highlanders, at Marfaux in France on 20 July 1918. Born at Kirkintilloch on 11 September 1898. Died at Marfaux on 16 September 1918 and is buried in the Marfaux British Cemetery. Also awarded the Military Medal.

MILES, Private Francis George, 1/5 Gloucestershire Regiment, at Bois de L'Eveque, Landrecies on 23 October 1918. Born at Clearwell in Gloucestershire on 9 July 1896 and died there on 8 November 1961.

MUGFORD, Lance Corporal (later Sergeant) Harold Sandford, 8 Machine Gun Corps, (Essex Yeomanry) at Monchy le Preux on 11 April 1917. Born at St James's in London on 31 August 1894 and died at Chelmsford in Essex on 16 June 1958.

NEEDHAM, Private Samuel, 1/5 Bedfordshire Regiment, at Kefa Kasim on 10 and 11 September 1918. Born at Great Limber, Lincolnshire on 16 August 1885 and died at Kantara in Egypt on 4 November 1918. He is buried in the Kantara War Memorial Cemetery.

POLLARD, Second Lieutenant Alfred Oliver, 1 HAC, at Gavrelle, France on 29 April 1917. Born in Wallington, Surrey on 4 May 1893 and died at Bournemouth on 5 December 1960. Also awarded the Military Cross and bar, and the Distinguished Conduct Medal.

POTTS, Private, Frederick William Owen, 1/1 Berkshire Yeomanry, at Hill 70, Gallipoli, 21 August 1915. Born at Reading on 18 December 1892, where he died on 3 November 1943.

POULTER, Private Arthur, 1/4 Duke of Wellington's WR Regiment, at Erquinghem in 10 April 1918. Born at Kilgrambridge in North Yorkshire on 16 December 1893 and died in Leeds 29 August 1956.

PROCTOR, Private Arthur Herbert, 1/5 King's

Liverpool Regiment, at Ficheux on 4 June 1916. Born at Bootle in Lancashire on 11 August 1890 and died at Sheffield on 27 January 1973. Ordained in 1927 and was an RAF Chaplain during the Second World War.

RIGGS, Sergeant Frederick Charles, 6 Yorkshire and Lancashire Regiment at Epincy on 1 October 1918, posthumous. He was born in Bournemouth on 28 July 1888 and is remembered on the Vis-en-Artois Memorial to the Missing.

RIVERS, Private Jacob, 1 Nottinghamshire and Derbyshire Regiment at Neuve Chapelle on 12 March 1915, posthumous. Born at Bridgegate in Derby in 1881 and is remembered on the Le Touret Memorial to the Missing.

RUSSELL, Captain John Fox, Royal Army Medical Corps attached to 1/6 Royal Welch Fusiliers, at Tel-el Khuweilfeh on 6 November 1917, posthumous. Born at Holyhead on Anglesey on 27 January 1893. Buried in Beersheba War Cemetery and there is a plaque to him at St Bees School Holyhead.

SANDERS, Corporal (later Captain) George, 1/7 West Yorkshire Regiment, at Thiepval on 1 July 1916. Born at New Wortley in Leeds on 8 July 1894 and died in Leeds on 4 July 1950.

SCHOFIELD, Second Lieutenant John, 2/5 Lancashire Fusiliers, at Givenchy on 9 April 1918, posthumous. Born at Blackburn in Lancashire and buried at Vielle Chapelle British Cemetery.

SMITH, Second Lieutenant Alfred Victor, 1/5 East Lancashire Regiment at Helles, Gallipoli on 23 December 1915, posthumous. Born at Guildford in Surrey on 22 July 1891 and buried in Twelve Tree Copse Cemetery, with memorials in Blackpool and Burnley.

SMITH, Lance Sergeant (later Lieutenant) Edward, 1/5 Lancashire Fusiliers, at Serre from 21 to 23 August 1918. He was born at Maryport, Cumberland on 10 November 1898 and died at Beuvry on 21 January 1940 when serving with the 2 Lancashire Fusiliers and is buried in the Beuvry Commonwealth Cemetery extension, and is commemorated on the Maryport War Memorial.

TANDEY, Private (later Sergeant) Henry, 5 Duke of Wellington's Regiment, at Marcoing on 28 September 1918. Born at Leamington Spa on 30 August 1891 and died in Coventry on 20 December 1977.

THOMAS, Lance Corporal John, 2/5 North Staffordshire Regiment, at Fontaine 30 November 1917. Born at Openshaw in Manchester on 10 May 1885 and died at Stockport in Cheshire on 28 February 1954.

TRAIN, Corporal (later Sergeant) Charles William, 2/14 London Regiment (London Scottish) in Palestine on 8 December 1917. Born at Finsbury Park in London on 21 September 1890 and died in

Vancouver, British Columbia on 28 March 1965. Buried in the Field of Honour, Forest Lawn Memorial Park, Barnaby, BC.

VANN, Lieutenant-Colonel Bernard William, 1/8 Nottinghamshire and Derbyshire Regiment attached to 1/6 Battalion, at Bellinglise on 29 September 1918. Born at Rushden in Northamptonshire on 9 July 1887 and died at Ramicourt in France on 3 October 1918. Buried in the Bellincourt British Cemetery. Also awarded the Military Cross and bar, and the Croix de Guerre avec Palmes (France).

VICKERS, Captain (later Colonel) Charles Geoffrey, 1/7 Nottinghamshire and Derbyshire Regiment at Hohenzollern Redoubt on 14 October 1915. He was born in Nottingham on 13 October 1894 and died at Goring-on-Thames on 16 March 1982. Also awarded the Belgian Croix de Guerre and the US Medal of Freedom. Later knighted.

WARING, Lance Sergeant William, 25 Royal Welch Fusiliers, at Ronssoy on 18 September 1918. Born at Welshpool on 13 October 1885 and died at Le Havre on 8 October 1918. He is buried in St Marie Cemetery, Le Havre.

WEST, Major then Lieutenant-Colonel Richard Annesley, North Irish Horse, seconded to 6 Tank Corps, at Courcelles and Vaux on 21 August 1918 and 2 September 1918, posthumous. He was born at Cheltenham on 26 September 1878 and is buried in Mory Abbey British Cemetery. Also awarded the Distinguished Service Order and bar and the Military Cross.

WHITFIELD, Private (later Sergeant) Harold, 10 Shropshire Light Infantry, at Burj el Lisaneh, Egypt on 10 March 1918. Born at Oswestry on 11 June 1886 where he died on 19 December 1956.

WILCOX, Lance Corporal Alfred, 2/4 Oxfordshire and Buckinghamshire Light Infantry at Laventie on 12 September 1918. Born at Aston on 16 December 1884 and died in Birmingham on 30 March 1951.

WILKINSON, Private (later Lieutenant) Alfred Robert, 1/5 Manchester Regiment, at Marou on 20 October 1918. Born at Leigh in Lancashire on 5 December 1896 where he died on 23 October 1940.

WOOLEY, Second Lieutenant (later Captain) Geoffrey Harold, 9 London Regiment (Queen Victoria's Rifles) at Hill 60, Belgium, 20 and 21 April 1915. Born at Bethnal Green in East London on 14 May 1892, died at West Chiltington in Sussex on 10 December 1968.

YOUNG, Second Lieutenant Frank Edward, 1 Hertfordshire Regiment, at Havrincourt 18 September 1918 posthumous. Born at Cherat, NWP India on 2 October 1895 and buried in Hermies Hill British Cemetery and is on the memorial in Hitchin.

YOUNG, Private Thomas, 9 Durham Light Infantry, at Bucquoy from 25 to 31 March 1918. Born at Bolden Colliery, County Durham on 28 January 1895 and died at Whickham in Durham on 15 October 1966. His real name was Morrell.

Second World War

ANDERSON, Private Eric, 5 East Yorkshire Regiment, at Wadi Akarit, Tunisia on 6 April 1943, posthumous. Born at Fagley, Eccleshall, Bradford on 15 September 1915 and is buried at Sfax War Cemetery and recorded on the Beverley Minster war memorial.

ANDERSON, John Thomas McKellar, Acting Major, 8 Argyll and Sutherland Highlanders, at Long Stop Hill, Tunisia on 26 April 1943, where he assumed command of the Battalion after the Commanding Officer had been killed. He died on 5 October 1943 at Termoli, Italy and is buried in the Sangro River War Cemetery.

CAMPBELL, Lieutenant-Colonel (later Brigadier) Lorne Maclaine, 7 Argyll and Sutherland Highlanders, at Wadi Akarit, Tunisia on 6 April 1943. Born at The Airds, Argyll, on 22 July 1902. Also awarded the Distinguished Service Order and bar and the Territorial Decoration.

CHAPMAN, Corporal (later Sergeant) Edward Thomas, 3 Monmouthshire Regiment, at Dortmund-Ems Canal, 2 April 1945. He was born at Pontlottyn, Glamorgan on 13 January 1920.

CLARKE, Lieutenant Wilwood Alexander Sandys, 5 Loyal Regiment, at Guerat-el-Ataq, Tunisia, 23 April 1943, posthumously. Born at Southport in Lancashire on 8 June 1919 and is buried in the Massicault War Cemetery in Tunisia.

DONNINI, Fusilier Denis, 4/5 Royal Scots Fusiliers, at Hongen, Holland, on 18 January 1945, posthumously. Born at Easington Colliery, County Durham on 17 November 1925 and is buried in the Sittard War Cemetery, at Limburg in Holland.

EARDLEY, Company Sergeant Major George Harold, 4 Kings Shropshire Light Infantry at Overloon in Holland on 16 October 1944. Born at Congleton in Cheshire on 6 May 1912, he was also awarded the Military Medal.

HARMAN, Lance Corporal John Pennington, 4 Royal West Kent Regiment, at Kohima, Assam on 9 April 1944, posthumously. He had been born at Beckenham in Kent on 20 July 1914 and is buried in Kohima War Cemetery and there is a memorial on Lundy Isle.

HARPER, Corporal John William, 4 Yorkshire and Lancashire Regiment, at Antwerp on 29 September 1944, posthumously. He had been born in Doncaster on 6 August 1915 and is buried in the Leopoldsburg British Cemetery in Belgium.

HOLLIS, Company Sergeant Major Stanley Elton, 6 Green Howards, at Le Hamel-Vers Mer, on 6 June 1944. He was born at Middlesbrough on 21 September 1912 where he died on 8 February 1972. This was the only VC awarded for action on D-Day.

JAMIESON, Captain (later Major) David Auldgo, Royal Norfolk Regiment, at Grimbosq in Normandy on 7 and 8 August 1944. He was born at Thornham, King's Lynn on 1 October 1920. The memorial at Grimbosq was unveiled by Major Jamieson in 1986.

MITCHELL, Private George Allan, London Scottish, at Damiano, Italy, on 23 and 24 January 1944, posthumously. He was born at Highgate in London on 30 August 1911 and is buried in the Minturno War Cemetery. His old school at Walthamstow has been renamed after him.

NEWMAN, Lieutenant-Colonel Augustus Charles, 4 Essex Regiment, attached to No. 2 Commando, at St Nazaire on 17 and 18 March 1942. Born at Buckhurst Hill in Essex on 19 August 1904 and died at Sandwich in Kent on 26 April 1972. Also awarded the OBE, Territorial Decoration, the French Legion D'Honour and Croix de Guerre. Appointed Deputy Lord-Lieutenant for Essex.

SEAGRIM, Lieutenant-Colonel Derek Anthony, 7 Green Howards, on the Mareth Line, Tunisia, 20 and 21 March, 1943, posthumously. Born at Bournemouth on 24 September 1913 and buried in Sfax War Cemetery. His brother, Major H.P. Seagrim was awarded the poshumous George Cross in Burma in 1944.

WAKEFORD, Captain (later Major) Richard, 2/4 Hampshire Regiment, at Cassino on 13 April 1944. Born in London on 23 July 1921 and died at Leatherhead in Surrey on 27 August 1972.

WAKENSHAW, Private Adam Herbert, 9 Durham Light Infantry, at Mersa Matruh on 27 June 1942, posthumously. Born in Newcastle upon Tyne on 9 June 1914 and buried at the El Alamein British Cemetery in Egypt.

WATKINS, Lieutenant (later Major) Tasker, 1/5 Welch Regiment at Martigny in France on 16 August 1944. Born at Nelson in Glamorgan on 18 November 1918, and later as a judge was knighted.

The George Cross

ARCHER, Lieutenant Bertram, Royal Engineers, in August 1940 for bomb disposal. Ended the war as a Major (Emergency Commission) then joined the Territorial Army, 137 Bomb Disposal Regiment RE (AER) and served to 10 June 1961, retiring as a Brevet Colonel.

ELLIS, Lieutenant Bernard George, 1/5 The Buffs, at Shahraban, Mesopotamia in 1918. The award was for the Albert Medal, exchanged for GC

in 1972. Born at Surbiton in Surrey on 21 November 1890 and died at Letchworth, Hertfordshire on 1 July 1979.

REYNOLDS, Lieutenant Edward Womersley, Royal Engineers, for bomb disposal work, with 101 BD Section at Congresbury on 17 August 1940 and with 102 BD Section in Bristol on 3 September 1940. Born on 27 June 1917 in Birmingham and joined the TA on 8 April 1936.

SPILLETT, Lance Bombadier, Brian, 'P' Battery, 289 Commando Battery, Royal Artillery, TA, on 16 January 1962, posthumous for his gallantry in attempting to rescue a neighbour from a burning house at Waltham Cross in Hertfordshire.

WILLIAMS, Sergeant Sidney, 6 City of London Rifles, on 4 January 1918. The award was for the Albert Medal, exchanged for the GC in 1972. Born at Lambeth on 23 December 1887 and died in London on 12 October 1976. He was a freeman of the City of London, and served as ARP in the Second World War.

Appendix 5 Territorial Army Order of Precedence

Details of the orders of precedence of Corps and Regiments in the British Army are outlined in Part One of The Army List. This is a publication printed annually and obtainable from Her Majesty's Stationery Office.

The first anomaly that strikes a student of the TA is that its regiments and corps are not included in that list, except at item 31, following the WRAC is the Royal Monmouthshire Royal Engineers, followed at 32 by The Honourable Artillery Company, then at 33 the rest of the Territorial Army. But, one asks, is it not so that today there is no 'separate' Territorial Army? Surely the British Army is operating under a concept of One Army? Why, therefore are the gallant, and honourable units manned by the members of the TA relegated to the lowliest of positions, being senior only to the Ulster Defence Regiment?

In time of war, all soldiers, whatever their background, don the same uniform and face the same rigours and dangers. The past has shown that members of the TA, in common with all other reserve forces, do not flinch from their duties, fighting and dying with the same patriotic zeal as their regular colleagues. With the much vaunted 'one army' concept, surely the time has come to look at this order of precedence in a new light.

To alter the order of precedence would, I have no doubt, cause much anxiety and heart searching, especially among the Regular Army units, and especially the various Colonels of the Regiments and Corps. If this anomaly is to be rectified, however, this will be necessary. Two solutions come immediately to mind. The first, which would be most unpopular with the regulars, would be a complete merger of the lists, with the TA regiments taking their rightful places within the order of seniority, irrespective of their volunteer status. There would be no problems in placing the TA units of the Corps, as they would be junior within their own Corps' lists, but take precedence with them. The TA battalions of established regular army regiments would be in a similar position, taking precedence with that regiment, but in battalion number order. The problems would start with the Yeomanry, who either become the junior regiments of the Royal Armoured Corps, or take precedence within the Cavalry list based on their seniority by age of their ancestry. The Royal Monmouthshires and the HAC will present peculiar problems, and would really need to be listed along with the Household Cavalry and RHA at the very top of the list.

There would also be difficulties with the Infantry list in placing those TA regiments which are not numbered battalions of regular regiments, such as the two Scottish regiments, and the Yorkshire and Wessex Volunteers. Research, however, would probably place them fairly based on the dates of formation of the earlier regiments from which they were formed.

The other solution might be to take the TA out of the list of precedence altogether and have its own special list. This would be easy to arrive at, as the order of precedence exists already; however, a major drawback would be that instructions would still be needed as to the order of precedence when regular and volunteer units parade together. The first solution, although the more drastic, is my favourite, and one that in my view correctly reflects the status of the volunteer.

Perhaps one day these views will hold sway, and the anomaly will be corrected. In the meantime, however, the TA units remain subordinate to the whole of the Regular Army, and this appendix shows the order of precedence as at 1988. The regiment and corps abbreviations are shown against each entry. This short way to refer to a unit may be used in correspondence or orders, but battalions of a regiment precede the abbreviation with the battalion number.

Infantry divisions group the various regiments of the Army, and they have their order of precedence as shown in chapter seven of this book. However, the regimental order of precedence remains the same as it was prior to the grouping of regiments into these divisions. Where members of the Women's Royal Army Corps are on the establishment of a mixed unit, they parade immediately after the male element.

List of Order of Precedence

1 Royal Monmouthshire Royal Engineers (Militia) — R MON RE(M)
2 Honourable Artillery Company — HAC
3 Royal Armoured Corps (see Yeomanry list)
4 Royal Regiment of Artillery — RA
5 Corps of Royal Engineers — RE
6 Royal Corps of Signals — R SIGNALS
7 Regiments of Infantry (see Infantry list)
8 Special Air Service Regiment — SAS
9 Army Air Corps — AAC
10 Royal Army Chaplains Department — RAChD
11 Royal Corps of Transport — RCT
12 Royal Army Medical Corps — RAMC
13 Royal Army Ordnance Corps — RAOC
14 Corps of Royal Electrical and Mechanical Engineers — REME
15 Corps of Royal Military Police — RMP
16 Royal Army Pay Corps — RAPC
17 Royal Army Veterinary Corps — RAVC
18 Royal Army Dental Corps — RADC
19 Royal Pioneer Corps — RPC
20 Intelligence Corps — INT CORPS
21 Army Catering Corps — ACC
22 General Service Corps — GSC
23 Queen Alexandra's Royal Army Nursing Corps — QARANC
24 Womens Royal Army Corps — WRAC
25 Officer Training Corps — UOTC

Precedence of Yeomanry Regiments Royal Armoured Corps:

The Royal Yeomanry — RY
The Royal Wessex Yeomanry — R WX Y
The Queen's Own Mercian Yeomanry — QOMY
The Queen's Own Yeomanry — QOY
The Duke of Lancaster's Own Yeomanry — DLOY

Precedence of Infantry Regiments

52nd Lowland Volunteers — 52 LOWLAND
The Queen's Regiment — QUEENS
The Queen's Fusiliers — QF
The King's Own Royal Border Regiment — KINGS OWN BORDER
The Royal Regiment of Fusiliers — RRF
The King's Regiment — KINGS
The Royal Anglian Regiment — R ANGLIAN
The Devonshire and Dorset Regiment — D and D (note: the 4th Battalion has the additional title of 1st Rifle Volunteers.)
Light Infantry — LI

Yorkshire Volunteers — YORKS
The Cheshire Regiment — CHESHIRE
The Royal Welch Fusiliers — RWF
The Royal Regiment of Wales — RRW
The Royal Irish Rangers — R IRISH
Wessex Regiment (Rifle Volunteers) — WESSEX
The Worcestershire and Sherwood Foresters Regiment — WRF
The Queen's Lancashire Regiment — QLR
The Staffordshire Regiment (The Prince of Wales's) — STAFFORDS
51st Highland Volunteers — 51 HIGHLAND
The Parachute Regiment — PARA
The Royal Green Jackets — RGJ

Notes: confusion could arise where a former regular army officer or soldier joins the TA, but because of attachment to a CVHQ or specialist pool, he retains his former cavalry or infantry regiment's cap badge. In these cases he would take precedence with the TA in the order of the regular army, but not preceding the HAC. For example an officer of the 1st The Queen's Dragoon Guards would take precedence ahead of the Yeomanry.

The order of precedence of the infantry regiments who are not numbered battalions of regular army regiments is dictated by the status of the senior regiment from which they were originally formed.

Appendix 6 The Regimental Quick Marches of the Territorial Army

Honourable Artillery Company — *The British Grenadiers;*
The Royal Yeomanry — *The Farmer's Boy,* and
A Squadron (Royal Wiltshire Yeomanry) — *God Bless The Prince of Wales;*
B Squadron (Sherwood Rangers Yeomanry) — *The Sherwood Rangers;*
C Squadron (Kent and Sharpshooters Yeomanry) — *The Sharpshooters;*
The Royal Wessex Yeomanry, as the squadrons:
A and C Squadrons (Royal Gloucestershire Hussars) — *D'ye Ken John Peel;*
B Squadron (Royal Wiltshire Yeomanry) — *God Bless The Prince of Wales;*
D Squadron (Royal Devon Yeomanry) — *Widecombe Fair* (unofficial).
The Queen's Own Mercian Yeomanry — *The Light of Foot;* and

A Squadron (Warwickshire and Worcestershire Yeomanry) — *The Warwickshire Lads;*
B Squadron (Staffordshire Yeomanry) — *Lilli Marlene;*
C Squadron (Shropshire Yeomanry) — *The Farmer's Boy;*
The Queen's Own Yeomanry — *D'ye Ken John Peel;*
The Duke of Lancaster's Own Yeomanry — *John o' Gaunt;*
Royal Regiment of Artillery — *The Royal Artillery Quick March;*
Corps of Royal Engineers — *Wings;*
The Royal Corps of Signals — *The Royal Signals March* (based on *Begone Dull Care* and *Newcastle.*)
52nd Lowland Volunteers — *Scotland the Brave;*
The Queen's Regiment — *The Soldiers of the Queen;*
King's Own Royal Border Regiment — an arrangement of *John Peel, The Lass of Gowrie* and *The Corn Riggs are Bonnie;*
The Royal Regiment of Fusiliers — (i) *The British Grenadiers,* and (ii) *The New Fusilier;*
The King's Regiment — *Kingsman;*
The Royal Anglian Regiment — *Rule, Britannia!* and *Speed the Plough;*
The Devonshire and Dorset Regiment — an arrangement of *Widecombe Fair, We've Lived and Loved Together* and *Maid of Glenconnel.*
The Light Infantry — *Light Infantry,* and the Regimental Double Past is *The Keel Row;*
Yorkshire Volunteers — *Ilkley Moor;*
The Cheshire Regiment — *Wha wadna fecht for Charlie?*
The Royal Welch Fusiliers — *The British Grenadiers;*
The Royal Regiment of Wales — *Men of Harlech;*
The Royal Irish Rangers — The Regimental March of the Royal Irish Rangers *Killaloe.*
The Wessex Regiment (Rifle Volunteers) — *The Farmer's Boy;*
The Worcestershire and Sherwood Foresters Regiment — An arrangement of *Young May Moon* and *Royal Windsor;*
The Queen's Lancashire Regiment — *L'Attaque* and *The Red Rose;*
The Staffordshire Regiment (The Prince of Wales's) — *The Staffordshire Regiment,* an arrangement of *Come Lassies and Lads* and *The Days we went a Gipsying;*
51st Highland Volunteers — A quick march of *Highland Laddie* and *51st Highland Division of Wadi Akarit.*
The Parachute Regiment — *The Ride of the Valkyries;*
The Royal Green Jackets — an arrangement of *Huntsman's Chorus* and *Italian Song,* and the Regimental Double past is *The Road to the Isles.*
Special Air Service Regiment — *March du Regiment Parachutist* Belge;
Army Air Corps — *Recce Flight;*
Royal Army Chaplain's Department — *Trumpet Voluntary;*
Royal Corps of Transport — *Wait for the Wagon;*

Royal Army Medical Corps — *Here's a Health unto His Majesty;*

Royal Army Ordnance Corps — *The Village Blacksmith;*

Corps of Royal Electrical and Mechanical Engineers — *Lillibulero* and *Aupres de ma Blonde;*

Corps of Royal Military Police — *The Watchtower.*

Royal Army Pay Corps — *Imperial Echoes;*

Royal Army Veterinary Corps — an arrangement of *Drink Puppy Drink* and *A Hunting We Will Go.*

Royal Army Dental Corps — *Green Facings;*

Royal Pioneer Corps — *The Pioneer Corps;*

Intelligence Corps — *The Rose and The Laurel;*

Army Catering Corps — *Sugar and Spice;*

Queen Alexandra's Royal Army Nursing Corps — *Grey and Scarlet;*

Womens Royal Army Corps — an arrangement of *Lass of Richmond Hill* and *Early one Morning.*

Acknowledgements

It would be impossible to thank everyone who contributed to the production of the book, so to those whose names are not recorded in this representative list, many thanks.

Brigadier (now Major-General) The Hon. W.E. Rous OBE, Director of Public Relations (Army), and Brigadier W.K.L. Prosser CBE MC, Director of Army Reserves and Cadets, for their approval and the co-operation of their staff in the production of this book.

Major-General M. Matthews CB, Secretary and the Council of TAVRAS.

Chapter three: Captain J.J. Powe RY: Col. D.R.B. Thompson TD ADC, CVHQ RAC; Major C.A. Le Hardy RWY; Capt. A.J. Clay QOMY; Capt. P.J.A. Darling QOY; Capt. M.A.C. Williams DLOY.

Chapter four: Lt-Col. D.R. Kersley Baker RA; Major E.R.C. Herron TD RA(V); Lt-Col. G.E.J. Blythe RA; Lt-Col. D.J. Cameron TD RA(V); Capt. G.W.C. Waddell RA; Capt. A. Mears RA; Capt. W.G. Hunt HAC; Capt. R.J. Boyce RA(V).

Chapter five: Col. G.W.A. Napier MA, The Institution of Royal Engineers; Capt. R.L.S. Philpot MBE RE(V); Capt. J.A. Hick RE; Capt. J.J. Greaves RE; Capt. R. Matthews WRAC(V); Lt-Col. W.J.R. Hughes RE; Capt. H.R.I. Berridge RE; Capt. C.M. Knights RE; Maj. M. Banks RE; Mr R.G. Harding; Capt. R.C.A. MacGregor RE(V); Maj. B.W.P. Bennett MA RE; Maj. A.J. Johnstone RE; Mr J.P. Coulson; Capt. R.A. Kerns RE(V); Mr G. Hudswell; Maj. D.L. Marshall RE(V); Capt. P.W. Kennedy RE(V); Capt. G.T. Reilly RE(V); Capt. R.S. Small RE.

Chapter six: Capt. F.M. Dempster; Capt. R.J. Sheldon; Capt. E. Butterworth; Capt. B. Smith; Capt. S.K. Reed WRAC; Maj. F. Jepson; Lt-Col. C. Gale OBE TD; Maj. D.C. Podevin; Lt-Col. J.D. Cox; Lt-Col. S.A. Coltman; Maj. A.A. Maude; Lt-Col. I.C. Shuker; Maj H.R. Kinkhead; Capt. S.P. Forkes.

Chapter seven: Capt. H.C.D. Cameron RHF; Capt. A.J. Loudon KOSB; Capt. A.A.S. MacDonald BW; Capt. S. Robertson GORDONS; Capt. N.W. Scott A&SH; Regimental Secretary QUEENS; Capt. J. Dixon QUEENS; Capt. D.J. Greenfield QUEENS; Capt. P.A. Stack RRF; Capt. F.A. Calvert MBE TD; Capt. G.R. Witbey RRF; Capt. S.B. Brunt; Capt. R.J. Hare; Capt. P.T. Hampson; Capt. H. Clarke MBE KINGS; Capt. D.J. Sanderson; Maj. A.J. Podmore TD YORKS; Capt. A.D. Lane; Capt. J.S.C. Baker; Capt. W.M. Sharpe; Capt J.M.C. Rylands; Capt. M. Maund; Capt. J.C.St.J. Kilmister RRW; Maj. R.V. Williams RRW; Lt-Col. M.J.H. Harry RRW; Capt. M.S.M. Simpson; Capt. C.J. Joynson STAFFORDS; Capt. R.J. Montagu LI; Capt. R.J. Tolhurst LI; Capt. P.A. Kellett LI; Lt-Col. N.A. Johnson TD RGJ(V); Capt. R.L.S. Bolton RGJ.

Chapter eight: Capt. M.R. Oates; Capt. A.B. Robertson; Maj. A.W. Lees AAC.

Chapter nine: Lt-Col. R.W. Nye; Col. J.S. Riggall MBE TAHQ RCT; Capt. R.N. Howard RCT; Capt. J. Boyce RCT(V); Maj. G.P. Arnold TD RCT(V); Lt. N.P. Browne RCT(V); Maj. P.W. Baker; Capt. R.H. Allen; Mr D. Oliver; Lt-Col. F. Davis RAMC; Capt. J.A. Doolan; Maj. D.A. Campbell RAMC; Maj. M.D. Riley RAMC(V); Maj. G.H. Barker TD RAMC(V); Maj. S.N. Quayle QARANC(V); Maj. S.F. Bloom; Maj. M.A.W. Thompson RAOC; Maj. J.A. Kneale RAVC; Capt. R. Kemp RMP; Capt. R. Crook REME; Capt. T.E. Wilson REME; Lt-Col. A.C. Monk ACC; Maj. A.G. Howard Harwood RAPC; Lt-Col. R.F. Carson TD RCT(V); Lt-Col. I.C. Brooking Thomas TD RY; S.Sgt. T.H. Johnson; S.Sgt. J. Robinson; Mr S. Cook QUEENS; Mr C.G. Collins; Mr R.B. Creasey; Mr R.W.E. Macdonald; Mr D.A. McCarthy; Mr D.D. Thompson; Mr M.P. Feehily RAMC; S.Sgt. M.J. Germany R ANGLIAN.

For his photographic work, Capt. P. Brown RRF(V), Capt. R. Tutt QUEENS (V).

Additional information: Major Jim Peck, LI; Captain C.M. Deuchars RE(V); Capt. Robson RWF; Mrs M. Magnuson, Royal Engineers Library; and the Librarian of the Military Section of the M.O.D. Library.

Index